FRANCE
TRAVELBOOK™

SECOND EDITION

AAA

President & CEO: Robert Darbelnet
*Executive Vice President, Publishing &
    Administration:* Rick Rinner
Managing Director, Travel Information: Bob
    Hopkins

Director, Product Development: Bill Wood
Director, Sales & Marketing: John Coerper
Director, Purchasing & Corporate Services:
    Becky Barrett
Director, Business Development: Gary Sisco
*Director, Tourism Information Development
    (TID):* Michael Petrone
Director, Travel Information: Jeff
    Zimmerman
Director, Publishing Operations: Susan Sears
Director, GIS/Cartography: Jan Coyne
*Director, Publishing/GIS Systems &
    Development:* Ramin Kalhor

Managing Editor, Product Development:
    Margaret Cavanaugh
Development Editor: Greg Weekes

Marketing Manager: Bart Peluso
AAA Travel Store & e-store Manager: Sharon
    Edwards

Manager, Product Support: Linda Indolfi
Manager, Electronic Media Design: Mike
    McCrary
Manager, Pre-Press; Quality Services: Tim
    Johnson

Published by AAA Publishing, 1000 AAA
Drive, Heathrow, Florida 32746

The *AAA France TravelBook* was created and
produced for AAA Publishing by AA
Publishing, AA Developments Limited,
Millstream, Maidenhead Road, Windsor,
Berkshire SL4 5GD, England.

Written by Laurence Phillips
Second edition verified by Colin Follett
Page make-up by Anton Graphics Ltd.

Cover photos
Main photo: Cathédrale Notre-Dame
© Mike Howell/Camerique Inc.
Intl./H. Armstrong Roberts
Cover inset: French chef in garden
© Owen Franken/Corbis
Spine: Eiffel Tower
© Spectrum/EuroStock/H. Armstrong
Roberts

ISBN 1-56251-819-4

Cataloging-in-Publication Data is on file
with the Library of Congress.

Color separations by Leo Reprographic
Ltd., Hong Kong

Printed in Dubai by Oriental Press

A01235

Preparing to play *boules*

FOREWORD

Welcome to the AAA France TravelBook!

As you plan your vacation in France, let this book guide you through the fascinating places that this country can offer. Visit the places you've always heard of: Paris, with its gracious boulevards and elegant open spaces that make the city such a delight; thriving and cultured Bordeaux, center of its wine region; Strasbourg, laced with canals and topped by its wonderful cathedral; and the glitter of the Côte d'Azur.

But vary your trip and be tempted by some of France's quieter corners. The small town of Sarlat-la-Canéda is an exquisitely beautiful medieval melange of cobbled passageways and stone houses. Tiny Rocamadour clings improbably to the side of its cliff, with steps instead of streets. Escape inland from the frantic Riviera to the edges of the Alps and the quieter "perched villages," where stunning views of the coast and sea below are around every corner. And try the northwest region of Brittany, protruding far out into the Atlantic, with bustling towns, rugged coastlines, and the freshest seafood you've ever tasted.

Be sure to experience the finer pleasures of French life – eating wonderful food, enjoying fine French wines, joining in the life and color of street markets, exploring the great cathedrals and châteaux, seeing one of the many festivals, or just watching a local game of *boules*.

Let the AAA TravelBook, with its informative text and colorful illustrations, stir your imagination. Practical information will help you decide what you want to do, there are maps to find your way and useful suggestions for eating, drinking and shopping; everything to help you get the most from your French vacation.

FRANCE TRAVELBOOK™

CONTENTS

INTRODUCTION TO
FRANCE

" F RANCE is the largest country in western Europe, geographically one of the most diverse, and certainly among the most beautiful. "

Introduction to France

Opposite: Château Brissac by the banks of the Aubance river near the town of Brissac-Quince

Introduction to France

FRANCE

"How is it possible to govern a country which produces more than 370 different cheeses?" So demanded Charles de Gaulle, war hero and the nation's most famous 20th-century leader. It's no easier to define the land that also boasts 450 registered wines. The very essence of France is in its diversity.

Administrative boundaries may change on the whim of politicians, but tradition is made of sterner stuff. Local pride and a healthy mistrust of other regions stem from the different cultures that created each part of the land, which first united against outside invasion in the sixth century. Such pride means towns and villages still nurse their centuries-old prejudices, lick their wounds and respect their heritage, offering the visitor to France a selection of some 4,000 museums and 38,152 historic monuments, with 1,500 private châteaux open to the public.

Culture

The arts are part of everyday life. The Académie Française may rail against Americanization of French culture, complaining of words such as *le weekend* falling into their dictionaries and insisting on the spelling *mél* to replace the blatantly Anglo-Saxon "e-mail." However, France has always loved its American dream. Its youth icons remain Marilyn Monroe and 1950s Hollywood. France gave America

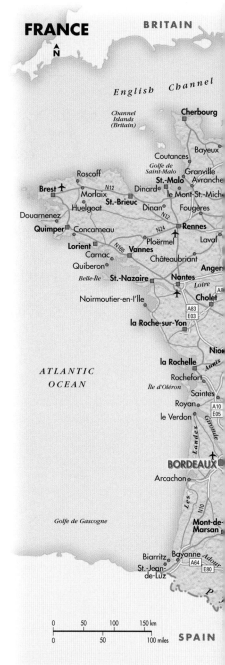

its denim, and the U.S. returned it wrapping up James Dean, just as literature and philosophy share French

prime-time television with imported soaps and game shows. Culture is not reserved for the elite: Many museums are open free once a month, and some stay open late at night since art appreciation is regarded as a social activity. When the country feels good about itself, art flourishes. The wealth that built châteaux lured Renaissance artists from Italy. The 19th-century reinvention of France as a republic saw the beginnings of the Impressionist movement.

Take-out Tradition

Although large supermarkets on the edge of towns have tolled the death knell of many small businesses, the French still support specialist food stores. France has 35,000 *boulangeries* (bakeries), where *baguettes* and *flûtes* (stick loafs) are freshly baked throughout the day. After a hard day's work, people choose quality prepared foods from the local *traiteur* – a cross between a caterer and a deli – rather than a mass-produced TV dinner. The art of the pastry chef is widely respected (even restaurants have specialist chefs to prepare desserts), so there is no shame in buying a fruit tart

or rich gâteau for dessert. All towns have at least one *pâtisserie* selling wonderful homemade cakes.

Religion and Race

Although church and state are formally separate entities and marriages are sanctioned at the local town hall, 63 percent of French people still consider themselves Catholic. Thirty percent declare themselves without religion. Minority religions are most active. Less than two percent of the population are Protestant, persecuted throughout the nation's history, and immigrant Jewish and Muslim communities thrive in major cities.

The well-documented rise of the National Front, under Jean-Marie Le Pen, led to the extreme right-wing party gaining political control in some areas of the south. However, a strong anti-racist movement – S.O.S. Racisme, founded by the improbably named Harlem Desir with the slogan *Touche pas à mon pote* (hands off my pal) – did much to unite the country in support of minority groups in the 1980s. When neo-Nazis attacked a Jewish cemetery in Carpentras at that time, President Mitterand himself joined protesters marching against racism.

The mainstream has adopted the distinctive youth culture and music of second generation north Africans (*les Beurs*) and black communities, and success for multiracial national sports teams has built many bridges. Visitors are unlikely to encounter any tension outside the poorer suburbs of the large cities.

National Pride

With the revival of its sporting fortunes in the late 1990s came proof that despite regional affiliations, *la patrie* (the homeland) is alive and well. For most of the past 150 years, France has

---

The Nobility

France may be a republic, but it still has its aristocracy. Although international banks own most vineyard châteaux in Bordeaux, many châteaux of the Loire still belong to dukes, counts and princes.

Laws have been relaxed to allow heirs and pretenders to the French throne to live in France. Even until the late 20th century they were forced into exile. Since 1998, the once-ruling classes annually return to Versailles to host a sumptuous New Year's Eve charity ball as in the days of Louis XIV.

Association Bienvenue au Château (the association of château owners, offering bed and breakfast) Manoir de la Motte, 28340 La Ferté-Vidame, France ☎ 02 37 37 51 69, fax 02 37 37 51 56; website: www.bienvenue-au-chateau.com; e-mail: info@bienvenue-au-chateau.com.

Opposite: There's only room to walk between the houses in the Dordogne village of Issigeac

The national pastime of *boules* is a serious matter across towns and villages in France

been a republic, with the French Revolution giving the world a model for liberty, equality and brotherhood. The blue, white and red *tricolore* flag flies above most public buildings. The symbol of France is the face of Marianne, displayed in city halls and on stamps and coins. Models for the figure have included actresses Brigitte Bardot and Catherine Deneuve. There was a cause célèbre in April 2000 when the latest Marianne, L'Oréal and Victoria's Secret model Laetitia Casta, decided to live in London; politicians regarded her action as treason.

Pastimes

Winter sports, particularly skiing and boarding in the mountains from the Pyrénées to the Alps, thrive in France, which has the largest skiing area in Europe. Rugby is the game of the southwest, especially around Toulouse, and soccer is a national obsession. The wide beaches of the north and west attract sailboarders, and surfers congregate at Biarritz. *Pétanque,* the great game of *boules* from the south, is played in public squares all over France.

Geography

Known as the "hexagon," France has mountain or sea borders on all six sides. The coastline – 3,418 miles – faces the English Channel (la Manche), the Atlantic Ocean and the Mediterranean Sea. Europe's largest beach is attributed to France at la Baule-Escoublac.

southern Europe. France's temperate climate covers several climatic zones: cold winters and hot summers in much of the country's mountainous regions, a moist western seaboard with cool summers, and the Mediterranean zone in the south with mild winters and sweltering summers.

The regional traditions of daily life permitted each corner of the country to exist in isolation for centuries. However, the 1970s witnessed a railroad revolution that united the country and allowed it to become a leading player in the European community. Reaching speeds up to 200 m.p.h., the TGV (Train à Grande Vitesse) slashed journey times between major cities and allowed depressed agricultural and mining regions to reinvent themselves as European business centers. The northern city of Lille, with a population of less than 150,000, went from a depressed industrial zone with 40 percent unemployment to a major financial hub when the trains brought Brussels, Paris, Britain and Germany within 90 minutes. As former Prime Minister Pierre Mauroy explained, "Distance in France is now measured in time not kilometers."

Private Pleasures

On the bridge that spans the fast-flowing Vézère river in the tiny hamlet of le Saillant, local lads gather to fish, smoke and watch the occasional traffic that passes through from nearby Brive to the Limousin countryside. Ask the boys if there is anything special to see in le Saillant, and they shrug, inhale and laughingly suggest the chapel. There is no chapel in sight. "Yes, the chapel – in that house over there," they say, pointing to a workman's terraced cottage. "A man came from Provence to do the windows."

Within the hexagon are some 58 million people, clustered in cities or spread over the vast and varied countryside, which, at 210,000 square miles in area, is roughly the size of Texas. The country's 36,000 towns and villages are linked by 604,000 miles of roads and 19,847 miles of railroad.

France is divided into 95 administrative départements (departments), numbered in their alphabetical order and often named after the rivers or mountain ranges that cross them. Each department is run by a prefect and general council. Car license plates and postal codes contain the department number; Paris is 75.

Six mountain ranges and 37 million acres of forests run through a land at the heart of both northern and

Naturally, the house is locked, but perhaps a neighbor lends a key. Inside, the tiny parlor-sized chapel is lit by six stained-glass windows by Marc Chagall: luminous sketches of the harvest, the forest and the fishing, in blues and reds, gold and black.

This is the magic of traveling through France. Every corner presents a treasure. Chagall's art attracts countless thousands to the museum in Nice, the Paris Opéra and Rheims Cathedral, but for the villagers of le Saillant, his glasswork remains a mirror of their working lives.

The modest village is featured on no holiday map, and France delights in many such private pleasures. Hikers' paths and vacation freeways can be pathways to serendipity.

Public Joys

Food and drink are naturally part of any celebration. Turkeys trot through the streets of Licques as their brethren are sacrificed at Christmas. Cherries in the east and olive oil in the south inspire music and dancing. And wine flows throughout the year.

Jazz is another favorite for a festival: twilight jam sessions under springtime Normandy apple blossoms in Coutances, or living legends playing by starlight in the pine groves of Antibes or among Roman ruins in Nice and Vienne.

Classical music, too, is not always restrained within the plush velvet of the concert hall. Strasbourg's summer festival has the great orchestras. In Reims, the *Flanneries d'Été* are a glorious game of hide and seek with free recitals tucked away in street corners and spilling into parks. Winter is the season of gala concerts at Évian-les-Bains, beneath the backdrop of snowcapped peaks.

Local people add that special touch.

After a *fest-noz* (after-dark party) of sea shanties and feasting in a Brittany port, take a moonlight boat trip and listen to fishermen's tales as a sound-and-light enactment of *Jonathon Livingston Seagull* teases the horizon from a distant cliff top. Or at Charleville's puppet festival, stumble across a full-scale curbside production of "Dracula" at 11 p.m., the Transylvanian spell broken only by the sound of a motorcycle and the furious yapping of a nervous terrier.

Enviable collections of Impressionist canvases vie for gallery space with local sources of pride. Grasse has its perfume, Lorraine its glassware, Limoges that famous porcelain. Some collections bordering on the eccentric can be found in the most unlikely

The Beaujolais vineyards at Fleurie, overlooking the Saône river plain

places – a beret collection in Franche-Comté, or the Musée Imaginaire de la Sardine in Hérault. The private Melon in Art collection, accumulated by restaurateur Jean-Jacques Prévot in Cavaillon, features watercolors with paint made from local melon seeds and skins.

France en Fête
But no one better exemplifies French *joie de vivre* than ordinary people at their local town fairs and festivals. Year round, there is always some excuse to dress up and take to the streets. February is carnival time on the Riviera. Summer sees sound-and-light shows at Loire châteaux. Sometimes you find a pageant where you least

expect it, as a village commemorates a long-forgotten poet or local hero. In the most unassuming of farmsteads, 10, 20, 40, 50, then 60 masked figures might creep into the courtyard softly singing sacred music, the flames from their torches licking the night sky. Later, audience and players will adjourn to the farmhouse cellar for food, wine and general conviviality. Someone may start to sing a country song; one by one, other voices will join in the chorus.

Later, as you wander through the trees to the parking lot and turn toward the unblinking stars of a summer night, reflect that once again France has opened one of her private doors to you – as she may to other lucky souls in a Brittany fishing boat, jazz lovers in

Roman theaters of the south or anyone lucky enough to cross the bridge over the Vézère at le Saillant.

Dining

Fatty foods, creamy sauces and strong red wine – yet this nation has one of the lowest incidences of heart disease in the world. Rich French cuisine appears to break all the rules without clogging the arteries.

Food is an essential part of French life. Even in the age of business and fitness – when lunchtime wine may be replaced by mineral water, and heavy casseroles by fish – the midday meal can still last two hours.

Fortunately, *nouvelle cuisine*, once described as "a little bit of nothing on a big white plate," has faded from fashion, although the food presentation itself remains an art form. Regional cuisine has its own robust identity, where local produce always has pride of place; look for it on the *menu du terroir* of Logis de France restaurants.

Supermarket convenience foods may be found in the freezers of Parisian department stores, and fast-food emporia sprout on many a city street corner. However, in provincial France and family homes throughout the land, evening and weekend meals remain social occasions. At Christmas and family celebrations, six-, seven- or eight-course meals are not uncommon, with wine and spirits served to nudge the digestion.

Dining out is always a joy whether in smart formal restaurants or local bistros. Choose your restaurant with the same care you would select a show, concert or other entertainment. Menus must be displayed outside, so browse. Often the humble café complete with locals will be more rewarding than the starchy establishment along the road.

Three to four courses are the norm. Eat à la carte from the wider menu or choose from recommended set menus at a fixed price. A range is usually available, from modest two- to three-course options to the *menu gastronomique* (gourmet selection) in high-class venues, perhaps featuring an *amuse-gueule*, appetizer, soup, salad, fish, main course (usually meat), cheese,

dessert, then coffee with *gourmandises* (candies). Often a sorbet or calvados (apple brandy) is served before the main course as a *trou normand* (see page 61).

All restaurants offer the fixed-price option. Budget diners should opt for the plat du jour (dish of the day), usually an excellent-value local specialty. Top-of-the-range restaurants often have lunch menus at less than half the price of the dinner ones. (Also, it's easier to get a table at midday.) Top restaurants often close in August and January.

Wine

The French have a word for it: *terroir*. It's what makes every French wine different from its neighbor bottled across the valley. It's that magic something a wine gets from its own soil, its hometown and the people who love and raise it. To meet a wine on its home soil is a bit like being introduced to the family. That is how a wine lover goes from a one-glass stand to a serious affair.

Each wine region proclaims that its *terroir* (native soil) makes its wines special, and a willingness to try something local wherever you travel will bring its own rewards. Of course the grand *crus* of Bordeaux (those classified wines within the individual château areas) and the celebrated Burgundy vintages will take pride of place on a top restaurant wine list in Paris. However, if you take advice from your local waiter in the provinces, you will be pleasantly surprised for far fewer francs.

Invariably, local cuisine evolves around the characteristics of local wines, so sometimes a modest table wine will better serve your meal than the town's most expensive bottle.

Bistros in Lille spill onto the sidewalk

Wines labeled *appellation d'origine contrôlée (A.O.C.)* meet strict standards before they are permitted to be sold under the regional or vineyard name. *Vin du pays* (country wine) will name the region, and *vin de table* is an unpretentious everyday wine sometimes blended from various sources.

The principal wine-producing regions are:

Alsace, which is known for refreshing white wines. Unlike most French wines, bottles boldly state the grape variety rather than town of origin, such as Reisling (dry), Gerwurztraminer (more complex) and Pinot Gris (nutty dry).

Beaujolais Produces respected wines as well as the famous *nouveau* wines.

Bordeaux Bergerac provides a budget alternative to the pricier *crus.* Sauternes dessert wines include the legendary Château d'Yquem.

Burgundy Where classic wines are celebrated with a calendar of traditional festivals.

Champagne The world's finest fizz founded the region's fortunes.

Jura in Franche-Comté; try the excellent *vin jaune.*

Languedoc-Roussillon, which is beginning to gain a reputation for extremely palatable everyday wines at reasonable prices.

Loire, which boasts more than 100 wines – mainly whites, but also a popular rosé d'Anjou and a fine red Gamay – grown along the longest river in France. Saumur produces the best sparkling wines outside Champagne.

Provence, which includes such surprises as the local Bellet rosé and white wines served by both café owners and award-winning restaurateurs alike. Provence wines are unlikely to be offered outside the region.

Rhône From Châteauneuf du Pape to favorite table wines, vineyards line the river.

Events

January Monte Carlo Rally, Paris fashion shows

February Nice and Menton carnivals

March Paris Book Show

April Paris Marathon

May Cannes Film Festival, Paris International Tennis, Monaco Grand Prix

June Le Mans 24-Hour Car Race, Day of Music

July Bastille Day celebrations, Tour de France, Avignon Festival

September Braderie street market in Lille (last weekend in August or first weekend in September), Paris fashion shows, National Heritage Days (third weekend)

October Grand Prix de l'Arc de Triomphe horse race in Paris

November Beaujolais Nouveau released on second or third Thursday

December St. Nicolas' Day celebrations in Alsace, Lorraine and Franche-Comté (5th) St. Sylvestre's Day – New Year's Eve (31st)

The Summer Break

The French tend to take their vacations within France and at the same time. For six weeks from the Bastille Day celebrations to the first week in September, Parisians leave their city for the coasts and countryside. Many families have second homes and decamp to them for the duration.

Meanwhile the wealthier quarters of Paris are strangely deserted. Major restaurants and many shops and theaters close their doors. Even the best ice-cream parlor shuts down for July and August. On the plus side, you can always find a parking space. The last weekend of the summer holiday, known as the *Rentrée,* is the busiest time of the

Chasing for the leader's yellow jersey in the annual Tour de France bicycle race

year on French roads.

Highways to the sunshine can be a nightmare in July and August as 35 million travelers clog the network and contribute to record numbers of accidents. To combat this, the state organizes summer festivals at rest areas to persuade motorists to pull over for a break every two hours.

The *relais bébé* sign designates staffed baby changing and feeding units. Local history and wildlife excursions are offered in some areas, as are free eye and reflex tests for drivers.

Autoroute-Infos, Europe's largest highway information system, continuously broadcasts information about more than 800 miles of highway and on a single frequency (107.7 MHz).

Some facilities are offered only on peak travel days, but leaflets detailing busy periods and programs of events are available from service areas. Ports and national tourist offices offer a free road map called *Le Bison Futé*, which features alternative routes to the congested freeways.

Tour de France

The best way to see the infinite variety of France is through the Tour de France. For three weeks in July, the world's greatest bicycle race covers 2,260 miles of the country – from the harshest mountain passes to the coast roads, from Disneyland's Sleeping Beauty Castle to the châteaux of the Loire. Each grueling daily stage and time trial brings thousands of well-wishers to cheer on the leading media caravan and the riders following in its wake who vie to win the coveted yellow jersey. Despite drug-taking scandals in recent years, teamwork is the key to the Tour's success and nationalism comes second place to hero worship. When Texan Lance Armstrong cycled up the Champs-Élysées to win the 1999, 2000 and 2001 tours, even Parisian taxi drivers tooted their horns in congratulation.

TIMELINE

15,000 BC	Prehistoric groups occupy caves in southwest France.
4,000 BC	Tribes in Brittany erect megalithic tombs.
600 BC	Greek traders found Marseilles as a trading post.
58–51 BC	Julius Caesar conquers Gaul and begins cultural Romanization.
AD 300	Paris (Lutetia) becomes home to Roman emperors.
AD 500	King Clovis unites tribes to form Francia.
AD 800	Charlemagne, king of the Franks, is crowned Holy Roman Emperor.
1309–77	The popes reside at Avignon during their exile from Rome.
1333	Edward III of England claims the throne of France, leading to the Hundred Years War (1337–1453).
1431	Patriotism movement begins after Joan of Arc is burned at the stake in Rouen as a heretic.
1547–59	Henri II persecutes the Huguenots. After his death, his widow Catherine de Médicis becomes politically influential.
1603	A French colony is established in Canada.
1624-42	Cardinal Richelieu becomes Louis XIII's chief minister.
1635	The Académie Française is established to promote art and learning.
1661–1715	Louis XIV, the Sun King, reigns as a patron of the arts.
1715–74	During the reign of Louis XV, France loses its American colonies to Britain after the Seven Years War.
1774–93	Louis XVI (see panel).
1804–15	Napoléon Bonaparte, emperor of France, seizes power across Europe. He is defeated by the British at Waterloo in 1815.
1814–24	The Bourbon monarchy is restored. King Louis XVIII creates a new constitution.

THE FRENCH REVOLUTION

Political factions at court, and later revisionism, liked to paint Queen Marie Antoinette as the Austrian bimbo who shrugged, "Let them eat cake," when told that the poor were starving. Yet it was economic mismanagement of the country during the reign of Louis XVI that ultimately led to civil unrest. The storming of the Bastille prison July 14, 1789, began mass execution of the aristocracy and the supremacy of Madame la Guillotine. Robespierre, the Committee of Public Safety and revolutionary tribunals orchestrated the Reign of Terror. Louis XVI and Marie Antoinette were executed in 1793. When Robespierre himself lost his head in 1794, normal life resumed.

1824–30	Charles X tries to restore old-style monarchy. Paris revolts against him in 1830 and Charles abdicates. Louis-Philippe, duke of Orléans, becomes the *roi citoyen* (citizen king).
1848	February Revolution leads to abdication and the establishment of the Second Republic and democratic elections to the National Assembly.
1870	The Republic is restored.
1874	The first exhibition of Impressionist art is held.
1889	The Eiffel Tower is built for the Paris Exhibition. The belle epoque begins.
1894	The Lumière brothers develop the cinematograph.

D-Day: American troops land at Normandy in June 1944

1896–1906	Jewish officer Alfred Dreyfus is falsely imprisoned for spying. The issue is resolved after Émile Zola publishes *J'Accuse*.
1914–18	France joins Britain and Russia against Germany and Austria-Hungary in World War I. Victory for the Allies is finalized in the Treaty of Versailles (1919).
1939–45	World War II is declared in September 1939. Charles de Gaulle forms government in exile in Britain.
1944–45	June D-Day landings take place in Normandy. Paris is liberated. Charles de Gaulle becomes president.
1946	The Fourth Republic is declared.
1958	France is a founding member of the European Economic Community (called the European Union since 1993).
1968	Students protest the way in which universities are governed.
1981–95	François Mitterand's two-term socialist presidency launches the *grands projets,* through which major monuments are constructed around the country.
1994	The tunnel under the Channel links France and Britain.
1995	Conservative Jacques Chirac is elected president.
1999	France is among the first E.U. nations to debut the euro currency. Christmas storms damage forests and parkland.
2000	The Green Meridian project plants a line of trees along the meridian from Dunkerque to the Pyrénées.
2002	France adopts the euro as its new national currency.

SURVIVAL GUIDE

- Although in Paris, the Riviera and most cities English is spoken in the more obvious tourist areas, people generally prefer you to at least begin a conversation in French. The phrase *"Parlez-vous anglais?"* is the polite opener.
- Remember that in southern and eastern border areas, English will not be the principal foreign language. Expect fewer English brochures and guidebooks. Spanish, German or Italian may be spoken more widely.
- Good manners are highly regarded. It's customary to shake hands on meeting, to address shopkeepers as monsieur or madame, always to say *bonjour* or *bonsoir* and *merci,* and to bid a general *au revoir* when leaving a café or bar.
- Smart appearance is appreciated. Even in bars, the well-dressed will receive better service.
- At concerts and in cinemas and theaters tip the attendant 20–50 cents. They receive no other payment.
- Bars and cafés always display a list of drink charges with two prices for every drink. Usually the first column shows the lower rate for drinks taken standing or sitting at the bar. The second price – 30 to 50 percent higher – is that charged for drinks served at a table or on the terrace. In some trendy Parisian bars, the second column is the cost of drinks served after 10 p.m.
- Unless a bar is crowded or an obvious tourist trap, it isn't customary to pay for drinks in advance. Each drink comes with a price ticket that the bartender or waiter will tear when you pay. Before leaving the bar, settle up for all drinks.
- Coffee is usually served black unless you request *café au lait, un crème* or *un grand crème.* French coffee is strong espresso. For weaker, filtered coffee ask for *café américain,* or order a glass of water (*un verre d'eau*) on the side.
- Sodas and soft drinks are often more expensive than wine and beer.
- Tap water is safe for drinking. Restaurants are legally obligated to provide a glass or carafe on request, so don't be forced to buy mineral water against your wishes.
- Smoking is part of the national culture. Under new regulations, no-smoking areas are designated in certain restaurants. This may sometimes be one seat by the kitchen or a solitary table in the street.
- Vegetarianism isn't widely understood. A meatless meal might include bacon, a cheese sandwich could include ham unless you specify otherwise, and vegetable dishes are often prepared in a meat stock. Always be specific about dietary requirements.
- When invited to a French home, bring a gift of pastry for your hostess. If you wish to take flowers, seek advice from the florist since some blooms are at the heart of local superstitions or have religious significance, and might cause offense.
- Many offices and small shops close for a long lunch break. Most shops close Sundays although bakers and florists open Sunday mornings.
- Numbered seats on the subway and buses are reserved for the war wounded, pregnant, elderly or infirm.
- When telephoning for a taxi you will be charged for the driver's journey to meet you, in addition to your own journey.

- Keep small bags with you in taxis, as a charge is made for each case carried in the trunk.
- French motorists are often aggressive, and city driving often may be intimidating. Since local insurance companies refuse to pay when accidents occur on place Charles-de-Gaulle in Paris, you will often find cars being pushed into side streets after collisions, in order that the crash may be recorded as occurring elsewhere. Highways (except some stretches around major urban areas) and tunnels charge tolls (*péage*).
- The euro replaced the French franc as the national currency in January 2002.
- Restrooms: Most restrooms in museums and modern restaurants are equipped with flushing toilets. However, in small cafés and rural areas the old-fashioned hole in the ground with porcelain footrests for squatting may still be in use. Use facilities in hotels and restaurants whenever possible.
- Many restroom facilities have an attendant – slang nickname "Madame Pipi" (pronounced "Peepee"), but never to her face – who will expect a tip of about 30 cents. The price is usually displayed.
- Bidets: These low-level fixtures resembling toilets with faucets are designed for purposes of intimate hygiene.
- Telephones: Since hotels usually mark up call charges 100 to 200 percent, phone from public pay phones. Most use phone cards (*une télécarte*), which are available from post offices and tobacco shops (*tabacs*) in 50- and 120-unit versions. The cheapest time to call the United States and Canada, with 50 percent extra time, is from 7:30 p.m.

Captured on canvas: The ancient village of Blesle

to 1:30 a.m. daily and all weekend. Some phone cards include a list of discount rates. Alternatively, details can be obtained from any post office. Phone booths displaying a blue bell sign may receive incoming calls.

- If your credit card is refused, don't panic. Most French credit cards are now equipped with a microchip (*puce*) to avoid fraud. International cards often contain the same information on a magnetic strip, which may not always be easily read. If a clerk or waiter is suspicious of your card, simply explain: *"Les cartes internationales ne sont pas des cartes à puce, mais à bande magnétique."*

PARIS AND THE ÎLE DE FRANCE

"EUROPE'S most exciting and vibrant city is at the heart of a region loved by kings and the Impressionists."

Opposite: Elegant chandeliers in the Hall of Mirrors at Versailles

PARIS AND THE ÎLE DE FRANCE

Arrogant and romantic, flirtatious and self-indulgent, the city of lights with a million secret shadows, Paris belongs to the world. So it's always a shock to find it nestled in the heart of a sleepy, gentle and oh-so-French region, the Île de France.

Long, unbending, tree-lined country roads. Extravagant, wide-open spaces. Rural farms and medieval churches. These are the timeless treats for which Francophiles will cheerfully trek to the most inaccessible corners of the land.

An Island City

Yet, so close to the city much of the region is served by the RER underground and overground express rail service that runs parallel with the urban subway network *(métro)*. These connections, and the fact that all roads in France seem to lead to and from Paris, offer the opportunity to escape from the bustle of the city for a few hours or a weekend.

Perhaps spend an afternoon browsing in the 13th-century marketplace of Luzarches or discovering the medieval underground world of the town of Pontoise. Or enjoy a couple of days of total self-indulgence at the region's only lakeside thermal spa resort, Enghien-les-Bains. Stroll the promenade, wrap, steam and spray

War memorial in the village of la Roche-Guyon

yourself fit, or dress to the nines for a night at the casino.

A ring of illustrious châteaux and royal palaces, standing in vast parks and estates, are a reminder that the woods and waterways were once the playground of kings and princes. Even today, successors to the royal throne of France choose to live in the region. The count of Paris, direct descendant of the last king, set up his Fondation Condé at Chantilly, where the pretty château seems to float on a lake.

The Impressionists were drawn to the Île de France, seeing similarities to the moody skies and ambiguous landscapes of Normandy nearby.

The countryside and rivers of the Oise valley attracted Pierre-Auguste Renoir, Paul Cézanne, Paul Gauguin and Vincent van Gogh, and many views are familiar from their gallery versions. Lovers of Claude Monet will instantly recognize the Seine at Vétheuil. You

What's in store – a fine vintage?

can explore Impressionists country by boat on the Oise or by hot air balloon.

Tickets

A standard single central Paris subway ticket won't take you out to the Île de France. Either buy a tourist pass that includes the wider region, or type your destination at an automatic ticket machine to buy a one-way *(aller simple)* or round-trip *(aller-retour)* ticket to the châteaux or market towns.

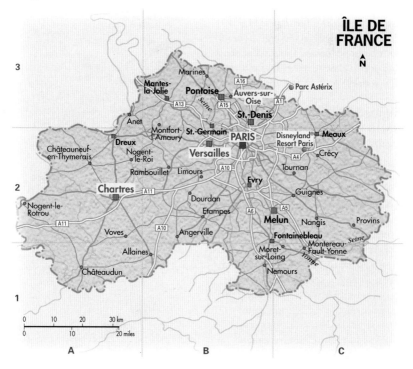

PARIS

Even if you've never visited Paris, you are likely to know the city is divided into the southern, left bank and the right bank. Once you arrive, you discover life is never that simple. The city is divided into a shell-like spiral of 20 *arrondissements* (districts), each an individual village in its own right. Literary romantics need never leave the Latin Quarter. Lovers of glamour stay firmly in the area between the Champs-Élysées and the Opéra.

True bohemia departed the left bank and Montmartre many years ago, but young cosmopolitan artistic communities thrive in the northeast of the city at Belleville. For four days each May, potters and painters throw open the doors and skylights of their studios and garrets and welcome visitors to a Paris most of us dream about.

The two million genuine Parisians live within the 21-mile ring-road (La Périphérique). In a city of high fashion, don't be afraid to wear comfortable shoes. Sites are so close together that you may find yourself on your feet for hours.

Sightseeing

Riverboats (see page 33) offer spectacular views of Paris from the Seine.

Pick Up the Card

Direct admission to the popular collections, which saves hours standing in line in peak season, and unlimited access to some 70 museums and monuments in and around Paris are guaranteed with the Paris museum pass *(la carte musées-monuments)*. The pass is available for 1, 3 or 5 days from participating museums and monuments, main subway stations, tourist offices and FNAC ticket counters.

Best are the dinner cruises at night on the Bateaux Mouches, which illuminate monuments as you pass.

L'Open Tour, an open-top double-decker bus with English commentary, travels from the Arc de Triomphe to Notre-Dame, with branches up to Montmartre and across to Bercy. One ticket allows one or two consecutive

days of unlimited use. Buses depart at 15- to 30-minute intervals for the full two-hour 15-minute circuit all day, every day. Tickets may be purchased on board, at principal subway stations and tourist offices. More traditional guided tours with cassette commentary are offered on distinctive buses marked Cityrama and Paris Vision. If you have

a travel pass, ordinary buses provide an excellent Parisian's eye view of the city. Route 47 crosses the river, passes Notre-Dame on the Île de la Cité and glimpses the Pompidou Center. The 24 travels along the banks of the romantic Seine, taking in the Madeleine, place de la Concorde, the Louvre, the Musée d'Orsay and both islands in the Seine.

Paris and the Île de France

Paris and the Île de France

Paris Music

Cole Porter and the Gershwins hinted at it. But there is a headiness about the combination of Paris and music that suggests it should be kept out of the reach of children and the easily led.

In most cities, music is played. In Paris, music happens. Walk through a subway station and hear tribal sounds. Travelers happily miss their trains and lean against poster-shellacked walls to be entertained. Past midnight on rue St.-André-des-Arts on the left bank, sheltered from the misty rain in a doorway, a lone sax player might play the blues as a window opens across the narrow street and a piano jams along. This is what the French call a *boeuf* – and Anglo-Saxons call improbable.

Midsummer's Eve is Fête de la Musique – a sleep-free city on June 21 and a party spirit from the gutters to the skies. Every year the orgy of song takes over street corners and railway termini. At 3 a.m., having closed up shop, café proprietors take chairs to the sidewalk to enjoy the music. Many a lively grandmother decides a smart, young American should be next on her dance card.

When opera houses close for summer, 20 parks provide free jazz. Another seasonal idyll may not be free, but it's certainly priceless: a season of Frederic Chopin recitals in the Parc de Bagatelle's Orangerie in June and July and at the Musée de la Vie Romantique (George Sand Museum), 16 rue Chaptal. Most major museums stage concerts for a modest door charge.

Parisians regard music as a basic human right. Just as the city provides clean drinking water and a constant supply of *haute* and cold running couture and Impressionist painting, year-round music is available practically on demand. Churches offer fabulous free performances of Johann Sebastian Bach and Antonio Vivaldi. The Sunday concert at Notre-Dame, at 5:30 p.m., is always packed and is superb if you can ignore the video-whirring and camera-clicking. The American Church on quai d'Orsay has frequent piano and guitar recitals. In the heart of the Marais, the Église des Billettes hosts great choral concerts. St.-Merri, next to the Pompidou Center, gives performances of world music and contemporary sounds on Saturday night and Sunday afternoon.

That's Entertainment

The box office of the Comédie Française doesn't recommend its cheaper seats. Apparently, all one can see from these is the play. At the Comédie Française, one still goes to the theater to be seen and to notice who is sitting with whom. Accordingly, the more expensive seats are at right angles to the stage, facing the audience. In nearly all other Paris theaters, keen enthusiasm for the plays and shows suppresses that snobbery.

Street musicians entertain passers-by in the Latin Quarter

Paris loves American and English theater. Larger playhouses offer Arthur Miller, William Shakespeare and Neil Simon in French. Smaller bilingual companies stage English-language productions. American actors often perform free English-language play readings in the left bank's famous Café de Flore. Monday performances begin at 8 p.m. Broadway musicals are treated like opera, with English performances subtitled in French. But new French musicals are worth catching. (Remember, *Les Misérables* started here.)

Most theaters close on Monday but offer Sunday matinées. Prices are much cheaper than New York, and half-price, same-day tickets are sold from midday at a booth in place de la Madeleine.

Paris has more cinema screens than any other city and a choice of more than 300 movies every week. On advertisements "vf" means dubbed versions are shown and "vo" usually means the original English version is screened with subtitles. The Opéra de Paris-Bastille stages operas, and the Opéra Garnier is home to the ballet.

The traditional Parisian cabaret exists for the city's visitors, as locals tend to prefer jazz and comedy clubs. Regardless, the slick productions provide enjoyable, undemanding entertainment with no language barriers. Since the image of the leggy showgirl is about six inches taller than the average Parisienne, today's belle of Belleville is most likely to hail from Portland, Oregon, or Baltimore, Maryland. The Moulin Rouge cancan pays homage to the days of Maurice Chevalier and Joséphine Baker, and The Lido's Vegas-style floor show flourishes with special effects. The Folies Bergères now stages French rock 'n' roll musicals.

Information about the theater, movies and operas is the focus of the Wednesday magazine *Pariscope*, which has an English-language supplement edited by *Time Out*.

Bric-a-brac stalls at the antique market by place de Bastille

Shopping

In a city of the arts, the greatest talent is shopping. Big department stores on boulevard Haussmann spread over several buildings. At the biggest, Galeries Lafayette and Printemps, show your passport at the welcome desk to get a 10 percent discount on your purchases and an invitation to the weekly fashion shows, the best way to see all the season's ready-to-wear apparel in one morning. Individual fashion houses will present their collections to serious shoppers by appointment. Bargains at the lower end of the market may be found between Gare du Nord and Montmartre (see page 41). Visit the covered arcades of the Grands Boulevards (see page 38). For fine foods as gifts try Fauchon and its neighbors on place de la Madeleine.

Buried Treasure

There are several flea markets in Paris, but the best – indeed, in Europe – is the Marché aux Puces at Porte de St.-Ouen/Clignancourt every weekend and Mondays from 7:30 a.m. Antiques, rugs, clothes, bric-a-brac and furniture are among the varied offerings. To snap up a real bargain, arrive before dawn

and try the small dealers on the outskirts of this enormous market. These smaller markets are well signed: Marché Malik for old clothes and bric-a-brac, records, canes and tin boxes; Marché Jules Vallès for dolls, toys and theatrical trunks; Marché Paul Bert for crystal, mirrors and furniture; Marché Michelet for new clothes and shoes; and Marché Vernaison for antique furniture and silverware. Pickpockets frequent the market, so keep a close eye on your belongings.

Antique shops abound in the back streets of poorer districts. Find shops with an eye for the tourist trade around place des Vosges. Dealers around avenue Matignon and the St.-Honoré district advertise in the trade press and have showings in their own houses. The classiest – and most expensive – area is the Carré Rive Gauche, where numerous shops and galleries are lined along rues Allent, du Bac, de Beaune, de Lille, Jacob, des St.-Pères, de l'Université, de Verneuil and quai Voltaire. Details are on the website: www.carrerivegauche.com. The right bank version, the Louvre des Antiquaires, place du Palais-Royal, in the shadow of the Louvre, is a collectors' corner for the incurably wealthy. Like many dealers, shops are closed in summer and on Sundays.

Parks and Gardens

Most visitors tend to stroll in the Jardin des Tuileries, in front of the Louvre, but Paris is a city of green outdoors. The two main expanses of city-center countryside are the Bois de Boulogne and Bois de Vincennes, where each spring sees the famous Foire du Trône fair. Bois de Boulogne has 2,000 acres of woodland with open-air restaurants, seven lakes, a Shakespearean garden, amusement park and racetrack. It also has a notorious red-light district, so take local advice before nighttime strolls. Victor Hugo set up *Les Misérables* lovers in the Jardin du Luxembourg, now home to old men playing *boules*, students laden with books and friends engaged in genteel games of croquet. The rugged Parc des Buttes Chaumont hides ravines, hills and a temple of love in a quiet dormitory quarter, and on the left bank, the Arènes de Lutèce Roman arena is a legacy of the city that ancient Rome named Lubetia.

Paris and the Île de France

ESSENTIAL INFORMATION

 TOURIST INFORMATION
• 127 avenue des Champs-Élysées ☎ 08 36 68 31 12 (toll call); www.paris-touristoffice.com Ⓜ Charles-de-Gaulle-Étoile.
• Gare de Lyon
• Tour Eiffel 🕐 May–Sep. only

 URBAN TRANSPORTATION
You are never more than 200 yards from a *métro* (subway) station. Trains run from 5:30 a.m. to 12:30 a.m. When you leave a subway train, follow either the blue and white signs marked "Sortie" for the exit or the orange and white signs marked "Correspondances" for interchanges and the connecting service. The subway links with an underground-overground express service called the RER, which stretches into the Île de France, Disneyland Paris, the airports and Versailles. Buses run Mon.–Sat. 6:30 a.m. to 8:30 p.m.; some have a reduced service until 12:30 a.m. and on Sunday. Night buses – Noctambus, which require separate tickets – cover the city from place du Châtelet when the subway is closed. Tickets are available individually or in books of 10 from subway stations, where free maps also may be obtained, and are interchangeable. Tourist tickets – Paris-Visite – are valid for 1, 2, 3 or 5 days. Buses and bus stops display route maps. Validate and keep your ticket with you, as you can be fined for traveling without a valid ticket. For information in English call ☎ 08 36 68 41 14, website www.ratp.fr.

From April through October, Batobus operates a hop-on, hop-off river bus at sights between Eiffel Tower and the Jardin des Plantes ☎ 01 44 11 33 99 🕐 Every 15–25 minutes daily 10–9, Jun.–Sep.; 10–7, rest of year.
Taxi stands can be found near subway and main train stations although there is often an extra charge for pick-ups from the stands. Hail a taxi in the street if the white light on the roof is switched on. The maximum number of passengers most taxis will carry is three. At night, all three of you may have to squeeze in the back seat, as it isn't unusual for the driver's dog to sit in front. Call taxis on ☎ 01 49 36 10 10 or 01 47 39 47 39. The Eurostar Channel Tunnel train (3 hours from London) and other high-speed TGV services from northern Europe arrive at Gare du Nord. Trains for the east depart from Gare de l'Est, the south from Gare de Lyon, the southwest from Gare d'Austerlitz, Brittany and Aquitaine from Gare Montparnasse, and Normandy from Gare St.-Lazarre.

❌ **AIRPORT INFORMATION**
Paris has two international airports, Roissy-Charles-de-Gaulle (☎ 01 48 62 22 80) and Orly (☎ 01 49 75 15 15). Most U.S. flights arrive at Roissy, 14 miles north of Paris. Air France has shuttle buses every 20 minutes to and from both airports, but the quickest route is the RER connection to the subway, which runs every 15 minutes around 5 a.m. to midnight.

CLIMATE – Average highs and lows

JAN.	FEB.	MAR.	APR.	MAY	JUN.	JUL.	AUG.	SEP.	OCT.	NOV.	DEC.
6°C	7°C	10°C	13°C	18°C	21°C	24°C	24°C	20°C	14°C	9°C	8°C
43°F	45°F	50°F	55°F	64°F	70°F	75°F	75°F	68°F	57°F	48°F	46°F
2°C	2°C	4°C	5°C	9°C	12°C	14°C	14°C	12°C	8°C	4°C	2°C
36°F	36°F	39°F	41°F	48°F	54°F	57°F	57°F	54°F	46°F	39°F	36°F

Paris and the Île de France

PARIS SIGHTS

Key to symbols

⊞ map coordinates refer to the Paris map on pages 28–29; sights below are highlighted in yellow on the map.

⊠ address or location ☎ telephone number
🕐 opening times 🍴 restaurant on site or nearby
🚌 nearest bus route Ⓜ nearest métro
ℹ information 🎟 admission charge: $$$ more than €10, $$ €5–10, $ less than €5

BASTILLE

The famous Bastille prison that started the French Revolution was completely destroyed on July 14, 1789, although the outline of the fortress is marked on the paving stones of the square. Place de la Bastille has at its center the July Column topped by the winged *Spirit of Liberty*, sculpted in memory of the victims of the 1830 and 1848 uprisings immortalized in *Les Misérables*. The new opera house, designed by Canadian Carlos Ott, is a confection of gray, silver and sunlight and seats 2,700 music lovers. Rue de Lappe is the gateway to trendy jazzland and old-style dance halls, once the haunt of Edith Piaf and her lovers. Some platforms of the busy subway interchange rise above ground to overlook the Arsenal Basin, pleasure port of the Seine. After years of decline, this area from Bastille to place de la République has been reborn as eatery country, with fashionable restaurants on the edge of the new bohemia of the Marais.

⊞ E2 ⊠ place de la Bastille, 75012 ☎ 01 40 01 17 89 🍴 Bofinger, see page 258 Ⓜ Bastille

BEAUBOURG

Known internationally as the Pompidou Center, this is probably more famous for its architecture than its collections. The controversial inside-out design by Richard Rodgers and Renzo Piano makes it as much a landmark meeting place as an exhibition center. Fully renovated for the new millennium, the Musée National d'Art Moderne housed in the center now has two distinct themes: 1905–60 modern art, and works from the 1960s to the present day. Henri Matisse, Salvador Dalí, Amedeo Modigliani, Marc Chagall and

The July Column at place de la Bastille

An enormous ossuary: Six million skeletons are stacked in the Catacombs below Paris

Andy Warhol are among 20th-century giants whose creations span movements from cubism and surrealism to pop art. Outside, a sunken piazza is a popular sprawling ground for backpackers and a showplace for street entertainers.
✚ D3 ✉ place Beaubourg, 75004 ☎ 01 44 78 12 33; www.centrepompidou.fr ◷ Wed.–Mon. 11–10. Museum and exhibitions close at 9 p.m. 🍴 Café Beaubourg, see page 258 🚇 Hôtel de Ville ♿ $$ (free first Sun. of the month)

LES CATACOMBES AND LES ÉGOUTS

The Catacombs – a labyrinth of man-made tunnels beneath Paris – aren't for the claustrophobic. Dating back to Roman times, one corner of the vast network was given over to a ghoulish rehousing program for the dead. When Paris was being redesigned after the Revolution, it was decided to rebuild the cemeteries. Remains of 6 million occupants of the former graveyards were taken to the old catacombs and reburied in 1810. In the true spirit of post-Revolutionary bureaucratic efficiency, the remains weren't classified by name but stacked neatly as femurs and skulls for the discerning visitor who braves the winding tunnels. Some unintentionally kitschy postcards are displayed in the kiosk at the end of the tunnel. Elsewhere, the remarkable sewer system, Les Égouts, is well worth a visit. Ventilated with fresh air, a small section of the elaborate network of tunnels and squares, which mirror the street grid of the city, is open for guided tours. Although an illegal youth subculture may have colonized some of the huge main drains elsewhere in town, this well-maintained showcase features an exhibition about the history of sanitation that is actually almost entertaining and glimpses Paris' most-hidden architecture. As for the museum shop, the most outrageous souvenirs include cuddly rats, but the pride of the collection, bar none, is the ultimate designer accessory: a chic wristwatch filled with blue-rinsed, guaranteed-genuine Parisian sewage.

Catacombs de Paris ✚ C1 ✉ 1 place Denfert-Rochereau, 75014 ☎ 01 43 22 47 63 ◷ Tue. 11–4, Wed.–Sun. 9–4 🚇 Denfert-Rochereau ♿ $$
Musée des Égouts de Paris ✚ A3 ✉ Opposite 93 quai d'Orsay, 75007 ☎ 01 53 68 27 81 ◷ Sat.–Wed. 11–5, May–Sep.; 11–4, rest of year. Closed the last three weeks Jan. 🚇 Alma-Marceau ♿ $

Symbol of victory and power: The Arc de Triomphe that stands at the head of the Champs-Élysées

WALK: ALONG THE CHAMPS-ÉLYSÉES

Refer to route marked on city map on pages 28–29

Here Parisians gathers to see in the New Year, to welcome the Tour de France, to cheer the marathon and to toot horns on election night. Bustling and brilliant until the small hours, France's most famous avenue has never looked lovelier.

After decades of erosion by traffic, building and fast-food emporia, the Champs-Élysées has been reborn as the most civilized downhill stroll in town. At its crest – and at the center of the Étoile, a star-shaped junction of 12 avenues – is the Arc de Triomphe, a 164-foot Napoleonic monument and home to the tomb of the unknown soldier. Here, at the Arc de Triomphe, this 1.5-mile walk begins.

Cross to the top of the avenue des Champs-Élysées

Stepping out on the avenue is something of a fashion parade since sidewalks were widened, parking moved underground and broad paths were planted with trees reflecting the original design of landscape gardener André Le Nôtre. The top section is lined with cafés, car showrooms, cinemas, restaurants and shops. Most famous are the Lido floor show and celebrated restaurant Fouquet's (you pronounce the T) on the corner of avenue George-V. The haunt of

aging rock stars and starlets, Fouquet's still forbids single women to drink at the bar.

Midway down the avenue cross the intersection of Rond-Point, with its fountains and pretty flowerbeds, marking the start of the true champs or fields.

Gardens to the right border the 1900 art and exhibition galleries Grand Palais and Petit Palais; opposite is a memorial to Jean Moulin, French Resistance hero. The avenue opens out to the magnificent 18th-century place de la Concorde, which boasts a central pink granite obelisk from the Palace of Luxor in Egypt. To the right is the Seine, with the Assemblée Nationale parliament building across the bridge. To the left is the start of the colonnades of rue de Rivoli. Straight ahead is the majestic Jardin des Tuileries and the Louvre beyond.

Arc de Triomphe ✉ place Charles-de-Gaulle, 75008 ☎ 01 55 37 73 77 🕐 Daily 10 a.m.–11 p.m., Apr.–Sep.; 10 a.m.–10:30 p.m., rest of year 🚇 Charles de Gaulle-Étoile 💶 $$ (free first Sun. of the month)
Grand Palais ✉ 3 avenue du Général-Eisenhower ☎ 01 44 13 17 17 🕐 Wed.–Mon. 10–8 (also Wed. 8–10 p.m.) 🚇 Champs-Élysées-Clémenceau 💶 $$$
Petit Palais ✉ Avenue Winston-Churchill, 75008 ☎ 01 42 65 12 73 🕐 Closed for renovation 🚇 Charles de Gaulle-Étoile 💶 $$ (reduced price on Mon.)
Assemblée Nationale ✉ 126 rue de l'Université, 75007 ☎ 01 40 63 69 81 🕐 Sat., tours at 10, 11 and 3. except when the parliament is in session 🚇 Assemblée Nationale 💶 Free

Turning the corner: The Grande Arche de la Défense

CONCIERGERIE

Poor Marie Antoinette has had bad press over the years. The "let them eat cake" remark was taken out of context, and accounts of her eccentric lifestyle at Versailles (see page 55) denied her public sympathy. A visit to her prison cell at the well-scrubbed fortress of the Conciergerie on the Île de la Cité should soften the hardest hearts.

It was here – at this former royal palace, a prison since the 14th century – that the queen and other victims of the Reign of Terror were held before being taken across the river to their public execution at the guillotine. Here also were spent the final turbulent nights of Danton and Madame du Barry, Robespierre and the poet André Chénier. Cells, the guard house, the vaulted Gothic great hall and the kitchens with their huge, open fires are open to the public. The address, quai de l'Horloge, is named after the first public clock in Paris, on the building's great square tower.

➕ C2 ✉ Palais de la Cité, 1 quai de l'Horloge, 75001 ☎ 01 53 73 78 50 🕐 Daily 9:30–6:30, Apr.–Sep.; 10–5, rest of year. 🚇 Cité 💲 $$ (free first Sun. of the month)

LA DÉFENSE

The most impressive view in Paris is from the top of the Grande Arche de la Défense, the newest of the triumphant gateways to the city. Less a traditional arch and more a gigantic hollow cube of glass and white Carrara marble, from here one can see the major sites of Paris in a straight line from this newest business district right to the heart of the Louvre itself. Inaugurated in 1989 for the bicentennial of the French Revolution, the arch dominates the Parvis, a modern square studded with contemporary statuary and home to an IMAX cinema (the Dome) and a superb shopping complex (Les Quatre Temps).

At first in the 1960s, La Defénse seemed harsh and alien, but it has softened over time into a modern community, and this dream of president and war hero Charles de Gaulle is now matched by the other grand monuments conceived across town by his 1980s successor, François Mitterand. At the foot of the Grande Arch is the Center of New Industries and Technologies (CNIT), an important conference and exhibition center.

Good restaurants serve the business community, and fast public transportation links this most western quarter of Paris with the city center in just minutes.

Grande Arche ➕ A4 ✉ Paris la Défense, 92044 ☎ 01 49 07 27 57 🕐 Daily 9:30–8, in summer; 10–7, rest of year 🍴 Restaurant 🚇 La-Défense-Grande-Arche 💲 $$

GRANDS BOULEVARDS

Choked by traffic snarling from République to the Opéra and beyond, Haussman's wide streets might be dismissed as mere rat runs. Don't miss out on the real Paris. On wide sidewalks shaded from the sun by tall trees and taller buildings, smart bankers on skates avoid the rush-hour crowds on the subway, and honeymooners stroll in no particular hurry to find a nice spot for coffee.

A fair smattering of 19th-century theaters, which put on light entertainment and farces, offer performances late enough that patrons can grab an early supper at a neighboring restaurant. Famous Parisian galleries and passages and glass-roofed shopping arcades have discreet entrances on the boulevards themselves. Within are art shops, toy shops, the occasional small theater or such tucked-away sights as the Musée Grévin, Paris' waxworks museum.

The eastern section of the boulevards, nearer République, was once home to indoor circuses but now is a bit run-down. However, the two gateways to Paris, the Porte St.-Denis and Porte St.-Martin, have been beautifully restored. The sophisticated west serves the Opéra and Opéra-Comique audiences. As a rule of thumb, side streets in the southern financial district, home to great restaurants, are quieter, and streets in the north, which serve the more working-class districts between the boulevards and the fleshpots of Pigalle, are livelier. A well-chosen café table can afford a superb glimpse of Montmartre.

Musée Grévin ➕ C3 ✉ 10 boulevard Montmartre, 75009 ☎ 01 47 70 85 05 🕐 Daily 10–7 🍴 Chez Georges, see page 258 🚇 Grands-Boulevards 💷 $$$

LES HALLES

Despite the less than flattering local nickname "le Trou" (the hole), this is one hole in the ground that is well worth a visit. When the old wrought-iron framed halls of the market – the city's principal food market for 800 years – were demolished in 1969, an ambitious glass cascade was constructed to bathe the underground shopping mall in natural light. Although the fortunes of the shops have fluctuated, it's now a good place to find clothes by young designers. The streets above have become a pedestrian-friendly zone of restaurants, bars, cafés and nightlife, from the seedy, neon promises of the rue St.-Denis red-light district to the bistros and restaurants serving seafood to theatergoers at midnight and onion soup to party revelers

Offbeat Museums

Experienced shoppers start at the Musée de la Contrefaçon, where you can test your skills in discriminating between quality and junk. This is one of Paris' most unusual museums (this in a city that boasts a gallery devoted to 4,500 years of bread!), where the discerning can show shrewd skills in detecting forgery. Here one can see counterfeit Cartiers and Louis Vuittons that never saw the inside of a designer's workroom. A shrine to the greatest French singer of the 20th century makes a touching detour: Les Amis d'Edith Piaf is a private museum dedicated to her memory and life. Enjoy a dash of whimsy at the Curiosities and Magic Museum in the Marais, something of an interactive wonderland with 19th-century curios, magic tricks and futuristic robots.

Musée de la Contrefaçon ➕ A3 ✉ 16 rue de la Faisanderie, 75116 ☎ 01 56 26 14 00 🕐 Mon.–Thu. 2–5, Fri. 9:30–noon 🚇 Porte Dauphine 💷 $

Les Amis d'Edith Piaf ➕ E3 ✉ 5 rue Crespin-du-Gast, 75011 ☎ 01 43 55 52 72 🕐 Open by appointment, Mon.–Thu. 3–6 🚇 Menilmontant 💷 Donation

Musée de la Curiosité et de la Magie ➕ E2 ✉ École de Magie, 11 rue St.-Paul, 75004 ☎ 01 42 72 13 26 🕐 Wed. and Sat.-Sun. 2–7 🚇 St.-Paul 💷 $

at dawn. At all hours this is the vibrant hub of the city, welcoming new arrivals from the busy subway interchange below to the cultural overspill from the Pompidou Center and the Théâtre du Châtelet.

➕ D3 ✉ Rue Pierre Lescot, rue Rambuteau, rue Berger 🍴 Grand Vefour, see page 259 🚇 Les Halles

HÔTEL DES INVALIDES

The elegance of Louis XIV military architecture is never more striking than around the grand arcaded courtyard of Les Invalides. Some visitors just make a whistlestop halt here to see Napoléon's tomb, but time is recommended to see the other treasures in this 17th-century retreat from modern Paris. Originally constructed as a home for military pensioners, it's still the residence of 100 veterans. The soldiers' Église St.-Louis-des-Invalides is decked with flags and pennants from 300 years of military campaigns. The other church in the complex is the imposing Église du Dôme, designed by Jules Hardouin-Mansart, housing the six-layer coffin of Emperor Napoléon. The Musée de l'Armée is among the world's finest museums of warfare and strategy, and the fourth-floor Musée des Plans-Reliefs contains a unique national treasure, hidden from the public for some 200 years. Louis XIV commissioned the military architect Sébastien le Prestre de Vauban to create miniature models of all the fortified towns in the kingdom. The bulk of the collection is on display here; the remaining section, covering northern France and Flanders, is held at the Palais des Beaux-Arts in Lille.

➕ B2 ✉ Esplanade des Invalides, 75007 ☎ 01 44 42 37 72 🕐 Daily 10–7; mid-Jun. through Aug. 31; 10–6, Apr. 1 to mid-Jun. and in Sep.; 10–5, rest of year 🍴 Restaurant 🚇 Latour-Maubourg 🎫 Combined ticket $$

LE MARAIS

Mozart and matzos, majesty and marshland: the treasures of the Marais are hidden behind high walls in the quaint 17th-century streets and alleys of the

Napoléon's imperial tomb at Les Invalides

right bank, just north of Notre-Dame, and east of the Pompidou Center. Past narrow byways and creaking houses where the young Wolfgang Amadeus Mozart once played, come upon place des Vosges – once place Royale – the last great pre-Revolution square where ladies lunch under shady arcades while nannies and babies take in fresh air at the gardens. Victor Hugo's house at No. 6 is now a museum dedicated to the author.

The area was once a slushy bog to the north of the island that was Paris, uninhabitable until the 13th century when monks reclaimed the swamps around rue St.-Antoine for farmland. Gradually the Marais became a fashionable alternative to the city center. In the late 14th century, it even became a royal retreat for Charles VI.

The joy of the Marais lies in its many secret courtyards. *Hôtels particuliers* are grand private residences whose tall street gates hide some stunning entrances. Worth a visit are the Hôtels Carnavalet, now a museum of Paris history, Salé (Picasso Museum, see pages 44–45), Rohan-Guéménée (Maison de Victor Hugo) and Soubise. The buildings are floodlit at certain times of the year.

For generations the Marais was best known for its Jewish quarter, restaurants

The final steps up to the marble basilica of Sacré-Coeur

and bakers of the ghetto along rue des Rosiers. Since the 1980s, when the gay community adopted rue Ste.-Croix-de-la-Bretonnerie and its tributaries, unlikely neighbors have become the best of friends and the area has become very fashionable. Town planners readily issue preservation orders, and every season ushers in new museums such as the little-known Musée de la Poupée, home to hundreds of dolls in impasse Berthaud. Café theater flourishes at Point-Virgule and Les Blancs Manteaux, and you might find a thing of beauty, if not quite a bargain, from the antique dealers around Église St.-Paul-St.-Louis. Today's Marais attracts a fashionable element whose penthouse apartments overlook old streets where new shopfronts are more likely to display designer cuff links than meat and vegetables. Nonetheless, a true sense of people and place remains.

Musée Carnavalet-Musée de l'Histoire de Paris
✚ D2 ✉ 23 rue de Sévigné, 75003 ☎ 01 44 59 58 58
🕐 Tue.–Sun. 10–5:40 🚇 St.-Paul ♿ Free
(temporary exhibitions $–$$)

Musée de la Poupée ✚ D3 ✉ Impasse Berthaud, 75003 ☎ 01 42 72 73 11 🕐 Tue.–Sun. 10–6 🍴 Café Beaubourg, see page 258 🚇 Rambuteau ♿ $$

Maison de Victor-Hugo ✚ E2 ✉ Hôtel de Rohan-Guéménée, 6 place des Vosges ☎ 01 42 72 10 16
🕐 Tue.–Sun. 10–5:40 🚇 Bastille ♿ Free
(temporary exhibitions $–$$)

MONTMARTRE

Montmartre was always a village. Originally outside the city limits when the cancan was banned from Paris theaters, the public balls of Montmartre welcomed revelers to enjoy the shameless gavotte performed by the prostitutes of the hill. Today, a sanitized dance is the finale of the floor show at the Moulin Rouge, named for the windmills that once dotted the hill. Pierre-Auguste Renoir's quaint "Moulin de la Galette" can still be seen here.

Take the funicular train up the final slopes to the Sacré-Coeur basilica, completed in 1910 as penance for the Franco-Prussian War. Hardy types climb the extra 295 feet to the dome. Around the corner at place du Tertre, a permanent rush hour of arrogant waiters and portrait-hustlers continues as accordion tunes mingle with the constant honking of coaches passing the white marble domes. If the garish daubs of the street artists don't appeal, the nearby Espace Dalí, a museum devoted to the great surrealist, may prove more interesting. However, only the fantastically wealthy might be able to buy an exhibit or two.

Montmartre remains true to its past. Private mansions lie behind locked gates and rickety steps climb sidewalks so steep that they have banisters in the middle of the street. Snack on *frites* and mustard under a 19th-century lamp with the city spread at your feet, or savor a midnight crêpe and modern jazz in a cramped basement bar.

The village is home to a tiny vineyard, an exclusive cemetery and more than one alley or face that might have been painted by Toulouse-Lautrec or the bohemians of a glorious past. Montmartre's past poverty is today's nostalgia.

The lower slopes lead to the bustling cliché of Clichy, home to a Museum of Erotica (Musée de l'Érotisme), fairground shows and Tati, the famous bazaar where store security guards keep at bay hordes of local shoppers determined to secure a pair of trousers for €3, a €6 skirt or an entire wardrobe for less than €30. The carnival spirit bustles all year round, and it isn't only locals who come here. The well-to-

Fouquet's boutique in the Musée Carnavalet

do put on dark glasses and Hermès scarves to join the crush. A world leader once arrived late for a summit conference because the lure of the Tati racks proved too strong for his wife.

Basilique du Sacré-Coeur 🔂 D4 ✉ Parvis-du-Sacré-Coeur, 75018 ☎ 01 53 41 89 00 🕐 Basilica open daily 6 a.m.–10:30 p.m. Dome and crypt open daily 10–5:45 🚇 Anvers 🎫 Basilica free; dome and crypt $$

Espace Dalí 🔂 C4 ✉ 11 rue Poulbot, 75018 ☎ 01 42 64 40 10 🕐 Daily 10–9:30, Jul.–Aug.; 10–6:30, rest of year 🚇 Abbesses 🎫 $$

Musée de l'Érotisme 🔂 C4 ✉ 72 boulevard de Clichy, 75018 ☎ 01 42 58 28 73 🕐 Daily 10 a.m.–2 a.m. 🚇 Blanche 🎫 $$

MUSÉE D'ART ET D'HISTOIRE DU JUDAISME

The Hôtel de Saint-Aignan in the Marais is the elegant setting for the Jewish Art and History Museum, containing relics of French Jewish communities dating back hundreds of years before the Spanish Inquisition. Artifacts and icons from the Diaspora across Europe and North Africa are at the heart of a fascinating, informative and moving collection depicting Jewish life. Paintings of religious festivities in Venice, menorahs and Chanukah candleholders from Poland to the Ottoman Empire and models of *shtetl* villages and synagogues from eastern Europe are among highlights of the historical wings.

Paris and the Île de France

Contemporary sculpture in Musée d'Art Moderne de la Ville de Paris

The works of Marc Chagall and fellow Jewish artists form the second collection. Visitors may use an interactive audio guide, which provides fascinating insight into Jewish history and the Sephardi and Ashkenazi cultures. Original papers and pamphlets from the Dreyfus Affair and firsthand accounts of anti-Semitism bring the collection into the 20th century. The Holocaust is referred to only by an exhibit charting the fate of the wartime inhabitants of the Marais mansion itself. For a sobering reflection of life in occupied France, the Memorial to the Unknown Jewish Martyr is dedicated to the memory of 6 million Jews who died during World War II.
➕ D3 ✉ Hôtel de St.-Aignan, 71 rue du Temple, 75003 ☎ 01 53 01 86 60 ⏱ Mon.–Fri. 11–6, Sun. 10–6. Closed some Jewish holidays 🍴 Restaurant 🚇 Rambuteau ♿ $$ ℹ Audio-guided tours available
Memorial du Martyr-Juif-Inconnu ✉ 37 rue de Turenne, 75003 ☎ 01 42 77 44 72 ⏱ Sun.–Fri. 11–5:30. Closed until summer 2003 🚇 St.-Paul ♿ $

MUSÉE D'ART MODERNE DE LA VILLE DE PARIS

In a city that positively groans under the weight of the greatest artworks from the Renaissance to the Impressionists, it would be all too easy to forget that the 20th century has left its own treasure chest.

Not to be confused with the national collection at Beaubourg (see page 34), light, airy rooms in the Museum of Modern Art at the Palais de Tokyo – itself a fabulous example of 1937 modern architecture – are the fitting home to a collection of works by Henri Matisse, Pablo Picasso, Maurice Utrillo and Georges Braque. A prominent place goes to Raoul Dufy's *La Fée Electricité*, which was created for the building's opening at the 1937 World Exhibition. No mere gallery of canvasses, the permanent collection gives prominence to a range of art-deco furniture and modern tapestries.

The museum holds several temporary exhibitions each year and can arrange guided tours by appointment.
➕ A3 ✉ Palais de Tokyo, 11 avenue du Président-Wilson, 75116 ☎ 01 53 67 40 00 ⏱ Tue.–Fri. 10–5:30, Sat.–Sun. 10–6:45 🍴 Restaurant 🚇 Iéna Free (temporary exhibitions $)

MUSÉE JACQUEMART-ANDRÉ

Only recently renovated and opened to the public, the perfect contrast to the sprawling Louvre is an elegant private art collection in a charming 19th-century home on boulevard Haussmann. Banker Edouard André and his wife Nélie Jacquemart accumulated a fabulous collection of art and furniture, bequeathed to the Institut de France. Mostly 18th-century French art from François Boucher to Antoine Watteau and 17th-century Flemish masters is housed in the library. A Renaissance collection includes works by Donatello and Sandro Botticelli. Visitors may also enjoy a glimpse of life as it was once lived behind the high walls of this city mansion, with some of the family rooms restored to their original splendor. An audio guide is available in six languages. The small tearoom is a popular meeting place for genteel Parisian widows and wives.
➕ B4 ✉ 158 boulevard Haussmann, 75008 ☎ 01 45 62 11 59 ⏱ Daily 10–6 🚇 St.-Philippe-du-Roule ♿ $$ (includes audio guide)

MUSÉE DE LOUVRE

The only way to arrive at I. M. Pei's Pyramide is from below. Leaving the subway, enter the Carrousel du Louvre, a high-class shopping mall and underground temple to today's highest culture. Inside the glass pyramid, a balletic spiral staircase whisks into daylight, and the most surprisingly glamorous wheelchair elevator spins to street level. The great glass structure itself reflects the grandeur of its setting in a kaleidoscope of constant architecture and ever-changing skies. This was the first sign of Grand Louvre, President François Mitterand's imperial plan to revive a building that was museum, royal palace, government offices and city landmark three subway stations long.

Because the Louvre is really seven museums in one sprawling three-winged palace, the Pyramide offers three entrances. It's impossible to walk the reputed 5 miles of galleries in one day, so first-timers should take the Sully entrance to see the 12th-century fortress, hidden underneath the Royal Palace until 1989. Above on two levels are Egyptian collections. Discover daily life from bread-making to mummification, then walk through to explore the reigns of the pharaohs.

The Apollo Gallery in the Denon wing houses the Crown Jewels, removed from regal necks before Madame Guillotine descended. See the dynamic *Winged Victory of Samothrace* atop the staircase, then wander among 13th- through 15th-century Italian paintings, including Leonardo da Vinci's *Mona Lisa* behind bullet-proof glass in room six. The renowned piece is smaller and more like the postcard than you might expect.

Back on the first floor, pass through the first sculpture gallery, taking in Michaelangelo's *Dying Slave*, and stroll through treasures of ancient Greece and Rome until you see the *Venus de Milo*. Poised above the surging crowd, she almost comes to life.

The Richelieu wing has two covered courtyards studded with marble statues of the gods – all of which are woefully overlooked by the beautiful people noshing at Café Marly. Upstairs are the Renaissance galleries, Napoléon III's state

The Louvre in a Hurry

If you simply want to see the three most famous attractions in record time, then beat the crowds in the Denon wing. Take the elevator to the first floor, turn into room six for *Mona Lisa*, back past the elevator for *Winged Victory*, then head downstairs and double back to room 12 for *Venus de Milo*. When you are done, follow the exit sign to the subway.

Sculptures by Pierre Puget in the Louvre

Art has replaced trains in the former railroad station that is now the Musée d'Orsay

apartments and the works of French, Flemish and Dutch old masters, including Jean Baptiste Camille Corot, Antoine Watteau and Jan Vermeer.

✚ C3 ✉ La Pyramide, cour Napoléon, 75001 ☎ 01 40 20 51 51; www.louvre.fr 🕐 Thu.–Sun. 9–6, Mon. and Wed. 9 a.m.–9:45 p.m. 🍴 Restaurant 🚇 Palais-Royal-Musée du Louvre 💶 $$ (less expensive after 3 p.m. and all day Sun.; free first Sun. of the month)

MUSÉE D'ORSAY

Every pane in the glass roof, the big clock and the vast light and airy space itself conjures the tingle of anticipation that only a railroad station built in 1900 could inspire. In 1986, the building was reincarnated as the home of 1848–1914 art, the missing link between the Louvre and the Modern Art Museum (see page 42). Fine examples of art nouveau and realism fill the first two levels, but the pride of Paris is the upper floor's prestigious collection of Impressionist and post-Impressionist art. Claude Monet's *Houses of Parliament* and *Rouen Cathedral*, Vincent van Gogh's *Church at Auvers–sur–Oise*, Pierre-Auguste Renoir's *Bathers* and Edgar Degas' *Blue Dancers*, to name but a few, highlight a line-up that features the best of Paul Cézanne, Paul Gauguin, Edouard Manet, Alfred Sisley and Henri

de Toulouse-Lautrec. The belle-epoque station decor reflects an age of inspiration and encourages visitors to linger. The tearoom, whose window is the huge clock, is a wonderful place to sit at sunset, watching the great hands orchestrate shadows across the Seine.

✚ C2 ✉ 1 rue de la Légion-d'Honneur, 75007 ☎ 01 40 49 48 14; www.musee-orsay.fr 🕐 Tue.–Sun. 9–6 (also Thu. 6–9:45 p.m.), late Jun. through Sep. 30; Tue.–Sat. 10–6 (also Thu. 6–9:45 p.m.), Sun. 9–6, rest of year 🍴 Restaurant and Café 🚇 Solférino 💶 $$ (less expensive on Sun.; free first Sun. of the month)

MUSÉE NATIONAL PICASSO

Some 200 of Pablo Picasso's paintings, dozens of sculptures and hundreds of drawings and sketches are housed in the elegant Hôtel Salé, an imposing Marais mansion rescued from years of neglect by a major cultural project. The visit takes the form of a chronological walk through the various ages, periods and styles of the artist from the early blue to the pink to the final cubist phases in what is probably the most comprehensive collection of the most-prominent and prolific painter of the 20th century. The sensitivity and detail of the young painter's canvasses often strike visitors, who are mostly familiar with his later work.

The collection, donated to the state by the family in lieu of death duties, also features works acquired by Picasso during his lifetime, in particular paintings by Pierre-Auguste Renoir, Paul Cézanne, and his contemporary Georges Braque.

✚ E2 ✉ Hôtel Salé, 5 rue de Thorigny, 75003 ☎ 01 42 71 25 21 🕐 Wed.–Mon. 9:30–6 (also Thu. 6–8 p.m.), Apr.–Sep.; Wed.–Mon. 9:30–5:30 (also Thu. 5:30–8 p.m.), rest of year ⍾ Restaurant Ⓜ St.-Paul ⬛ $$ free (first Sun. of the month) ℹ Guided tour in English first Mon. of the month at 11 a.m.

MUSÉE RODIN

The most-celebrated work of the great sculptor Auguste Rodin (1840–1917) cannot be found in any room of the museum that bears his name. *The Thinker,* along with the *Burghers of Calais,* is discovered in the tranquil gardens that make this left-bank gallery so special. The roses, trees and pathways in the grounds of the 18th-century Hôtel Biron set off the larger works in this excellent collection. The mansion was home to Rodin in his later years and also numbered Jean Cocteau, Henri Matisse and Isadora Duncan among its illustrious residents. After the artist's death, the state opened the house as a permanent memorial to a national hero. His much-copied work, *The Kiss,* is among exhibits displayed within the indoor galleries.

✚ B2 ✉ Hôtel Biron, 77 rue de Varenne, 75007 ☎ 01 44 18 61 10 🕐 Tue.–Sun. 9:30-5:45 (park closes at 6:45), Apr.–Sep.; 9:30–4:45, rest of year ⍾ Restaurant Ⓜ Varenne ⬛ $$ (free first Sun. of the month)

PÈRE-LACHAISE, CIMETIÈRE DU

A vast sprawling town in its own right, this cemetery is a true necropolis: a city of those who have gone before, the last home of some of the world's greatest talents. The most-famous resident is Oscar Wilde, whose once-magnificent Sphinx-guarded tomb has been hacked by souvenir hunters. His most private trinkets are said to serve as a paperweight in some curator's office.

Père-Lachaise Cemetery is a full day out. Pay your respects to Marcel Proust, Balzac, Sarah Bernhardt, Gertrude Stein, Abelard and Héloïse and of course Edith

Mère et Enfant (1907), in the Musée National Picasso

Piaf and Yves Montand. Jim Morrison's graffiti-spattered monument is a gathering point for most visitors to this vast park of past glories. But there are quiet corners for reflection. The Mur des Fédérés, for example, is where more than 100 of the last members of the Commune were lined against the cemetery wall and shot dead.

Père-Lachaise is only one of Paris' many last resting places. The arty guest list at Montmartre Cemetery includes Jacques Offenbach, Hector Berlioz, Alexandre Dumas, François Truffaut and Vaslav Nijinsky. Jean Seberg, Jean-Paul Sartre and Charles Baudelaire lie at Montparnasse Cemetery.

✚ E3 ✉ boulevard de Ménilmontant, 75020 ☎ 01 55 25 82 10 🕐 Mon.–Fri. 8–6, Sat. 8:30–6, Sun. 9–6, mid-Mar. to early Nov.; closes 5:30, rest of year ⍾ Pavillon Peubla, see page 259 Ⓜ Père Lachaise ⬛ Free (guided tours $$)

Cimetière de Montmartre ✚ C4 ✉ 20 avenue Rachel, 75018 ☎ 01 43 87 64 24 🕐 Mon.–Fri. 8–6, Sat. 8.30–6, Sun. 9–6, mid-Mar. to early Nov.; closes 5:30, rest of year Ⓜ Place de Clichy ⬛ Free ℹ Guided tours (☎ 01 40 71 75 23)

Cimitière du Montparnasse ✚ B1–C1 ✉ 3 boulevard Edgar-Quinet, 75014 ☎ 01 44 10 86 50 🕐 Mon.–Fri. 8–6, Sat. 8.30–6, Sun. 9–6 mid-Mar. to early Nov.; closes 5:30, rest of year Ⓜ Raspail ⬛ Free ℹ Guided tours ($$) (☎ 01 40 71 75 23)

A sightseeing boat on the Seine river passes the Gothic cathedral of Notre-Dame

THE SEINE AND THE ISLANDS

When Paris was born, the Seine ran around it – the Île de la Cité. That island and its more subdued twin, the Île St.-Louis, are the heart of Paris to this day, between the bustle and commerce of the modern right bank and the more romantic reflections of the left bank (see page 47). The Île de la Cité is home to the Conciergerie (see page 37), the Palais de Justice, the bird and flower market at place Louis-Lépine and the peaceful, old-style place Dauphine.

The main attraction is the Gothic Cathédrale Notre-Dame. Built from 1163 to 1345, the edifice is 426 feet long, with towers creating a skyline at 226 feet. It's a magnet for tourists who tend to crowd the place with too many camcorders. Arrive early in the day to appreciate the exquisite

rose window and the view from the top of the towers of Eugène Viollet-le-Duc's celebrated 19th-century gargoyles. Two areas of contemplation sit beside the cathedral: the Hôtel Dieu's cloister across the parvis, and at the eastern tip of the island, the tiny cell that serves as a memorial to deported concentration-camp prisoners. A little bridge leads to the Île St.-Louis, much quieter with many discreet restaurants and hotels.

On both banks are *bouquinistes*, dealers of second-hand books and prints who trade from lock-up cabinets at street level. Below by the waterside are dusty, shaded footpaths where lovers stroll into the evening and where on summer Sunday mornings, fire-service cadets practice their water drill below quai Voltaire.

The metal Pont des Arts footbridge offers the best view of the city's prettiest

Cafés in the Latin Quarter are places for refreshing debate or studied reflection

Paris and the Île de France

RIVE GAUCHE

The *rive gauche*, or left bank, is more than simply the southern half of Paris. Marked by boulevards St.-Germain and St.-Michel, the left bank is a time and place apart.

The Romans developed the Latin Quarter at the time the Île de la Cité was being colonized, but it was the establishment of the universities in the Middle Ages that gave the area its name and character. The 13th-century Sorbonne is the heart of the scholastic district. Largely escaping the grand designs that shaped the boulevards of the rest of Paris, the left bank remains a place where students argue in cafés and cheap bookstores and where midnight is no excuse to retire. History happens at the table. Around place St.-Germain-des-Près, people flock to the Deux Magots and Café de Flore seeking Jean-Paul Sartre and Ernest Hemingway. At restaurants like Le Procope, the American Constitution was drafted and debated.

The quarter's true spirit is its love of the arts: Théâtre de la Huchette with Paris' longest-running play, Eugène Ionesco's *La Cantatrice Chauve* (The Bald Prima Donna), a play still going after 40 years; scores of tiny cinemas, especially the essential Action chain, screening late-night Cary Grant and Katharine Hepburn classics; and, most of all, Shakespeare & Co. on rue de la Bûcherie, the American bookshop that published James Joyce when the literary establishment scorned his work and where to this day, penniless travelers are offered shelter and rest. The sign over the door reads, "Be not inhospitable to strangers, lest they be angels in disguise."

The left bank is the Paris of legend for sitting and sipping rather than rushing and ticking a checklist of sights. Should you need a soundtrack, the Roman ruins of Musée de Cluny and the nearby small 13th-century Église St.-Julien-le-Pauvre, where student councils were held until tempers flew too high in the 16th century, both host classical concerts on midweek afternoons. As the boulevards reach the area around the Musée d'Orsay and rue du Bac, streets become less bohemian and art galleries more and more exclusive.

The Eiffel Tower – a temporary exhibit that became Paris' most enduring landmark

sunset. Other bridges to cross include the famous Pont Neuf (literally new bridge, but actually the oldest surviving crossing in town) by Île de la Cité, with its statue of a horseback Henry IV who galloped across on its opening in 1607, and the flamboyant Pont Alexandre-III, a gift from the czar in 1900 with gilded cupids atop columns. Cross the Pont de Grenelle for its miniature Statue of Liberty facing westward to her big sister across the Atlantic.

Bateaux Mouche floating restaurants depart from Pont de l'Alma and smaller sightseeing craft from Pont Neuf. The Batobus plies the central stretch of the Seine in summer months as a hop-on, hop-off alternative to the subway.

Notre-Dame ✚ D2 ✉ place du Parvis-de-Notre-Dame, 75004 ☎ 01 42 34 56 10 ⏰ Mon.–Fri. 8–6:45, Sat.–Sun. 8–7:45. Visits are limited during religious services ⓜ Cité 🎟 Free

TOUR EIFFEL

More than a triumph of 19th-century engineering, this 1,040-foot hunk of ironwork is one of the great personalities of Paris. Built by Gustave Eiffel for the 1889 World Exhibition, the temporary exhibit is still going strong. The world's tallest structure until New York's Chrysler Building was built in 1930, the Eiffel Tower took just two years to build and was saved from demolition in 1909 thanks to its radio mast, later boosted another 65 feet to serve as a weather station and TV antenna. Radio signals intercepted during World War I led to the capture of spy Mata Hari. Every fact – it weighs 7,000 tons and is repainted every seven years – is matched by a better anecdote: During the Nazi occupation, resistance fighters hid vital elevator parts so Hitler couldn't be

The Géode movie theater at futuristic La Villette

photographed atop the symbol of France. Elevators and 1,710 steps serve the three levels. Information, a gift shop and a post office for specially postmarked mail are available on the second floor. The Jules Verne Restaurant occupies the third. A panoramic viewing platform is perched 906 feet up on the highest level. Here, until his death in 1923, Eiffel maintained an office with the unique address, "Mr. Gustave Eiffel, Tour Eiffel, Paris." Although on a clear day you can see some 40 miles, the best view in town is of the illuminated tower itself by night, as seen from the Trocadéro. Among the more than 185 million visitors in its first 100 years were an 85-year-old circus elephant that made it to the first level and golfer Arnold Palmer, who teed off from the viewing platform.

➕ A2 ✉ Champs de Mars, 75007 ☎ 01 44 11 23 23; www.tour-eiffel.fr Ⓜ Bir-Hakeim

LA VILLETTE

The canals and slaughterhouses of northeast Paris had long been dismissed as an area beyond the pale when the Cité des Sciences et de l'Industrie opened its daringly futuristic complex at La Villette. The spherical Géode movie theater is the landmark seen by traffic roaring by on the Périphérique highway circling Paris, but within the museums' halls and

auditoriums are plenty of worlds to uncover. From an aquarium to a planetarium, all life is explored and tested at the science museum, using up-to-the-minute cinema and computer technology. Across the modernist gardens is a piazza ding to the Cité de la Musique and its Grande Halle, home to classical music and jazz festivals, open-air movies in summer and major exhibitions. Concert halls and displays of musical instruments dating back to the Renaissance and art inspired by music are part of the Musée de la Musique (Museum of Music) housed within the complex. Just a few steps from La Villette are the Canal de l'Dureq and the Canal St.-Martin, which originally fed the city's fountains and provide quiet walks from the outskirts of Paris to the Gare de l'Est train station. The arrival of the museums has led to several fashionable cafés and restaurants opening by the canal locks and riverbanks of this newly discovered waterside district.

➕ E4

Cité des Sciences et de l'Industrie ✉ Parc de la Villette, 30 avenue Corentin-Cariou, 75019 ☎ 01 40 05 80 00; www.cite-sciences.fr Ⓒ Tue.–Sat. 10–6, Sun. 10–7 🍴 Restaurant Ⓜ Porte de la Villette 🎫 $$

Musée de la Musique ✉ 221 avenue Jean-Jaures, 75019 ☎ 01 44 84 44 84 Ⓒ Tue.–Sat. noon–6, Sun. 10–6 🍴 Restaurant Ⓜ Porte de Pantin 🎫 $$

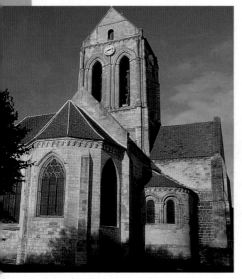

Auvers-sur-Oise church made famous by van Gogh

REGIONAL SIGHTS

Key to symbols

✚ map coordinates refer to the region map on page 27; sights below are highlighted in yellow on the map.
✉ address or location ☎ telephone number
🕐 opening times 🍽 restaurant on site or nearby
Ⓜ nearest metro ⓘ information 🖐 admission charge: $$$ more than €10, $$ €5–€10, $ less than €5

AUVERS-SUR-OISE

Immortalized by the Impressionists – Vincent van Gogh's famous painting of the church surrounded by slanting rooftops, Paul Cézanne's *House of Dr. Gachet* and countless local views by Jean-Baptiste-Camille Corot and Camille Pissarro – the little town on the banks of the Oise river is still something of an artists' colony. Van Gogh spent the last 70 days of his life here in 1890, creating 70 canvasses in a painting frenzy before committing suicide. His room at the Auberge Ravoux – still a restaurant today – has been preserved as he left it and can be visited by up to five people at a time.

Van Gogh is buried in the Auvers cemetery beside his brother Théo, and a statue sculpted by Ossip Zadkine in 1961 stands in Van Gogh Park between the restaurant and the train station. A walk along the "old road" at the foot of the cliffs reveals many of the vistas and 19th-century houses that inspired so many famous works of art.

The tourist office in the 17th-century Manoir des Colombières has many walking and driving routes around the town, dubbed the cradle of Impressionism. The first floor of the manor is a museum devoted to the father of the Auvers art community, Charles François Daubigny, whose own descendents show visitors around his studio in the family home nearby. Another 19th-century quirk was the drinking of absinthe, now banned. The culture of the liqueur is explored at the local Musée de l'Absinthe. Château d'Auvers offers a multimedia tour of over 500 virtual Impressionist works and a three-dimensional film biography of Van Gogh.
✚ B3

Tourist information ✉ Manoir des Colombières, rue de la Sansonne ☎ 01 34 64 85 15; www.auvers-sur-oise.com

Maison de Van Gogh ✉ Auberge Ravoux, 52 rue du Gal-de-Gaulle ☎ 01 30 36 60 60 🕐 Tue.–Sun. 10–6 🖐 $$

Musée Daubigny ✉ Manoir des Colombières, rue de la Sansonne ☎ 01 30 36 80 20 🕐 Wed.–Sun. 2–6 🍽 Café 🖐 $

Musée de l'Absinthe ✉ 44 rue Alphonse-Callé ☎ 01 30 36 83 26 🕐 Wed.– Sun. 11–6, Jun.–Sep.; Sat.–Sun. 11–6, rest of year 🖐 $

Château d'Auvers ✉ Rue de Léry ☎ 01 34 48 48 40 🕐 Tue.–Fri. 10:30–6, Sat.–Sun. 10:30–6:30, Mon. 2–6, Apr.–Sep.; Tue.–Fri. 10:30–4:30, Sat.–Sun. 10:30–5:30, Mon. 2–4:30, rest of year. Closed first Mon. of the month 🖐 $$$

CHARTRES

The great Gothic Cathédrale Notre-Dame is well worth the 50-mile drive from Paris. Unlike its magnificent sisters throughout Europe, this 13th-century masterpiece shimmering above the cornfields has remained untouched by the ravages of war and revolution. Survival has marked the site since the original ninth-century church, built to house the tunic of the Virgin Mary, was burned to the ground in 1194, leaving the holy relic untouched by the flames.

Particularly spectacular are the 25,000 square feet of original stained-glass windows, most dating from the 13th century. Chartres blue glass gives the cathedral a particular light, notably from the Blue Madonna near the steps to the crypt. Each generation adds to the stained-glass heritage. In 1971 the American Society of Architects donated a window to the south transept. Chartres has been a place of pilgrimage since the days of the first church on the site. The labyrinth in the nave is traditionally followed by pilgrims shuffling on their knees.

In town, the 17th-century streets have been well-restored, a grain store from the 12th century remains as a stained-glass center, and old mills survive along the Eure river.

✚ A2

Tourist information ✉ place Cathédrale ☎ 02 37 18 26 23; www.ville-chartres.fr

Cathédrale Notre-Dame ✉ Place Cathédrale ☎ 02 37 21 75 02 ⊙ Daily 8:30–6:45 ⒲ Free ✚ Guided visits Mon.–Sat. at noon and 2:45

Statues of Old Testament kings and queens at Chartres' cathedral

DISNEYLAND PARIS

Since opening as Euro Disney, changes of name and management and a distinctly French twist on the American dream, especially the serving of alcohol at previously "dry" restaurants, resulted in Disneyland Paris being reborn in a "happy ending." The park is spread over the usual Fantasy, Adventure and Frontier Lands, as well as a suitably Gallic Discoveryland, with a nicely European 360-degree film adventure featuring Jules Verne and H. G. Wells. White-knuckle rides, flights of fancy and street parades are textbook Disney. Christmas is perhaps the best season to visit, as the domestic charm creates the cozy feel of Charles Dickens meets the *Nutcracker Suite*. Festival Disney, outside the gates, and cheap summer-evening rates for the park attract locals to Disney by night. The train station links to the Paris subway and airports and a direct international service to London.

✚ C2 ✉ Marne-la-Vallée, 77777 ☎ 01 60 30 60 30

⊙ Hours vary between 9 a.m. and 11 p.m., early Jan. to early Sep. (call to confirm) ✚ Choice on site ⒭ RER: Marne-la-Vallée-Chessy ⒲ $$$

PARC ASTÉRIX

Disneyland may be more famous, but Parc Astérix is far more European. Based on the local cartoon characters Astérix and Obelix, the park is themed around the Roman occupation of Gaul, as France formerly was known. With the usual rides and splashes and the conventional themed foods and souvenirs, Astérix has the added value of an educational subtext for the young and unaware, with Latin puns for the mature and overeducated. There are nonscary family rides for younger children. Smaller than Uncle Walt's place at Marne-la-Vallée and just 21 miles north of Paris, the park boasts five zones, a hotel and enough entertainment to keep a young family happy for a day or two.

✚ C3 ✉ Plailly, 60128 ☎ 03 44 62 34 34 ⊙ Daily 9:30–7, Jul.–Aug.; daily 10–6, Apr.–Jun; Wed. and Sat.–Sun. 9.30–7, Sep. 1–Oct. 15 ✚ Choice on site ⒭ RER: Aéroport-Charles-de-Gaulle 1 then shuttle bus ⒲ $$$

DRIVE: THE PALACES OF THE ÎLE DE FRANCE

Distance: 150 miles Time: 3 to 4 days

Much of France claims royal status. Reims in Champagne and Rouen in Normandy have staged coronations, but the Île-de-France has more than its fair share of castles, palaces and hunting estates. Some, like Vincennes, can be found within the Paris subway network for a brief detour from the usual city sights. However, the great châteaux and royal towns that encircle the capital make for a country drive in itself.

From Paris take the A1 to St.-Denis
Better known today for its national sports stadium, St.-Denis has a rich 2,000-year history. The Basilique St.-Denis is the last

resting place of 70 kings and other royals who reigned before Louis XVIII. No mere mausoleum, the early Gothic church has a spectacular collection of medieval and Renaissance sculpture. Both the original architect and the 19th-century restorer also worked on the Cathédrale Notre-Dame in Paris. The city's Museum of Art and History is housed in a Carmelite convent that once was home to Louise de France, sister of Louis XVI. In spring, St.-Denis hosts major jazz and film festivals.

Take the A86 for 5 miles to Pont de Chatou then the D186 to St.-Germain-en-Laye
Before the move to Versailles in 1682, St.-Germain-en-Laye was Louis XIV's birthplace and country estate, famous for its hunting parties in the nearby state forest. A strategic fortress since the 14th century, the site was restored and embellished by successive kings in its 17th-century heyday. Royal favorite garden designer Le Nôtre designed the

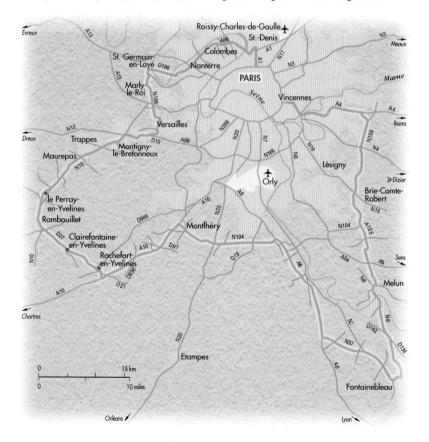

Rich wall coverings in the Tapestry Salon of the château at Fontainebleau

Grande Terrasse, which stretches for nearly 1.5 miles and offers magnificent views of the Seine valley. The garden is best enjoyed in summer, when concerts are held on the terrace bandstand. The château was restored under Napoléon III, who inaugurated the Museum of National Antiquities, with France's archeological treasures displayed in 17 rooms. In town, the birthplace of composer Claude Debussy is open to the public.

Leave St.-Germain on the N284, following signs to le Pecq for a mile, then follow the N13 for 130 yards to join the D7 for almost a mile.

You have to hand it to Louis XIV. Settled into his new and improved home of Versailles, he immediately decided the main palace was a little too large for entertaining friends. So he commissioned a second country estate at Marly-le-Roi. Less formal than the court, a modest royal pavilion with separate buildings for guests was conceived and constructed by the architect Jules Hardouin-Mansart, who spent the rest of his life perfecting the project. It's said that the king himself enjoyed gardening on the grounds. Today, the buildings have gone, but visitors may drive and stroll through the royal park. A must see is the wonderful Marly Machine, designed to pump water from the Seine to supply the fountains of Marly and Versailles. Madame du Barry's music pavilion remains from the Golden Age. Worth a visit is the Château of

Monte Cristo, a delightful Moorish-Renaissance folly built by Alexandre Dumas from the proceeds of his successful novels the *Count of Monte Cristo* and *The Three Musketeers*. The author worked in his Gothic Château d'If nearby. Marly Forest comprises 5,000 acres of woodland. Some roads may be closed to traffic.

Leave Marly on the D386, drive a mile to the N186, leading to the D186 into Versailles.

Visit the stunning Palace of Versailles (see page 55).

Take the D91 and turn right onto N286 to the N12. At the Rambouillet exit, turn left to the A12 continuing on the N10 for 14 miles.

Something of a storybook castle with creeper-covered towers at each corner, Rambouillet is the official summer residence of the French president. Another of Louis IV's collected châteaux, it was given to the count of Toulouse and repurchased by Louis XVI, who enjoyed the hunting grounds. Queen Marie Antoinette was less enchanted, so the king commissioned a modest dairy pavilion for her pleasures. Another pretty outbuilding is the seashell-encrusted cottage in the park. The grounds are blanketed with flowerbeds and water gardens fit for regal and presidential strolls. Two other attractions on the estate are the National Sheep Farm, founded by Louis XVI, and the Musée

The French president's Château de Rambouillet

Rambolitrain with 1,300 feet of miniature railroad track and some 4,000 models.

Drive southeast on the D27 for 8 miles, the D149 toward Paris for a mile, then join the A10 for 10 miles leaving at the Lyon-Évry-Orléans exit for the N104. Continue for 11 miles, then take the A6 toward Lyon for 11 miles. Take the Fontainebleau-Montargis exit and turn left onto the N37, then N7, following signs for the château.

The spring of Bleau gave its name to the regal pleasure ground of Fontainebleau. François I tore down much of the medieval palace, and the great Renaissance estate was planned throughout the 16th century, with statuary copied from Rome and painting and stucco supervised by Giovanni Battista Rosso. Fontainebleau gave its name to a school of Renaissance art. Each reign saw new improvements or additions to the magnificent building, and after the revolution, Napoléon and his successors maintained the estate. The grounds, vast ponds and lakes, neat formal lawns and well tended forest have been classified, along with the château, as a World Heritage Site. The Carp Pool shouldn't be missed. Around the forest sits the village of Barbizon, home to great landscape artists and early Impressionists, Jean-François Millet, Pierre-Auguste Renoir and Claude Monet.

Take the N6 north to Melun. Two miles north of the town turn onto the N105 for half a mile to the A5B for 6 miles. Then go north on the N104 for 13 miles. At the Paris exit, turn left and take the A4 for 7 miles. At the Joinville go right onto the N4 and follow signs for the château.

On the boundary of Paris, the Château de Vincennes is the last habitable, medieval royal fortress in France. Since Vincennes fell from royal favor, the buildings have served as a state prison, porcelain factory and military base. An on-site museum of army insignia is open twice a week, and the cartridge factory *(cartoucherie)* is now a theater complex, from where a shuttle bus operates to the nearest subway station. Two royal pavilions and a chapel are among the buildings open to the public, and Paris' zoo and pleasure park of the Bois de Vincennes are favorite Sunday outings for Parisians.

Château St.-Germain-en-Laye ☎ 01 39 10 13 00 🕐 Wed.–Mon. 9–5:15 ✋ $
Maison Claude Debussy ✉ 38 rue au Pain, St.-Germain-en-Laye ☎ 01 34 51 05 12 🕐 Tue.–Sat. 2–6 ✋ Free
Musée-promenade de Marly-Le-Roi ✉ La Grille Royale, Parc de Marly, Louveciennes ☎ 01 39 69 06 26 🕐 Wed.–Sun. 2–6 ✋ $
Château de Rambouillet ✉ place de la Libération, 78120 Rambouillet ☎ 01 34 83 00 25 🕐 Wed.– Mon. 10–11:30 and 2–5, Apr.–Sep.; Wed.–Mon. 10–11:30 and 2–4:30, rest of year. Closed during presidential stays ✋ $$ (includes Laiterie de la Reine)
Château de Rambouillet, Laiterie de la Reine (Queen's Dairy) ✉ Parc de Château ☎ 01 34 83 29 09 🕐 Wed.–Mon. 10–noon and 2–5, Apr.–Sep.; Wed.–Mon. 10–noon and 2–3:30, rest of year. Closed during presidential stays ✋ $$ (includes Château)
Château de Rambouillet , La Bergerie Nationale (National Sheep Farm) ✉ Parc de Château ☎ 01 61 08 68 00 🕐 Wed.–Sun. and public holidays 2–5 ✋ $
Château de Rambouillet , Le Musée Rambolitrain ✉ 4 place Jeanne-d'Arc ☎ 01 34 83 15 93 🕐 Wed.–Sun. 10–noon and 2–5:30 ✋ $
Château de Fontainebleau ✉ Place du Général-de-Gaulle, 77300 Fontainebleau ☎ 01 60 71 50 60 🕐 Wed.–Mon. 9:30–6, Jul.–Aug; 9:30–5, in Jun. and Sep.–Oct., 9:30–noon and 2–5, rest of year ✋ $$
Barbizon tourist information ✉ 55 Grand Rue ☎ 01 60 66 41 87; www.iplus.fr/barbizon
Château de Vincennes ✉ avenue de Paris, 94300 Vincennes ☎ 01 48 08 31 20 🕐 Daily 10–11:45 and 1:15–6, Apr.–Sep.; 10–11:45 and 1:15–5, rest of year ✋ $$

Spectacular fountains and statues in the Apollo Basin at Versailles

VERSAILLES

Versailles is unique. For 100 years it served as the center of French government, and for posterity it's the legacy of a magnificent ego. Louis XIV inherited a modest hunting lodge from his father and throughout his reign hired the greatest architects and landscape artists to embellish the site, from château to palace to a veritable kingdom in its own right. The result is a palace standing in 2,350 acres of nature tamed to a royal will.

It is impossible to see everything in a day, so content yourself with the essential visit to the great apartments and the grounds. The best of the château is on the first floor, with the state apartments and the king's rooms along one wing and the queen's suite on the other. The wings are linked by the magnificent Hall of Mirrors designed by Jules Hardouin-Mansart in 1687. The hall, with its unrivaled view over the great perspective of fountains and waterways, hosted royal banquets and the signing of the Treaty of Versailles in 1919. Despite the grandeur of decor and

furnishings, human aspects still echo through the centuries. Discreet passageways link the bedrooms, where much of court life took place in private. The mantelpiece in Marie Antoinette's bedroom still bears scars of a scramble for a good view of the queen giving birth. Visit the private opera house – used in the film *Dangerous Liaisons* – and the royal chapel before discovering the grounds. The spectacular fountains and statues, particularly the Apollo Basin, are among the set pieces viewed from the flowerbeds. The Hameau was Marie Antoinette's own pastoral idyll, a model farm where the Austrian outsider might escape from the machinations of the court.

The least known of the gardens is the Potager du Roi, the royal kitchen garden adjoining the estate. Now the national agricultural college, it boasts trellised fruit trees and fascinating vegetable varieties.

🗺 B2 ✉ Versailles, 78000 ☎ 01 30 83 78 00 🕐 Château open Tue.–Sun. 9–6:30, Apr.–Oct.; 9–5:30, rest of year. Various times for other attractions 🍴 Restaurant 🚇 RER: Versailles Rive Gauche 🎫 Château $$; other attractions $–$$. Free first Sun., Oct.–Mar.

NORMANDY AND BRITTANY

" *N* *ORMANDY'S apple orchards and the D-Day beaches, Brittany's rugged cliffs and Celtic charm – two contrasting lands of conquest and mysticism.* *"*

Opposite: Residents of le Folgoët gather with banners in front of the church for the *pardon* procession

Normandy and Brittany

NORMANDY AND BRITTANY

Even though Normandy and Brittany share the northwest coast of France, these two regions have fiercely independent histories and identities. The Normans, named Norsemen after fierce Vikings who descended from Scandinavia to take the land and tame a lush fertile region of farms and abundant seas, settled the area in the ninth century. Within 200 years, their regime of churches and ducal government had extended from here to England, and two nations' histories were bound together for centuries to come.

Normandy's Heritage

The year 1944 saw the Allied D-Day landings and the Battle of Normandy

Fishing boats in the harbor of Dieppe

that eventually liberated France. Post-war recuperation and tourism saw Normandy's traditional cuisine of cream, cheeses and seafood being discovered and it has influenced the world's menus ever since.

The distinctive landscape will likely be familiar to first-time visitors from its interpretation by the great Impressionists: Claude Monet on land and Pierre Bonnard and Eugène Boudin on the coasts. Sea ports such as Honfleur and Dieppe are popular with fishermen and tourists alike, Deauville is an unashamed holiday resort, and Caen and Cherbourg are principal cities, with their ferry and container ports and thriving commercial centers.

The Normandy capital is Rouen on the Seine, which periodically welcomes international armadas, festivals of ships great and small from all over the world. The upper-eastern section of the region, Haute-Normandie, is more industrial and certainly wealthier. The lower half, Basse-Normandie, is far more rural, its economy relying on farms and fishing. Signs on the roadside announce homemade cider for tasting and buying, in an area that has plenty in common with the neighboring region of Brittany.

The Land of the Sea

Any resemblance to Normandy is superficial, for Brittany is France's kingdom of the Celts. The past is only ever a few yards away in a land that still guards its identity and joined France only in 1547. Its Breton name is Armorica, the land of the sea. Once a harsh, barren land, today Brittany has a strong farming community, celebrated for its arable produce, including onions and artichokes. The landscape is no less dramatic: from the cliffs ablaze with gorse on the emerald coast, to the treacherous rocks around coves that none but a local could ever navigate, to the salt marshes on the Guérande peninsula, where egrets and purple herons stand sentinel over lagoons and pools as salt flakes crystallize while the sea trickles away.

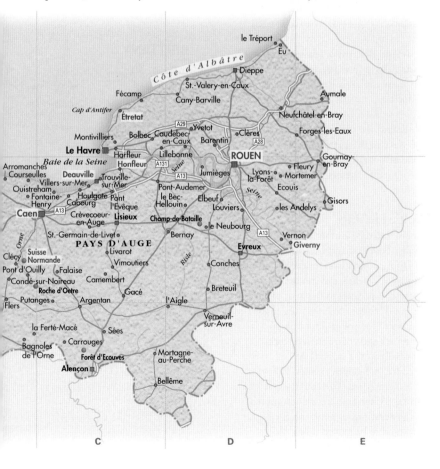

Camembert is Normandy's best-known cheese

stone remains of long-lost cultures can still be seen.

Food

Oysters in Brittany and Normandy, or Brittany's *bélons* from the Bélon river, are rare treasures on any menu, and the region produces many of the finest varieties of oysters in France. In Normandy, choose the oysters from St.-Vaast-la-Hougue (see page 77). Brittany's celebrated *crêpes*, flat pancakes folded into fan-shaped wedges, are fabulous, savory or sweet. Every village has its *crêperie*, where fast food is an art. Chefs prize the local sea salt, farmed on the salt marshes and sold in shops and by the roadside.

Normandy's lush pastures produce

Inland Brittany is less interesting for visitors, with few cities worth a detour. The new capital is Rennes, though the historic capital was Nantes, where Gilles de Rais, better known as Bluebeard the pirate, was burned at the stake in the 15th century by the duke of Brittany. Nantes has since been reassigned to the neighboring Loire region.

Celtic Heritage

Celtic festivals, uniting Brittany with Wales, Scotland and Ireland, take place in Quimper and Lorient every summer. Myths of witches and strange creatures abound, especially to the west of the region. Plenty of folk festivals enable visitors to see colorful traditional costumes and charming lacework, especially in the *coiffes* (lace headdresses) elderly women still wear to Sunday Mass. The country crafts of Brittany's heritage are well promoted, but generations of piracy on the high seas tend to be played down. With history evident to pagan times, strange

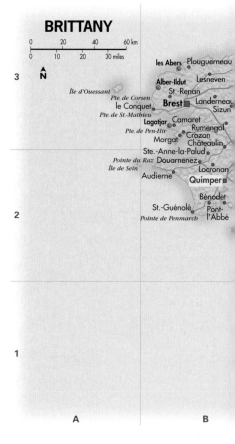

great cheeses – Camembert is the best known – and wonderful butter from Isigny-sur-Mer. *Tripes à la mode de Caen* (a savory offal dish) is a delicacy, as is a starter of *rillettes* (course pâté) or *boudin noir* (black pudding). The main seafood dish is a fish and shellfish stew, *marmite Dieppoise*. *Tarte Normande* is a delicious pastry made with apples or pears. Those apples provide the staple drink, cider. In Normandy and Brittany, order cider rather than wine with your meal and maybe try a glass of calvados, a potent apple brandy. Calvados is often served as a *trou Normand* (Norman hole), to be downed in one gulp midway through a meal to increase the appetite and make way for yet another few courses.

Les Pardons

The traditional Brittany *pardon* is a colorful local pilgrimage with costumes, parades and feasting. *Pardons* occur during summer months and details are available from local tourist offices.

Language

There has been a keen revival of Celtic, the ancient Breton language, in recent years. It's said that a fisherman from St.-Malo may converse freely with a Celtic trawlerman from Cornwall in England. Signage is bilingual and in Finistère even hotels are moving away from the standard international or French styles, now involving traditional folk color and design schemes and using the local language on menus.

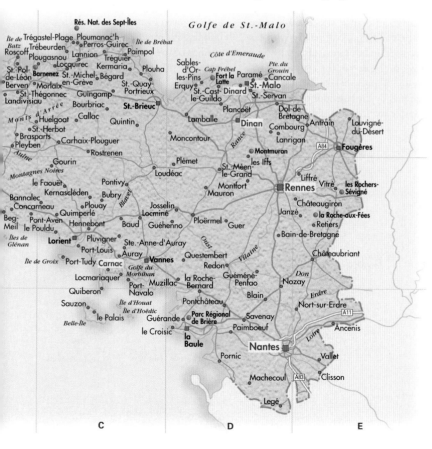

Timber-framed houses front the old marketplace in Rouen

ROUEN

Rouen is the city of Joan of Arc. The Norman capital may be an important modern port, but it can never escape its association with one of the great folk martyrs of France. It's centrally placed in rich and rural Normandy, with easy access (rare in France) along the Seine river to the east or through the new tunnel from Abbeville. Visitors are greeted by the splendor of the city's Gothic cathedral. Arrival at sunset,

when the spire and towers glow with sparkling rich sculptures twinkling like a fairy tale castle, is an unforgettable experience.

But there is much more to Rouen than St. Joan. Its old quarters haven't been allowed to stagnate. Modern building is not self-conscious, and all periods of the port's historic wealth and influence may be seen in the style of buildings and the busy shops and streets. The city is compact and easy to walk around. Begin any visit by

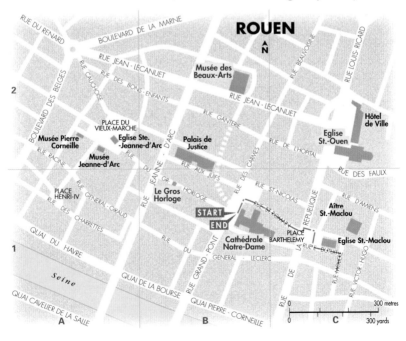

The City of St. Joan

The warrior saint, who heard the voice of St. Catherine and scandalized society by wearing male clothing, was burned at the stake May 30, 1431, in the old marketplace (place du Vieux-Marché) after Bishop Pierre Cauchon tried her for heresy. A modern commemorative cross stands on the spot where she died. Visit the striking Église Ste.-Jeanne-d'Arc, created in 1981 by a local architect to mark the 550th anniversary of her martyrdom. The boat-shaped church dominates the square where markets still take place under a canopy matching the new building. The interior is impressive, with notable stained glass, including Renaissance panels removed from Église St.-Vincent before bombings destroyed the original church. Excavations revealed the foundation of another church, St.-Sauveur, destroyed in 1833. The complex is surrounded by gardens and a museum dedicated to St. Joan, with waxwork scenes from her life.

Église Ste.-Jeanne-d'Arc ✚ A2 ⊠ Place du Vieux-Marché ⏱ Mon.–Thu. and Sat. 10–12:15 and 2–6, Fri., 11–12:15 and 2–6, Sun. 2–6 🚇 Théâtre des Arts ✋ Free

Musée Jeanne-d'Arc ✚ A2 ⊠ 33 place du Vieux-Marché ☎ 02 35 88 02 70 ⏱ Daily 9:30–1 and 1;30–7, mid-Apr. to mid-Sep.; 10–noon and 2–6:30, rest of year 🚇 Théâtre des Arts ✋ $

stopping off at the tourist office on the main courtyard of the cathedral. Based in a historic timbered house, the office can organize guided tours. If you plan to stay a while, buy a map – the free version handed out here is plastered with advertisements for shops, obscuring details of historic sites.

Shopping is excellent, mainly in the pedestrian-friendly zone, a maze of cobbled side streets and half-timbered houses. The best area is around the huge clock that straddles rue du Gros-Horloge.

ESSENTIAL INFORMATION

TOURIST INFORMATION
25 place de la Cathédrale ☎ 02 32 08 32 40; www.mairie-rouen.fr

URBAN TRANSPORTATION
A bus and subway system known as Métrobus serves Rouen and its outlying districts. However, the central historic part of town is best explored on foot, and all sights are within a short walk of the Théâtre des Arts subway station. Tickets are inexpensive and should be validated in machines at stations and on boarding buses. The Découverte pass is valid for 1, 2 or 3 days. Transportion information is

available at the bus station Espace Métrobus, rue Jeanne-d'Arc ☎ 02 35 52 52 52. Taxis can be hailed in the street or at stands, including those outside Espace Métrobus and the main railroad station.
Trains to Paris and other towns in Normandy arrive and depart from the SNCF (Gare-rue Verte) ⊠ Place Bernard-Tissot ☎ 08 36 35 35 35 (premium-rate call).

AIRPORT INFORMATION
Aéroport Rouen-Vallée-de-Seine is at Boos, 10 miles east of Rouen. Taxis serve the city center ☎ 02 35 79 41 00.

CLIMATE – Average highs and lows

JAN.	FEB.	MAR.	APR.	MAY	JUN.	JUL.	AUG.	SEP.	OCT.	NOV.	DEC.
8°C	8°C	10°C	12°C	15°C	18°C	19°C	20°C	19°C	15°C	12°C	10°C
46°F	46°F	50°F	54°F	59°F	64°F	66°F	68°F	66°F	59°F	54°F	50°F
4°C	4°C	5°C	7°C	9°C	12°C	14°C	14°C	13°C	10°C	8°C	5°C
39°F	39°F	41°F	45°F	48°F	54°F	57°F	57°F	55°F	50°F	46°F	41°F

Normandy and Brittany

The Gros Horloge – "Great Clock"

ROUEN SIGHTS

Key to symbols

⊞ map coordinates refer to the Rouen map on page 62; sights below are highlighted in yellow on the map.

✉ address or location ☎ telephone number

⏱ opening times 🍴 restaurant on site or nearby

🚌 nearest bus or tram route 🚇 nearest métro

ℹ information

✋ admission charge: $$$ more than €10, $$ €5–€10, $ less than €5

CATHÉDRALE NOTRE-DAME

The white stone of the beautifully restored Gothic facade dazzles visitors. The dusky interior is nonetheless impressive, with seemingly tenuous arches beside the airy nave. Among the medieval legacies are several stained-glass windows – still in place despite centuries of assault – with vivid, deep-blue panes. The tombs of dukes and princes outdo each other with their opulence and dignity. Soaring above is the 499-foot 14th-century cast-iron spire, which dominates the city and is floodlit every night until 1 a.m.

⊞ B1 ✉ Place de la Cathédrale ⏱ Mon.–Sat. 8–7, Sun. 8–6 🚇 Théâtre des Arts ✋ Free ℹ Guided tours daily at 4, Apr.–Sep.; Sat.–Sun. at 3, rest of year

ÉGLISE ST.-OUEN

It's best to visit during one of the many concerts held in this massive light and airy Gothic arched church. Only an unattractive modern altar mars the splendor of the windows and the sanctuary, with 18th-century choir gates. The 15th-century abbey church by the town hall is famous for the excellent quality of its organs, which may be heard in rehearsal during the days leading up to a concert. The church has its own tower and spires to augment Rouen's skyline. The building is seen to best effect from the peaceful gardens at the rear.

⊞ C2 ✉ Place du Général-de-Gaulle ⏱ Wed.–Mon. 10–12:30 and 2–6, mid-Mar. through Oct. 31; Wed. and Sat.–Sun. 10–12:30 and 2–4:30, mid-Jan. to mid-Mar. and Nov. 1 to mid-Dec. Closed mid-Dec. to mid-Jan. 🚇 Théâtre des Arts ✋ Free

LE GROS HORLOGE

One glance at the huge clock face straddling an archway across the bustling rue du Gros-Horloge and you are tempted to laugh at the original criticism that locals had trouble seeing it. But keep in mind that originally it was placed out of sight high on the clock tower next door. Moved by public demand to its present location, the fascinating "Great Clock," with its complicated, gilded double face showing both time and date, is now part of a potpourri of architectural styles. The building is framed with other unusual details, from its medieval tower to 17th-century carved fripperies and an ancient stone sculpture set in the arch under the clock. Enjoy a pleasant walk underneath through this old part of the town.

⊞ B1 ✉ Rue du Gros-Horloge ☎ 02 35 71 28 40 ⏱ call for opening times 🚇 Palais de Justice

MUSÉE DES BEAUX-ARTS

The elegant square Verdrel has waterfalls and exotic trees to distract the visitor from entering the Classical fine arts museum that takes up one side of the square. Within is a fine collection of paintings from François Clouet's fleshy nudes to Claude Monet's hazy *The Seine at Vétheuil*. Michelangelo da Caravaggio's *Flagellation of Christ* shouldn't be missed. Regular exhibitions are also held here and guided tours are available.

⊞ B2 ✉ Square Verdrel ☎ 02 35 71 28 40 ⏱ Wed.–Mon. 10–6. Closed holidays 🚇 Palais de Justice ✋ $

WALK: ROUEN'S ANTIQUES SHOPS

Refer to route marked on city map on page 62

You will take some of Rouen's past home with you if you spend a hour or so foraging through the back streets around the cathedral quarter. This area is rich with good small antiques shops. Dealers in this quarter are generally helpful and accommodating, and since most shops are in the city's famous old buildings, there is no need for guilt – it isn't consumerism, it's art!

Start this mile long walk facing the cathedral's facade. Go left and walk along the narrow rue St.–Romain, checking out the shops on the left side.

A specialist in old glass, porcelain, silver and furniture at Nos. 10–14 is Max Tetelin. Newer, but no less stylish, tableware is sold at Augy-Carpentier (No. 26).

Arriving at the busy shopping street of rue de la République, turn left to find Les Ans Chanteurs, at No. 47, stocked with art-deco tableware, curiosities and 19th-century household goods. Cross the road to walk through one of the narrow side streets into the intimate place St.-Barthélémy

Take time to appreciate the enchanting Gothic Église St.-Maclou with its five porches and carved wooden doors dating from 1552. Charming galleries cluster opposite the bow fronted church. Signs lead to the church's unusual Aître, a cloistered cemetery with wall designs created from bones.

Walk behind the church to reach place Barthélémy.

At No. 11 a fascinating old house contains a shop called Vieux Rouen, specializing in faience, a local craft with centuries of examples on display in the city's museums. Also, you will find old maps and vintage travel books on the bookshelves, excellent souvenirs of a seafaring town.

Leave the square on rue Eugène-Dutuit, leading to rue Molière.

Bertran at Nos. 108–110 has a fine selection of porcelain, jewelry and small paintings.

Turn back along rue Eugène-Dutuit and cross the square to return to rue St.-Romain and the cathedral shops, which are open Monday through Saturday until 7 p.m.

Église St.-Maclou ➕ C1 ✉ Place Barthélémy 🕐 Mon.–Sat. 10–noon and 2–6 (5:30 from Nov.–Feb.), Sun. 3–5:30. Closed some holidays 🚇 Théâtre des Arts ♿ Free ℹ Audio-guided visits available
Aître St.-Maclou ➕ C1 ✉ Rue Martainville 🕐 Daily 8–8 🚇 Théâtre des Arts ♿ Free

The cloistered garden at Église St.-Maclou

Normandy and Brittany

REGIONAL SIGHTS

Key to symbols

➕ map coordinates refer to the region maps on pages 58 and 60 (N refers to the Normandy map, B to the Brittany map); sights below are highlighted in yellow on the maps.

✉ address or location ☎ telephone number

🕐 opening times 🚌 nearest bus or tram route

🍴 restaurant on site or nearby ℹ️ information

🎟 admission charge: $$$ more than €10, $$ €5–€10, $ less than €5

BAYEUX

Timbered buildings, clean streets and the splashing of watermills: this city would be worth a visit even without its rich history. However, there is never any escaping the past in Bayeux. The Musée Mémorial de la Bataille de Normandie tells of the 1944 battle.

The 11th-century cathedral, with its frescoes depicting the murder of St. Thomas, was the original home to the Bayeux Tapestry, now displayed nearby. This remarkable 230-foot embroidered epic, commissioned by Odo, bishop of Bayeux and half-brother of William the Conqueror, relates the frame-by-frame drama of William's triumph at the Battle of Hastings and how the duke of Normandy won the crown of England in 1066. More than just propaganda, the incredibly detailed craftwork is an 11th-century soap opera, with scenes showing servants preparing food, religious intrigue, shipwreck and panic when Halley's

Comet warns Saxon king Harold of impending disaster. An excellent exhibition highlights the storytelling and stitching techniques, and an audio guide explains the drama.

➕ B2–N

Tourist information ✉ Pont St.-Jean ☎ 02 31 51 28 28; www.bayeux-tourism.com

Musée Mémorial de la Bataille de Normandie
✉ Boulevard Fabien-Ware ☎ 02 31 51 49 90
🕐 Daily 9:30–6:30, May 1 to mid-Sept.; 10–12:30 and 2–6, Feb. 1 to Apr. 30 and mid-Sep.–mid-Jan. 🎟 $$

Tapisserie de Bayeux ✉ Centre Guillaume-le-Conquerant, rue de Nesmond ☎ 02 31 51 25 50 🕐 Daily 9–7, May–Aug.; 9–6:30, in Apr. and Sep.; 9:30–12:30 and 2–6, rest of year 🎟 $$

CAEN

With a castle and two abbeys founded by William the Conqueror as a penance for marrying his cousin, enough of old Caen survived the bombing to make a visit worthwhile. And don't miss the (Peace Memorial) just outside town. Through bunker walls, confront the past. From the 1919 peace pledges, the gallery descends an unstoppable spiral past politicians, press and daily life into the inferno of World War II. Linked cinemas take you from D-Day to the present; you will see a split-screen perception of the landings through home movies of both sides, then a multimedia diary of events. *Esperance* (Hope), the third film, which ends this strange history, is a painful barrage of clips of the great peace the world has achieved. Churchill, Ike, de Gaulle,

"Here Duke William …" – an animated section of the Bayeux Tapestry

Stories in stones: Visitors check the plan at Carnac's prehistoric site

Hitler, JFK, King, Stalin, Nixon, Mao – it's impossible to tell hero from villain. Nazis at Nuremberg declare their innocence to the children of Auschwitz. Nelson Mandela walks free. Rwanda denies food to its own people. From Yalta to the United Nations, Hanoi to Sarajevo, the relentless screen is an unforgiving mirror to the face of world peace.

🞦 C2–N

Tourist information ✉ Place St.–Pierre ☎ 02 31 27 14 14; www.ville-caen-fr

Le Mémorial, Un Musée pour la Paix ✉ Esplanade D.D. Eisenhower ☎ 02 31 06 06 44 🍴 Café 🍷 $$$

CARNAC

Come to wonder at the riddle of the stones, strange alignments erected up to 6,000 years ago and still standing to the north of the town. The megaliths are said to have been arranged for some long-forgotten religious or ritual purpose, and the more distinctive lines can be seen from viewing platforms. Most are now roped off from the public to avoid erosion and vandalism. Pamphlets proposing local myths and legends about the stones can be found at the tourist office. Details of guided tours and seasonal opening hours are available from the tourist office. For a more recent historical era, visit Église St.-Cornély, dedicated to the patron saint of horned beasts. To worship the sun, find your way past the lagoons to Carnac Plage, a modern seaside resort.

🞦 C2–B

Tourist information ✉ 74 avenue des Druides (Carnac-Plage) ☎ 02 97 52 13 52; www.ot-carnac.fr

COTENTIN

From the granite cliffs of Cap de la Hague, the Cotentin peninsula is the finger of France pointing toward the British Channel Islands. The rugged coastline from Cherbourg to Caen is better known for the D-Day circuits, but the northern side of the peninsula is worth a visit in its own right. William the Conqueror and Richard the Lion-Heart both sailed from Barfleur, which boasts a lifeboat museum and Normandy's tallest lighthouse (233 feet) at Gateville. St.-Vaast-la-Hougue and Tatihou (see page 77) are across the atmospheric Val de Saire, an area with France's tiniest town hall at la Pernelle. At Isigny-sur-Mer, discover France's best butter and cream. Volognes, another city ravaged by bombings, has the regional cider and calvados museums. On the other side of the peninsula, where the coast has unspoiled dunes, visit the Cathédrale Notre-Dame at Coutances and Christian Dior's childhood home in the busy fishing port of Granville, which, like nearby Barneville-Cartaret, has ferries to the Channel Islands.

🞦 A2, A3, B2, B3–N

Barfleur tourist information ✉ Rd-Point Guillaume-le-Conquérant ☎ 02 33 54 02 48; www.ville-barfleur.fr

Coutances tourist information ✉ Place Georges-Leclerc ☎ 02 33 19 08 10; www.manchetourisme.com

Granville tourist information ✉ 4 cours Jonville ☎ 02 33 91 30 03; www.ville-granville.com

Musée Christian-Dior ✉ Rue de la Falaise, Granville ☎ 02 33 61 48 21 🕐 Daily 10–12:30 and 2–6:30, late May to late Sep. 🍷 $$

Sun and shade on the beach at Deauville

CÔTE D'ALBÂTRE

The northeastern strip of coastline from le Tréport to Le Havre is named for its fast-retreating cliff faces. The white chalk is eroded by several yards each year, and the sea is dotted with lonely shards of rock, showing where a previous generation once stood. Beaches of smooth, blue-gray pebbles and stones are a particular attraction of the many coves and harbors nestling under the cliffs. Most charming is Étretat (see page 70), and most interesting is Fécamp, where the 12th-century Église de la Trinité harbors a relic said to be the blood of Christ and a palace still makes the monastic liqueur Bénédictine. Tours and tastings are offered daily.

Le Havre is uncompromisingly modern, with an industrial approach road and little remaining of the prewar port. By contrast, Dieppe, though a little run-down, has lovely old streets linking the port and the town center, many good seafood restaurants and its 15th-century château containing a museum with a fabulous ivory collection and paintings by Pierre-Auguste Renoir, Eugène Boudin and Camille Pissarro. Alas the fishermen's stalls that once lined the quayside have been moved to a less picturesque modern market. ✚ C3–D3–N

Fécamp tourist information ✉ 113 rue Alexandre-le-Grand ☎ 02 35 28 88 29; www.ville-fecamp.fr

Palais Bénédictine ✉ 110 rue Alexandre-le-Grand ☎ 02 35 10 26 10 ⊙ Daily 10–7:30, mid-Jul. through Aug. 31; 10–1 and 2–6:30, Apr. 1 to mid-Jul. and in Sep.; 10:30–12:45 and 2–6, Feb.–Mar. and Oct.–Dec. ✋ $$

Dieppe tourist information ✉ Pont Jehan-Ango, quai du Carénage ☎ 02 32 14 40 60; www.mairie-dieppe.fr

Château Musée ✉ Rue de Chastes ☎ 02 35 84 19 76 ⊙ Daily 10–noon and 2–6, Jun.–Sep.; Wed.–Mon. 10–noon and 2–5 (also Sun. 5–6 p.m.) rest of year ✋ $

DEAUVILLE

A pleasure ground designed for summer with its eye keenly focused on Parisian and American weekenders, Deauville built its boardwalk (promenade des Planches), casino and racecourse in 1910. Here Gabrielle "Coco" Chanel invented herself as a couturier making women's fashions out of fishermen's jerseys, Hollywood stars come for the annual American Film Festival in September or the races, and casino gamblers take time out to enjoy the feathers and sequins of the floor show. At its best during July and August, the city has its share of vacation residences. The mock-Riviera buzz is great fun, and everyone is in on the joke of southern chic transplanted north for the season. ✚ C2–N

Tourist information ✉ Place de la Mairie ☎ 02 31 14 40 00; www.deauville.org

DINAN

If possible, try to arrive at this charming medieval town by boat. As you sail from St.-Malo along the Rance river, you will stock up on lifelong memories. This most perfectly preserved of walled towns is built on such a human scale that you will hardly believe its charm – from the little pleasure port, past the black-roofed gray-stone buildings to the fertile green fields and trees on the sloping hillside. Start your walk from the town museum in the castle, and stroll on the almost complete ramparts dating from the 13th century. Best views are from the promenade de la Duchesse-Anne. Streets are storybook narrow, steep and arcaded. Many old shops, especially along the medieval rue du Jerzual, are now tasteful boutiques selling handicrafts and antiques.

In good weather, take a turn around the neat Jardin Anglais; on duller days, step inside Église St.-Sauveur, which holds the heart of Bertrand du Guesclin, who famously fought a duel with one Thomas of Canterbury in Dinan's main square in 1357. Today, a statue of the hero stands in the square.

🔒 D3–B

Tourist information ✉ 6 rue de l'Horlage ☎ 02 96 87 69 76; www.dinan-tourisme.com

Château ✉ Rue du Château ⏰ Daily 10–6:30, Jun. 1 to mid-Oct.; daily 10–noon, 2–6, mid-Mar. through May 31 and mid-Oct. to mid-Nov.; Wed.–Mon. 1:30–5:30, Feb. to mid-Mar. and mid-Nov. through Dec. 31 ♿ $

DINARD

Probably the prettiest of the popular resorts of Brittany is Dinard, with its lovely Grande Plage and surprisingly warm summer climate that comes courtesy of the Gulf Stream, which blesses mimosa and camellia blossoms from spring onward. Just across the estuary from St.-Malo (see page 76), the resort was discovered by Americans in the mid-19th century, and since then, every year sees new striped bathing tents and familiar faces returning to the favorite beach.

The season brings regattas by day, sound-and-light shows by night, and thalassotherapy by way of alternative pampering. The romantically named Promenade du Clair de Lune (Moonlight Promenade) leads to the aquarium and sea museum.

Dinard is a good base for exploring the Côte d'Emeraude (Emerald Coast) – ideally hiring a boat, but just as interesting by car. Cross the bridge for St.-Malo and the tidal dam that provides Brittany's electricity, enjoy the beaches of les Sables-d'Or or explore the magnificent 230-foot-high cliffs of Cap Fréhel and its lighthouse.

🔒 D3–B

Tourist information ✉ 2 boulevard Féart ☎ 02 99 46 94 12; www.ville-dinard.fr

Aquarium de Dinard ✉ 17 avenue Georges-V ☎ 02 99 46 13 90 ⏰ Currently closed

Cobbled streets lead to the clock tower in Dinan

Carved out by the sea – the chalk cliffs at Étretat

ÉTRETAT

Without question, Normandy's most-stunning beach resort, Étretat is best enjoyed out of season, when the bay is deserted and the magnificent chalk headlands, with their imposing arches astride the sea, may be admired in peace. A cathedral-size cave is accessible from the pebbled beach. Atop the Falaise d'Amont cliff is a sailor's chapel, Notre-Dame de la Garde, and a memorial to aviators Charles Nungesser and François Coli, whose plane l'Oiseau Blanc was last seen from these cliffs on its ill-fated bid to fly from Paris to New York in 1927. Their story is told in a nearby museum. In the sea just beyond the other cliff, the Falaise d'Aval, stands a 230-foot rock stack known as the Aiguille d'Étretat (the needle). These rocks inspired the great landscape and Impressionist artists Claude Monet, Jean-Baptiste-Camille Corot and Eugène Boudin, who returned here year after year. In place du Maréchal-Foch, the town built its wooden covered market in 1926, surrounded by charming 16th-century town houses. A commemorative plaque recalls a World War I American hospital on the square.

☩ C3–N
Tourist information ✉ Place M.-Guillard ☎ 02 35 27 05 21; www.etretat.net
Musée Nungesser et Coli ✉ Falaise d'Amont
☎ 02 35 27 07 47 ◷ Daily 10–noon and 2–6, mid-Jun. to mid-Sep.; Sat.–Sun. 10–noon and 2–6, Apr. 1 to mid-Jun. ✋ $

GIVERNY

You won't find a single, famous canvas by Claude Monet himself in the charming pink and green house where the artist lived until his death in 1926. But where else can you step inside a painting? The gardens, with the water-lily pond and bridge, are so well-known the world over that the air around this most visited site is filled with sighs of recognition.

Just like a Claude Monet painting – the gardens at the artist's house in Giverny

Maintained with old-style planting, exactly as they've been immortalized in the world's art galleries, these gardens were the artist's constant subject from 1895, when he finally bought the house he had rented since 1883. Monet traveled and painted a great deal in the countryside and coasts of Normandy. His family home was at Le Havre, and he studied in Honfleur. However, it was his later study, *Nymphéas*, Water Lilies, that many consider his masterwork.

The house and gardens, the lily pond and the Clos Normand are best seen in early summer (when blooms are at their best) and early in the day (before crowds arrive). The favorite spot for photographs is the little green bridge, where delays can occur as almost everyone takes the same snapshot. Reproductions of Monet's classic paintings, as well as his collection of Japanese prints, are displayed in the house.

The nearby Musée d'Art Américain Giverney displays works by disciples of Monet and American artists. It has a restaurant on its grounds and is convenient for art pilgrims doing the full tour, since Giverny is also close to the Impressionist site of Auvers-sur-Oise (see page 50).

✚ D2–N

Fondation Claude Monet ☎ 02 32 51 28 21 🕐 Tue.–Sun. (also Mon. public holidays) 10–6, Apr.–Oct. 🍴 Café 🖐 $$ (gardens only $)

Musée d'Art Américain Giverney ✉ 99 rue Claude Monet ☎ 02 32 51 94 65 🕐 Tue.–Sun. 10–6 (also 6–9 p.m., first Thu. of the month) Apr.–Oct. 🍴 Restaurant and café 🖐 $$

The harbor at Honfleur

HONFLEUR

The prettiest working port in northern France positively hums with visitors seeking the best table for a seafood dinner, yet it still retains its charm. The quayside view of the Vieux Bassin is always seen through a haze of bobbing masts from little fishing boats and pleasure craft in the harbor. Tall slate-and-oak fronted timber-framed buildings jostle for position and their ground floors are now yacht chandlers, art galleries and of course restaurants. Many an adventurer departed from here. A plaque on the wall of the 16th-century Lieutenant building records Samuel de Champlain setting sail for Quebec. Local fishermen worked the Newfoundland banks, using Honfleur's great salt store to preserve their catch. René-Robert Cavelier de La Salle embarked for the Mississippi to found Louisiana. Here came artists: The Musée Eugène-Boudin – named for the town's most-celebrated son, Eugène Boudin, the son of a ferryman – has the artist's works along with views by Jean-Baptiste-Camille Corot, Raoul Dufy and Boudin's student, Claude Monet. The marketplace Église Ste.-Catherine was built of wood in the 15th century by shipbuilders. From here photograph the 18th-century bell tower across the square.

✚ C2–N

Tourist information ✉ Place Arthur-Boudin
☎ 02 31 89 23 30; www.ville-honfleur.fr
Musée Eugène-Boudin ✉ Rue de l'Homme-de-Bois
☎ 02 31 89 54 00 ◉ Wed.–Mon. 10–noon and 2–6, mid-Mar. through Sep. 30; Mon. and Wed.–Fri. 2:30–5, Sat.–Sun. 10– noon and 2:30–5, mid-Feb. to mid-Mar. and Oct.–Dec. ✋ $$

LE MONT-ST.-MICHEL

An awe-inspiring sight, this centuries-old monastery appears to rise from the sea in the early mist. Mont-St.-Michel has been a symbol of France and French ingenuity long before the Eiffel Tower was a twinkle in an engineer's toolbox.

A 260-foot granite island in the mudflats and salt marshes of the

The tidal granite island of le Mont-St.-Michel is approached across a modern causeway

Couesnon estuary stands on the Norman side of the border with Brittany. Quicksand and sudden tides separate the rock from the mainland. The mount is reached via a modern causeway.

Believed originally to be a pagan burial ground, le Mont-St.-Michel had the early name Mont Tombe. In the eighth century, the bishop of Avranches had a vision of the Archangel Michael, who is said to have ordered the building of a chapel on the site. Successive Carolingian, Romanesque and Gothic buildings crowded on the precarious rock to create the abbey known since the Middle Ages as *la Merveille* (the wonder). A place of worship and impregnable fortress, the wonder was finally topped out with the placing of a statue of St. Michael atop the 515-foot spire in the late 19th century.

The trek through the compact streets to the ramparts is worth the effort. Don't complain about the tourists squeezed into the inaccurately named Grande Rue. In the past it would have been just as crowded, but with pilgrims and penitents rather than tourists. Key religious festivals see candlelight processions across from the mainland, winding through the streets to the church, and every evening except Monday from June through October brings a sound-and-light display.

✠ A1–N

Tourist information ✉ Boulevard Advencée
☎ 02 33 60 14 30; www.mont-saint-michel.com
Le Mont-St.-Michel 🕐 24 hours
Abbey of le Mont-St.-Michel ☎ 02 33 60 14 14
🕐 Daily 9–5:30, May–Sep.; 9:30–4:30, rest of year
🖐 $$

Normandy and Brittany

Stalls displaying crafts add to the bustle of a town-center street in Quimper

NANTES

Nantes, the former capital of Brittany, now reigns over the neighboring region of Pays de la Loire, where it proves a useful gateway for excursions into the fabulous vineyards and château country of the Loire region. The city may have been overrun with modern development, but its cultural life continues apace with carnivals, fairs and folk festivals. Worth a visit is the Cathédrale St.-Pierre-et-St.-Paul, built of local gleaming white tufa stone. Built in the 15th through 17th centuries, the airy cathedral holds the extravagant Renaissance tomb of François II, last duke of Brittany, who died in 1488. A few steps away is the ducal château, whose moat is now gardens. The fortress dates from the 15th to 16th centuries and has a 15th-century well at the entrance. Within are various small museums of local history and traditions. Boat trips along the Erdre river are a pleasant way to view some charming smaller private châteaux.

➕ D1–B
Tourist information ✉ Place du Commerce
☎ 02 40 20 60 00; www.mairie-nantes.fr
Château ✉ 4 place Marc-Elder ☎ 02 40 41 56 56
🕐 Daily 10–noon and 2–6, Jul.–Aug.; Wed.–Mon. 10–noon and 2–6, rest of year. Closed holidays 💳 $$

QUIMPER

The ancient Celtic kingdom of Cornouaille chose Quimper as its capital after the original city of Ys sank beneath the waters of Douarnenez bay in the sixth century. A statue of King Gradlon, founder of the city, stands between the twin spires of the 13th-century Gothic cathedral. A pottery museum a little way out of town in the Locmaria district displays the best of 300 years of local crafts. Modern variants are manufactured and painted by hand in workshops that are open to the public or sold in the many souvenir and craft shops in the bustling town center.

Served by its own airport for domestic flights, Quimper is the focus of several Breton-Celtic gatherings and festivals throughout the year. The other local tradition is lace making, and the summer sees picturesque roadside stalls appear from which doilies, shawls and tablecloths are sold. With its attractive timber-framed houses, cobbled streets and an unmistakable air of gentility, this large town manages to present an air of discreet intimacy.

➕ B2–B
Tourist information ✉ Place de la Résistance
☎ 02 98 53 04 05; www.bretagne-4villes.com

Normandy and Brittany

The city of Rennes stands on the confluence of the Ille and Vilaine rivers. The canalized Vilaine neatly separates the northern and southern districts. The tale of two cities is just as neatly divided by time. The 1720 great fire raged for eight days and destroyed large parts of the medieval town. About a thousand houses were destroyed, and Jacques Gabriel laid out the new section with two wide regal squares and Paris-style streets.

Rennes is often compared unfavorably with Nantes, the former seat of the dukes of Brittany (see page 74). But traces of unmistakable Breton charm can be found in any stroll through the oldest corners of the town, with its bulging beamed Renaissance buildings tottering over narrow streets and the aroma of cider from open windows and freshly made *crêpes* from sidewalk cafés.

Just north of the canal, the remaining byways of old Rennes make for a revealing walk. The tourist office is housed in the Chapelle St.-Yves, just off quai Duguay-Trouin, and has a free exhibition of Rennes history in a medieval setting.

From here, explore narrow streets lined with ancient houses around Église St.-Sauveur. The nearby cathedral is an unremarkable baroque building, but the area around it is intriguing. Follow rue des Dames to the Portes Mordelaises, a medieval corner with entry gate and fortifications. Close by is place des Lices with its colorful Saturday market. The city's larger main market, in the south section, is open every weekday.

Visit the restored Breton Parliament, imposingly placed on place du Palais with gardens, and the Hôtel de Ville on place de la Mairie, a pedestrian square with an

A carving mounted on a building in the old part of Rennes

CAPITAL OF BRITTANY

impressive Classical opera house.

Dining is fine across town, but the old quarter is especially charming for informal meals.

The city walks off its excellent lunches in the Jardin du Thabor gardens. Admission is free, and one enters from either rue de Paris or place St.-Mélaine. The 40-acre green space has wide formal walks, terraces and flower beds.

On the eastern side of town, explore the gardens around the Abbaye St.-Georges, which now serves as office space.

South of the Vilaine, the Musée des Beaux-Arts boasts displays of Egyptian artifacts and an art gallery with the inevitable collection of Impressionist pieces, augmented by a selection of works by Breton artists. The museum's jewel is a painting from the 17th century, Georges de la Tour's *The Newborn*, a masterpiece of rich color. This side of town is where most top restaurants and international class hotels are found. Less-expensive establishments are strung around the modern station, which welcomes fast train services from Paris and the west coast. This is also a popular haunt for students and young people on Saturday nights, when livelier bars accommodate Breton artists and musicians. When entering the city, follow signs for Rennes-Sud in order to park near your hotel. The canal and northern section are a good 15-minute walk away, but a taxi to the town center should cost approximately €5.

✚ D2–B

Tourist information ✉ 11 rue St.-Yves ☎ 02 99 67 11 11; www.ville-rennes.fr

Musée des Beaux-Arts ✉ 20 Quai Émile-Zola ☎ 02 99 28 55 85 🕐 Wed.–Mon. 10–noon and 2–6 ♿ $$

The neat gardens of the Marché aux Légumes (Vegetable Market) in St.-Malo

ST.-MALO

The seafaring town of St.-Malo was the homeport for the notorious Corsairs, state-licensed pirates who would board foreign vessels and claim their cargo for France. Officially operating in French waters, these adventurers managed to ride and raid the high seas as far away as the south Atlantic. At the mouth of the Rance estuary is a walled town – St.-Malo-Intra-Muros – all faithfully restored after wartime bombing. A tour of the sympathetically renovated ramparts is an essential part of any visit. Many imposing 18th-century family homes were built on the proceeds of piracy. Jacques Cartier, discoverer of Canada, is buried in the cathedral. If the weather is pleasant and the tide is out, walk across the sands to the two islands in the bay. Back on the mainland, there are many fine seafood restaurants both in St.-Malo itself and the neighboring resort of St.-Servan, which has a maritime museum in the medieval Tour Solidor and a pleasantly landscaped path, the Aleth Corniche.

✚ D3–B

Tourist information ✉ Esplanade St-Vincent
☎ 02 99 56 64 48; www.ville-saint-malo.fr

SUISSE NORMANDE

It may not have any Alps and winter sports are a world away, but the "Norman Switzerland" area around the Orne valley, south of Caen, offers some charming half-timbered buildings, the opportunity for modest rock climbing and plenty of outdoor sports in summer. The river weaves through its attractive valleys, and both rafting and canoeing are popular ways to see the countryside. Horseback riding and hang-gliding are other alternatives. The "Route de la Suisse Normande," a

Just 69 acres, Tatihou is known for its Vauban fort. The island may be reached on foot across the oyster beds at low tide or by amphibious boat May through September, which is included in admission charges to the fort and maritime and marine heritage museum. Ecology rules limit the maximum number of visitors to 500 per day. Free supervised bird-watching excursions take place during summer months. Also offshore are the Îles St.-Marcouf – Île de Terre and Île du Large – once home to pirates. Each winter 30,000 gulls come here to nest and rest among cormorants and herons. In summer, fishermen and lifeboat crews take groups for a closer view of these seabird sanctuaries, with their abandoned 19th-century military buildings. In August, Tatihou hosts an international open-air music festival, with free fringe events on the St.-Vaast wharf and music in local bars until late. The port of St.-Vaast has excellent restaurants and superb food shops.
🚩 B3–N

Tatihou visitor center ✉ Quai Vauban, St.-Vaast-la-Hougue ☎ 02 33 23 19 92 🕐 Boat departs daily every 30 minutes (ebb tide) or every hour (flood tide), May–Sep. 🚤 Boat (includes fort and museum) $$ ℹ Ornithological and historical tours (free), daily, Jul.–Aug.
St.-Vaast-la-Hougue tourist information
✉ 1 place du Général-de-Gaulle ☎ 02 33 23 19 32; www.saint-vaast-reville.com

signposted circular driving route, is an easier option. Picturesque drives offer ample opportunity to sample local food and drink. Calvados (apple brandy) and farmhouse cider are everywhere, and tastings are offered at the roadside. Thury-Harcourt, with its bombed-out château, has attractive parks and gardens. During summer a scenic train takes picturesque excursions to the coast near Caen or inland to Clécy, a pretty stone village that is the unofficial capital of the Suisse Normande. A popular and none-too-strenuous walk features views from the Pain de Sucre (sugar-loaf) hill.
🚩 B2–N

Clécy tourist information ✉ Place du Triport ☎ 02 31 69 79 95; www.clecy.com or www.suisse-normande.com

ÎLE DE TATIHOU

One of Normandy's least known attractions lies just off the coast of the celebrated oyster-fishing port of St.-Vaast-la-Hougue.

The Orne river at Pont Ouilly, Suisse Normande

DRIVE: THE D-DAY COAST

Distance: 130 miles Time: 2 to 3 days

D-Day: June 6, 1944. Allied forces stormed the beaches of Normandy to the east of the Cotentin peninsula to mark the beginning of the end of the war in Europe and the liberation of France. The coast is marked with cemeteries, memorials and scores of local museums, each telling the tale of a remarkable day and its aftermath from the viewpoint of those who lived through the events.

Starting at Caen, visit its stunning Le Mémorial, Un Musée pour la Paix (see page 66), then take the D515 to Benouville.
The first target captured by the Allies on D-Day, the Pegasus Bridge on the Caen-Ouistreham canal was a vital strategic link that needed to be preserved. Three gliders crash-landed just after midnight, and Pegasus Bridge was in Allied hands by the time reinforcements arrived from Sword Beach. The original bridge was removed in 1999, amid much controversy, when plans were made to rebuild the original within a dedicated museum. Columns near the bridge mark the glider landings.

Take the D35C then the D514 to the port of Ouistreham.
Visit the Musée du Mur de l'Atlantique (Atlantic Wall Museum). Follow the D514 beside

American Cemetery, Colleville-sur-Mer

Sword, Juno and Gold beaches, with a detour at Bernières-sur-Mer to turn left on D79A for the Canadian Cemetery at Bény-sur-Mer. Turn back to the coast road, stopping perhaps at Ver-sur-Mer's museum, commemorating both the Gold Beach landings and the 1927 airmail race between Paris and New York. Then head for Arromanches-les Bains. The remains of Mulberry Harbor's prefabricated landing pontoons can still be seen. The Musée du Débarquement explains this remarkable feat. Also visit Arromanches 360 to view an 18-minute, 360-degree cinema re-enactment.

Take the D516 to Bayeux (see page 66). Follow the D6 to Port-en-Bessin.
At Omaha Beach, visit the Musée des Épaves-Sous-Marines du Débarquement for the artifacts of salvage operations from wrecks of warships lost at D-Day. The Cimetière Américain (American Cemetery) at Colleville-sur-Mer – 170 acres laid with 9,000 white crosses – overlooks Omaha Beach itself, serving as a sobering reminder of the devastating cost of the bloody battle. An orientation table above the beach shows how the German defenses were able to inflict such damage. At St.-Laurent-sur-Mer, the Musée Omaha-6-Juin-1944 has vehicles and weapons found on the beaches. Past the cliffs of Pointe du Hoc, where German fortifications were taken by the brave young Americans of Colonel Rudder's elite Rangers, Grandcamp-Maisy has an exhibition devoted to the Rangers.

From the intersection of D514 and N13, follow signs for Cherbourg to Ste.-Mère-Église.
The true story of the American 82nd and 101st Airborne Divisions is told at the Musée Airborne.

From the D423, turn right onto D115 then D14 to Ste.-Marie-du-Mont. Turn left toward the beach on D913 to reach the Musée de Débarquement d'Utah-Beach.
Along the coast from here as far as Belgium are distinctive milestones of liberty, including the Mémorial de Montormel. The Musée de la Liberté at Quinéville recalls life under the Nazi occupation.

Follow D42 for 5 miles to join the N13 to Cherbourg.
A ferry and cruise liner port, Cherbourg was badly damaged by wartime bombings. Find propaganda posters and the dramatic story of the liberation at the Musée de la Libération.
✚ C2, B2, B3, A3–N

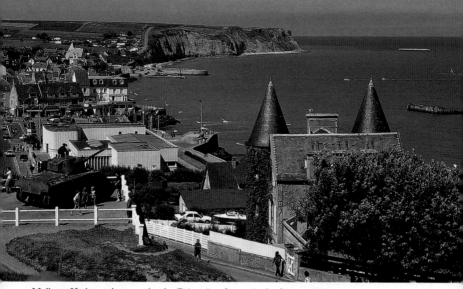

Mulberry Harbor at Arromanches-les-Bains, site of a massive landing operation

Musée du Mur de l'Atlantique ✉ 6 avenue du 6-Juin, Ouistreham ☎ 02 31 97 28 69 🕐 Daily, early Feb. to mid–Nov. ✋ $$

Musée América Gold Beach ✉ Place Amiral-Byrd, Ver-sur-Mer ☎ 02 31 22 58 58 🕐 Daily, May–Oct. ✋ $

Musée du Débarquement ✉ Place du 6-Juin, Arromanches-les Bains ☎ 02 31 22 34 31 🕐 Daily, Feb.–Dec. ✋ $$

Arromanches 360 ✉ Chemin du Calvaire, Arromanches-les-Bains ☎ 02 31 22 30 30 🕐 Half-hour screening daily from 10 a.m., Feb.–Dec. ✋ $

Musée des Épaves-Sous-Marines-du-Débarquement ✉ Route de Bayeux, Port-en-Bessin ☎ 02 31 21 17 06 🕐 Daily in Jun.; Sat.–Sun. in May ✋ $$

Cimetière Américain ✉ Colleville-sur-Mer ☎ 02 31 51 62 00

Musée Omaha-6-Juin-1944 ✉ Rue de la Mer, St.-Laurent-sur-Mer ☎ 02 31 21 97 44 🕐 Daily, mid-Feb. to late Nov. ✋ $$

Musée des Rangers ✉ 30 quai Crampon, Grandcamp-Maisy ☎ 02 31 92 33 51 🕐 Daily, Jun.–Aug.; Tue.–Sun., Apr.–May and in Sep. ✋ $

Musée Airborne ✉ Place du 6-Juin, Ste.-Mère-Église ☎ 02 33 41 41 35 🕐 Daily, Feb.–Nov. ✋ $$

Musée de Débarquement d'Utah-Beach ✉ Opposite Utah-Beach, Ste.-Marie-du-Mont ☎ 02 33 71 53 35 🕐 Daily, Apr. 1 to mid-Nov.; Sat.–Sun. and school holidays, rest of year ✋ $

Musée de la Liberté ✉ Quinéville ☎ 02 33 21 40 44 🕐 Daily, mid-Mar. to mid-Nov. ✋ $

Musée de la Libération ✉ Fort du Roule, Cherbourg ☎ 02 33 20 14 12 🕐 Daily in summer, Mon.–Sat. winter ✋ $

ℹ Call individual museums for opening times

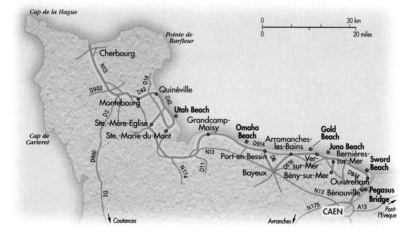

LOIRE VALLEY AND THE ATLANTIC COAST

> " *A LANDSCAPE studded with improbable châteaux, the garden of France is the country of enchanted journeys.* "

Opposite: Formal gardens at the Château de Villandry

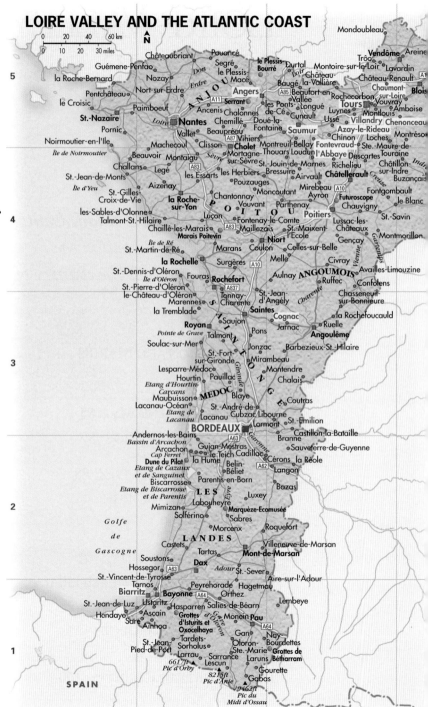

LOIRE VALLEY AND THE ATLANTIC COAST

D   E

LOIRE VALLEY AND THE ATLANTIC COAST

The Loire is the picture book of France. Every mile offers spectacular Renaissance indulgences on hilltops and islands and medieval fortresses guarding bridgeheads and towns. The Loire river, with its many tributaries, serves countless creamy-white châteaux whose turrets and gardens literally inspired the authors and illustrators of the great European fairy tales.

Like every fairy tale, it has its fabulous matriarchs and wicked queens. Eleanor of Aquitaine, Catherine de Médicis, and many a king's mistress shaped French history. Every journey is but a few steps behind the paths of the women who took on the world of men: Joan of Arc and George Sand are remembered in châteaux and festivities.

Sound and Light

Celebration in summer often takes the form of sound-and-light presentations at the grand palaces. Lights, lasers and even fireworks tell the stories of great houses and the kings and princes who lived there.

Best is the *Puy du Fou:* Its name means madman's well, but the spectacle is anything but crazy. Conceived by a local politician, the show – which brings to life 1,000 years of history in an hour and 40 minutes – has entertained more than 5 million people. The entire populations of 15 villages in the heart of the Vendée country spend all year preparing for the stunt-riding re-enactments of the glory days of a ruined fortress. France's greatest actors and musicians provide the soundtrack for the largest show of its kind in the country. Twenty-eight performances are given each summer.

Monarchs and Windmills

The Vendée has always been independently minded, remaining staunchly monarchist after the revolution and signaling its underground movement across the countryside by coded positioning of the sails of its windmills.

The Marais-Poitevin, habitat of herons and marsh birds, is known as the Venice of the Atlantic, a network of unending green waterways seen through a haze of willow trees. The tranquility seems a world away from the

Loire Valley and the Atlantic Coast

Loire Valley and the Atlantic Coast

Grapes that produce the great wines of Bordeaux

campsites and tourists on the coast and at such island resorts as La Rochelle.

Further south, the Aquitaine coastline borders on the great forests of the Dordogne and Limousin.

Wining and Dining

This area includes two great wine regions: the Loire and Bordeaux. The whites of the Loire – Hollywood star Gérard Depardieu is counted among the region's winemakers – are crisp and refreshing. The great wines of Bordeaux, of course, are the stuff of legends. Various *crus* are as carefully considered as gilt-edged stocks and bonds, and large château estates are owned and managed mostly by leading banks and multinational businesses.

Cognac and Armagnac are the splendid brandies of Aquitaine and Cointreau the *digestif* of Anjou. Where no wines are made, western France is always inventive. What apples are to Normandy, pears are to the Mayenne. Here drink *pommeau*, calvados mixed with apple or fruit juice, or *poiré*, an

alcoholic fermentation of pears alone.

Fine dining is the order of the day. Generally, restaurants of the Loire serve a lighter, but no less satisfying, cuisine. Freshwater *sandre* (pike perch) and Chalon duck are among delights to discover. This is the region of frogs legs, button mushrooms and *mogettes* (white beans). When dining in Les Landes, don't be surprised to find prunes served with meats and poultry. Bordelais food is richer and more classical, while foie gras, walnuts and truffles define the tables of neighboring Dordogne.

Overindulgence and most other conditions can be treated at one of the many thalassotherapy centers on the coast from Nantes to Biarritz. Seawater treatment is considered essential for such things as asthma or maintaining a general sense of well-being. These spa resorts usually boast highly prized chefs, and the "cure" is taken by the French as a luxury vacation rather than a medical emergency.

Grape Expectations

Au revoir lettuce leaves, *adieu* pills and potions, and *bonjour* and *bienvenue* to the bottle and its bounty. Fitness through claret and its byproducts is the latest treat for the clinically wealthy. Vinotherapy, a range of anti-ageing and slimming treatments, is based on extracts from vines and wine, in particular grape-seed polyphenols that protect against ultraviolet rays. The technique was developed in the heart of the Graves vineyards, a stone's throw from Bordeaux. Whether you go for a day's quick fix or a week of indulgence, you will be pampered. After wine and a honey wrap or a barrel-bath in which fresh grape-seed extracts are added to the whirlpool bath, you may set off to discover all the appellations of Bordeaux wine with a tour of some of the world's most valuable grapes.

BORDEAUX

Naturally enough, in a city of so many classic wines, Bordeaux is rich, dignified and discreet with many fine flavors. A classic city by any standards, Bordeaux enables visitors to enjoy fine architecture from the 18th century and earlier, as well as grandiose public sculpture added over several periods.

The abiding impression is of unostentatious wealth and well-tended good taste. Mansions have wrought-iron balconies and sculpted facades, both in the central streets and along the wide Garonne river. A particularly fine, if rather run-down, parade of family houses faces the river itself. Sightseeing boats chug along the port to provide an excellent introduction to the city and its region.

Like any thriving French city of its size, Bordeaux is divided into distinct quarters. The northern Chartrons quarter lines the quayside of the old wine trade. If you are on a short visit, concentrate on the St.-Pierre, Ste.-Croix and St.-Michel districts where all the principal sites can be found.

There is little overtly modern building to detract from the classic layout of the city, designed in the Paris mold. However, the tourist office will provide information about a walking tour for those keen on discovering 20th-century buildings. The joy of the center is that it remains surprisingly intimate and convenient for *flâneurs* (strollers). If you arrive with a car, your best bet is to park up near the Pont de Pierre bridge that arches across the Garonne river.

Loire Valley and the Atlantic Coast

Liberty atop the monument to the Girondins

Loire Valley and the Atlantic Coast

Wines

Since the city perches on the Dordogne and Garonne routes to the Atlantic, is the capital of the region and is surrounded by the great château vineyards, Bordeaux has developed as much by marketing as by producing fine wines. During their various occupations of the region, the English developed the wine known as claret. The original *clairette* is still on sale here. The classification of the wines was carried out by Thomas Jefferson before he became president of the United States. It was then that the thriving export business began.

The grand Maison du Vin, opposite the theater, is as much a financial and commercial institution as an information point. The public inquiry desk in the spacious lobby can arrange tours and day or half-day visits to the surrounding wine country. Red wines are produced to the north: Médoc on the west bank of the Gironde, Bourg on the east and St.-Emilion and Pomerol north of the Dordogne. The rest of the area mostly produces white wines: Graves, Sauternes and Entre Deux Mers. Staff at the Maison du Vin can point you in the right direction for free wine tastings in the city, suburbs and countryside, and let you know of any wine festivals.

Culture

In town, people are elegant and have a real sense of civic pride. The compact yet well-laid-out center is always busy, with well-dressed ladies at lunch and suited business types meeting over a glass of wine and easily outnumbering more-obvious tourists. There is a friendly hum on commercial streets such as cours de l'Intendance.

Early in the evening, people loiter on café terraces or meet with friends at the botanic gardens or around place Gambetta. Chic and unmistakably French, this handsome square with an English garden is the best place in town for people-watching. Originally known as place Dauphine, the square boasts 18th-century arcades and mansard roofs from which revolutionary executions were witnessed in 1790. To one side is the 1748 Porte Dijeaux. Off to the rear, the elegant tree-lined cours Clemenceau stretches up to the public garden and Église St.-Louis.

The area fosters a vibrant cultural scene and season. Check at the tourist office for details of temporary exhibitions and performances. Permanent pleasures and treasures include the famous Grosse Cloche, a well-preserved gate from the 14th through 18th centuries. Set beside a section of the 13th-century town wall, this former chunk of the town hall features a fine profile of stonework and pointed slate roofs, a bell suspended in the arch, carved water spouts and clock faces on both sides.

The Hôtel de Ville – once the 1784 Hôtel de Rohan – on the wide cathedral square is an early example of French neoclassicism. Pass through a

The Pont de Pierre across the wide Garonne river

courtyard and enter to discover a memorable staircase and fine paneled salons. Outside the two wings of the art gallery (see page 89), gilded gateways and a grille of railings surround a formal French garden with a classic carpet of bedding plants, fountains and statues. The garden remains open until early evening.

At the south of the city near Église Ste.-Eulalie, see the monument to the Girondin victims of Robespierre's regime: a 164-foot column with a figure of Liberty throwing off her shackles.

ESSENTIAL INFORMATION

 TOURIST INFORMATION
• 12 cours du 30-Juillet, just behind the theater ☎ 05 56 00 66 00; www.bordeaux-tourisme.com 🚌 7, 8
• St.-Jean railroad station, rue Charles-Domercq ☎ 05 56 91 64 70 🚌 1, 7, 8, 9

PUBLIC TRANSPORTATION
There is frequent bus service all over the city from 5 a.m. to 10 p.m. CGFTE special tickets offer one hour of travel (cheaper on Sundays). Tickets are also sold at newsstands and bookstores. The Carte Bordeaux Découverte offers unlimited travel on buses for 1–6 days. The city's many limited-access streets are welcoming to pedestrians. For bus information ☎ 05 57 57 88 88. Taxis can be hailed from stands at Gare St.-Jean (☎ 05 56 91 48 11) and in the city center (Grand Théâtre ☎ 05 56 81 99 15 and cours Georges Clemenceau ☎ 05 56 81 99 05). Frequent fast trains leave for Paris from the Gare St.-Jean (☎ 08 36 35 35 35), south of the main center.

AIRPORT INFORMATION
Bordeaux–Merignac Airport services national and international flights ☎ 05 56 34 50 50, website www.bordeaux.aeroport.fr. A shuttle to several town-center stops, including Gare St.-Jean (45 minutes) and place Gambetta (30 minutes), operates every 30 minutes on weekdays and every 45 minutes on weekends. Jet'bus ☎ 05 56 34 50 50.

CLIMATE – Average highs and lows

JAN.	FEB.	MAR.	APR.	MAY	JUN.	JUL.	AUG.	SEP.	OCT.	NOV.	DEC.
9°C	11°C	14°C	16°C	19°C	23°C	26°C	26°C	23°C	18°C	13°C	10°C
48°F	52°F	57°F	61°F	66°F	73°F	79°F	79°F	73°F	64°F	55°F	50°F
2°C	3°C	5°C	6°C	10°C	13°C	15°C	15°C	12°C	9°C	5°C	3°C
36°F	37°F	41°F	43°F	50°F	55°F	59°F	59°F	54°F	48°F	41°F	37°F

Gothic splendor – the Cathédrale St.-André

BORDEAUX SIGHTS

Key to symbols

✚ map coordinates refer to the Bordeaux map on page 85; sights below are highlighted in yellow on the map.

✉ address or location ☎ telephone number

🕐 opening times 🚌 nearest bus or tram route

🍴 restaurant on site or nearby

ℹ information

💶 admission charge: $$$ more than €10, $$ €5–€10, $ less than €5

CATHÉDRALE ST.-ANDRÉ

Listed as a World Heritage Site in 1998, the Cathedral of St. André is mostly Gothic but has gathered touches from most successive periods. A devastating fire in 1787 destroyed many early features: The nave survives from the original church in which Eleanor of Aquitaine was first married in 1137 to the future king of France. Today the large sanctuary and extensive chapels impress visitors. A timeless, gentle light from stained glass gives the effect of an endless elegant nave.

The church faces the Hôtel de Ville across a wide open square. Twin spires on the cathedral itself are complemented by a separate bell tower (the Tour Pey-Berland, 1440) with a burdensome statue perched atop like a cork in a bottle. All around the building is a cluster of supporting arches and flying buttresses. Neat gardens alongside offer seclusion for private reflection.

✛ A1 ✉ place Pey Berland 🚌 12, 19

ÉGLISE ST.-MICHEL

Colorful glass casts blue, red and gray light in the handsome 14th-century Gothic basilica. Inside is an extravagant swollen wooden pulpit and a vast organ set on stone. To one side of the main building is a separate bell tower, La Flèche. The original tower, finished in 1492, was struck by lightning in 1574 and 1608 and lashed by a hurricane in 1768. Despite the ravages of the elements and a period of service as a telegraph station, the tower was only reconstructed in 1865. It's the highest tower in the south of France at 370 feet. The nation's tallest is at Rouen cathedral. The market square spreading around the church offers a junky mixture of trash and treasures spread on the cobblestones.

✛ C1 ✉ place Canteloup ☎ 05 56 94 30 50 🕐 Daily 9–noon and 2–6 🚌 22, 23

GRAND THÉÂTRE

Considered the finest theater in the country, this handsome Classical building opened its doors to the wealthy citizens of Bordeaux in 1780. With 12 Corinthian pillars supporting carved figures of the muses and gods, the facility is the masterwork of architect Louis Victor. Dominating the town center, it spreads across a vast city block almost 300 feet long. The focus of the stone lobby is its sweeping double stairway, said to have inspired the Paris opera house. Here you will find the box office for a varied program of opera and ballet classics, as well as popular productions of William Shakespeare. Some Sunday mornings see less formal concerts and wine-tasting events. The spacious interior is

Muses and gods atop the Grand Théâtre

exceptional. If you aren't planning to take in a performance, then consider arranging a guided visit of the building (bookable at the tourist offices, see page 87) to see the luxurious gilding and blue and red velvet. Splendid cantilevered boxes and elegant pillars complete the majestic effect.

✛ B2 ✉ place de la Comédie 🚌 7, 8, 31 🎟 Guided tour $$$

MUSÉE DES BEAUX-ARTS

Beautifully set in a pair of Classical two-story pavilions flanking the gardens of the Hôtel de Ville (see page 86), the Musée des Beaux-Arts (Fine Arts Museum) houses works dating up to the 19th century in one section and a second wing with modern and contemporary art. A varied collection ranges from Dutch and Flemish classics to 19th-century bourgeois erotica, such as Henri Gervix's *Rolla*. Eugène Delacroix's *Greece Surveying the Ruins of Missolonghi* is among the city's prized artworks. Sculpture surrounds the entry desk.

Regular temporary art shows are held at nearby Galerie des Beaux-Arts, place du Colonel-Raynal.

✛ A1 ✉ Jardin de la Mairie, 20 cours d'Albret ☎ 05 56 10 20 56 🕐 Wed.–Mon. 11–6 🚌 17, 8 🎟 $ (temporary exhibitions $$); free first Sun. of the month

Loire Valley and the Atlantic Coast

WALK: STROLL THROUGH BORDEAUX

Refer to route marked on city map on page 85

This 3-hour stroll through the city is about 2 miles long and begins at the oldest bridge in town, the Pont de Pierre, built by Napoleon.

Turn left along rue de la Fusterie right into narrow, cobbled rue des Faures up past Église St.-Michel (see page 89). Continue to turn left along the shopping street of cours Victor-Hugo and cross right to rue St.-James.

Pause at Grosse Cloche (see page 86). Still on rue St.-James, peek (right) into rue St.-Eloi to see the church, and don't miss a view of cathedral spires on your left. Cross place Lafargue and continue along rue St.-James to turn left into cours d'Alsace-et-Lorraine to place Pey-Berland, with Cathédrale St.-André and the Hôtel de Ville. Take time to visit the sites and gardens (see page 87).

From the northwest corner of the square, follow rue des Remparts past the Musée des Arts-Décoratifs (Museum of Decorative Arts) and continue up to charming place Gambetta (see page 86).

Turn right along busy and wide cours de l'Intendance.

Handsome buildings go up to the big block of the theater, with the wine center nearby.

Continue on cours de l'Intendance to cours du Chapeau-Rouge, down to the river. Turn right onto place de la Bourse, with its Musée Nationale des Douanes (Customs House Museum) on the corner.

This wide riverside space on quai de la Douane has a statue of the Three Graces replacing the original figure of Louis XV. In the early 18th century, the square was known as place Royale.

Retrace your steps behind the Bourse along rue Phillipart.

Note the pretty Second Empire-style place du Parlement with its fountain. Turn left down rue St.-Pierre, crossing the site of the old port of Bordeaux past Église St.-Pierre.

At the end of rue des Argentiers turn left at the bottom to see the 15th-century arch of the Porte Cailhau, then right, along quai Richelieu.

Take time to enjoy the riverside from Porte Cailhau all the way down to place de Bir-Hakeim passing some fine restaurants. The splendid crescent and arch of Porte de la Bourgogne faces the Pont de Pierre from where the walk began.

The leafy gardens in place Gambetta

The unspoiled château at Azay-le-Rideau beside the Indre river

REGIONAL SIGHTS

Key to symbols

⊕ map coordinates refer to the region map on page 82; sights below are highlighted in yellow on the map.

⊠ address or location ☎ telephone number

⊕ opening times 🚌 nearest bus or tram route

🍴 restaurant on site or nearby ℹ information

💰 admission charge: $$$ more than €10, $$ €5–€10, $ less than €5

ANGERS

Angers is a city protected by a fortress of poets and heroes. Looming above the town and built to protect a flourishing river trade, 17 mossy gray-and-white towers of the medieval château proclaim this was originally constructed as a fortress rather than a palace. The first duke of Anjou, Louis I, commissioned artworks and remodeling to adapt the château to a family home in the 14th century. By the time of the last duke, poet and patron of the arts Good King René (1409–80), Angers had acquired royal status, formal gardens and a private menagerie of lions and monkeys. The greatest of Louis' acquisitions was the remarkable series of tapestries, *The Apocalypse of St. John the Evangelist*. Woven by Nicolas Bataille, the finest artist in his field, these spectacular, sometimes shocking, works stand 16 feet high and wrap 328 feet around a specially customized gallery. Having been lost in the Revolution, each fragment was sought and found by the city's bishop, who commissioned a major restoration work in 1843. Take time to enjoy the gardens in the former moat. Compare the tapestries with contemporary Jean Lurçat tapestries at the Musée Jean Lurçat in the Ancien Hôpital St.-Jean, across the river.

⊕ B5

Tourist information ⊠ Place du Président-Kennedy ☎ 02 41 23 50 00; www.angers-tourisme.com

Château ⊠ 2 promenade du Bout de Monde ☎ 02 41 87 43 47 ⊕ Daily 9:30–7:30, Jun. 1 to mid-Sep.; 10–6, mid-Mar. through May 31 and mid–Sep. through Oct. 31; 10–5, rest of year 💰 $$

Musée Jean Lurçat ⊠ Ancien Hôpital St.-Jean, 4 Boulevard Arago ☎ 02 41 24 18 45 ⊕ Daily 9:30–6:30, in summer; Tue.–Sun. 10–noon and 2–6, rest of year 💰 $

AZAY-LE-RIDEAU

A rich, dappled, tree-framed vision of an enchanted château floating on the water lures summer wanderers to the ordinary village of Azay-le-Rideau. The blue-black slate turrets and conical spires top Rapunzel towers like icing on a cake. The pretty château is unusual in that it was built in just 11 years from 1518 and remained faithful to the original plans of the architect

Bastien François. Perched on the river foundations of a previous building, the château, remarkably, has been left alone by generations of owners who, in a rare instance of restraint, managed not to rebuild or add to the finished gem in almost 500 years. The towers are delicate adornments, as this was never a fortress, merely a country retreat. Note the carved salamander, a symbol of François I, over the main entrance and the lavish grand staircase, among Renaissance tapestries.

⊞ C5

Tourist information ✉ 5 place de l'Europe
☎ 02 47 45 44 40; www.tourisme.fr/office-de-tourisme/azay-le-rideau

Château d'Azay-le-Rideau ☎ 02 47 45 42 04
⊕ Daily 9:30–7, Jul.–Aug.; daily 9:30–6, Apr.–Jun. and Sep.–Oct.; Tue.–Sun. 10–12:30 and 2–5:45, rest of year
⛉ Castle $$ (free first Sun., Nov.–Apr.)

CHÂTEAU DE CHAUMONT

Don't be misled by first impressions. The stern drawbridge, cylindrical keep and pathways atop of its high ramparts suggest a military fortification. The approach is impressive, as white walls rise behind a veil of spreading cedar trees. From the austerity of the western facade you might expect to find weaponry and bare stone walls. But once inside, prepare to savor the pleasant indulgences of a modest Renaissance home with a good selection of tapestries from the

15th through 19th centuries and period furnishings, but no overwhelming display of ostentation. Surprising when you consider that this was the residence of the

Carriage rides in the park outside the Château de Chaumont

The Château de Chenonceau is built on a series of arches over the Cher river

manipulative Catherine de Médicis, wife of King Henri II and proof positive that scheming villainy does not a homemaker make. Venture out on the 18th-century terrace for a superb views across the Loire.

✠ D5

✉ Chaumont-sur-Loire ☎ 02 54 51 26 26 ⊙ Daily 9:30–6, Mar. 15–Sep. 30; 10–4:30, rest of year 🎫 $$

CHÂTEAU DE CHENONCEAU

The most popular of the Loire châteaux is famous for its extravagant gallery, which spans the Cher river. Originally a graceful 200-foot bridge in the style of the main château, the gallery was commissioned by Diane de Poitiers, mistress of Henri II. On the king's death, his vengeful wife Catherine de Médicis ousted Diane from her home, embellished the bridge with a two-tier gallery and ordered a landscaped park over Diane's gardens. Diane was sent to live at Chaumont. The grace of the château reflects the styles of many powerful women who shaped its history, including the Scottish Mary Stuart. You will find no whimsical spiral steps – the main flight is a strong straight staircase designed for making an entrance.

Well-presented pamphlets (in English) explain art, furnishings and hangings. For an additional fee, a wax exhibition features 15 tableaux from the glory days. The story also is told in a nightly 45-minute sound-and-light show, *The Days of the Women of Chenonceau*, at 10:15 p.m. in July and August. The château's owines, labeled Des Dômes de Chenonceau, are sold in the Bâtiment des Dômes in the Jardin Vert.

✠ D5

✉ Chenonceaux ☎ 02 47 23 90 07 ⊙ Daily 9–7, Mar. 16 to Sep. 15; 9–6:30, Sep. 16–30; 9–6, Mar. 1–15 and Oct. 1–15; 9–5:30, Feb. 16–28 and Oct. 16–31; 9–5, Feb. 1–15 and Nov. 1–15; 9–4:30, rest of year 🍴 Restaurant 🎫 $$ (additional $ for wax exhibition; $$ for sound and light show)

Loire Valley and the Atlantic Coast

Unquestionably one of the elegant towns in France, Biarritz was little more than a whaling port until an empress discovered and adopted it. Just along the coast from the Basque port of St.-Jean-de-Luz (see page 133) and within easy reach of Spain and the Pyrénées, the resort is the southern showcase of France's Atlantic coast.

In 1854, when the Spanish-born empress Eugénie was the darling of society, she brought her husband Napoléon III to stay in the town. Almost overnight, Biarritz became regarded as the Atlantic's answer to the Riviera, the playground of the rich and famous. A popular saying declared: "If you have to choose between two beaches – one of them is always Biarritz." Life still revolves around the villa Napoléon

Above: Vantage point above the shore
Below: Sun umbrellas on the beach

BIARRITZ: THE IMPERIAL RESORT

commissioned for his empress. The town's fortunes continued to rise even after the imperial couple left town, and the ostentatious brick and stone villa became Hôtel du Palais, keeping its imposing gates and pretty formal gardens and adding new wings and even a swimming pool with a sea view. The lobby is over the top, packed with grandiose and pretentious furnishings, ponderous sculpted chandeliers and light fittings.

No visit is complete without enjoying a cup of coffee or tea while taking in the great sea views from the *salle rotonde,* a belle-epoque addition to the building. A decided whiff of money lingers in the air even today, from the classy staff to the assured demeanor of the

regular guests. Even if today's Biarritz lacks the Parisian chic of Deauville (see page 68), reminders abound as to the great guests of the past. At the beginning of the 20th century all European and Russian royals came here to relax and a marble tablet records the presence of several crowned heads over the centuries, including Queen Victoria, the Shah of Persia, and Eugénie's natural successors as magazine fodder: Edward and Mrs. Simpson.

Touring visitors will arrive through a well-signed knot of narrow streets although the town is served by good rail and air links. The area is ideal for exploring on foot and inevitably is busy from mid-June to mid-September. Hotels are usually open year round although some close during February. Regardless, there is plenty of life even out of season on a cold, wet March day. Visit Eugénie's imperial chapel for a sense of the flamboyant early days of the resort. Shopping is good. Golf and tennis are options for more active visitors. From the tourist office in the main square d'Ixelles, one can easily stroll the entire town in half a day. Narrow streets introduce you to clumpy stone arcades, nice art-deco hotels and casinos, a handful of original 19th-century villas and plenty of views of the fretting sea.

The bulk of the town is spread along the rocky sea front, a welcome route for driving or strolling along the promenades and gardens. On fine days genteel vacationers take in the air. At the cry "surf's up," a young, fit and tanned generation materializes to make the most of France's best breakers. When strong winds agitate the Bay of Biscay, there is something impressive about green and white spray hurling itself at the lighthouse and headlands. The sea also washes the town's symbol, a modest statue of the Virgin Mary designed by Gustave Eiffel and perched on a rock in the sea just opposite the old port. Seals and sharks await rainy-day visitors to the sea museum, and buses leave place de l'Hôtel-de-Ville during the day for the lighthouse and suburbs.

➕ B1

Tourist information ✉ Javalquinto, 1 square d'Ixelles ☎ 05 59 22 37 00; www.biarritz.tm.fr

Loire Valley and the Atlantic Coast

COGNAC

Don't ask for brandy here. The quality tipple is called cognac, after the town. The Dutch developed the drink as "burnt wine" (*brande-wijn* – gently corrupted to brandy) and distilled here as a means of storing wine and avoiding tax since Cognac was a major wine port on the Charente river. Drive around the countryside to see the exclusive area of just 250,000 acres of vines that make the white wine matured in barrels of Limousin oak. The areas are divided into Grande Champagne, Petite Champagne, Borderies, Fins Bois, Bons Bois and Bois Ordinaires. A tour and tasting visit to a cellar enables you to learn how the wines are blended. The big names, including Courvoisier, Martel and Rémy-Martin, all have visitor centers. Some lesser-known houses often prove more interesting. Otard, for example, is made in the 13th-century Château de Cognac, birthplace of François I.

✚ C3

Tourist information ✉ 16 rue du 14-Juillet
☎ 05 45 82 10 71; www.cognac-france.com or www.ville-cognac.fr

Otard, Château de Cognac ✉ 127 boulevard Denfert-Rochereau ☎ 05 45 36 88 86 ⏰ Daily 10–noon and 1:30–7, Jul.–Aug.; daily 10–noon and 2–6, Apr.–Jun.

and Sep.–Oct.; Tours depart Mon.–Thu. at 11, 2:30, 3:45 and 5, Fri. at 11, 2:30 and 4, Nov.– Dec. 🖐 $

FONTEVRAUD-L'ABBAYE

To atone for the death of St. Thomas of Canterbury (Thomas Becket), England's Henry II built the Abbaye Royale de Fontevraud near Saumur. The abbey was home to nuns, monks and lepers, and 14 abbesses were royal princesses, each retiring from the material world with dozens of personal servants. Unsurprisingly, entering this cloistered community was something of a social event. Henry's dysfunctional family, the house of Angers, which governed England as the Plantagenets, included his wife Eleanor of Aquitaine (see page 106), who decreed that her favorite son, Richard the Lion-Heart, should be king of England. Richard kept the job 10 years, never learned English and spent less than 10 months in England.

Many abbey buildings are gone, but you may visit huge kitchens, cloisters and an herb garden and see the tombs of Richard, Eleanor and Henry in the church itself.

✚ C5

✉ Fontevraud-l'Abbaye ☎ 02 41 51 71 41 ⏰ Daily 9–6:30, Jun. 1 to mid-Sep.; 9:30–12:30 and 2–5:30 (or dusk if earlier), rest of year 🖐 $$

Effigies of Eleanor and Henry repose in the abbey church at Fontevraud l'Abbaye

Nohant-Vic – a discreet hamlet with its tree-lined square and countryside of hedgerows – is set in a sleepy corner of the Berry region. It slipped onto the map thanks to a dynamic woman who lived from 1804 to 1876.

Although Amandine-Aurore-Lucile Dudevant (née Dupin) lived at the château of Nohant, the baronness was no ordinary chatelaine. "My profession is to be free," she wrote. So at night she would disguise herself as a man and sneak out to live the heartier peasant life of nearby La Châtre. Dudevant had another life: She achieved immortality as novelist and playwright George Sand.

Marionettes perform in the little theater designed by the composer, Chopin

WHEN GEORGE MET FRÉDÉRIC

Separated from her husband in 1831 at the age of 27, she wrote novels set in the countryside she called the Vallée Noire. She scandalized Paris society by smoking and wearing men's clothes.

The great love of her life was the Polish-born composer Frédéric Chopin, and the château, now a museum, holds many mementos of their life together. Visit in July for the Chopin Music Festival, when pianists revive the passion of the 19th century's most romantic composer in the house where he created so many masterpieces.

Even if you miss out on the concert season, Sand's home is always worth a visit. Delights include the novelist's additions to the 18th-century château, including the little theater Chopin designed for her. Here she staged private performances of her own plays. The varied marionettes, made by the novelist's son Maurice, are attired in costumes she sewed.

Details in her boudoir and study intrigue and delight, but it's the salon that captures the spirit of her secret artistic life. The table is laid ready for a dinner party, and one can almost anticipate the arrival of Gustave Flaubert, Franz Liszt and the guest of honor, Chopin himself.

Château de la Vallée Bleue, a nearby manor house once home to the couple's doctor, is now a family-run hotel offering musical candlelit dinners beside the fire and tours of Sand's favorite places.

Tourist information
✉ square George-Sand, La Châtre ☎ 02 54 48 22 64; www.tourisme.fr/office-de-tourisme/la-chartre

Maison de George Sand
✉ Domaine de George Sand, Nohant–Vic ☎ 02 54 31 06 04 ⏰ Daily 9–7:30, Jul.–Aug.; 9–12:15 and 2–6:30, Apr.–Jun. and Sep. 1–Oct. 15; 10–12:15 and 2–4:30. rest of year. Closed Sun. p.m. 🚽 $$

Château de la Vallée Bleue ✉ route de Vermeuil, St.-Chartier ☎ 02 54 31 01 91; 02 54 31 04 48

An elegant staircase in the Château de Nohant

POITIERS

Famous for Romanesque churches and a history of key battles against the English and Arabs, Poitiers is the nearest large town to Futuroscope (see panel) and a diversion on the way to the island beach resort of la Rochelle. The city's main architectural trophy is Église Notre-Dame la Grande, which is surrounded by a local market. Elsewhere, the fourth-century Baptistère St.-Jean is the oldest Christian building in France and has some medieval frescoes. In the 12th- to 13th-century Great Hall of the mainly 18th-century Palais de Justice, Joan of Arc successfully faced an ecclesiastical committee.

✚ C4

Tourist information ✉ 45 place Charles-de-Gaulle ☎ 05 49 41 21 24; www.mairie-poitiers.fr

SAUMUR

Horses, mushrooms and sparkling wine carry Saumur's fame from its gleaming white château on the banks of the Loire to the outside world. The École Nationale d'Équitation (National Riding School) – with its museums, cavalry horses and legendary Cadre Noir display team – puts on displays in July and sometimes allows visitors to see equestrian training and rehearsals.

Half of France's mushrooms are cultivated in underground cellars and tunnels that aren't used for storing the fabulous red and white still and sparkling wines. The bridge was a crossing point for pilgrims on the Santiago de Compostela route. The château, built of tufa stone, won immortality when it found its way into the

Ride the Future

Futuroscope is the theme park that predated Disney crossing the Atlantic and anticipates wonderful tomorrows. But unlike Disney, it is a theme park that deals not in making fantasies seem real, but in making reality seem an improbable adventure. Futuroscope is the European park of the moving image (Parc Européen de l'Image).

Cinema's second century is Futuroscope's second decade. Rides involve more IMAX perspectives than anywhere else on the Continent and use the latest technology to overload visitors' senses through filmmaking. The architecture around the verdant landscape is as challenging as the movies featured: A gigantic domed screen envelops its audience in a program of relativity that shoots participants from DNA to the stars. Another massive screen rises into the air as the auditorium finds itself by a man-made lake with amazing glass mountains.

The past features in one ride through great movies, and the local region is explored and exploited in a dynamic reactive cinema. An on-site tourist office provides information about attractions and days out in the Poitou-Charentes region. Accommodations, meals and admission fees are inexpensive compared to other parks.

Futuroscope, Parc Européen de l'Image
✉ Jaunay-Clan, 86130 ☎ 05 49 49 30 80; www.futuroscope.fr 🕐 Daily from 9 or 10 a.m. until between 6 p.m. and 11 p.m., depending on season 🍴 Choice on site 💷 $$$

The glazed exterior of the Kinemax

The ornate central porch of Cathédrale St.-Gatien in Tours

illustrations of the illuminated medieval book of hours, the *Très Riches Heures des Ducs de Berry*. From the towers and castle walls, summer brings unfor-gettable views of the old town at its feet and the Loire dried up to a mere stream, its bed a green park of trees and bushes.

✚ C5

Tourist information ✉ Place de la Bilange
☎ 02 41 40 20 60; www.saumur-tourisme.com
Château ✉ Avenue du Dr.-Peton ☎ 02 41 40 24 40
⏰ Daily 9:30–6, Jun.–Sep.; daily 9:30–noon and 2–5:30, Apr.–May; Wed.–Mon. 9:30–noon and 2–5:30, rest of year. Also Wed. and Sat. 8:30–10:30 p.m., Jul.–Aug. 🎫 $$
École Nationale d'Équitation ✉ Sammur-Terrefort, 49411 ☎ 02 41 53 50 60 ⏰ Tue.–Fri. 9:30–11 and 2–6, Sat. 9:30–11, Mon. 2–6, Apr.–Sep. 🎫 $$

TOURS

After the heavy bombing of World War II, Tours was all but left for dead. For nearly two decades, the ruins of once-prosperous houses and districts were sold off as architectural salvage. Then, in the 1960s plans were made to transform the slums and derelict shells of houses into a conservation area and build the charming city center we see today.

Old Tours is a skillfully blended mixture of those few buildings that survived the bombs and contemporary creations constructed from traditional materials. Now fashionable cafés, artists' quarters, galleries and chic boutiques cluster together in a vibrant district that houses the new university. Fifteenth-century timber-framed houses bracket place Plumereau. Gothic and Renaissance architecture lines rue Briçonnet, and the mansion of the dukes of Touraine stands in rue du Change. Two towers of the original basilica can still be seen, as can the Gothic-Renaissance concoction of buttresses and spires that make up Cathédrale St.-Gatien.

✚ C5

Tourist information ✉ 78 rue Bernard-Palissy
☎ 02 47 70 37 37; www.mairie-tours.fr

DRIVE: CHÂTEAU COUNTRY

Distance: 260 miles Time: 3 to 4 days

The fashion for building Renaissance châteaux in the Loire region came with a surge of national pride after the expulsion of the English from France in 1453. The nobility hired Italian architects, designers and gardeners, and design schools were established from Tours to Fontainebleau as each great family created its dream palace.

From Tours take the D751.
The well-preserved remains of the great Renaissance château of Amboise are noteworthy for the queen's chapel on the ramparts and Aubusson tapestries in the king's apartments. Nearby Clos Lucé has a museum devoted to Leonardo da Vinci, who died here.

Follow the D31 toward Loches.
The road climbs behind the town and two miles along is the Pagode de Chanteloup, a remnant of an 18th-century imitation of Versailles built by the Duke of Choiseul. Views are great from the top.

Continue on the D31, then turn left to the D40.
Visit the Château de Chenonceau (see page 93) from the village, spelled Chenonceaux.

Take the D40 to Chisseaux, turning right for the D80 to Francueil. Bear left to the D81. Drive south to turn left onto the D760 at Nouans les Fontaines. Then take a left on D960 to Valençay.
Actually in Berry rather than the Loire region, the stunning Renaissance and baroque chateau of Valençay is well worth the long detour. Patrolled by black swans, flamingos, peacocks, deer and llamas, the grounds are as regal as the interior.

Go north on the D4 then the D128 and turn right on the D724.
The heart of the Sologne region is the charming town of Romorantin-Lanthenay on the Sauldre river – a good starting point for an hour or two discovering the surrounding countryside.

The D49 takes you to la Sologne area, with its thatched red-brick houses, heaths and woodland. At St.-Viâtre, turn

right on the D93 to Nouan-le-Fuzelier. Take the D44 to turn right onto the D923. At Clémont, turn right on D176 toward the Étang du Puits. Go right on the D948 to Argent-sur-Sauldre, then left on D940.
The château at Gien is a river stronghold, unusual in eschewing the local white stone in favor of sturdy red brick. The 15th-century château was restored after World War II bombing. The modern pink-brick church nearby is dedicated to Joan of Arc. The tower of the original church remains.

Return back across the river and turn right on the D951.
Beautifully maintained, the fabulous moated château of Sully-sur-Loire retains its original timber roofs. To create the 30-foot arches, chestnut trees were tied together as saplings so that the wood would grow in the right shape. Here, Voltaire staged his early plays, and Joân of Arc met King Charles VII.

Follow the D948 and the D952 via Chateauneuf-sur-Loire, then take the N460 to Orléans.
Although May is the prime season for commemorations of the Maid of Orléans, Joan of Arc, plenty of year-round monuments honor the woman who broke the English

Towers, spires, cupolas, belfries and chimneys crown the grandiose Château de Chambord

siege of Orléans in 1429. Follow her story through the stained-glass windows of the cathedral.

Be careful as you leave the city not to filter onto the highway; watch for signs for the N152, signed for Blois. At Beaugency, cross the river on the D925 to la Ferté-St.-Cyr, then go right onto the D103, filtering onto the D33 through the walled estate of Chambord.

The epitome of the Loire valley châteaux, Chambord is the jewel in this royal region's crown. Constructed in the heart of a hunting forest with no views nor even a convenient water supply, the "simple" lodge ordered by François I incorporated 440 rooms,

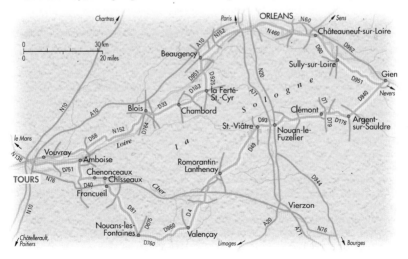

In the round: The superb spiral staircase at the Château de Blois

63 staircases and a roof studded with 365 ornate chimneys, spires, gables and dormer windows. Naturally it became home to huge regal hunting parties, plots, intrigues and scandals. Eventually it received a moat and glorious furnishings, including a riddle of a double spiral staircase, attributed to Leonardo da Vinci, which allows people to ascend and descend without crossing each other's path. It is said the king loved Chambord so much he spent money on its finery rather than pay ransom for his two sons.

Follow the D33 under the bridge of St.-Gervais-la-Foret, then turn right on the D956.

Blois, the city of Louis XII, bustles as much today with visitors as it did in the days of the court. The splendid Renaissance château has as many styles of decoration as there were kings and queens in the Loire. Followers of Médicis intrigues will delight in discovering secret cupboards and doors behind the panels in Catherine's apartments. Like Chambord (above), this is a château to be enjoyed through summer sound-and-light shows, which recount the gore and the glamour of the past. Blois is a useful base for exploring the region on guided tours.

Follow the N152 toward Tours, then turn right on the D65 and left onto D58, which becomes the D1. Follow signs for Vouvray, coming into town on the D46.

A wine-tasting and shopping stop, Vouvray lets you discover white, sparkling aperitifs and sweet dessert wines, as well as visit troglodyte houses (see page 103).

The N152 leads back to Tours.

Loire Valley and the Atlantic Coast

A cave bedroom in the extensive underground display at Doué-la-Fontaine

TROGLODYTE VILLAGES

If you believe the last cave dwellers in western France decorated their homes with primitive hunting scenes, then think again. The caves of the Loire have washing machines and cable TV. The soft, creamy-white tufa used for building châteaux hides hundreds of caves. Quarries created semi-underground villages, houses, churches and schools carved into the rock face. Most were active communities until inexpensive ground-level housing lured underground families to the surface in the 1940s and '50s. Visit Doué-la-Fontaine, near Saumur, and Rochecorbon, near Tours. Exhibitions show images of 20th-century troglodyte village life. Since the 1990s, many of these caves have been developed as holiday homes and restaurants. Don't expect primitive fireplaces. The caves have all usual facilities, including electricity. Tufa, cool in summer and warm in winter, is considered ecologically sound. Spend a night or two self-catering in a comfy cave as a base for exploring château country.

⊞ C5

Tourist information ✉ place des Fontaines, Doué-la-Fontaine ☎ 02 41 59 20 49; www.tourisme.fr/office-de-tourisme/doue-la-fontaine

Tourist information ✉ place du Croissant, Rochecorbon ☎ 02 2 47 52 80 22; www.mairie-rochecorbon.fr

Troglodyte accommodations ☎ 02 40 89 89 89

VILLANDRY, CHÂTEAU DE

The other châteaux may have greater staircases, tapestries and grandeur, but nowhere else in the Loire will you find gardens like those of Villandry. Dr. Joachim Carvallo, whose family still lives here, was the 19th-century historian who decided to re-create great 16th-century English gardens for his own pleasure. Magnificent terraces surround the château, as neat box and yew hedges create interesting geometric patterns. Admire the design of the gardens of Love and Music, and breathe in the aromatic sensations of an herb garden where a brush against wild thyme and rosemary releases fresh fragrances. Climb to the upper level, where enveloped within a cloister of lime trees, a shimmering lake collects rainwater to feed the gardens and fountains below. Graceful canals and water features irrigate the estate. The lowest tier is a well-stocked kitchen garden. Replanted twice a year, but no less decorative than the other gardens, the crops are clustered in attractive shapes. Pergolas and bowers abound for those who wish to wallow.

⊞ C5

✉ Villandry ☎ 02 47 50 02 09 ⏰ Daily 8:30–8, Jul.–Aug.; 9–7:30, May–Jun. and first 3 weeks of Sep.; 9–7, in Apr. and late Sep. to late Oct.; 9–6, in Mar. and late Oct. to mid-Nov.; 9–5:30, rest of year

🏰 Castle $$; gardens $

DORDOGNE

Dordogne

"T HE Dordogne flows through richly forested countryside of gastronomic delights, warring châteaux and prehistoric caves. "

Opposite: The fortress at Castlenaud guards the Dordogne river

Dordogne

DORDOGNE

Shaded from the rest of France by its vast forests, the Dordogne region is a timeless sanctuary where simple country values hold sway and city life is held firmly at bay. The Dordogne river itself flows from the mountains of the Massif Central to the Gironde estuary at Bordeaux, through countryside of unmatched fertility and beauty.

The traditional regions of Périgord and Quercy are today known as the Dordogne and Lot departments. Quercy is the country of winemakers and shepherds. Rivers divide Périgord into four colorful areas: Black Périgord, with its walnut forests and treasured truffles; White Périgord, grazing ground of veal herds; Green Périgord, with lush Limousin farmland; and Purple Périgord, home to the vineyards of Bergerac.

Secret History

For years people spoke of the history of Périgord as contemporary to its neighbors. Gallic dry-stone huts, called *bories*, and Roman remains were believed to date from the start of the region's history and were taken up again with repopulation in the 11th century. Until the end of the Middle Ages, the land batted between the French and English during the Hundred Years War and the Wars of Religion between the Catholics and Protestants. Thus, the tree-topped skyline gained round French-style towers, square towers in the English style, fortified towns and many châteaux.

In the 19th century came the discovery of Périgord's secret life in the Stone Age. Simple tools and caves announced a civilization that flourished tens of thousands of years ago. The early years of the 20th century brought about the revelation of cave paintings, proving that prehistory had an artistic tradition to match any period over the past millennium.

A major political pawn, Périgord became French when it was added to the dowry Eleanor of Aquitaine brought to her 1137 marriage to Louis VII. But when the marriage was dissolved in 1152, Eleanor presented the land to her new husband Henri, count of Anjou, lord of Maine, Touraine and Normandy, and eventual Plantagenet King Henry II of England. The land wouldn't be French for another 300 years.

Lots More Lot

The best way to explore the Dordogne is by water. Since 30 miles of the lower reaches of the Lot river opened up to pleasure craft, it's now possible to sail from the plum orchards of Villeneuve-sur-Lot to the Garonne. Tourists may be towed by tugboats and take 39-foot lock drops, then chug between the Atlantic and Mediterranean on the Canal des Deux Mers or float along the Baïse into Armagnac country, which lends itself to the prospect of fortifying brandy tastings.

Birth of the Forest

Périgord Noir (Black Périgord) gets its name from the vast forests that cover the land. However, at the time of the Roman occupation in the fourth century, much of this land was

Dordogne

DORDOGNE

0   20   40   60 km
0   10   20   30 miles

N

Aigurande
Crozant   Boussac
le Dorat   la Souterraine
M A R C H E   Gouzon
Bellac   Guéret
Oradour-   Moutier-d'Ahun
sur-Glane   Plateaux   Ambazac   Aubusson   Auzances
St.-Junien   Bourganeuf   Felletin
Rochechouart   Limoges   St-Léonard-de-Noblat
Aix-sur-Vienne   Eymoutiers
Châlus   du Limousin   Vienne   Plateau de Millevaches
St-Yrieix-   Coussac-
Nontron   la-Perche   Bonneval   Treignac   Meymac   Ussel
L   Jumilhac   Uzerche   Egletons
Mareuil   I   Seilhac   Ventadour
Brantôme   Thiviers   M   O   U   S   I   N   Massif Central
Bourdeilles   Excideuil
Hautefort   Tulle
Ribérac   Périgueux   Terrasson-   Brive-la-
la-Villedieu   Gaillarde
Montignac   Souillac   Turenne   Argentat
Montpon-   Isle   Grotte de Lascaux   Curemonte   Beaulieu-
Ménesterol   Mussidan   le Moustier   sur-Dordogne
les Eyzies-de-Tayac   SARLAT-   Martel   Carennac
Bergerac   Trémolat   LA-CANÉDA   Montal   Castelnau
Beynac-et-Cazenac   La Roque-   la Treyne   St.-Céré
Monbazillac   Cadouin   Gageac   Gouffre de Padirac
Eymet   Beaumont   Castelnaud   Domme   Gramat
Castillonnès   Villeréal   Monpazier   Gourdon   Rocamadour
Marmande   Monflanquin   Biron   Villefranche-   Figeac
Bonaguil   du-Périgord   Grotte du Pech-Merle
Fumel   Cabrerets   Montbrun
Tonneins   G   Cahors   St.-Cirq-Lapopie
Lot   Villeneuve-sur-Lot   U   E
Casteljaloux   Aiguillon   Montpezat-   Y   N
Lauzerte   de-Quercy   E
Houeillès   Caylus
Nérac   Valence   Caussade
Agen   Moissac
Condom   Castelsarrasin   Cordes-sur-Ciel
Lectoure   Montauban   Carmaux
Eauze   Fleurance   Gaillac   Albi   Tarn
Beaumont-   Lisle-sur-Tarn
de-Lomagne   Rabastens   Réalmont
Vic-Fezensac   Gironde   St.-Sulpice
G A S C O G N E   Auch   Graulhet   Lacaune
Gimont   Lavaur   Castres   Monts de Lacaune   413 ft
l'Isle-Jourdain   Monts de
Lombez   Labruguière   l'Espinous
Mazamet
Montage Noire

5   4   3   2   1

A   B   C

cultivated by farmers. For the next 800 years, successive barbarian invasions forced the local population away from southwest France, and thick forests grew where once were small Roman walnut groves.

SARLAT-LA-CANÉDA

The former capital of Périgord is so improbably beautiful it hardly seems real. In fact, Sarlat by night is nearly too gorgeous to believe. The main square and its side streets are so remarkably illuminated that the entire town resembles a cardboard cutout set from an expensive operetta.

The civic illumination, including picturesque gas lamps, is one of the more visible aspects of a conservation project started more than 30 years ago

to guarantee that the town was no anticlimax after the long scenic drive through the dramatic Dordogne region. Well indicated along food- and wine-tasting routes from Bordeaux and Bergerac, the historic center of Sarlat-la-Canéda is restrained by a ring road, where it's best to find a parking space and rely on your feet for the city visit.

The medieval center of town is full of narrow stone-paved streets that dip steeply up and down between houses and mansions of golden and gray stone. Every corner provides inspiration for another snapshot. In the early 19th century, rue de la République divided the town into two unequal halves. The

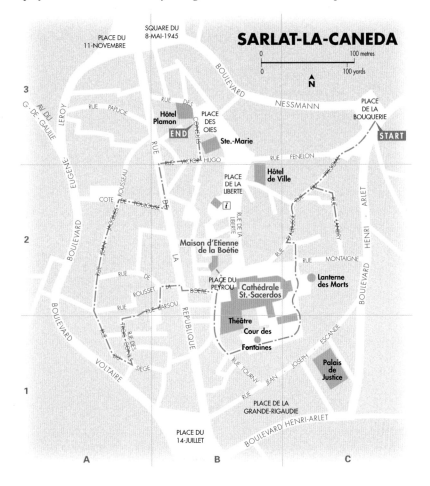

larger section is a haven of wonderful little houses, terraces, gardens and tiny squares. The old quarter (Quartier des Clercs), no mere museum piece, remains very much a thriving community with people as full of local character as their surroundings. Sarlat folk have strong country faces, with the weathered complexion of the south. See an elderly widow in black sitting in her doorway or an open window with a cat purring on her lap and a caged canary on the window sill. Watch old men in caps exchanging greetings as they puff their way up steep stepped streets.

In the heat of the summer, a siesta break isn't uncommon during the afternoon. Some local farmers have been known to spend the early evening in the city deep in conversation with their friends and neighbors before heading off to work their fields after midnight, when temperatures drop to a more tolerable level.

Rather than retreating to your hotel, slip into a museum when it's too hot for climbing hilly streets. The unexpected automobile museum on avenue Thiers displays a range of old and classic cars May through September.

A Renaissance building in the town center

Whether it's early or late in the day, take time to explore and look for the details. There is a fascinating variety of stone-carved doorways from Classical to high Gothic that merit an entire roll of film. Wednesday and Saturday morning markets on place de la Liberté sell local produce (see page 112), and summertime brings international music and theater festivals.

ESSENTIAL INFORMATION

TOURIST INFORMATION
The main office is in a striking late-Renaissance house ✉ Hôtel de Maleville, place de la Liberté ☎ 05 53 31 45 45; www.sarlat-tourisme.com. English is spoken, and useful maps and 90-minute walking tours (Apr.–Oct.) are provided.

URBAN TRANSPORTATION
There is no public transportation within the city. Rail services travel from Paris and Bordeaux to the Sarlat SNCF station (☎ 05 53 59 00 21). Taxis ☎ 05 53 59 02 43

AIRPORT INFORMATION
Local airfields are at Périgueux (☎ 05 53 02 79 79), Bergerac (☎ 05 53 22 25 25) and Brive (☎ 05 55 86 88 36). The closest national and international airport is Bordeaux (see page 87), which is two and a half hours away by rail.

CLIMATE – Average highs and lows

JAN.	FEB.	MAR.	APR.	MAY	JUN.	JUL.	AUG.	SEP.	OCT.	NOV.	DEC.
9°C	11°C	14°C	16°C	19°C	23°C	26°C	26°C	23°C	18°C	13°C	10°C
48°F	52°F	57°F	61°F	66°F	73°F	79°F	79°F	73°F	64°F	55°F	50°F
2°C	4°C	5°C	6°C	10°C	13°C	15°C	15°C	12°C	9°C	5°C	4°C
36°F	39°F	41°F	43°F	50°F	55°F	59°F	59°F	54°F	48°F	41°F	39°F

The exuberant facade of the Maison d'Etienne de la Boétie

SARLAT SIGHTS

Key to symbols

⊞ map coordinates refer to the Sarlat map on page 108; sights below are highlighted in yellow on the map.

⊠ address or location ☎ telephone number
⊘ opening times 🎟 admission charge:
$$$ more than €10, $$ €5–€10, $ less than €5

CATHÉDRALE ST.-SACERDOS

The Cathedral of St. Sacerdos is interesting as much for its surroundings of courts and chapels – which are clustered near the one-time abbey that ran the town – as for the building itself. The bulky monument dominates the town with its state-capped tower, appropriate since

Sarlat had been the seat of a bishop from the 14th century until the Revolution. The present church dates from the late-16th to 17th century. A Romanesque tower and ancient sculpture over the main door remain from the original building. The effects of glittering stained glass soften the cavernous and stern interior. Note the handsome organ and large wooden pulpit. On the south side is the Bishop's Palace. Behind the cathedral is a strange 12th-century bullet-shaped building with a conical roof. Called the Lanterne des Morts (Dead Men's Lantern), it's believed to have been used for funeral purposes although its actual history is unknown.
⊞ B2 ⊠ Place du Peyrou

MAISON D'ETIENNE DE LA BOÉTIE

Unfortunately, because the building is a working office suite that houses the Sarlat Chamber of Commerce and Industry, the interior of this strikingly handsome Renaissance-style house remains a mystery to most visitors. Opposite the cathedral, the splendid stone house was built in 1525 by a local magistrate, father of the poet Etienne de La Boétie, who grew up to inspire Jean-Jacques Rousseau's celebrated *Social Contract*. Step across the road to get the full effect of the facade, with its exuberant sculpture, stone pilasters and medallions. Compare and contrast with the Gothic windows and trailing flowers of the quaintly medieval Hôtel Plamon, across place de la Liberté. Enter the courtyard, once a covered market, to admire an elegant staircase.
⊞ B2
Chambre de Commerce et de L'Industrie ⊠ place du Peyrou ☎ 05 53 31 73 73

WALK: EXPLORING SECRET SARLAT

Refer to route marked on city map on page 108

From place de la Bouquerie, walk down rue Présidial and turn left onto rue Landry. Continue up a narrow stone-flagged passage to peer through a gate into the gardens of the 17th-century Palace of Justice, now a grand restaurant. Return to rue Présidial, and note the handsome Classical doorway at No. 6.

Turn left onto rue d'Albusse, with its corner Gothic doorway, then take a left behind the church to admire some wrought-iron balconies and follow a narrow winding stepped passage that leads to the Lanterne des Morts. Keep following the path down into the churchyard behind the cathedral and cross into cours des Fountaines to view a Classical stone arch. Turn right on rue Tourny. Continue to place du Peyrou. Here, pause by the Maison d'Etienne de la Boétie. To the right is rue de la Liberté with ancient wooden houses. For a small circular tour, follow along this road and turn left at the tourist office, which takes you through a lovely quarter of old houses returning to place du Peyrou.

Turn right along rue de La Boétie, cross rue de la République, and enter the western section. Turn left and then right to mount rue Liarsou, then wind up rue des Trois-Conils. This street is notable for its modern shops cunningly tucked into old buildings. Old city walls still border the main boulevard, belting the town. A nearby 16th-century tower is one of only two remaining from a set of 18 that once studded the fortifications.

Turn right onto rue du Siège. Enjoy the view down to the town and a charming towered house. Steps take you along the narrow and unusually straight rue Jean-Jacques-Rousseau, which is noteworthy for its handsome gold stone houses.

Turn right where côte de Toulouse crosses and go down to rue de la République, and swing a swift left and right down rue Victor-Hugo. Take a left before the large Église Ste.-Marie, with the cloth-makers' house, Hôtel Plamon, and the old well and sculpture of three bronze geese opposite. Turn left at the church and climb the street for a fine view down to the marketplace.

Alfresco refreshments in Sarlat's place de la Liberté

Dordogne

Country ham, bread and fruit are staple ingredients

TASTE OF PÉRIGORD

The Dordogne provides nearly half of France's luxury foods. The welcome is open and warm to guests who wish to taste, buy or learn to cook legendary poultry and mushroom dishes. However, locals jealously guard their sources, and too many questions as to where to find your own wild mushrooms and truffles will be met with a polite smile and determined silence.

The gathering and traditional preparation of conserves are an essential part of family life here, and each household has its secret supply of raw materials. Sunny mornings after rain in early autumn are spent trudging into the forest to collect *cèpes* and other wild mushrooms. The inexperienced take their finds to the nearest pharmacy to sort the savory from the lethal. While some mushrooms are enjoyed immediately, the majority are cooked, bottled and stored for the rest of the year.

In December, geese and ducks are plucked and prepared for the pot. Anglo-Saxon sensibilities often recoil at the force-feeding that creates foie gras, but here, what elsewhere might be considered goose abuse is regarded as high art. The liver is weighed separately and put aside for the alchemy of foie gras. Wings and legs are preserved in fat to recipes as old as the woods. Some birds are served *demoiselle*, grilled whole over a wood fire.

Mid-winter is time for farmers to snuffle for truffles. Some use pigs and others hunt with hounds to find the rare fungi. Back at the farm, these nuggets are bottled in their own juice. Pigs are slaughtered in the winter and the meat preserved. Walnuts and chestnuts are harvested in season, and these too find their way into bottles, cans and jars. The intensely flavored preserves are deployed year round in small doses to enliven simple foods and create gastronomic delights at little expense. Even an omelet becomes an occasion with a dash of truffle juice. Just a mist of *liqueur de noix* (walnut liqueur) can transform a summer ice cream.

In summer months, farmers grow asparagus, winemakers tend their vines, and farmers' wives open their kitchens to visitors for half-day and weekend cookery courses that teach vacationers how to make the most of pre-cooked confits and succulent *magret de canard* (duck cutlet). You can obtain details from the local tourist offices.

Cathédrale Ste.-Cécile rises above the Pont Vieux and Tarn river at Albi

REGIONAL SIGHTS

Key to symbols

⊞ map coordinates refer to the Dordogne map on page 107; sights below are highlighted in yellow on the map.

⊠ address or location ☎ telephone number

🕒 opening times 🚍 nearest bus or tram route

🍽 restaurant on site or nearby ℹ information

🎟 admission charge: $$$ more than €10, $$ €5–€10, $ less than €5

ALBI

Count Henri Marie Raymond de Toulouse-Lautrec (1864–1901) was born into minor nobility in the fiery red brick town of Albi. The medieval Pont Vieux spanning the Tarn river, as well as the flour mills, ocher dusty lanes and cypress trees of the hardy wine-producing area, may have kindled the young artist's passion for painting. However, it was the debauched fleshpots of Paris' Montmartre that lured him away from the family château in Naucelle and took him to the city where he was to find fame and wealth.

Crippled and stunted at the age of 14, Toulouse-Lautrec had been sheltered by his family. Life among the outcasts of Paris stimulated both the artist and his art. His paintings of prostitutes and showgirls at the Moulin Rouge and other public balls made his name even more famous than the dancers Jane Avril and La Goulue, whom he immortalized in the posters that defined late-19th-century nightlife.

Cathédrale Ste.-Cécile, the world's largest brick building, represents the restraint of his hometown. Apart from the flamboyant 16th-century porch, the edifice is austere. There are no stained-glass windows, merely fortress slits keeping daylight from the sumptuous interior, whose treasures include a masterly fresco of the Last Judgment, slightly damaged in the 17th century but still impressive.

Below the cathedral is Old Albi, with houses of timber and brick. Make your way to rue Toulouse-Lautrec to see the artist's birthplace, the Hôtel du Bosc.

The Palais de la Berbie, a 13th-century palace fortified by civil unrest, is now a museum devoted to Toulouse-Lautrec. The collection of his work before Paris features family portraits and local landscapes and offers clues to the compassion he later showed for harsher subjects.

A 30-mile drive northeast of town, the Château du Bosc, as well as its estate at

Dordogne

Naucelle, was the artist's childhood home and lifelong summer retreat. Here, his great-nieces and great-nephews welcome visitors to the family's richly furnished medieval château.

⊞ C2

Tourist information ✉ place de la Berbie, place Ste.-Cécile ☎ 05 63 49 48 80; www.mairie-albi.fr
Musée Toulouse-Lautrec ✉ Palais de la Berbie, place Ste.-Cécile ☎ 05 63 49 48 70 ◷ Daily 9–6, Jul.–Aug.; daily 9–noon and 2–6, Jun. and Sep.; daily 10–noon and 2–6, Apr.–May; Wed.–Mon. 10–noon and 2–5:30, Mar. and Oct.; Wed.–Mon. 10–noon and 2–5, Nov.–Feb. ☝ $ (palace terraces and gardens free) ⓘ Audio-guided tours available
Château du Bosc ✉ Camjac, 12800 Naucelle ☎ 05 65 69 20 83 ◷ Daily 9–7, in summer; 9–5, rest of year ☝ $

AUBUSSON

A town whose name is synonymous with the world's finest tapestries, Aubusson had its fame assured when Flemish weavers set up shop on the banks of the Creuse river in the 14th century. With each century, newer and greater craftsmen came to town, and each reign brought fresh royal warrants to weave finer and more ornate hangings for the châteaux and palaces being built by kings and princes along the Loire and around Paris. From the reigns of Louis XIV to Louis XVI, noble clients commissioned needlework copies of famous paintings. The popularity of pastoral and mythical themes is told at the town's museum of the history of weaving, the 16th-century Maison du Vieux-Tapissier. Modern tapestries can be seen in various private workshops and at the Musée Départemental de la Tapisserie, which exhibits contemporary examples as well as cubist-inspired work by the modern master Lurçat himself.

⊞ C4

Tourist information ✉ rue Vieille ☎ 05 55 66 32 12
Maison du Vieux-Tapissier ✉ rue Vieille ☎ 05 55 66 32 12 ◷ Daily 9–noon and 2–7, Jun. 15–Sep. 30 ☝ $

BEYNAC-ET-CAZENAC

If you like a romantic and extravagant view of history and its heroes, then drive out to see the improbably spectacular

château of Beynac looming atop rugged limestone rocks and soaking up the sunshine that blesses the village rooftops on the riverside below. The fortress known locally as Satan's Archway comes complete with a lifetime's supply of legendary heroes. Richard the Lion-Heart captured the original building in the 12th century, and Simon de Montfort destroyed it during his crusades. It eventually was rebuilt and changed hands several times during the Hundred Years War. When peace finally was restored, Beynac became a stronghold of the barons of Périgord and was embroiled in local rivalries with the Château de Castelnaud (see page 115).

It's worth the climb for the views and to see a fresco of the Last Supper in the principal stateroom. Bronze Age and Roman history can be discovered in a small museum in the attractive town below.

The town of Beynac-et-Cazenac is dominated by the château

🔲 A3
Château Féodal de Beynac ☎ 05 53 29 50 40
🕐 Daily 10–dusk, Oct.–Nov.; 10–6:30, Jun.–Sep.;
10–6, Mar.–May; noon–dusk, rest of year 🖐 $$

CAHORS

Cahors is best known overseas for the hardy red wine that bears its name. It was the holy spring, worshiped by the ancient Gauls and Romans, that led to a town developing in this natural moat formed by the Lot river. Coveted and taken by the English during the Hundred Years War, the town sustained little damage to its buildings and walls. Many early turrets and battlements are still dotted around town. Today, visitors come to admire the magnificent 14th-century Pont Valentré, with seven arches gracefully sweeping across the river and three square towers standing sturdily atop. For years no one could place the final stone on top of the central tower, known as the Devil's Tower, because, it is said, the devil quarreled with the architect and was appeased only when his image was carved on the tower. Cross the bridge into town to visit the Renaissance cloisters of the cathedral. The old quarter is famed for its ornate doorways dating from the 12th to 19th centuries.

🔲 B3
Tourist information ✉ place François Mitterand
☎ 05 65 53 20 65; www.quercy-tourisme.com/cahors

CHÂTEAU DE CASTELNAUD

The château was rescued from virtual ruin when it was declared a national monument in 1966. Now it's the Musée de la Guerre au Moyen Âge (Museum of

The Romanesque cloisters of the Benedictine abbey at Moissac

Medieval Warfare), with many fascinating exhibits. Its history is indelibly linked with that of its neighbor across the water, Beynac (see page 114). Both shared similar fluctuating fortunes during the Hundred Years War as the lords of the two houses bitterly vied for control of the region, spying on each other and splitting the loyalty of the community without ever actually declaring war. In 1317, Pope Jean XXII ordered a marriage between the families to end the conflict. As the château fell into disrepair, the family moved to nearby les Milandes (see page 120), abandoning Castelnaud to the ravages of the weather and raids of builders seeking local stone.

Finally restored in 1998, it welcomes visitors as much for the wonderful views as for the museum. On summer evenings (July through August), actors re-create scenes from the castle's glory days. Summer courses for children include calligraphy, heraldry and siege strategy.

✠ B3

Château de Castelnaud ✉ Castelnaud-la-Chapelle
☎ 05 53 31 30 00 🕐 Daily 9–8, Jul.–Aug.; 10–7, May–Jun. and in Sep.; 10–6, mid-Feb. through Apr. 30 and Oct. 1 to mid-Nov.; 2–5, rest of year 🍴 Café 💰 $$

LIMOGES

Elegant blue and gold tableware bearing the Limoges name is recognized throughout the world, but before the porcelain industry was even conceived, this town on the banks of the Vienne river had discovered another sought-after talent: champlevé. From the 12th to 18th centuries, Limoges was the world center of the art, which involves multilayering enamel onto copper to create perfect luster and sheen. The Musée Municipal has an extensive collection of classic pieces, and the craft is demonstrated at the Enamel Workshop, 31 rue des Tanneurs. The town's ceramic and porcelain making is celebrated at the Musée Adrien Dubouché.

Visit the eight-arch 13th-century bridge and the nearby Gothic Cathédrale St.-Étienne, inaugurated in the same era and completed 600 years later. The old streets, especially rue des Bouchers, make for a pleasant stroll. Plenty of shops sell genuine Limoges porcelain.

✠ B4

Tourist information ✉ boulevard de Fleurus
☎ 05 55 34 46 87; www.ville-limoges.fr

Arcades line place Nationale in Montauban

Abbatiale St.-Pierre ✉ place Durand de Bredon
☎ 05 63 04 01 85 🕐 Cloisters open daily 9–7,
Jul.–Aug.; 9–6 in Jun. and Sep.; 9–12:30 and 2–6,
Apr.–May; 10–noon and 2–5, rest of year 💶 $$
ℹ Guided tours Sun. at 3

MOISSAC

World Heritage Site canals, bustling
farmers' markets and orchards of succulent
plums, pears, peaches, apples and cherries;
modern Moissac has all of this. But it's
Abbatiale St.-Pierre (St. Peter's Abbey
Church) that entices people into this
modest settlement between the Tarn and
Garonne rivers. Despite serious bruising
during the French Revolution, the remains
of the Benedictine abbey church and
cloisters are among the most treasured in
France. Ornate carved capitals from the
11th through 13th centuries may be
viewed in the cool shade of a summer's
day. A museum next door displays
remaining stonework from the abbey. The
monks acquired many great artworks since
its founding in the seventh century. Most
impressive is the 12th-century southern
doorway depicting St. John's vision of the
apocalypse. The best time to visit the town
is on a market day, when you can sip a
glass or two of the local wines. Some street
names are bilingual, as the locals once
spoke the old language of Occitan.

 B2
Tourist information ✉ place Durand de Bredon
☎ 05 63 04 01 85; www.frenchcom.com/moissac

MONTAUBAN

Ignore the bland suburbs surrounding the
original old *bastide* – the name for a
fortified town with streets narrow enough
to avoid being taken by marauding
horsemen. The rose-tinted brickwork is
most striking at dawn and dusk. Garlands
of arcades border place Nationale with
angled porticoes linking 17th-century
houses. The quarter's alleys and bars provide
an evocative setting for the fringe events of
a jazz festival in July. The festival attracts
musicians from Louisiana to the Paris
suburbs, with main events taking place in
the park below the old town walls. The civic
history of this Protestant stronghold that
held out for 100 days against Louis XIII's
forces in 1621 has been overshadowed by
its art collection. The Bishop's Palace, by
the banks of the Tarn, houses a lavish
collection of religious and melodramatic
canvases by the popular 19th-century
painter Jean-Auguste-Dominique Ingres.

➕ B2
Tourist information ✉ place Prax ☎ 05 63 63 60 60;
www.ville-montauban.fr

DRIVE: HISTORIC AND PREHISTORIC TOUR

Distance: 238 miles Time: 4 days

From prehistoric caves to Roman streets, medieval miracles to the home of a 20th-century American heroine, this drive starts and finishes at Périgueux, the old capital of Périgord.

A carved Neanderthal man at Les Eyzies-de-Tayac

Taking the N2089 toward Brive, go right on the D710, then left on the D45, turning right along the D47.

Pause on the steps leading to the stalactites and stalagmites of the first cave of the tour, Grotte du Grand Roc, and gaze at breathtaking views over the Vézère valley.

Continue along the D47.

The heart of prehistoric Dordogne is Les Eyzies-de-Tayac, with the Musée National de Préhistoire (National Museum of Prehistory) in a 13th-century castle guarded by a giant statue of Neanderthal man. The Vézère river created the caves that make this one of the world's key prehistoric regions. The tourist office will direct you toward the key sites: cave paintings at Font de Gaume or the caving museum at Tayac.

On the D706 toward Montignac, you will pass the 20 reconstructions of Neanderthal and Cro-Magnon sites. Turn right on the D704, then right again.

Known as the "Sistine Chapel of Périgord," Lascaux cave was discovered by four boys and a dog in 1940. The dog fell into a hole, and the boys scrambled after it to find

themselves facing the greatest prehistoric art collection known to man. The lads told their teacher, who told expert Abbé Breuil, who told the world. The ravages of tourism, light and moss led to the cave being sealed in 1963, but a precise replica was opened in 1983 at Lascaux II. Painstakingly precise reproductions of the 25,000-year-old drawings use the original pigments. Once again, visitors may marvel at the famous picture of a man being chased by a wounded bison and other scenes from another world.

From Montignac, take the D704 to Sarlat-la-Canéda (see pages 108–111). Follow the D46 to Vitrac, turning left on the D703.

Souillac provides diversions from so much history. Enjoy the museum of automated toys, which houses 1,000 of them, including an entire jazz band. Then visit the 12th-century Romanesque church.

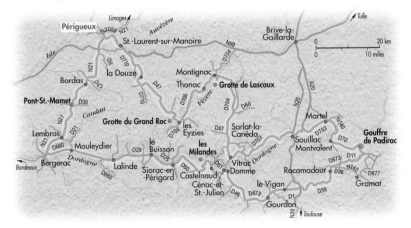

Opposite: The village of Rocamadour is steeped in legend

Strolling along a street in Rocamadour

Take the D703 to Martel, turning right on the N140 and left on the D70. Take a right for the D11 to Miers then left on the D91. Turn left and continue along the D60, taking the right fork by a stone cross. Turn right again at the T-junction.
At Gouffre de Padirac, take a boat trip along an underground river from the cave where Edward Martel discovered 200,000-year-old bones and human remains from nearly 50,000 years ago. Walk the 455 steps down or use the elevator to descend into an underworld of eerie and fascinating beauty.
Take the D90 to Padirac, then turn left onto the D673 to Rocamadour.
Yet another of Mother Nature's greatest photo opportunities (from the Belvedere of l'Hospitalet on the D32 below), the medieval village of Rocamadour clings improbably to a cliff face. The town flourished in the 12th century when a body of a man – thought to be Zaccheus, the tax collector turned philanthropist after meeting Jesus – was discovered. Miracles and pilgrims inevitably followed the discovery, and when Protestants seized the village and tried to burn the body, it remained untouched by the flames. Rocher des Aigles nearby has displays of flying birds of prey.
Follow the D32 to Couzou, turning right on the D39 through St.-Projet. Head right on the D1 and join the D673 to Gourdon.

Leave Gourdon on the D673, turning right on the D6/D46 to Domme.
Visit the quaint covered market in the fortified town of Domme atop a sheer rock face to buy picnic supplies for the journey ahead. An interesting local history museum sits on the square.
From Cénac, take the D50 toward Siorac-en-Périgord. In Pont de Cause go straight on for Castelnaud, then continue straight toward Fayrac and les Milandes. Turn left on the D53 toward Siorac-en-Périgord. After a bend sign, make a sharp right uphill to the château.
The star of the 1926 all-black cabaret *Revue Nègre*, Joséphine Baker left racism in America to find adulation in the *Folies Bergères*. The one-time topless dancer and French Resistance worker bought this 15th-century château at les Milandes to care for her Rainbow Tribe, the children of many races she adopted after the war. The multiracial family became a tourist attraction, and she built a golf course, hotel and restaurant to cater to the visitors. When bailiffs eventually came to evict her, she famously sat on the doorstep, holding her children to her, and refused to leave. After Princess Grace saw news film of the event, she offered Joséphine and the children a home in Monaco.
Continue along the road, bearing left to turn right on the D53. Take the D50 to Siorac-en-Périgord, then follow signs on the D25 for Lalinde and then Bergerac.
Not only a center of wine production but also once home to the French tobacco industry, Bergerac has museums of wine, tobacco and barrel making. Enjoy enchanting narrow streets and beautiful houses, not to mention the inevitable statue of Cyrano, who despite his name, in fact had nothing to do with the town.
The N21 takes you back to Périgueux.

Musée National de Préhistoire ⊠ Place de la Mairie, Les Eyzies-de-Tayac ☎ 05 53 06 45 45 🕐 Daily 9:30–7, Jul.–Aug.; Wed.–Mon. 9:30–noon and 2–6, mid-Mar. through Jun. 30 and Sep. 1 to mid-Nov.; Wed.–Mon. 9:30–noon, 2–5, rest of year 🚻 $
Grottes de Lascaux II ⊠ Montignac ☎ 05 53 35 50 10 🕐 Daily 9–8, Jul.–Aug.; daily 9:30–6:30, Apr.–Jun. and in Sep.; Tue.–Sun. 10–noon and 2–6, Feb.–Mar. and in Oct.; Tue.–Sun. 10–noon and 2–5:30, Nov.–Dec. 🚻 $$
Musée de l'Automate ⊠ Place de l'Abbaye, Souillac ☎ 05 65 37 07 07 🕐 Daily 10–noon and 3–6, Apr.–Oct.; Wed.–Sun., 2–5, rest of year 🚻 $$

The Manoir de Tarde, set into the cliffs at La Roque-Gageac

LA ROQUE-GAGEAC

Nestled among old trees at the foot of a limestone cliff with the river flowing gently by, the picturesque town of La Roque-Gageac is the epitome of the Dordogne. Tourists are escorted downstream on flat-bottomed boats known as *gabares*. Logs were floated downstream in the days when the town's fortunes were founded on the timber trade. The town looks its finest from the water, as the sun shines on rooftops of gray turrets and the local red tiles. The seemingly 15th-century château actually was built in the 20th century, but the Manoir de Tarde is the real thing. The cliffs crumbled too far in 1956, leading to tragedy when falling rock killed several people. Nowadays all is safely shored up, and the town receives a steady flow of visitors.

✚ B3

Tourist information ✉ La Bourg ☎ 05 53 29 17 01; www.perigord.com

PYRÉNÉES

*"*HIS *borderland rendezvous of many cultures is shaped by pioneers and pilgrims, mountains and miracles.* *"*

Opposite: The mountain abbey of St.-Martin-du-Canigou, south of Villefranche-de-Conflent

The snow-capped mountain of Pic de Font-Vive, east of the Col de Puymorens

PYRÉNÉES

To most strangers, the Pyrénées are the "other" mountain range of France. Ski resorts are less well-known than the glitzier destinations across the country. But the southwest corner of France boasts more than just peaks. The Pyrénées themselves rise from the plains of southwestern France to form a natural border with Spain. They span 250 miles between two seas, and though the highest peaks are on the Spanish side of the border, the French Pyrénées lure hikers in all seasons. The most spectacular scenery is preserved within an area defined as a national park. Here, ibex, chamois and bears roam the hills as golden eagles and three species of vulture – Egyptian, griffon and the rarer lammergeier – patrol the skies.

Where there are rocks, there are caves, and these encompass prehistoric paintings and picturesque stalactite-bordered subterranean waterways. Notable are the cavernous shrines at Bétharram and Lourdes.

Spanish Connection

The southwest of France is a funnel that distills all the Spanish influences that make the country such an intriguing and intoxicating cocktail. Just beyond are Catalan towns and villages, the principality of Andorra and the Basques. Summer bullfights, country dancing and cross-border pilgrim routes owe as much to Barcelona as to Toulouse.

French kings and leaders have long married Spanish princesses. This area recalls royal weddings and honeymoons from Louis XIV and Marie-Thérèse to the legendary pairing of Eugénie of Montijo with Emperor Napoléon III. Wars of religion and invasion have brought new blood from conquerors and refugees alike. The Romans opened spas, the Jews brought chocolate and the English gave the region foxhunting.

Two very different seas shape the region: the Atlantic, where surfers take on the turbulent Bay of Biscay and

Hikers enjoy the high pastures of the Pyrénées, along the border between France and Spain

royalty comes to play, and the calmer Mediterranean, rich with history.

Cutting-edge Tradition

Hikers often carry a traditional *makila* as they ascend the steepest paths. The Basque walking stick, used by

Pelota players hit a fast-moving ball in this single-wall court

shepherds and pilgrims since the Middle Ages, has been manufactured for centuries in the French village of Larressore. The name means "death giver," since the handle contains an ornate blade said to have inspired the blacksmiths of Bayonne to invent the bayonet. The stick is carved from a living tree six months before the branch is removed, and details include a metal band on the handle with the owner's name and family motto. The country's highest honor is to be publicly presented a *makila*. Recipients have included several popes, Ronald Reagan and Winston Churchill.

Sport

The region is said to have been the first in France to popularize golf. The Roman form of tennis *(pila)* is the main sport of the Basque country. Pelota is a type of jai alai played in the open air against one or more high walls called a *fronton*. Variants of the sport use specific mitts or gloves, but the most strenuous is indoor, bare-handed *cesta punta*, one of the world's fastest sports.

Pioneers

The lush hills and scrubland of the plains form an unlikely backdrop for an international center of business and technology. Yet Toulouse has pioneered the Continent's conquest of the skies, from the first airmail services to the Concorde airplane and the European space program. The exhibition halls of Toulouse's City of Space make a fascinating day out.

Crossing Borders

Apart from mountain passes, an essential cross-border link is with the port of Bilbao in northern Spain via the coastal route along the Bay of Biscay. A major attraction here is the remarkable Guggenheim Museum of avant-garde 20th-century and contemporary art (☎ [Spain 0034] 94 43 59 080). North American architect Frank Gehry's writhing combination of limestone, titanium and glass is a landmark collaboration between Americans and the Basques.

TOULOUSE

Toulouse is the fourth largest city in France and the capital of the skies. Since World War I, it has conquered flight, with legendary aviators such as Antoine de St.-Exupéry and Jean Mermoz pioneering routes to Casablanca and Rio. It may be home to the company Aérospatiale – the driving force behind the Concorde and space rockets – but ask any Frenchman about Toulouse's contribution to his country's wealth, and he will answer: *"cassoulet et rugby."*

Cassoulet, the bean and meat stew of the south, is served in every restaurant in town. And rugby is practically a religion, with the local team one of the best in France. During the championships, locals and students throng the streets dressed in the team's red and black colors.

Lively Nightlife

Youthful exuberance keeps Toulouse from becoming just another industrial and commercial center. The second-largest university in France brings fresh faces to the bars and cafés from place du Capitole to the circular place Wilson.

The mood is decidedly Latin, with more than a hint of the Mediterranean and Spain in both people and street culture. This hexagonal town along the Garonne river is ringed by boulevards and has seven theaters, legendary nightclubs and street scenes, and smartly dressed bar patrons lingering well after midnight.

Evenings begin in the hour before sundown, when the sky adds its special hues to the rosy tint of the buildings to cast warm shadows outside the Hôtel de Ville at the Capitole.

The Pink City

The Pink City gets its nickname from the red bricks used to build its magnificent houses and public buildings when local quarries died out in the Middle Ages. The pink building boom also was funded by another color. Trade in the bluish-black dye plant, woad, revived city fortunes in the 16th century. Previously the city had been an academic center, with literary societies promoting the ancient language of southern France, the Langue d'Oc.

Shopping

Although commerce today centers around smart shops by the main squares, the

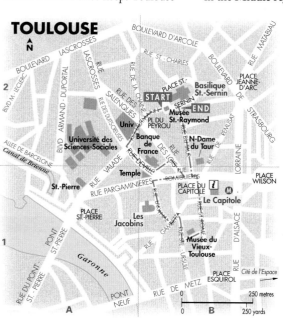

Markets take place outside the grand Capitole building in Toulouse

markets are much more fun. The main food market for sights, sounds and aromas is held every day but Monday outside the Capitole. A good book and prints market takes place at St.-Cyprien. For handicrafts and jewelry, try the market on place St.-Étienne all day on Saturday.

ESSENTIAL INFORMATION

TOURIST INFORMATION
Donjon du Capitole ☎ 05 61 11 02 22; www.ot-toulouse.fr The office has English-speaking assistants, and tours and river cruises can be booked here.

URBAN TRANSPORTATION
The single-line subway has seven stops across the center and isn't of much use to tourists. Tickets should be validated before journeys. The main sights are well-placed around the central town hall (Capitole subway station). However, there is a good bus service that runs from 5:30 a.m. to 11 p.m. ☎ 05 61 41 70 70. The SNCF Gare Matabiau, northeast of the center, has major national and local train connections ☎ 05 61 10 10 00. Taxis can be hailed on the street or call ☎ 05 61 42 38 38.

AIRPORT INFORMATION
Toulouse Blagnac airport is close to the city. ☎ 05 61 42 44 00; www.toulouse.aeroport.fr. Shuttle buses into town operate every 20 minutes from the first to the last flight ☎ 05 34 60 64 00; www.navettevia-toulouse.com

CLIMATE – Average highs and lows

JAN.	FEB.	MAR.	APR.	MAY	JUN.	JUL.	AUG.	SEP.	OCT.	NOV.	DEC.
9°C	11°C	14°C	16°C	19°C	23°C	26°C	26°C	23°C	18°C	13°C	10°C
48°F	52°F	57°F	61°F	66°F	73°F	79°F	79°F	73°F	64°F	55°F	50°F
2°C	4°C	5°C	6°C	10°C	13°C	15°C	15°C	12°C	9°C	5°C	4°C
36°F	39°F	41°F	43°F	50°F	55°F	59°F	59°F	54°F	48°F	41°F	39

Tier upon tier – Basilique St.-Sernin in Toulouse

TOULOUSE SIGHTS

Key to symbols

➕ map coordinates refer to the Toulouse map on page 127; sights below are highlighted in yellow on the map.

✉ address or location ☎ telephone number

🕐 opening times 🚌 nearest bus or tram route

🍴 restaurant on site or nearby

ℹ information

💷 admission charge: $$$ more than €10, $$ €5–€10, $ less than €5

BASILIQUE ST.-SERNIN

Among the most famous pilgrimage churches in France during the Middle Ages, the wedding-cake-like edifice attracted hordes of devout travelers en route to Santiago de Compostela in western Spain. Traditionally they stayed but one day, and you can still see their clearly marked route around the Romanesque basilica. Its twin-colored spire and long, brick nave are noteworthy, and there is an uncluttered and airy sense of space inside, with many chapels. The church stands amid well-tended gardens. It was consecrated in 1096, having been built to house the relics of St. Saturnin, who was martyred in AD 250. St.-Sernin impresses as the largest and one of the prettiest of its type in the West.

➕ B2 ✉ place St.-Sernin ☎ 05 61 21 80 45

LE CAPITOLE

Sitting grandly before colorful market stalls in the middle of the city, the grandest building in town is a full city block long. Containing both the city hall and the main theater, it's a particularly cheery place to be on a Saturday, as a constant procession of brides, grooms and bouquets spills out of the main doors on the day that weddings are registered. Looking as good as it has since the present building opened in 1759, the brick and stone has been restored and cleaned, and the eight marble columns positively gleam in the sunlight. Enter through the main carriageway to cour Henri-IV. On non-wedding days, climb the main staircase to some splendid

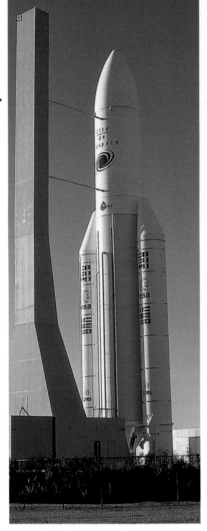

Ready for lift-off: The launch pad for Ariane 5 at
Cité de l'Espace

CITÉ DE L'ESPACE

Since the area around Blagnac Airport
continues to be the hub of Europe's
aerospace industry, it should come as no
surprise that Toulouse boasts a City of
Space.

Just on the outskirts of town (exit 17
of the Périphérique orbital road), the Cité
de l'Espace is easily recognizable by the
launch pad for the Ariane 5 – flagship of
the European space program. A full day
out includes a visit to the modern
planetarium, tours of the Mir space
station and close encounters with satellites
and stars. Hands-on experience includes a
course in controlling a simulated rocket
launch, close-up views of NASA and
Russian space vehicles and the
opportunity to forecast weather using the
latest technology. Temporary exhibitions
and an outdoor park complement the
main halls.

✚ B1 ✉ Parc de la Plaine, avenue Jean-Gonord
☎ 05 62 71 48 71; www.cite-espace.com
🕐 Tue.–Fri. 9–6, Sat.–Sun. 9–7 🎟 $$$

LES JACOBINS

The spectacular vaulting of this Gothic
church might never have been created but
for a fiery accident in a church in nearby
Narbonne. When the Dominican friars
came to rebuild their preaching base in
Toulouse, they remembered the
destruction at Narbonne and decided the
traditional timber ceiling of other
churches was too hazardous. Thus, when
they enlarged the church from 1275 to
1292, fireproof brick vaults rose from
seven tall columns running along the
center of the church, culminating in a
"palm-tree" vault that springs from the
final eastern pillar. The octagonal church
tower dates from the same period. A high
altar of gray marble contains the relics of
St. Thomas Aquinas. The cloister, a true
haven of peace in a busy town center,
comes into its own every September with
a month-long season of weekend piano
recitals. The Piano aux Jacobins season
attracts the world's finest musicians.

✚ B1 ✉ Parvis des Jacobins ☎ 05 61 22 23 82
🕐 Daily 10–7 🎟 $

staterooms adorned with 19th-century
paintings. The Galerie des Illustres, the
Marriage Room, contains busts of local
heroes and a fabulously restored painted
ceiling. The theater is grandly gilded and
draped. By the garden behind the
Capitole, the fortified Donjon houses the
tourist office. The Capitole takes up one
side of the wide square that bears its
name. The other three sides are mostly
hotels and shopping arcades.

✚ B1 ✉ Galerie des Illustres, place du Capitole
☎ 05 61 22 29 22 🕐 Mon.–Fri. 10–noon, 2–5. Closed
holidays 🎟 Free

Pyrénées

The Jacobins church has brick vaulting that spreads from seven tall columns

WALK: CLOISTERS AND COURTYARDS

Refer to route marked on city map on page 127

This walk around Toulouse will take about 2 to 3 hours.

Starting at place St.-Sernin, visit the pilgrims' church and the Musée St.-Raymond, a 16th-century college with high, light rooms for its collection of Roman and medieval treasures.

Take narrow rue Emile Cartailhac.
Admire brick courts that open out into the busy student quarter of tall slender houses with shutters, lively cafés and bookshops.

Continue across place du Peyrou to rue Albert Lautmann and the main Law Faculty on your right. Turn left on rue Déville.
The facades on this street have been cleaned and have typical wrought-iron balconies. At the end on the left is the Banque de France, with its elegant court and frontage.

Turn left here on rue du Collège-de-Foix, noting the massive broken arch and a tall ruined window of an ancient college, then right onto rue des Lois, and take

another sharp right to rue Romiguières.
Strolling through this typical, old-town street with red brick and courtyards, note the Vieux Temple on your right, then turn left on rue Lakanal to the Jacobins' church.

At the end of rue Lakanal to turn left on rue Gambetta, then right on rue Ste.-Ursule. Left onto rue du May.
The fine brick Hôtel du May at No. 7 houses the Museum du Vieux-Toulouse. Seize the opportunity to see the inside of a typical aristocratic house. This is right in the heart of the ancient residential quarter.

Go left on rue St.-Rome to return to the shopping center and place du Capitole.
Walk around the arcades of the square and take in a visit to the Capitole. The main central subway station and tourist office are nearby. Take the atmospheric rue du Taur and allow tempting old streets and courtyards to lure you off course. On the right is the gaunt brick facade of Notre-Dame du Taur. Step inside to see mosaics and faded 19th-century wall paintings. Browse the many small antique shops and galleries. The best buy is the celebrated Toulouse earthenware. The road ends at place St.-Sernin.

Stunning mountain scenery in Andorra

REGIONAL SIGHTS

Key to symbols

🞖 map coordinates refer to the Pyrénées map on page 124; sights below are highlighted in yellow on the map.

✉ address or location ☎ telephone number

🕘 opening times 🚍 nearest bus or tram route

🍴 restaurant on site or nearby

ℹ information

💶 admission charge: $$$ more than €10, $$ €5–€10, $ less than €5

ANDORRA

The other principality, clear across the country from Monaco, boasts two princes, stunning scenery, the best skiing in the Pyrénées and some of the top shopping bargains in western Europe.

Myths blur Andorra's history. A popular tale is that the original Gallic inhabitants fought Hannibal. The generally accepted view is that Charlemagne granted independence in the ninth century and that its princes have nominally governed the country since the 12th century. Princely honors are still shared between the French president and the Spanish bishop of Urgel. However, a 1993 referendum handed real power to an autonomous 28-seat assembly.

Measuring just 16 by 20 miles, Andorra is little more than a loop in the border between France and Spain, midway between Toulouse and Barcelona. Its official languages are French, Spanish and Catalan; the latter two are the most widely spoken. You are likely to hear English only at top hotels or in the crush of liquor, hi-fi and electronic stores that crowd the main streets of the capital, Andorra la Vella.

Since the principality isn't a member of the European Union and imposes no taxes, prices are on average 30 percent below those of the rest of the Continent. Trade all but dominates life in the capital, though the original old quarter, the Barri Antic, retains much of the charm of the original Pyrenean village. Among the whimsical stone houses lining cobbled streets is the 16th-century Casa de la Vall (House of the Valley), the Parliament building since 1702. Recognize it by the arms of the principality over the door. The house contains Andorra's only courtroom on the ground floor; the Parliament chamber, Sala del Consell, is upstairs.

Ski season runs from December to Easter, but many peaks are capped with snow well into the warm summer, when hiking takes over as the main sporting activity. The goal for many visitors is the highest point, the 9,650-foot Pic de Coma Pedrosa on the Spanish border. Caldea at les Escaldes is a modern spa resort of baths fed by natural thermal springs.

Catalan cuisine, which reflects strong French and Italian influences, dominates. Try *cunillo* (rabbit cooked in tomato sauce) or *escudella* (a stew of chicken, sausage and meatballs).

Since Andorra has no international rail or air links, the only access is by road. From France, pass through the highest pass in the Pyrénées, the 7,900-foot Port d'Envalira.

🞖 D1

Tourist information: Office du Tourisme de la Principauté d'Andorre ✉ 26 avenue de l'Opéra, 75001 Paris, France ☎ 01 42 61 50 55 or **Ministry of Tourism and Culture** ✉ Prat de la Creu 62, Andorra la Vella, Andorra ☎ 875700; www.tourisme.ad

Pyrénées

The most independently minded of the many lands that time has absorbed into France, the Basque Country straddles France and Spain. While the larger and wealthier part of this fiery nation occupies mineral-rich Spanish land, the French Pays Basque comprises three provinces: Basse Navarre, Labourd and Soule. Fishing and farming occupied daily life here until the advent of tourism.

The modern world knows the Basque Country through terrorism. The militant Basque separatist group ETA announces periodic cease-fires from its constant campaign for independence, but violent political activity tends to center on the Spanish section of the land. Within France, aside from occasional marches, Basque culture is predominantly folkloric.

A Basque in traditional costume

BASQUE COUNTRY

Country dancing, sports, such as pelota (see page 126), and shops selling berets and rope-soled espadrille shoes – these are the picturesque elements of Basque life in southwest France.

The convoluted Euskaldunak language dates back at least to the original tribes of eighth-century mountain men who fought Charlemagne's armies. Local legend claims it predates the Tower of Babel. Don't worry if you can't pick up the basics: The same tradition declares the devil himself managed to learn only three words. Unlike their colleagues over the Spanish border, French Basques will speak the language of the dominant country.

Cuisine combines peppers, pimentos, tomatoes, garlic and onions. Mixed with eggs, these make piperade, similar to an omelet. Pepper and garlic sauces are traditional *à la basquaise* accompaniments to grilled tuna or chicken with kidneys. Ham from Bayonne is famous (see page 134). The local dessert is *gâteau Basque*, a lemon and cherry cake. In fishing ports such as St.-Jean-de-Luz, taste the savory monkfish-rich mariners' stew, *ttoro*.

St.-Jean-de-Luz is the prettiest resort in the Labourd coastal region. Once a key port for the Atlantic whaling industry, today St.-Jean provides a picturesque stopover for travelers driving along the coast toward Spain. Stroll the old town, with its echoes of piracy and royal romance. See the harbor-side house where Louis XIV spent the month before his marriage to the Spanish infanta Marie-Thérèse, and the ornate Église St.-Jean-Baptiste, where they exchanged their vows.

Green hills, sandy beaches and neat red and white timbered villages – such as Sare, Ascain and Aïnhoa – line the coast. Inland look out for *pottocks*, half-wild horses roaming the hills and traded at the end of January during a colorful fair at the town of Espelette.

St.-Jean-du-Luz tourist information ✚ A1
✉ place du Maréchal-Foch ☎ 05 59 26 03 16;
www.saint-jean-de-luz.com

Costumed giants parade at a Bayonne fair

BAYONNE

Capital of the Basque Country (see page 133), Bayonne is the gastronomic highlight of the region. The town that gave the world the bayonet won fame through an unlikely pairing of pig farmers and chocolate makers. In the markets here locally cured ham and chocolate, brought to France by Jews fleeing Spain, is on sale.

Rue Neuve has quaint, old-fashioned tea rooms and *confiseries*, where the local confectionery is best enjoyed as a mid-morning or mid-afternoon snack. Place de la Liberté is lively in the early evening.

Two sites for any itinerary are the impressive Cathédrale Ste.-Marie – with its 14th-century cloister, 16th-century stained glass and twin towers from the 19th century – and the Musée Bonnat, with works by Francisco José de Goya, Sandro Botticelli and Peter Paul Rubens.

Learn more about the Euskaldunak language and culture of the Basque people, not to mention berets, folklore and bayonets, at the Musée Basque (Basque Museum), which outlines the history of the town.

✚ A2
Tourist information ✉ place des Basques ☎ 05 59 46 01 46; www.ville-bayonne.fr or www.bayonne-tourisme.com

Musée Bonnat ✉ 5 rue Jacques-Laffitte ☎ 05 59 08 52 ⏰ Wed.–Mon. 10–6:30 May–Oct.; 10–12:30 and

2–6, rest of year 🖐 $$ (free first Sun. of the month; joint ticket with Musée Basque available)

Musée Basque ✉ Maison Dragourette, 37 quai des Corsaires ☎ 05 59 46 61 90 ⏰ Tue.–Sun. 10–6:30, Apr.–Oct.; 10:30–12:30 and 2–6, rest of year 🖐 $$ (free first Sun. of the month)

BÉTHARRAM, GROTTES DE

Considered something of a sideshow to the more serious pilgrimage to Lourdes (see page 137), seven miles to the east, this slick underground excursion gets absolutely packed with tourists during the high season. The sheer noise of excited school parties can sometimes detract from the spirit of the occasion. However, a well-run transportation system keeps visitors flowing steadily through the attraction.

The medieval outline of la Cité, the old town of Carcassonne

More than three miles of stalactite- and stalagmite-packed chambers feature in a highly entertaining journey. The caves are reached by cable-car, then passengers transfer to a boat and train to follow the course of the underground river and its phosphorous-coated stone figures.

The name *bét arram* means beautiful branch, and the story is told of a young girl who slipped and fell in the nearby Gave de Pau. As she started to drown, a vision of the Virgin Mary reached out and threw her a branch and the girl was saved.

✚ B1

✉ Bétharram, 65270 St.-Pé-de-Bigorre ☎ 05 62 41 80 04 🕐 Daily 9–noon and 1:30–5:30, late Mar.–late Oct.; Mon.–Fri., 2:30–4, early Jan.–late Mar. (groups by reservation only) 🍴 Café 💰 $$$

CARCASSONNE

Like an ornamental cake, Carcassonne is so much nicer on the outside than within. Views of the completely walled old town dominate the countryside, seemingly promising a great deal. Unfortunately, the city is more than aware of the fact, and a barrage of Kodak signs, T-shirt racks and souvenir stalls clogs a warren of winding lanes inside the walls.

Just to the southeast of the modern town, the old Cité stands 485 feet high and is marked by 2 miles of double walls fortified with 52 towers. Round and square towers from the 12th and 13th centuries appear in pristine condition. This is because in the 19th century – on

PAS DE VOUS RENDRE ⬩ ⬩ HEUREUSE DANS C

⬩ VIII ⬩
⬩ APPARITION ⬩ ⬩ ELLE ⬩ NOUS ⬩ SALUE ⬩ ET ⬩ NOUS ⬩ SOURIT ⬩ ⬩ 16 JUILLET 1858 ⬩

⬩ VII ⬩
⬩ APPARITION ⬩ ⬩ VOULEZ ⬩ VOUS ⬩ ME ⬩ FAIRE ⬩ LA ⬩ GRACE ⬩ DE ⬩ VENIR ⬩ ICI ⬩ PENDANT ⬩ 15 ⬩ JOURS ⬩

Pyrénées

the orders of *Carmen* author Prosper Merimée (then government inspector of ancient monuments) – architect Eugène Emmanuel Viollet-le-Duc renovated the entire edifice as a lasting reminder of the golden age of fortification.

Like most memories, this re-creation is somewhat hazy on details, adding pretty pepper-pot roofs to some towers to please contemporary tastes. This scrubbed image of medieval defenses inspired Hollywood to film actor Kevin Costner here in the blockbuster movie *Robin Hood, Prince of Thieves,* with Carcassonne standing in for Nottingham, England.

In the space between the twin walls, known as les Lices Hautes and Basses (the upper and lower lists), knights of old would practice jousting. Re-enactments of tournaments, sound-and-light shows, concerts and theatrical presentations enliven summer evenings, and the end of October sees locals from the region celebrating the wine harvest within the old stone walls.

The town is entered through two gateways: the Porte d'Aude by the river and the twin-towered Porte Narbonnaise. Take a horse-drawn carriage from April through September, or explore on foot. After visiting the tomb of Simon de Montfort, climb to the top of the ramparts, turn away from the tourist hordes and gaze out on vineyards producing *vin du pays d'Aude.*

Likewise, visitors will do better to stay in hotels outside the Cité to appreciate views of what Carcassonne might have been, rather than to wake up to the commercial reality.

Across the Aude river, the Ville Basse, modestly wealthy from the wine trade, offers a pleasant Fine Arts Museum, the Gothic Église St.-Vincent with its unfinished tower, and the 14th-century Cathédrale St.-Michel. Half a mile from the Cité, Les Aigles de la Cité provides displays of medieval falconry.

➕ D1

Tourist information ✉ 15 boulevard Camille Pelletan
☎ 04 68 10 24 30; www.carcassonne.org
Les Aigles de la Cité ✉ Colline de Pech Mary
☎ 04 68 47 88 99 ⏰ Daily displays at 3 and 4:30,
Easter to Oct. 31 💲 $$

CASTRES

Castres owes its fortune to a heritage of textile manufacturing, and industry rings today's sprawling city. Its early wealth enabled the city fathers to commission the good and the great of the 17th century to design the public buildings. Thus the Hôtel de Ville has the stamp of the legendary architect Jules Hardouin-Mansart, who worked on Versailles and Paris' place Vendôme.

Mansart also is responsible for Castres' main attraction, the 1675 former Bishop's Palace (Evêché). This elegant building, on the edge of the old quarter, stands in grounds landscaped by royal favorite Le Nôtre. The palace is now the Musée Goya, holding a small yet superb collection of paintings and drawings by Francisco José de Goya himself, as well as an impressive collection of other Spanish canvases. The striking cathedral also dates from the 17th century.

Castres is a useful base for touring the Midi-Pyrénées region and the Haut Languedoc Regional Park near the Sodobre. The park is known for its unusual granite boulders, the *roches-tremblantes* (shifting rocks), which actually sway gently when touched. A product of natural erosion, this movement is said to help psychics or sensitive souls predict the future.

➕ D2

Tourist information ✉ 3 rue Milhau-Ducommun
☎ 05 63 62 63 62
Musée Goya ✉ L'Evêché de Castres ☎ 05 63 71 59
30 ⏰ Daily 9–noon and 2–6, Apr. 1 to mid-Sep.; 9–12
and 2–5, rest of year (Sun. from 10 a.m.). Closed Mon.
except Jul. and Aug.

LOURDES

The phenomenon of Lourdes – with its 4 million annual visitors, 300 hotels, three dozen campsites and efficient support system – is that despite the huge pilgrimage traffic, one may still find the spirit of Bernadette.

The town of Lourdes, which graces both banks of the Gave de Pau, is the summer residence of the bishop of Tarbes. Even now that the shrine has taken over the town, the elegant image remains one

Opposite: The shrine at Lourdes, one of the most-visited religious sites in the world

Pyrénées

of a gracefully arched bridge and gleaming church spire against green trees, snow-capped peaks and crystal blue Pyrenean skies.

On February 11, 1858, 14-year-old shepherdess Bernadette Soubirous (1844-79) had the first of 18 visions of the Virgin Mary at a nearby cave, the Grotte de Massabielle. Against her parents' wishes, Bernadette, frail and consumptive, returned time and again. Eventually Mary led Bernadette to a natural spring within the cave, which later was found to have healing qualities. Although Sainte Bernadette wasn't beatified until 1925 and wasn't canonized until 1933, the pilgrimages began during her lifetime.

Today, a nightly candlelit procession passes along the 550-yard Esplanade des Processions to the Esplanade du Rosaire for the blessing of the sick. Here is the ornate basilica, reached by two curving ramps. Below the church is the large crypt and the cave itself, with its marble figure of Mary according to Bernadette's description. Open-air Masses are held nearby. Below the esplanade is the remarkable Basilique souterraine St.-Pie-X (underground Church of St. Pious X), which can accommodate 20,000 pilgrims at a time.

Look beyond the sea of retail candles, holy water and plastic icons to discover the true town. Lourdes clusters around its place Peyramale. See Bernadette's birthplace, the Moulin de Boly, at 2 rue Bernadette-Soubirous. Take the elevator 260 feet above the town to the fortress, parts of which date back to the 13th century. The château's Pyrenean Museum has colorful folk costumes, and its terrace offers inspirational views of the mountains themselves.

Lourdes pioneered disabled accessibility, with the pilgrimage route designed to welcome those with restricted mobility. Appropriate dress is expected around the grotto area.

✚ B1

Tourist information ✉ place Peyramale ☎ 05 62 42 77 40; www.lourdes-france.com

Musée Pyrénéen ✉ rue du Bourg ☎ 05 62 42 37 37 🕐 Daily 9–noon and 2–6, Apr.–Sep.; Wed.–Mon. 9–noon and 2–6, rest of year 🚻 $

LUCHON

Something of a Roman holiday resort, Luchon (or as the maps would have it, les Bagnères-de-Luchon) was the fashionable mountain spa resort favored by Roman invaders. Even today the place exudes elegance and sophisticated leisure. The thermal baths are still reached through a well-maintained park with statues of visitors past. The local museum recalls the town's golden eras, with stories of such illustrious figures as mountaineer Count Henry Russell, who dynamited caves in the nearby mountains. Russell used one such artificial cavern near the top of the Vignemale for exclusive dinner parties. Naturally enough, Luchon boasts a casino to generate enough excitement and stress to guarantee a regular flow of customers to take to the calming, curative waters. A breathtaking drive from the valley climbs past waterfalls and mountain views, and leads to the smaller resort of Superbagnères. ✚ C1

Tourist information ✉ 18 allées d'Étigny ☎ 05 61 79 21 21; www.bagneres-de-luchon.com

NIAUX, GROTTE DE

Another well-preserved collection of cave paintings was discovered in 1906 in the Grotte de Niaux. Although copies of these 13,000-year-old images of bison are displayed nearby at Tarascon-sur-Ariège's Parc de l'Art Historique, the original works may be seen by torchlight. No free roaming is permitted, however; small, organized groups are escorted through the huge gaping mouth of the cave. Not simply the expected mammoth, bison and deer painted on the walls, the Salon Noir has black painted animal scenes, considered among the most remarkably preserved in Europe. Experts are divided as to the significance of dots and splashes accompanying the illustrations. Many believe this to be a primitive form of alphabet although none of the symbols has yet been deciphered. Perhaps because access is so restricted and none of the usual trappings of a tourist site get in the way, this particular setting brings visitors closer than ever to the individuals who

The ramparts of the Basque town of St.-Jean-Pied-de-Port

lived and painted here so long ago. The floor of the cave has amazingly preserved the footprints of the original artists – dating from 11,000 BC.

🔲 D1

Grotte de Niaux ✉ Tarascon-sur-Ariège ☎ /fax 05 61 05 88 37 🕐 Daily tours at 8:30, 11:30, 1:30, 2:15, 5 and 5:15, Jul.–Aug.; at 10, 11:30, 1:30, 2:15, 3, 3:45, 4:30 and 5:15, in Sep.; at 11, 2:30 and 4, rest of year 💵 $$ 🔳 Tours by reservation only (tours in English at 9:15 and 1, Jul.–Aug.; at 1, in Sep.)

St.-Jean-Pied-de-Port

St.-Jean-Pied-de-Port has welcomed travelers since the days before tourists. A rallying point for pilgrims on the popular trail of Santiago de Compostela, the port isn't a harbor but a mountain pass, and the name recalls the pious travelers that once walked the route. Today, it's one of the prettiest Basque towns in France, with old stone walls and clay tiles set against the lush greenery of a textured horizon of hazy hills and the peak of Roncevaux. The original cobbled path of the pilgrims' way, from the Porte St.-Jean to the Porte d'Espagne, is a favorite with hikers. Over the years, the way has been fortified, most notably by Louis XIV's builder of citadels, Sébastien Le Prestre de Vauban. The ramparts hold the reinforced Notre-Dame du Pont, over-looking the Nive river itself. St.-Jean manages the balancing act of retaining both its individual charm and a healthy tourist industry. Its souvenir shops sell walking sticks and climbing gear.

🔲 A1

Tourist information ✉ 14 place Charles-de-Gaulle ☎ 05 59 37 03 57

Pyrénées

DRIVE: THE HIGH PYRÉNÉES

Distance: 220 miles Time: 3–4 days

Since parts of this route are impassable in winter, save this drive for the summer months, when the spectacular scenery, hairpin bends and picturesque mountain passes make for some of the more dramatic moments of the Tour de France (see page 19). This tour starts in Tarbes.

Home to a French song festival in spring and a celebration of the humble bean in September, Tarbes spends its summer months wallowing in culture. The bandstand and open air theater of the charming Jardin Massey provide a varied program of concerts. Within the park, peacocks strut and call outside the Musée Massey, with its cavalry exhibition and art galleries.

From Tarbes take the D935 to Bagnères-de-Bigorre.

The fashionable spa town of Bagnères-de-Bigorre was popular in the Roman era and again in the 19th century. A less passive way to enjoy the waters is a white-water canoe ride along a stretch of the Adour river. The river later goes underground and flows through the Grottes de Médous. Cave visits include escorted boat rides along the subterranean waterway.

Take the D938 toward Toulouse, turning right on the D26 and again on the D929 through Hèches. As soon you see the sign for Rebouc over a railroad crossing, take a sharp left on the D26. Once at St.-Bertrand-de-Comminges, take a right uphill along the D26.

An endearing little medieval village of timbered houses, St.-Bertrand-de-Comminges owes its charm and its name to the 12th-century bishop Bertrand de l'Isle. Bishop Bertrand inspired the restoration of the village after years of neglect and oversaw the development of the impressive cathedral within which he was buried.

Continue along the D26 through Valcabrère. Turn right on the N125, following signs to Bagnères-de-Luchon (see page 138.) From Luchon the D618 goes over the Col de Peyresourde. At Arreau, go right on the D929, then bear left opposite the gas station, climbing uphill on the winding D918 over the Col d'Aspin. At Ste.-Marie-de-Campan, turn left following the D918 toward the Col du Tourmalet.

Ignore the name (bad detour), but do check local weather reports to ensure the road is open. This is the big one – at 6,939 feet the highest pass in the French Pyrénées – and its views are spectacular. The highest museum of astronomy in Europe is the 100-year-old Pic du Midi Observatory at 9,439 feet. To get closer to the stars, take a cable car from Taoulet station to the planetarium-style observatory, which affords a clear-day panorama from Biarritz to the Monts du Cantal. Even the elevator to the top floor is spectacular. Models, telescopes and special glasses help visitors discover the secrets of the sun, moon and stars, and exhibitions reveal the extent of France's space program.

Continue straight after the summit and bear left through Barèges to Luz-St.-Sauveur.

A delightful little spa town with a 14th-century fortified church, Luz-St.-Sauveur was established by the Knights of the Hospital of St. John at Jerusalem (or Knights Hospitallers), a military and religious order that offered travelers both spiritual and physical protection.

Take the D921 south to Gavarnie.

Gavarnie is to the Pyrénées what Chamonix is to the Alps. Its great natural treasure is the Cirque, an hour of challenging hiking or 20 minutes on horseback from Gavarnie. A glacial virtual amphitheater of rock with a sheer drop of 4,600 feet, the cliff face is awash with running water. The Grande Cascade plummets 1,450 feet to constitute one of Europe's longest falls. A statue of eccentric mountaineer Henry Russell can be seen in Gavarnie. His eyes are wistfully raised toward his beloved Vignemale mountain, which he climbed for the 33rd time at age 70. The mountain was presented to him as a gift.

Head back along the D921 past Luz-St.-Sauveur toward Lourdes, doubling back sharp left on leaving Soulom on the D920 to Cauterets.

Another spa town, Cauterets, houses an information center for the Pyrénées National Park. Use the town as a base for exploring as far as Pont d'Espagne and the Vignemale.

Back on the D920, turn left for Lourdes (see page 137) on the D921–N21. Follow signs on the D937 for Grottes de Bétharram, passing through St.-Pé-de-Bigorre. Turn left and left again to reach

The cathedral at St.-Bertrand-de-Comminges

the Grottes de Bétharram (see page 134). The D937 leads to Pau.

Once capital of the Béarn region, Pau (pronounced as in Edgar Allan Poe) was the hometown of one of France's favorite monarchs, Henri IV. Born a Protestant in 1553, he found his route to the capital barred when he came to take the throne, as the establishment insisted on a Roman Catholic king. He good-naturedly renounced his own tradition with the immortal line, "Paris is well worth a Mass." His cradle, a turtle shell, may be seen at the museum, a 19th-century restoration of a Renaissance restoration of a medieval château.

Grottes des Médous ✉ route des Cols, 65200 Asté ☎ 05 62 91 78 46 🕐 Daily 9–noon and 2–6, Jul.–Aug.; 9–11:30 and 2–5, Apr.–Jun. and Sep. 1–Oct. 15. Rest of year by appointment ᴨ Café 🎫 $$
Observetoire du Pic du Midi de Bigorre For visiting contact: Syndicat Mixte du Pic du Midi ✉ 6 rue Eugène Tenot, 65000 Tarbes ☎ 05 62 56 71 11
Cauterets tourist information ✉ Espace Cauterets, place Foch ☎ 05 62 92 50 27; www.cauterets.com
Musée National du Château de Pau ✉ 64000 Pau ☎ 05 59 82 38 00 🕐 Daily 9:30–12:15, and 1:30–5:45, Jun. 15–Sep. 15; 9:30–11:45 and 2–5, Jun. 1–14 and Sep. 16–Oct. 31; 9:30–11:45 and 2–4:15, rest of year 🎫 $ ℹ Visit by guided tour only

PROVENCE AND THE CÔTE D'AZUR

*"*D*RAMATIC rugged landscapes hide a region rich in great food, history and pleasure – from mountains to the Mediterranean. "*

Opposite: A quiet watering place in the unspoiled village of Crestet

PROVENCE AND THE CÔTE D'AZUR

The French know the south of France as the Midi. When you pass through the town of Valence on the long drive or fast rail journey south, something happens. The unmistakable air of the south overtakes the inconstancy of northern Europe. Even more than 100 miles from the Mediterranean, the area is warmer, drier, slower and of another age and culture.

Landscape

The region of Provence covers most of the ground, but Languedoc-Roussillon, with its Roman settlements and rugged scrubland, gives its own style to the countryside and coast west of Marseille.

The postcard image of Provence may be gentle, sun-kissed landscapes of olive groves and lavender fields, but the region has harsh mountainous terrain, dramatic gorges and some merciless winds – including the *mistral*, which whistles along the Rhône Valley to the coast, scattering roof tiles in its wake from late summer onward.

Vineyards – from the fine Châteauneuf du Pape and Côtes du Rhône to the stronger country vines that thrive along rare strips of flat land in rocky valleys around Narbonne – mark the countryside. On slopes, chestnut trees are kept for candied chestnuts and hundred-year-old olive groves for the oil. Rice is harvested in the Camargue wetlands, and farms grow melons, peaches and strawberries.

The People

Locals tend to be laconic. Conversation is not courted, and curt answers to questions should not be taken as a sign of rudeness. There is a notorious wariness of outsiders moving permanently into their towns and villages – anyone living 10 miles away is considered a foreigner – but visitors are assured a genuine welcome.

All caricatures of the Latin temperament have been applied to the folk of Provence: fiery jealousy and lazy procrastination. This makes for entertaining films and good reading, from the stories of Marcel Pagnol (see page 146) to Peter Mayle's *A Year In Provence*. The truth is the people here guard their family and village histories and ways of life. That very resistance to

Provence and the Côte d'Azur

change makes the region so attractive.

Provence has always been a summer retreat for Parisians. The major festivals in July and August bring the cultural establishment to the region when the capital closes down. Since the first high-speed train links brought the region within hours of Paris, main cities are far more open to year-round visitors. The area's rich heritage of arenas, temples and theaters from the Roman occupation of Gaul are the main attraction. However, a turbulent history of dukedoms, principalities and long-forgotten monarchies has left a rich and varied architectural legacy, with styles from the Italianate to Gothic to Moorish.

Languages

The distinctive Provençal accent itself is hard for many French people to understand (*vin* sounds like "ving," for example), and individual towns and districts have their own dialects and argots. The Catalan and Basque communities near the Spanish border are essentially bilingual. Nice's original Italian argot is not widely spoken. The old Langue d'Oc that gives the western region its name is today a historic curiosity. In Marseille, however, the old Provençal language is undergoing something of a revival and is being taught in schools and taken up by young musicians and a café subculture. Many street signs are now bilingual.

Local Sport

When afternoon shadows are long, older men take to the dusty squares to play *boules* or *pétanque* (slang for "feet together"), a traditional bowling game in which each player has two, three or four steel balls (depending on the number of players) to roll toward a

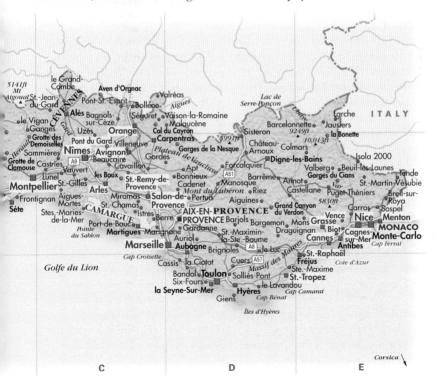

The huge Friday market in Carpentras is the local choice

small wooden aim ball called a *cochonnet* (little piggy). The closest ball wins. Notices in cafés and bars announce serious tournaments.

If watching from a bar, remember the local aperitif is pastis, a liqueur flavored with licorice and aniseed, taken with a carafe of water. If picnicking, inexpensive picnic wines can be bought from the local cooperative.

Lagoons

To understand what the Riviera was like before fashion reinvented the Mediterranean coastline, go east from the Camargue to the Spanish border and lose yourself in the beautiful rugged and natural coast of the Languedoc. Numberless vast lagoons *(étangs)* separate the shore from the hinterland where hardy vineyards grow rich *corbières* and *banyuls* wines. Molière's

home town of Pézenas, the stunning coastal lookout town of Agde and many quaint fishing villages guard the past, while modern resorts such as Leucate and Palavas sprout holiday apartments and villas. The African game reserve at Sigean, the Cistercian abbey of Fontefroide and the cities of Narbonne and Beziers serve sensation seekers, but the unspoiled land, the sea and the lagoons seduce the soul.

Pagnol

The cinema's love affair with the light, landscape and people of Provence is probably best seen in more than a dozen re-creations of the tales of author and filmmaker Marcel Pagnol (1895–1974). His *Jean de Florette* and *Manon des Sources*, a two-part story starring Yves Montand and Gérard Depardieu, is the most famous. The

Provence and the Côte d'Azur

town of le Castellet features in several movies. The small town of Aubagne is home to Le Petit Monde de Marcel Pagnol – featuring *santons* (see below) of his characters and stories. The tourist office in avenue Antide-Boyer offers a walking tour that takes in Manon's fountain and Pagnol's grave.

Christmas

Christmas in Provence is a wonderful occasion. The Christmas Eve meal, *gros souper*, has 13 traditional desserts. Nativity scenes are re-enacted December 24; local people come in costume for the midnight Mass. Every town, village and family has a *crèche*, a model stable with characters of Jesus, Mary and Joseph. These figurines and many more are sold at the remarkable *santon* markets. *Santons*, models of saints, have been made here for more than 300 years. Craftsmen's workshops in Aubagne are open year round, and Christmas markets in most towns and cities take place from late November until early January.

California to Europe

From the gorges of the Ardèche to Silicon Valley, the region Provence-Alpes-Côte-d'Azur is the technology center of France. Electronics, information technology and biotechnology are centered around six science parks, the best known being Sophia-Antopolis outside Antibes. Since 1991, the region has been "twinned" with California, highlighting its technology and climatic similarity.

Stars of the Med

The bulk of coastline is famous as the French Riviera. Intellectuals claim true magic left when the film stars arrived, and Cannes Film Festival is blamed as the beginning of the end. Hollywood movie moguls and starlets came in 1947, trodding the bulb-popping steps

of hyperbole, spoon-feeding glamour to the press and crushing the soul of the Côte d'Azur, they say.

Baloney, of course. Cannes never had a sensitive soul. She was ever a harlot, always a tramp, and that was her appeal. Never let anyone tell you Cannes was ever a lady. She has style, but remember the twin cupolas on the celebrated Carlton Hotel were modeled on the breasts of a well-known courtesan. Here, a supermarket check-out boy earns more in one week fluttering his lashes as gigolo to the stars than he does the rest of the year blinking bar codes.

No one comes from the Riviera. Rather, it's a place to which people go – and always have. Graham Greene and Noël Coward came, stayed and gossiped in print here. Henri Matisse discovered the azure blues that he painted into legend. And the rich and famous played, hid behind high walls and swam on the peak of Cap Ferrat.

Then Cannes created Woman. Femininity – led by Brigitte Bardot, who eventually fled to the very public obscurity of St.-Tropez with only cars, dogs, donkeys and the paparazzi for company – was paraded on the front page of the *Croisette* newspaper (with the street lined with paparazzi).

Museums

The Carte Musées Côte d'Azur (Riviera Museum Pass), valid for one, three or seven days, gives visitors access to 62 museums, monuments and gardens on the Riviera. It is on sale in participating museums and monuments, tourist offices, FNAC stores and Thomas Cook travel offices.

Carte Musées Côte d'Azur ✉ 2 boulevard Victor-Hugo, 06000 Nice ☎ 04 97 03 82 20; www.cmca.net

Provençal flavors stem from the native herbs

Nowadays, the whole stretch from the Pyrénées to the Alps is a haven for the nipped, tucked and liposucked. Though in the summer months, when the roads are bumper to bumper with traffic, this paradise becomes a hell for those not blessed with a private villa.

Survival Tip

Hedonists should be aware that unlike Cap d'Agde, where naturists are welcome in specialist supermarkets and banks, flesh isn't served on all streets of the Riviera. It's illegal to walk through the town of St.-Raphaël unless the upper and lower body is properly covered, and in Ste.-Maxime, bikini-clad sunbathers who stray from the beach may be fined.

Yet during the off-season, the Azur Coast is where deities take their sabbatical. Land at the whisper-thin airstrip on the beach; take the train past the ocher cliffs of St.-Raphaël, which reflect a never-ending sunset; and breathe the heady, unsteady perfume that is the secret soul of the late summer sun: citrus blossom, pine, violet and lavender.

Sniff the air, fruit and mimosa in the breath of a New Year and see the dancing sea clean and bright. Take to the hills, and wine and dine in one of the clifftop perched villages. A world away from film festivals, overguarded royals, fast-buck merchants and hangers-on, in springtime or fall you will discover what generations bemoan as lost forever – the true soul of the Riviera.

AIX-EN-PROVENCE

Today's city of fountains was, until 1790, the capital of Provence, and parliamentary and judicial history feeds what is still a cultural, artistic and social hub.

Its early fame came from thermal springs. Then in the 12th century, it was chosen as a civilized oasis in a rugged landscape to be the seat of the counts of Provence. The last of the line to live in the city was Good King René (1409–80), duke of Anjou, Lorraine and Bar and king of Naples. He completed the cathedral and was a patron of the arts. When Provence became part of France in 1486, its cultural life continued.

Known as the city of the waters, Aix-en-Provence bore the Latin name Aquae Sextiae. The streets of Aix are studded with nearly 100 fountains, refreshing in the hot summer sunshine.

In the 17th century under the guidance of Cardinal Jules Mazarin, the city was expanded. Medieval ramparts were torn down, and cours Mirabeau was created in their place (see page 151), which neatly divides Aix between the old town to the north, with its cathedral and market squares where residents come to sit under parasols, and the elegant residential quartier Mazarin below, with elegant town

Provence and the Côte d'Azur

AIX-EN-PROVENCE

| 0 | 100 | 200 metres |
| 0 | 100 | 200 yards |

Gracious statuary on a fountain in Aix

houses and mansions of the good and the great.

City of Artists

A fine university town since 1413, Aix has never been allowed to stagnate. The annual Lyric Art Festival showcases the finest young operatic talent in the world. Émile Zola (1840–1902) spent his youth here, and the Sainte-Victoire mountain that looms above the city inspired the great Impressionist painter Paul Cézanne (1839–1906), who reproduced the mountain in more than 60 of his paintings.

Aix retains many of the artist's greatest works, and the city is liberally sprinkled with reminders of his life. Using commemorative bronze plaques in the sidewalk as a guide, stroll through the streets to follow the Cézanne trail. The final address is 9 avenue Paul-Cézanne, the artist's garden and studio L'Atelier des Lauves, built in 1901 and where he spent the final years of his life. Everything is kept exactly as he left it: his old black hat, his paints, his still-life props and his unfinished canvases.

Eggs and Aches

Although the French word Aix is pronounced midway between the English words "eggs" and "aches," locals pronounce the city as Ais. The local candy of choice is *calissons,* a confection of almonds and fruits.

ESSENTIAL INFORMATION

TOURIST INFORMATION
✉ 2 place du Général-de-Gaulle
☎ 04 42 16 11 61;
www.aixenprovencetourism.com
Guided tours leave from the tourist office 🕒 Daily, Jul.–Sep.; Tue.–Wed. and Fri.–Sat., Apr.–Jun. and Oct.; Tue.–Wed. and Sat.–Sun., rest of year

URBAN TRANSPORTATION
Bus services link central Aix-en-Provence with outlying towns. The bus station (gare routière) is at boulevard de l'Europe ☎ 04 42 91 26 80. Within the city center, all sites can be reached on foot. Taxis can be hailed at stands, in the streets or call ☎ 04 42 27 71 11.

AIRPORT INFORMATION
The nearest aiport is Aéroport Marseille-Provence ☎ 04 42 14 14 14. Website www.marseille.aeroport.fr. Shuttle buses leave the airport for Aix every 45 minutes at peak times. Journey time is around 30 minutes. Regional rail services are available from Aix-en-Provence Gare SNCF. National and international services are routed via Marseille.

CLIMATE – Average highs and lows

JAN.	FEB.	MAR.	APR.	MAY	JUN.	JUL.	AUG.	SEP.	OCT.	NOV.	DEC.
10°C	12°C	15°C	18°C	22°C	26°C	29°C	28°C	25°C	20°C	15°C	11°C
50°F	54°F	64°F	72°F	79°F	84°F	82°F	77°F	68°F	59°F	59°F	52°F
2°C	2°C	5°C	8°C	11°C	15°C	17°C	17°C	15°C	10°C	6°C	3°C
36°F	36°F	41°F	46°F	52°F	59°F	63°F	63°F	59°F	50°F	43°F	37

AIX-EN-PROVENCE SIGHTS

Key to symbols

➕ map coordinates refer to the Aix-en-Provence map on page 149; sights below are highlighted in yellow on the map.

✉ address or location ☎ telephone number

🕐 opening times 🚌 nearest bus or tram route

🍴 restaurant on site or nearby ℹ information

💷 admission charge: $$$ more than €10, $$ €5–€10, $ less than €5

Architectural details of Cathédrale St.-Sauveur

CATHÉDRALE ST.-SAUVEUR

An architectural history lesson in its own right, the cathedral has a fifth-century baptistery, an 18th-century octagonal cupola supported by eight columns from a Roman temple of Apollo, a Romanesque doorway from the 12th century, a 15th-century belfry and an extravagant Gothic facade dating from the 16th century. Within is something of a treasure trove. In the nave is the 1645 Buisson Ardent, a triptych by Nicolas Froment that combines the Old Testament burning bush of Moses with an image of the Madonna and Child. The tranquil cloisters are built on the site of the original Roman forum. The Archbishop's Palace is now home to a museum of tapestry and its courtyard is transformed into a theater each summer for Aix's Festival d'Art Lyrique (see page 154).

➕ A3 ✉ 34 place des Martyrs de la Résistance ☎ 04 42 23 45 65

Musée des Tapisseries ✉ 28 place des Martyrs de la Résistance ☎ 04 42 23 09 91 🕐 Wed.–Mon. 10–11:45 and 2–5:45 💷 $

COURS MIRABEAU

A promenade in every sense of the word since 1651, cours Mirabeau is more than a street – it's an occasion. From late afternoon until well into the small hours, the very European phenomenon of *passagiata* takes place, in which people dress in their best clothes and walk up and down the sidewalk to see and be seen. After midnight, the peacock parade is augmented by young motorists in open-top cars cruising slowly

in front of café tables in Aix's peculiar blend of fashion show and mating ritual. During the day, old men shelter from the sun on benches, and far from impoverished would-be artists hold animated discussions in the Café des Deux Garçons. At festival time, people dine here very early or very late. The posing takes place on the north sidewalk, and narrow alleyways lead up to the old town.

➕ B2

MUSÉE GRANET

One room containing eight paintings by Paul Cézanne – including his *Nude at the Mirror* and the famous *Bathers,* all belatedly donated by the state to his hometown in the 1980s – is the main lure of Aix-en-Provence's main museum and gallery. The museum is housed in the neighboring Palais-de-Malte. A pleasant collection of 18th- and 19th-century art from France, Flanders and Italy, including works by Peter Paul Rubens and Rembrandt that mostly were collected by local painter François Granet (1775–1849), is overshadowed by archeological finds displayed in the basement. Noteworthy are statues and masks from the settlement known as Oppidum d'Entremont, which existed here before the Roman occupation of the area, as well as Roman remains from Aquae Sextiae.

➕ C1 ✉ place St.-Jean-de-Malte ☎ 04 42 38 14 70 🕐 Wed.–Mon. 10–noon and 2–6 (museum re-opens after renovation during summer 2002, please check to confirm opening times) 💷 $$

Provence and the Côte d'Azur

WALK: FOUNTAINS AND MARKETS

Refer to route marked on city map on page 149

Begin this 2.5-mile walk at the tourist office on place du Général-de-Gaulle, the meeting point of roads from Avignon, Nice and Marseille, at the foot of the great fountain built in 1860.

Walk along the right side of cours Mirabeau and turn right onto rue du 4-Septembre, with its collection of fine earthenware, statuary and rare books in the Musée Paul-Arbaud.
In front is the beautiful 1667 *Fontaine des Quatre Dauphins* by Jean-Claude Rambot. A left on rue Cardinale leads to the Musée Granet (see page 151). Next door is the 13th-century Église St.-Jean-de-Malte.
Turning left on rue d'Italie, return to cours Mirabeau.
A fountain dedicated to the city's patron, Good King René, stands in the middle of the road. Across the boulevard, the sign at No. 55 announces the Chapellerie du cours-Mirabeau, Cézanne's father's hat shop, where

young Paul spent much of his childhood. A narrow passageway beside the shop leads to place de Verdun, where the morning flea market in front of the 18th-century Palais de Justice spills across to the edge of place des Précheurs and its farmers' market on Tuesday, Thursday and Saturday mornings. Succumb to the aromatic lures of lavender, rosemary and mint. Salt cod, olive oil and Provençal herbs are the essential flavors of Aix. Climb steps to see the Peter Paul Rubens piece and other artwork displayed in the Église Ste.-Marie-Madeleine.
Take rue de Montigny opposite, then turn left through narrow streets to place Richelme, which has a daily market.
Here music students earn extra money by playing flutes, violins and guitars for shoppers. Behind the old corn market, now a post office, is the Italian-style 17th-century Hôtel de Ville, with its splendid 16th-century clock tower that announces the seasons as well as the time.
Follow rue Gaston de Saporta to the Cloître St.-Sauveur, where occasionally chamber concerts are staged, and the cathedral. Retrace your steps to place Richelme and filter through the little alleyways back to cours Mirabeau.

Country comes to town in a farmers' market in Aix-en-Provence

Awaiting the spectacle: Bullfights have replaced gladiators at the Arènes ampitheater in Arles

REGIONAL SIGHTS

Key to symbols

☩ map coordinates refer to the Provence map on page 144; sights below are highlighted in yellow on the map.

⊠ address or location ☎ telephone number

⊕ opening times 🍴 restaurant on site or nearby

🚌 nearest bus or tram route Ⓜ nearest métro

⛴ ferry 🛈 information 🎟 admission charge: $$$ more than €10, $$ €5–€10, $ less than €5

ARLES

On the banks of the Rhône sits the Roman capital of Provence. Plenty of reminders of the days of imperial occupation remain, most notably the remnants of the old theater and the vast Arènes, the largest amphitheater in the country at almost 450 feet in length and with a capacity to hold 20,000 gladiator-cheering visitors. Although the top tiers of marbled galleries are long gone, the stadium today hosts bullfights. Another place of entertainment was the Cirque Romain, where chariot races once were held. Now a base for archeological research, the site holds the Musée de l'Arles Antique, which tells the story of the town from the Romans to the Christian era.

On the edge of the Roman settlement is Les Alyscamps, which like its Parisian namesake, Champs-Élysées, is a tree-lined avenue. Unlike the more famous bustling thoroughfare, the quiet street is bordered with moss-covered stone coffins. This veritable city of the departed once boasted 19 temples and thousands of great tombs. So prestigious was the cemetery that bodies would be floated down the river with gold in their mouths to pay the gravediggers of Arles. The artist Vincent van Gogh is forever linked with the town, as it was here that he famously cut off his own ear. The hospital and gardens where the artist recovered from the episode are now the Espace Van-Gogh. The courtyard, laid out as in the artist's day, is free to visit.

☩ C2

Tourist information ⊠ Boulevard des Lices ☎ 04 90 18 41 20; www.arles.org

Arènes ⊠ Rond point-des-Arènes ☎ 04 90 96 03 70 ⊕ Daily 9–6:30, May–Sep.; 9–5:30, Mar.–Apr. and in Oct.; 10–4:30, rest of year 🎟 $

Provence and the Côte d'Azur

Festive drama on the streets of Avignon

AVIGNON FESTIVAL

Don't blame the sunshine, the heat or the last *pastis* on the café terrace. That really was the star of *Jean de Florette* addressing a television camera in your hotel foyer. Believe the improbable: Avignon is *en fête*.

In July, the world of arts and entertainment has a Provençal postal code. The reason: The Avignon Festival, now more than 50 years old, boasts about 50 official stage productions and countless more fringe events.

The old papal city bursts at its fortified seams with a glorious crush of talent and revelers. Every sipped espresso at a sidewalk table is accompanied by eager performers promoting one-man versions of Voltaire. So fascinating is the eavesdropping in restaurants that people nibble olives and forget to peruse the menu. Tall shady trees lining dusty, breezy streets are dressed in handbills, posters and enticements to sample something new, something different – something daring.

All the arts have their moment in the spotlight. Ballets may be inspired by rock albums of the 1970s. Nonetheless, the heart of the festival is quality drama. The top names in French theater and cinema appear in new productions of the classics, and the most successful transfer to Paris for the fall. Legendary productions of William Shakespeare may grab the headlines, but search the listings to find Eugene O'Neil, Tennessee Williams and Henry James, given a European twist for the contemporary stage.

Everything will be previewed and reviewed, and all Paris papers and TV shows move to Avignon for the festival. Hotel bars and restaurants are called into service as makeshift studios, with arc lamps and movie stars as commonplace as mini-bars and chambermaids.

Intoxicating stuff, but for a respite visit the two neighboring opera festivals. At Orange, pageant-scale productions of *Carmen*, *Aida* or *Tosca* are staged in the Roman theater in a season known as the Chorégies. At Aix's Festival d'Art Lyrique, famous for discovering the great divas of the future, the strains of works by George Frederic Handel and Wolfgang Amadeus Mozart ring out from a specially constructed playhouse within the courtyard of the Archbishop's Palace.

Provence and the Côte d'Azur

Musée de l'Arles Antique ✉ avenue 1ère-Division-France-Libre ☎ 04 90 18 88 88 🕐 Daily 9–7, Mar.–Oct. 10–5, rest of year 🎫 $$

Les Alyscamps ✉ avenue des Alyscamps ☎ 04 90 49 36 87 🕐 Daily 9–6:30, May–Sep.; 9–11:30 and 2–5:30, in Oct.; 10–11:30 and 2–4:30, rest of year 🎫 $

Espace Van Gogh ✉ Rue du Président-Wilson ☎ 04 90 49 37 53 🕐 Open access 🎫 Free

Fondation Vincent Van Gogh – Arles ✉ Hôtel de Luppé, 24 rond point des Arènes ☎ 04 90 49 94 04 🕐 Tue.–Sun. 9:30–noon and 2–5:30 🎫 $ ℹ️ Guided tours available

AVIGNON

Most visitors knowing the old song *"Sur le pont d'Avignon"* feel shortchanged on their first view of the famous 13th-century Pont St.-Bénézet, with its tiny Chapelle St.-Nicolas. Only a fraction of the bridge remains, jutting impotently into the Rhône. Just four of the original 22 arches stand lamely in the waters, with the rest destroyed by floods in the 17th century. Despite the lyrics "on the bridge of Avignon," locals traditionally danced under the bridge on the riverbanks. Rarely will visitors find disappointments elsewhere in town. Step inside the walled city to discover a wealth of architectural treasures. Known as the City of the Popes since Pope Clement moved his court here from the Vatican in 1309, Avignon developed as the church's center of power. Even when the papacy returned to Rome in 1377, a breakaway group continued to follow rival papal authority for four decades in what became known as the Great Schism. Walk around the ramparts to experience the intimacy and power of the old city, and look out on the sprawling suburbs across the river. The essential visit is a tour of the Palais des Papes, actually a complex of two palaces: the old palace of 1334 – austere and monastic, a place of prayer – and the newer grander chambers of 1348, reflecting the power of a wealthy church and patron of the arts. Although much of the ornate decoration has been lost, the Stag Room frescoes are worth seeing. To see medieval artwork and Italian paintings from the 13th through 16th centuries, visit the Petit Palais, former residence of bishops of Avignon and a museum since 1958.

More recent works are displayed at the Musée Anglandon. The collection encompasses works from Impressionists to Pablo Picasso and includes one of the few Vincent van Gogh paintings that remain in Provence. Throughout the year, especially during festival time (see page 154), enjoy watching the world go by from a table on place de l'Horloge.

➕ C2

Tourist information ✉ 41 cours Jean-Jaurés ☎ 04 32 74 32 74; www.ot-avignon.fr

Palais des Papes ✉ place du Palais ☎ 04 90 27 50 74 🕐 Daily 9–9, in Jul.; 9–8, Aug.–Sep.; 9–7, Apr.–Jun. and in Oct.; 9:30–5:45, rest of year 🎫 $$ ℹ️ Avignon Festival early to late Jul.

Musée du Petit Palais ✉ Place du Palais ☎ 04 90 86 44 58 🕐 Wed.–Mon. 10–1 and 2–6, Jun.–Sep.; 9:30–1 and 2–5:30, rest of year 🎫 $$

Musée Angladon ✉ 5 rue Laboureur ☎ 04 90 82 29 03 🕐 Wed.–Sun. 1–7, Jul.–Aug.; 1–6, rest of year 🎫 $

Pont St.-Bénézet ✉ Rue Ferruce ☎ 04 90 85 60 16 🕐 Daily 9:30–6:30, Apr.–Sep.; 9–1 and 2–5, rest of year 🎫 $

BIOT

Biot is to Provence what Murano is to Venice. The pretty arcaded main square, the window boxes ablaze with geraniums and steep cobbled streets in the orange-roofed village, perched high above Antibes-Juan-les-Pins, would merit a detour. Biot has long been home to potters and silversmiths who for centuries have created charming jars and bowls. Since the 1950s, it has become a center of glass-blowing, and the glass workshop is a visitor attraction in its own right. Biot glassware is sold in countless small galleries. The craft was pioneered by cubist Fernand Léger, whose own museum of glass and ceramics is housed at the edge of the village. Outside the museum is Léger's bright mosaic designed for the Hanover Olympic Stadium. At the southern side of place des Arcades, a modest doorway leads to the village church, which contains 16th-century altarpieces.

➕ E2

Tourist information ✉ 46 rue St.-Sébastien ☎ 04 93 65 78 00; www.biot-coteazur.com

Straggling along the hills between Menton and Monte Carlo is the medieval town of Roquebrune-Cap-Martin

Musée National Fernand-Léger ✉ chemin de Val de Pome ☎ 04 92 91 50 30 🕐 Wed.–Mon. 10:30–6, Jul.–Sep.; 10–12:30 and 2–5:30, rest of year 🍴 Café (Apr.–Sep. only) 🖐 $

CÔTE D'AZUR

The ribbon of coastline along the skirts of Provence from Marseille to the Italian border is known as the Côte d'Azur, a genuinely azure combination of sea and sky that tantalized Henri Matisse, wooed the rich and nurtured some of the Mediterranean's most charming resorts.

In many cases, the landscape itself stops picturesque coves from growing too big and losing their charms. Other resorts sprawl and drip proof of their fantastic wealth. However, it's the many bays and rocky cliffs that, despite the unattractive rash of concrete apartment blocks that mars city limits, stop the ports, towns and villages from merging into one homogenized vacation park. Nice, the main city of the Riviera, has the bustle of any capital but with the added pleasure of the sweeping coastline of the Baie des Anges. Other beaches are more compact, providing marinas for millionaires and wharfside markets for fishermen.

The great headlands are still the preserve of the rich and famous. Cap Ferrat's fairy-tale Rothschild estate is fantastic opulence. Cap d'Antibes juts out into the Mediterranean, with its private beaches and exclusive villas. The eastern side of the peninsula has a good-sized public beach. The cap separates Juan-les-Pins – the party side, where a fabulous July jazz festival takes place in the pine grove – from Antibes, which is more reflective, with ramparts, flower markets heady with the scent of mimosa or lavender, and a Picasso Museum in the artist's 13th-century Château Grimaldi.

High above the coastline are perched villages (see page 172). Strung along the rock face like garlands of white-knuckle rides are the three tiers of the *corniches*, daredevil mountain roads with harrowing hairpin bends and unrivaled views between Nice and Menton. And touching the sky are the Alps. Few people realize that in early spring, less than an hour's

at a fish restaurant in the port. Attractions in the château include the Olive Tree Museum and an art gallery boasting pieces by Marc Chagall, Henri Matisse and Pierre-Auguste Renoir, who came here when he was struck by rheumatoid arthritis. Renoir's villa, in ancient olive groves outside town, preserves his studio and art collection.

✚ E2

Tourist information ✉ 6 boulevard Maréchal-Juin ☎ 04 93 20 61 64; www.cagnes.com or www.cagnes-tourisme.com

Grimaldi Château-Musée ✉ place Grimaldi, Haut-de-Cagnes ☎ 04 92 02 47 30 ⏺ Wed.–Mon. 10–noon, 2–6, in summer; 10–noon, 2–5 in winter ✋ $

Musée Renoir ✉ 19 chemin des Collettes ☎ 04 93 20 61 07 ⏺ Wed.–Mon. 10–noon and 2–6, May–Oct.; 10–noon and 2–5, Dec.–Apr. ✋ $

CAMARGUE

White horses run free here through the waters, pink flamingos flaunt their plumage in the lagoons, and spectacular sunsets color the horizon. The Camargue is a spectacular nature reserve that spreads across the Rhône delta. The waterways, salt marshes and coastline are home to more than 400 species of birds and half-wild sheep, black bulls and horses, all managed by local cowboys known as *gardians*. The *gardians* work the ranches *(manades)*, where visitors can enjoy riding vacations. Local legend has it that the fishing village of les Stes.-Maries-de-la-Mer is where Maria Jacobé and Maria Salomé, half sisters of

drive separates the exhilaration of the ski slopes and the hedonism of an all-over tan on the Med.

No greater contrast exists than that between the neighboring towns on the coast itself. A local maxim says, "I sin in Cannes, I work in Nice, I play in Monte Carlo, and I will die in Menton."

✚ E2

Tourist information ✉ 11 place de Gaulle, Antibes ☎ 04 92 90 53 00; www.antibes-juan-lespins.com

Picasso Musée ✉ Château Grimaldi, Antibes ☎ 04 92 90 54 20 ⏺ Tue.–Sun. 10–6, Jun.–Sep.; 10–5, rest of year. ✋ $$

CAGNES-SUR-MER

Pretty painted fishing boats, known as *pointus*, bob in the harbor and terra-cotta roofs top whitewashed buildings. This looks like a typical busy coastal town, like so many others. But climb the hill to Haut-de-Cagnes to find the real charm of the medieval fortified village, with a 14th-century castle built by the Grimaldis as a lookout for pirate ships. Nicely gentrified with earthenware pots on sunny window sills and bougainvillea-dappled shadows, the walk is a leisurely diversion after lunch

The white horse – a true native of the Camargue

the Virgin Mary, arrived with their black serving maid Sarah, patron saint of gypsies. Their graves are marked by the Église Notre-Dame-de-la-Mer. Every year for two days around May International 25, gypsies from all over Europe make their pilgrimage here. In colorful traditional costumes, gypsies and *gardians* carry statues of Ste.-Sarah and the Marias into the sea for a blessing, then into the night, the revelers celebrate with rodeos, flamenco dancing, bullfights and fireworks.

✚ C2

Tourist information ✉ 5 avenue Van-Gogh, Les Stes.-Maries-de-la-Mer ☎ 04 90 97 82 55 or www.saintesmariesdelamer.com

Parc Ornithologique de Pont de Gau ✉ route d'Arles, Les Stes.-Maries-de-la-Mer ☎ 04 90 97 82 62 🕐 Daily 9–9, May–Sep.; 10–6:30, rest of year 💵 $$

CANNES

Cannes exists only for pleasure. What other town would have two branches of the same jeweler on opposite sides of the street to save clients the trouble of crossing a road? The city is famous for its May International Film Festival, where in successive generations Elizabeth Taylor, Brigitte Bardot and Madonna have dutifully stopped traffic to pander to paparazzi. The parade of starlets along the main thoroughfare, boulevard de la Croisette, feeds the world's front pages for two weeks and launches the vacation season. The only free beach is the area in front of the hideous orange Palais des Festivals et des Congrès; the rest of the sand is divided into private strips belonging to the seafront hotels – with the famous Carlton Inter-Continental probably the best known symbol of the town. To escape high prices, shop either in the back streets around rue Maynadier or take a boat trip to the Îles de Lérins. The larger island, Ste.-Margucrite, has a fortress said to have held the Man in the Iron Mask. The smaller, St.-Honorat, is a tranquil haven where Cistercian monks make liqueurs and honey, and where visitors forget that Cannes is just 30 minutes away.

✚ E2

Tourist information ✉ Palais des Festivals et des Congrès, La Croisette ☎ 04 93 39 24 53;

www.cannes.fr or www.cannes-on-line.com

Ferries to Îles de Lérins 🚢 Compagnie Maritime Cannoise ☎ 04 93 38 66 33 🕐 Timetables vary seasonally (15 minutes to Ste.-Marguerite, 25 minutes to St.-Honorat)

CAP FERRAT

Home to the Duke and Duchess of Windsor, David Niven, Charlie Chaplin and others who could afford absolute privacy, the villas of Cap Ferrat all are hidden from view by lush greenery. The casual visitor can do little more than gaze at treetops and imagine the splendors that exist behind imposing gateways. Fortunately, one of the finest estates is open to the public. The remarkable Villa Ephrussi, an exquisite pink belle-epoque palace, was commissioned by Beatrice, Baroness Ephrussi de Rothschild, of the great banking family. With the sea on three sides and nestling among re-creations of the great gardens of the world, the Italian-style villa houses the Rothschild collection of art and porcelain. Visitors must be escorted through the house but can wander the grounds at their own pace. If you aren't fortunate enough to be invited to a house party, then wine and dine in the former fishing village of St.-Jean-Cap-Ferrat.

✚ E2

Tourist information ✉ 59 avenue Denis Séméria, St.-Jean-Cap-Ferrat ☎ 04 93 76 08 90; www.franceplus.com/stjeancapferrat

Villa et Jardins Ephrussi de Rothschild ✉ 1 avenue Ephrussi de Rothschild, St.-Jean-Cap-Ferrat ☎ 04 93 01 45 90 🕐 Daily 10–7, Jul.–Aug.; daily 10–6, mid-Feb. through Jun. 30 and Sep.–Oct.; Mon.–Fri. 2–6, Sat.–Sun. 10–6, rest of year 💵 $$

CORSICA

Known as the birthplace of the all-conquering hero Napoléon, this rugged individual island is no stranger to conquest. Invaded by just about everyone who ventured into the Mediterranean in Classical times – Phoenicians, Greeks, Etruscans, Carthagineans and Romans – Corsica has been taken and influenced since then by barbarian, Byzantine, Saracen, Italian, Spanish, German and even English conquerors. French from

A ruined Genoese watchtower remains sentinel on the shore of Erbalunga in northern Corsica

1768 and a region of the country in its own right since 1970, Corsica boasts many listed parks on land and at sea and has a distinct identity.

A mountain in the sea and landscapes of peaks and lakes alternate with vast, tranquil plateaus. On the south and west coasts is a succession of wild rocky coves, fine sandy beaches and white chalky cliffs. Less rugged are the eastern shores, strewn with pools and long beaches. Inland are fast-flowing streams and waterfalls. The fragrant heather and myrtle led Napoléon to declare he could sense Corsica before her shores came into view.

The strongest image is of vivid bright colors: reds and blacks of penitants' Good Friday parades, when the brilliant Easter sunshine of Holy Week lights a million colorful fires on Cargèse's whitewashed walls; ocher Genoese fortifications and watchtowers that contrast with the shimmering slate rooftops of Cap Corse; and flecks of granite, vast red rocks, white cliff faces and lush, rich greens, which are framed as ever by a silver and blue horizon. It is no wonder the Greeks called the island *Kalliste* – the most beautiful one.

The tourist office suggests good drives, depending on the season. Winter snows create cross-country ski resorts from December to April and hikers could spend 15 grueling days on the best-known mountain hiking path, the GR20. Known locally as Fra I Monti, the path links Calenzana and Porto-Vecchio. Year-round sporting attractions include hang gliding, horseback riding and white-water rafting. Others may prefer comfortable inns and hotels in the resorts and towns of Bastia, Ajaccio, Bonifaccio and Calvi. Each has its museum with remnants of religious and military past.

The island has four airports and six ports. Car ferries from Marseille, Nice and Toulon cruise overnight. Express ferries from Nice cut the journey to less than three hours. Summer excursions to the neighboring Italian island of Sardinia are popular. ✈ E1

Tourist information ✉ 17 boulevard Roi-Jérôme, Ajaccio. ☎ 04 95 51 53 03; www.tourisme.fr/ajaccio. Useful website for Corsica: www.corsica.net
Ferries 🚢 Societé Nationale Maritime Corse Méditerranée (SNCM) ✉ 61 boulevard des Dames, Marseille ☎ 08 36 67 95 00 (toll call); www.sncm.fr

Marseille's daily fish market on quai des Belges

GRASSE

Although flowers are sold around the fountain in the marketplace at place aux Aires, the fragrance is enjoyed all over the world. Grasse has been the center of the global perfume industry for 400 years. Born of the custom of local Italian glove-makers to perfume their creations with local blossoms, the manufacture of scent soon overtook the leather-tanning industry as the source of Grasse's wealth. Light breezes now waft aromas of jasmine, roses and lavender from the acres of cultivated fields around town. At the perfume museum, the story of scent is told and a fabulous exhibit displays rare bottles. Two main perfume factories – Parfumerie Fragonard and Parfumerie Galimard – welcome tourists. The latter invites visitors to create their own personal fragrance, but at a price.

Elsewhere, see the town's two Peter Paul Rubens paintings, *The Crucifixion* and *Crown of Thorns*, in the cathedral, and discover local culture and traditions at the Musée d'Art et d'Histoire de Provence.

✚ E2
Tourist information ✉ Palais des Congrès, 22 cours Honoré-Cresp ☎ 04 93 36 66 66; www.ville-grasse.fr
Musée International de la Parfumerie ✉ 8 place du cours Honoré-Cresp ☎ 04 93 36 80 20 🕐 Daily 10–7, Jun.–Sep.; Wed.–Mon. 10–12:30 and 2–5:30, Oct. 1–early Nov. and early Dec.–May. 31 👆$
Musée Villa Jean-Honore Fragonard
✉ 23 boulevard Fragonard ☎ 04 93 36 01 61

🕐 As Musée International de la Parfumerie 👆$
Parfumerie Galimard ✉ 73 route de Cannes ☎ 04 93 09 20 00 🕐 Daily, by appointment 👆Free, $$$ to make your own perfume
Musée d'Art et d'Histoire de Provence ✉ 2 rue Mirabeau ☎ 04 93 36 01 61 🕐 As Musée International de la Parfumerie 👆$

MARSEILLE

Don't expect Riviera glamour. Marseille is a true mariners' port with a notorious underworld of crime and corruption, a promise of instant pleasures and the constant traffic of ships heading off to the wide world beyond. The wealthy live above the town; the city crush downtown is a web of ghettos and communities impenetrable to the casual tourist. The visitor shops are on La Canebière, the main boulevard leading down to the port. The name does mean "cannabis," but it has nothing to do with international drug running. The city is well-established in the hemp rope-making industry. You will sense 26 centuries of the city's history as a port, from ancient civilizations to today's popular diversion for cruise liners, while eavesdropping on conversations among old sea salts in Vieux Port bars or while browsing museum displays. A bronze plaque on quai des Belges marks the point where the Greeks first landed, and the wreck of a Roman merchant ship from the third century BC is displayed at the Musée d'Histoire de Marseille.

Like Paris, Marseille is divided into districts. Use the subway and bus system, as taxis can be something of an adventure. There are several beaches away from the ferry, freight and fishing ports. Take a trip to the island Château d'If, where the Count of Monte Cristo was imprisoned.

The magnificent Église Notre-Dame-de-la-Garde (1853–64) stands 525 feet above the port. A 32-foot gold Madonna balances above the dome of the Byzantine-style basilica. Inside the sailors' church, model ships and paintings created by mariners serve as votive offerings. Above the modern docks is the similarly exotic 19th-century Cathédrale de la Nouvelle-Major. The smaller, more-interesting 11th-century

Almost Italian: Menton offers the last French beach before the border with Italy

Romanesque cathedral it replaced is tucked behind it.

Marseille boasts an excellent cultural life, with a respected opera season, concerts and a famous biennial dance festival. Artwork by Peter Paul Rubens, Jean-Baptiste-Camille Corot and local 19th-century artists is exhibited at the Palais Longchamp fine arts museum, and on promenade Georges-Pompidou stands a 1903 copy of Michelangelo's *David*, by marble-sculptor Jules Cantini.

⊞ D2

Tourist information ✉ 4 La Canebière (1e) ☎ 04 91 13 89 00; www.marseille-tourisme.com ⓘ The tourist office runs escorted tours with such themes as maritime heritage and soap-making

Musée d'Histoire de Marseille ✉ Centre Bourse square Belsunce, (1e) ☎ 04 91 90 42 22 🚇 Vieux-Port ⏰ Mon.–Sat. noon–7 ✋ $

Musée des Beaux-Arts ✉ Palais Longchamp, place Bernex (4e) ☎ 04 91 14 59 30 ⏰ Tue.–Sun. 10–7, mid-Jun. to mid-Sep.; 10–5, rest of year 🚇 Cinq-Avenues Longchamp ✋ $

MENTON

A mile from Italy and half a century from the rest of the Riviera, the little town of Menton is a delightful curiosity. Its 19th-century heyday welcomed consumptive writers advised to take the sea air rather than risk city winters. The hilltop cemetery is a lasting ironic reminder of the unfortunate folly of ill-informed

doctors. A very English seaside resort (see the memorial to Queen Victoria), Menton reveals architecture that is pure Italian: ocher mountainside houses and baroque churches (St.-Michel and the Chapelle de la Conception). The other Italian touch comes from cross-border gamblers enjoying a Sunday flutter at the casino. By the 1920s, overtaken by rival resorts Nice and St.-Tropez, Menton settled into faded dowager gentility. Happily, Menton's famous son (celebrated in a pier museum dedicated to his work) was artist and filmmaker Jean Cocteau, whose little artistic scandals brought back the thrill last felt in the era of Britain's Prince of Wales, later Edward VII. Cocteau decorated the wedding room of the Hôtel de Ville with scenes of bacchanalia orgies, animal-print carpets and the face of his male lover as Marianne, emblem of France. The Jardin des Biovès lemon grove is Europe's biggest citrus garden, home to the annual Lemon Festival (see page 165).

⊞ E2

Tourist information ✉ palais de l'Europe, 8 avenue Boyer ☎ 04 92 41 76 76; www.villedementon.com

Musée Jean-Cocteau ✉ Bastion de Port ☎ 04 93 57 72 30 ⏰ Wed.–Mon. 10–noon and 3–7, mid-Jun. to mid-Sep.; 10–noon and 2–6, rest of year. Closed holidays ✋ Free

Sale des Mariages ✉ Hôtel de Ville, place Ardoïno ☎ 04 92 10 50 00 ⏰ Mon.–Fri. 8:.30–12:30 and 1:30–5 ✋ $

MONACO, MONTE-CARLO

The world's longest-reigning royal family still holds sway in one of Europe's smallest principalities, midway between Menton and Nice and a helicopter hop from the airport. Prince Rainier is the present head of the Grimaldi family, which has governed since 1297.

Once stretching from Antibes to Italy, the principality shrunk to its present size in the 19th century when citizens revolted against high taxes. In response, Prince Charles III created the new town of Monte Carlo, opening the casino to create additional revenue. It was such a success that all taxes soon were abolished. Casino profits funded the 1875 Romanesque-style cathedral in Monaco-Ville. The casino – and the tax-free status for residents – ensures Monte-Carlo's reputation as the playground of the fabulously wealthy. The casino building was designed by Charles Garnier, architect of the Paris Opéra, and a miniature opera house within the building, the Salle Garnier, allows the elite to enjoy Luciano Pavarotti and Placido Domingo. The decor throughout is as extravagant as the high rollers it attracts – marble floors, onyx columns and crystal chandeliers. Passports are needed for admission. The "man who broke the bank" of popular song was Charles Deville, who turned $400 into $40,000 back in 1891. Less fortunate gamblers have been known to end their misery by plunging from the cliffs behind the casino.

Down in Monaco-Ville, lower-budget tourist attractions include the audiovisual *Monte-Carlo Story* and the inevitable waxworks museum. For the real thing, take a tour of the royal palace, which is closed to the public when the Prince is in residence (indicated by the royal flag flown from the tower). Changing of the guard takes place daily at 11:55 a.m. Princess Grace, the former Hollywood actress Grace Kelly who died in a car accident on the Moyene Corniche in 1982, is immortalized by a statue in the rose garden bearing her name in the district of Fontevielle. Her tomb can be seen in the cathedral.

Present-day "stargazing" takes place in the marina, where only the elite may moor their yachts. The famous May Grand Prix commissioned Europe's first Tarmac roads.
✚ E2

Tourist information ✉ 2a boulevard des Moulins ☎ (Monaco 377) 92 16 61 16; www.monaco-congres.com

Above: Bronze statue of Princess Grace, former Hollywood actress

Opposite: Monte-Carlo seen from the Jardin Exotique

Place de la Comédie – center of life in Montpellier both by day and night

MONTPELLIER

A buzzing university town where social life takes place on the streets, Montpellier is the kind of place in which a well-chosen café table on place de la Comédie – with its fountain of the Three Graces and 19th-century theater – can give you a better sense of the town than any trek around the museums. The town grew around the medieval spice trade on the Lez river, with its spin-off early medical faculty. The gardens of esplanade Charles-de-Gaulle serve heritage at the Musée Fabre, with a collection of works by Italian and Dutch masters. Promenade du Peyrou is a park with an aqueduct, water tower, triumphal arch and sea views. A tramway makes getting around a breeze.

➕ B2
Tourist information ✉ 30 allée de Lattre-de-Tassigny ☎ 04 67 60 60 60; www.ot-montpellier.fr
Musée Fabre ✉ 39 boulevard Sarrail ☎ 04 67 14 83 00 ◉ Tue.–Fri. 9:30–5:30, Sat.–Sun. 10–5:30 🎫 $

NARBONNE

Narbonne is a delightful sea port that stands 10 miles away from the sea. Centuries of silting means Narbonne Plage is now a spectacular drive away though undulating country of vineyards and inland cliffs of La Clappe. The town itself, often overlooked by tourists, stands on the Canal de la Robine, which serves the Aude river, and disappears under the shops of the old quarter; boats may be hired for an hour's exploration of the canal. The ramparts of the 13th-century Archbishop's Palace – within which nestles today's town hall, tourist office and a museum of art and history – dominate the splendid place de l'Hôtel-de-Ville. The Madeleine Courtyard in the oldest part of the palace shouldn't be missed. Abutting the town hall is the unfinished 13th-century Cathédrale St.-Just. The 135-foot north French Gothic-style choir is one of the highest in France. Narbonne is liberally sprinkled with references to 2,000 years of uprisings and intrigues, from the memorial by the main square to martyrs of a peasant revolt to the Renaissance-style Maison des Trois-Nourrices, where Cinq Mars was arrested for conspiring against Cardinal Richelieu.

➕ B2
Tourist information ✉ place Roger-Salengo ☎ 04 68 65 15 60; www.mairie-narbonne.fr

Just when the rest of France is muffling and snuffling in blizzards and hardship, winter ends early on the Riviera – proclaimed by the centuries-old Mardi Gras tradition of Carnival. Nice goes to town during February with the Nice Carnaval (www.nicecarnaval.com). Magnificent floats are papier-maché fantasies parading along promenade des Anglais. Huge caricature heads skip beside trucks as marching bands "out-Disney" Disney along streets lined with grandstand seating. Streamers, whistles, singing and delight fill the air.

Daytime battles of the flowers are breathtaking shows, and nightly parades are a cue for open-air partying until the wee hours. On the last night, the massive figures take their final ride through place Masséna to the beach, to be set afire and adrift at sea in the Bay of the Angels. The Mardi Gras tradition dates back to the 13th century, but the modern burlesque procession, with its figures of the king and queen of Carnival, was begun in 1873.

During February,

CARNIVAL TIME IN NICE AND MENTON

the glamour continues but with less hullabaloo and more grace at the border town of Menton. The Lemon Festival is a carnival quite unique. There's no papier-maché here: Dozens of floats, scores of statues and countless street decorations all are constructed from half a million oranges and lemons. Locals spend dark winter months attaching fruit to chicken wire and unleashing citrus aromas throughout town. Local legend has it that Eve herself gave the fruit to the town, and Menton pays homage to her generosity with parades aplenty in the teasing, breezing 70-degree sunshine of late winter. The undoubted highlight of each of these events is the carnival ball; a joyous occasion when locals dressed in their Sunday best dance the night away.

The carnivals are essentially parties for the locals although visitors are always welcome to join in. In summer, Nice and Antibes-Juan-les-Pins invite the biggest names from the United States to come and perform at world-class jazz festivals to please a more international crowd.

Outrageous characters parade on floats during Mardi Gras in Nice

Provence and the Côte d'Azur

NICE

Nice combines all the thrills and pleasures of the Côte d'Azur in its picturesque old port, grand town center for shopping and gambling, broad sea front and the coast's principal airport. French only since 1860, Nice has its rich Italian heritage – from its years as part of the duchy of Savoy.

Nice is blessed with the magnificent sweep of the wide Baie des Anges, named for angels who carried the town's 15-year-old saint into the harbor after her martyrdom. The English discovered the bay in the late 18th century, and they built the famous promenade des Anglais in 1822. The British influence on the town was so strong that well into the 20th century, all foreigners, be they American or German, were known as "des Anglais." Today, the walk is lined with palm trees and hotels, from the monstrosities of recent years to the operetta extravagance of the 1912 Hôtel Négresco. The Négresco has as many legends as it has rooms. Staff tell stories of Isadora Duncan, the Beatles, Richard Burton and Elizabeth Taylor.

At the eastern end of the prome-nade, the road spills into place Masséna and its gardens, which make up the city's main square. Here is the more modern and swanky shopping district and the focus of music festivals and Carnival (see page 165). The old town (see page 168) is just across the square and behind quai des États-Unis, named for the town's American fans. Follow the coast road to its sudden sweep into the Quartier du Port, where 18th-century buildings and the Classical Église Notre-Dame line the quayside.

Between the port and the old quarter is the Colline du Château (Castle Hill), which despite its name can boast no castle. The French destroyed it in the 18th century. Climb the hill for pleasant gardens and views over the port and the rooftops of old Nice. Some remains of Classical times, housed in a small museum on the hill, are reminders that although the resort was a 19th-century creation, the ancient Greeks founded the town in the fourth century BC.

The Romans settled in the Cimiez district, an area that later found favor with Britain's Queen Victoria and became the smartest residential quarter. Here is the Musée Matisse, a stylish villa that houses works from all of Henri Matisse's periods in the location that inspired his brilliant blues.

There are many art collections in Nice, and the tourist office sells Carte Passe-Musées Nice (Nice's Museum Pass) that gives admission to most museums and galleries. The Musée National Message Biblique Marc-Chagall displays the nation's major collection of the great 20th-century artist's work. At the foot of the Cimiez hill, the museum is renowned for a series of 17 canvases inspired by Old

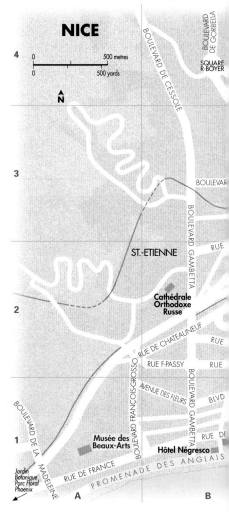

Testament tales. The third of Nice's local heroes was Raoul Dufy, who until recently had a seafront museum devoted to his work. Fears of damage by the sea air led to the entire collection being moved to the Musée des Beaux-Arts. Here, in the former mansion of a Ukrainian princess, is a superb fine arts collection spanning the Italian old masters to contemporary works.

The main home of modern and contemporary art is the Musée d'Art Moderne et d'Art Contemporain (MAMAC), a marble and glass temple to the last 40 years of American and French avant-garde art. Light and graffiti are explored as art forms.

E2

Tourist information 5 promenade des Anglais 04 92 14 48 00; www.nicetourism.com

Musée Matisse D4 164 avenue des Arènes-de-Cimiez 04 93 81 08 08 Wed.–Mon. 10–6, Apr.–Sep.; 10–5, rest of year $

Musée National Message Biblique Marc-Chagall C3 avenue du Docteur-Ménard 04 93 53 87 20 Wed.–Mon. 10–6, Jul..–Sep.; 10–5, rest of year $$

Musée des Beaux-Arts A1 33 avenue des Baumettes 04 92 15 28 28 Tue.–Sun. 10–noon and 2–6 $

Musée d'Art Moderne et d'Art Contemporain (MAMAC) D2 promenade des Arts 04 93 62 61 62 Wed.–Mon. 10–6 $

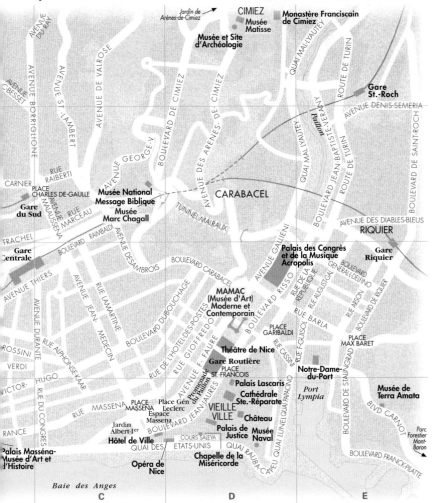

The flea market in cours Saleya – a colorful corner of old Nice

NICE: THE OLD TOWN

The old town of Nice was dismissed as a slum for most of the post-war years until the inevitable gentrification of the 1970s. Nowadays it is a picturesque, atmospheric place that is ideal to explore on foot. It flaunts its endearing Italian side with tempting side streets bedecked with garlands of laundry, cascades of flowers on window sills, quaint red-painted terrace houses and small chapels in hidden corners.

To gain the real flavor of this area, join local housewives and chefs with coffee from a street café and breathe in the aromas of the market in cours Saleya: flowers, of course, but also fresh fruits, honey and Provençal herbs. If you're here on Monday, however, you'll miss all of this, as Mondays welcome the flea market.

The yellow house in cours Saleya was once home to Henri Matisse. On the south side of the square are the squat houses known as *ponchettes*, many of which are now seafood restaurants. On the north side of the square, visit the 18th-century Chapelle de la Miséricorde, with its overtly rococo interior, and the sweet little seashell museum next door, the Galeric de Malacologie.

On place Rossetti is the distinctive, green-domed Cathédrale Ste.-Réparate, a 17th-century baroque tribute to the patron saint who was martyred in Asia Minor at age 15.

A more secular treat is the unmistakably Italian ice cream served from 9 a.m. until midnight every day except Wednesday at Fennochio.

For more aromas, follow your nose along rue Mascoînat and rue du Collet to place St.-François, site of the morning fish market, surprisingly some distance from the pier.

Check out some of the excellent art galleries and antique shops on rue Droite. Then visit the beautiful Palais Lascaris at No. 15. Restored by the town, the former palace of the counts of Castellar boasts a 1738 pharmacy on the first floor and state rooms, adorned by fine tapestries, that are reached up a magnificent staircase decorated by paintings and statues.

Galerie de Malacologie ✉ 3 cours Saleya ☎ 04 93 85 18 44 🕐 Tue.–Sat. 10:30–1 and 2–6:30, May–Sep.; 10:30–1 and 2–6, rest of year 🎟 $

Palais Lascaris ✉ 15 rue Droite ☎ 04 93 62 05 54 🕐 Tue.–Sun. 10–noon and 2–6, mid-Dec. to mid-Nov 🎟 Free

Provence and the Côte d'Azur

NÎMES

Although its greatest gifts to the world are the blue jeans made from the textile that bears its name (*serge de Nîmes* = denim), real life Nîmes is ancient Rome in Provence. For 500 years, gladiators fought to the death in the Arènes, an exceptionally fine example of a Roman amphitheater. The preservation is remarkable considering that generations of local families built houses inside the arena. The site was restored in the 19th century. Well worth a visit is the Maison Carrée, a first-century temple with neat Corinthian columns. Opposite a 20th-century reinterpretation of the Classical design is architect Norman Foster's Carré d'Art, home of the contemporary art museum. The Jardins de la Fontaine were France's first public park. The pedestrian-friendly historic center has charming cafés and little shops. The Cathédrale Notre-Dame et St.-Castor is near by.

Seasonal bullfights *(ferias)* take place during the February Carnival, Easter, Pentecost and the September harvest.

➕ C2

Tourist information ✉ 6 rue Auguste ☎ 04 66 58 38 00; www.ot-nimes.fr

Musée d'Art Contemporain ✉ Carré d'Art, place de la Maison-Carré ☎ 04 66 76 35 35 🕓 Tue.–Sun. 10–6, Apr.–Sep.; 11–6, rest of year 🎟 $

ORANGE

On summer nights, 10,000 people climb the steep stone steps of a playhouse that first opened nearly 2,000 years ago. The figure of Emperor Augustus dominates a red sandstone wall 337 feet long and 118 feet high – the only Roman theater backdrop that survives. Three ranks of seating divided the original audience by social status and divide today's by budget. The Théâtre Antique of Orange is one of the town's two great reminders of the Roman heritage of Provence. The other is a magnificent 73-foot Arc de Triomphe, the first Roman monument in France. Erected around 20 BC at the gateway to Provence across the old Via Agrippa, the arch proclaims Rome's victory over the Gauls. It illustrates imperial might, with carvings showing natives in chains, and the supremacy of the Roman fleet. Carefully cross a busy main road for a closer look, as the triple arch now stands in the center of Route 7.

➕ C3

Tourist information ✉ 5 cours Aristide-Briand ☎ 04 90 34 70 88; www.provence-orange.com

Théâtre Antique ✉ place des Frères-Mounet ☎ 04 90 51 45 00 🕓 Daily 9–6:30, Apr.–Sep.; 9–noon and 1:30–5, rest of year 🎟 $ (includes Musée Municipal, opposite)

The statue of Emperor Augustus still sits backstage at the Théâtre Antique in Orange

Provence and the Côte d'Azur

DRIVE: JEWISH HERITAGE TRAIL

Distance: 240 miles Time: 3 days

Jewish communities have existed in Provence for nearly 2,000 years, and they faced a turbulent history of exile and welcome. Some ghettos (*carrières*) were created during the influence of the papal state as sanctuary from persecution; others were virtual prison townships.

Start the tour in Avignon.

In 1221, the bishop of Avignon granted Jews the right to live within the city walls. The main synagogue by place de Jérusalem, rebuilt in 1848 after a fire, is a national monument. Its white colonnades and walnut furnishings are striking features. Nearby, rues Abraham and Jacob testify to the old Jewish quarter, as does rue Vieille-Juiverie, opposite the palace.

Take the D225 northeast out of town, and turn right on the D942, continuing 6 miles to Carpentras.

Notorious for 1980s fascist attacks on the city's 15th-century Jewish Cemetery that brought widespread condemnation of the National Front, Carpentras has one of the oldest Jewish communities in France. A synagogue has stood on place de la Mairie since 1367. The present building, restored in 1741, is considered the most beautiful in France, retains its *mikvah* ritual baths fed by natural springs and bakery ovens with separate stone tables for preparing *chollah* bread and *matzah*.

Take the D938 to nearby Pernes-les-Fontaines.

Take a quick detour at Pernes-les-Fontaines to see the old stone *mikvah* baths that tap into the water table of this spring town.

Take the D28 toward Avignon, turning left on the D31 south until it rejoins the D938 into Cavaillon.

In 1453, Jews were forced into the ghetto in Cavaillon. The state seized the 1772 synagogue above rues Hébraïque and Chabran in 1793, and now it is a museum. The unusual building had an external staircase and a grill between the women's level and the main prayer room that could be

raised so women could see the Torah (scrolls of the law). Two fine staircases reach an extraordinarily ornate pulpit for the rabbi. Many important texts are preserved at the Inguimbertine Library.

Return to the A7 for 41 miles to Marseille.

The major modern community, Marseille is home to 40 synagogues and 17 kosher restaurants. Jews settled from the 12th century until expulsion in 1501. At the beginning of the 20th century, refugees fled here from the pogroms of eastern Europe, and as a free zone from 1939, Marseille became a sanctuary for Jews escaping Nazi persecution until the German regime arrived in 1942. Marseille later became a major port for concentration-camp survivors leaving for Israel. On the plage du Prado, see the sculpture *Marseille: Gateway to the East*, a symbol of Israeli gratitude to the city. A memorial to deportees may be seen on quai St.-Jean. The oldest surviving synagogue is

an 1864 Romano-Byzantine temple with bronze lamps and a magnificent organ.

Take the A7 north for 7 miles, following signs for Aix-en-Provence. Filter onto the A51 for 10 miles, then continue on the A8 in the direction of St. Maximin–Cannes–Nice for 60 miles. At exit 36 for Draguignan, turn left on the N555 into Draguignan.

Draguignan was known as the haven of the Hebrews, its ghetto a thriving local community. On rue Jutarié, 75 feet of the medieval synagogue wall can be seen. Religious images on stonework are common in this part of town.

Back along the N555 to the A8, continue in the direction of Fréjus–Nice for 42 miles. Take exit 50 for Nice center, following the N202 for 250 yards and then the N7 for a mile into Nice.

The community settled around Nice's rues Droite and Masconat and the Limpia

Cemetery from 1408 until the Nazi roundups in 1942. In the old town, a plaque on rue Benoît-Bunico commemorates the founding of the ghetto, and the cemetery on the Colline du la Château bears witness to centuries of resident Jewish families. Visit the main synagogue on rue Deloye. It's renovated with magnificent windows by Théo Tobiasse. The Musée National Message Biblique Marc-Chagall (see page 166) shouldn't be missed.

Synagogue ✉ place de Jérusalem, Avignon ☎ 04 90 85 21 24
Synagogue ✉ place de Maurice-Charretier, Carpentras ☎ 04 90 63 39 97
Synagogue ✉ rue Hébraïque/Chabran, Cavaillon ☎ 04 90 71 32 01
Synagogue ✉ 117 rue Breteuil, Marseille ☎ 04 91 37 49 64
Synagogue ✉ 15 rue Observance, Draguignan ☎ 04 94 68 41 45
Synagogue ✉ rue Droite, Nice ☎ 04 93 92 11 38

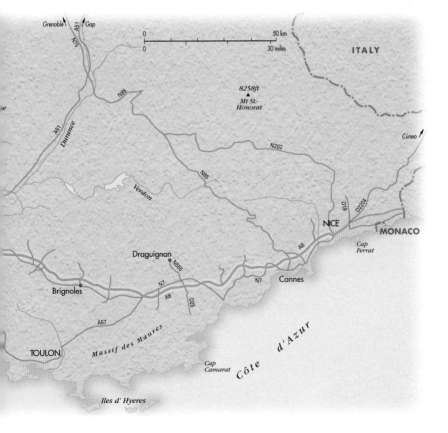

Provence and the Côte d'Azur

Known as *villages perchés* and *nids d'aigles* (eagles' nests), the small towns and hamlets literally perched on the rocks high above the Côte d'Azur are the last remaining outposts of ordinary life before the arrival of the Riviera. Originally created out of the reach of opportunist invaders, the villages remain difficult to access but are well worth the effort. Roads are so steep and winding that some houses have several addresses, with each storey of the houses being on a different street. Experienced motorists should pick one or two to visit on the map: Roquebrune, Vence (see page 175) and Eze. Eze, an outpost of the counts of Savoy, was fortified in the 12th century and belonged to Monaco until its citizens voted in the 19th century to join France. The exotic garden of

PERCHED VILLAGES

cacti and palms is worth a visit. Although St.-Paul-de-Vence is famous for its 16th-century walls and tower, not to mention its Provençal Museum, most people come to visit the hotel La Colombe d'Or. In the 1920s, it was a humble inn and the customers were struggling artists who paid the owner in paintings rather than cash. The shrewd hotelier amassed what is probably France's greatest collection of modern art: Henri Matisse, Amedeo Modigliani, Georges Braque, Pablo Picasso, Pierre Bonnard and Paul Signac. Dozens of the 20th century's greatest artists handed over works in exchange for a room or a meal. Inevitably, St.-Paul-de-Vence is now overrun with art galleries and high-priced shops.

Tourist information ✉ 2 rue Grande, St.-Paul-de-Vence ☎ 04 93 32 86 95

The highest village in Provence – Eze is perched 1,410 feet above the coast

One of the wonders of the ancient world: the Pont du Gard

PERPIGNAN

The second city of Catalonia – the capital is Barcelona, within Spain – is something of a curiosity, a nation within a nation. The town is home to the oldest palace in France – a French palace that served as the seat of the king of the island of Mallorca. A peculiar dynasty lasting only 68 years, it was created in 1276 by James I of Aragon as a treat for his youngest son. The palace, now standing within a pink brick citadel, still has its chapel, great hall and royal apartments. The Gothic Cathédrale St.-Jean boasts a 15th-century bell housed in an 18th-century cage. Next door, the Campo Santo, France's only cloistered cemetery, has four marbled galleries. Église St.-Jacques, built in two parts in the 14th and 18th centuries, stands in some charming gardens. Salvador Dalí proclaimed Perpignan's train station "the center of the universe." He painted his own vision of the building and inspired the decor of the roof and paving outside the modern station.
✚ B1

Tourist information ✉ Palais des Congrès, place Armand Lanoux ☎ 04 68 66 30 30; www.mairie-perpignan.fr

PONT DU GARD

A delightful detour, this magnificent triumph of Roman engineering is an imposing three-tiered aqueduct spanning the Gard river. Bringing fresh water to Nîmes (see page 169) from the spring at Uzès, about six miles away, the bridge was part of a 30-mile complex of man-made waterways constructed at the end of the first century BC. Rightly acclaimed as one of the wonders of the ancient world, the World Heritage Site has recently been refurbished to stunning effect. The triple row of arches complements the landscape and soars 160 feet above bathers and picnickers on the river banks below. Its top level spans a remarkable 902 feet. The massive blocks of stone, weighing up to 6 tons each, were assembled without the use of mortar. The aqueduct continued to supply water until the ninth century, when lime deposits and lack of maintenance finally impeded the flow.
✚ C2

ST.-RAPHAËL

St.-Raphaël is unable to flaunt the evidence of its heyday, when Hector Berlioz, Guy de Maupassant and Alexandre Dumas discovered the town's charms, since many of its 19th-century memories were destroyed in World War II bombing. The salons and hotels where literary giants once vacationed now are long gone. A fashionable seaside resort since the beginning of the 19th century, when Napoléon landed on its beaches following his Egyptian campaign, St.-Raphaël still attracts sun worshipers by day and casino lizards by night. Keep in mind, however, that beachwear isn't allowed in the town (see page 148). Dress respectably enough to visit the Byzantine Cathédrale Notre-Dame-de-la-Victoire and the Romanesque Église St.-Pierre, with its hint of the original medieval village that grew up here in the days before seaside resorts.
✚ E1–E2

Tourist information ✉ rue Waldeck Rousseau ☎ 04 94 19 52 52; www.saint-raphael.com

Fishing boats mingle with pleasure craft in the harbor at St.-Tropez

ST.-RÉMY-DE-PROVENCE

The prophet Nostradamus was born here and the composer Charles Gounod moved here, but the town's fame comes from the fact that Vincent van Gogh came to the St. Paul de Mausole hospital in May 1889 to recover from the famous depression when he cut off his own ear. Attracted by the light and landscapes around St.-Rémy, the artist warmed to the calm world of the nuns and nurses and created more than 150 paintings and numerous sketches during his year here – *The Irises* and *Starry Night* among them. He left St.-Rémy for Auvers-sur-Oise (see page 50), where he died little more than two months later. Visit Église St.-Paul-de-Mausole to see the cloister and a permanent exhibition (Galerie Valetudo) of pictures painted by patients and fine van Gogh reproductions, all of which are for sale. Proceeds go toward the hospital upkeep and making the facility as attractive as possible. The Centre d'Art Présence Vincent van Gogh in the Hôtel Estrine each year brings an exhibition on a different theme, using full-size reproductions of his paintings and slide shows. Contemporary artists exhibit in upstairs rooms. A signposted trail (follow the reproduction paintings) takes in locations the artist painted during his stay in St.-Rémy. Escorted 90-minute tours ($$) leave the tourist office every Tuesday, Thursday and Saturday at 10 a.m. from April to mid-October. Maps for individuals also are available.

✚ C2

Tourist information ✉ place J.-Jaurés ☎ 04 90 92 05 22; www.saintremy-de-provence.com

Centre d'Art Présence Vincent van Gogh ✉ rue Estrine ☎ 04 90 92 34 72 ⏰ Tue.–Sun. 10:30–12:30 and 2:30–6:30, Apr.–Dec. 👋 $

Galerie Valetudo ✉ Église St.-Paul-de-Mausole ⏰ Sat.–Sun. 10:30–6 👋 $

Provence and the Côte d'Azur

St.-Tropez

Forever linked with screen siren turned animal-rights activist Brigitte Bardot and promoted by the more salacious tabloid press for pioneering topless bathing, this former fishing village has a reputation as the playground of Hollywood in exile.

Named after a decapitated Roman martyr, the city's quaint streets and pretty market long have been appreciated by the good and the great. Here, 19th-century writers and composers escaped from city life. Raoul Dufy, Henri Matisse and Pierre Bonnard set up their easels; Jean Cocteau and Colette held house parties between the wars; movie stars moved in from the 1950s on. First-timers often come to glimpse the glitterati among locals at the fruit and fish markets. Regulars frequent the Musée de l'Annonciade to view paintings that reflect the town as it was seen by the Fauvists and Pointillists who knew it best. There are two addresses for the well-heeled and well-dressed to loiter with a glass of something cool. Place des Lices is where locals play *boules* and visitors hang out in arty cafés. Down by the Vieux Port, the merely rich watch the filthy rich dine on board the extravagant yachts moored just yards away. Detach yourself for photo opportunities, looking up at the town from the harbor walls, or down from the ramparts of the citadel (where there's a naval museum).

⊕ D1

Tourist information ✉ Quai Jean-Jaurès ☎ 04 94 97 45 21; www.ot-saint-tropez.com

Musée de l'Annonciade ✉ place Georges-Gramont ☎ 04 94 97 04 01 ◷ Wed.–Mon. 10–noon and 3–7, Jun.–Sep.; 10–noon and 2–6, in Oct. and Dec.–May 🖰 $

Musée Naval de la Citadelle ✉ Montée de la Citadelle ☎ 09 94 97 59 43 ◷ Wed.–Mon. 11–5:30, mid-Jun.–Oct. 31; 10–noon and 1–4, in Oct. and Dec.–mid-Jun. 🖰 $

Salon-de-Provence

The great riddler and seer Nostradamus moved to Salon in 1547 and spent the last two decades of his life in a house that is now a museum dedicated to his life. A doctor and astrologer, Michel de Nostredame was born in St.-Rémy-de-

The hand of Matisse at the Chapelle du Rosaire

Provence into a family of new converts from Judaism to Catholicism. His immortality was guaranteed by cryptic predictions reappraised by each successive generation to reveal visions of tyrants and natural disasters. The Maison de Nostradamus offers an audio-guided tour of his life and times. Nostradamus is buried in the town's Église St.-Laurent. Also worth seeing are the clock tower and Musée Grévin, featuring waxworks episodes from Provence's history.

⊕ C2

Tourist information ✉ 56 cours Gimon ☎ 04 90 56 27 60; www.salon-de-provence.org

Vence

Two miles north of St.-Paul-de-Vence is Vence itself – in its day, even more of an artist commune. Here D.H. Lawrence lived and died and Marc Chagall spent his final years. Chagall's mosaic is one of the sights of France's tiniest cathedral, Cathédrale St.-Véran, dating from the 10th century. Roman tombs are embedded in the walls. Henri Matisse declared that his finest work was the *Chapelle du Rosaire*, a labor of love created in gratitude to the Dominican sisters who nursed him to health when dangerously ill in 1941. He spent five years creating simple black line drawings of the stations of the cross, washed with colored light from the stained-glass windows.

⊕ E2

Tourist information ✉ place du Grand-Jardin ☎ 04 93 58 06 38; www.ville-vence.fr

Chapelle du Rosaire ✉ avenue Henri-Matisse ☎ 04 93 58 03 26 ◷ Tue. and Thu. 10–11:30 and 2–5:30, Mon., Wed. and Sat. (also Fri. during school holidays), 2–5:30, Oct.–Dec. 🖰 $

MASSIF CENTRAL

Massif Central

*"**A** civilized wilderness in the heart of France, Massif Central beckons you to enter the land of volcanoes and hot springs. "*

Opposite: The medieval bridge to the village of Estaing in the Gorges du Lot

Massif Central

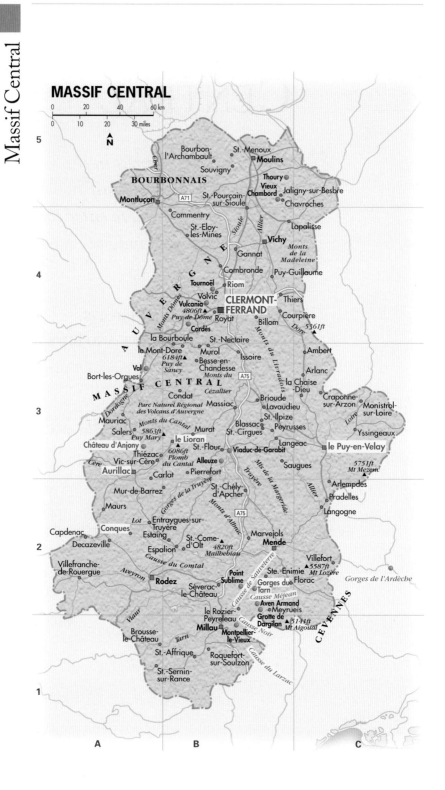

MASSIF CENTRAL

0   20   40   60 km
0   10   20   30 miles

N

BOURBONNAIS

Bourbon-l'Archambault
St.-Menoux
Moulins
Souvigny
Thoury
Vieux **Chambord**
Jaligny-sur-Besbre
Montluçon
A71
St.-Pourçain-sur-Sioule
Chavroches
Commentry
Lapalisse
St.-Eloy-les-Mines
Vichy
Gannat
Monts de la Madeleine
Combronde
Puy-Guillaume
Tournoël
Riom
Volvic
Thiers
Vulcania
4806ft ▲
Puy de Dôme Royat
CLERMONT-FERRAND
Courpière
Billom
Dore 5361ft ▲
Cordès
la Bourboule
St.-Nectaire
Monts du Livradois
le Mont-Dore
Murol
Issoire
Ambert
6184ft ▲
Besse-en-Chandesse
Val
Puy de Sancy
Monts du Cézallier
A75
la Chaise-Dieu
Bort-les-Orgues
Crapone-sur-Arzon
Monistrol-sur-Loire
MASSIF CENTRAL
Condat
Brioude
Lavaudieu
St.-Ilpize
Yssingeaux
Parc Naturel Régional des Volcans d'Auvergne
Massiac
Monts du Cantal
Mauriac
Peyrusses
Loire
Salers
5863ft ▲
Murat
Blassac
St.-Cirgues
le Puy-en-Velay
Puy Mary
le Lioran
St.-Flour
Langeac
Château d'Anjony
6086ft
Plomb du Cantal
Viaduc-de-Garabit
5751ft
Mt Mézenc ▲
Thiézac
Vic-sur-Cère
Alleuze
Cère
Sauges
Aurillac
Carlat
Pierrefort
Arlempdes
Mts de la Margeride
Pradelles
Mur-de-Barrez
St.-Chély-d'Apcher
Allier
Langogne
Maurs
Gorges de la Truyère
A75
Capdenac
Conques
Entraygues-sur-Truyère
Marvejols
Mende
Decazeville
Estaing
St.-Côme-d'Olt
Villefort
Espalion
4820ft
Mailhebiau
▲ 5587ft
Mt Lozère
Gorges de l'Ardèche
Villefranche-de-Rouergue
Causse du Comtal
Point Sublime
Ste.-Enimie
Florac
Aveyron
Rodez
Séverac-le-Château
Gorges du Tarn
Causse Méjean
le Rozier
Peyreleau
Aven Armand
Meyrueis
Causse de Sauveterre
Grotte de Dargilan
▲ 5141ft
Mt Aigoual
Brousse-le-Château
Millau
Montpellier-le-Vieux
Causse Noir
Tarn
St.-Affrique
Roquefort-sur-Soulzon
CÉVENNES
St.-Sernin-sur-Rance
Causse du Larzac

A   B   C

5

4

3

2

1

MASSIF CENTRAL

For lovers of the great outdoors, the Massif Central always comes as a surprise. Despite claiming a sixth of the country's land mass, the area boasts few major cities and therefore often fails to make it onto travel itineraries. However, this mountainous region is the missing link between the Alps and the Pyrénées, and it trickles out through the Loire, Dordogne and Lot rivers. The image the region has given the world is of vast expanses of volcanic landscapes, usually printed on plastic bottles of mineral water sold throughout France and the wider world. This anonymity works in the vacationers' favor. Untouched by some of the regrettable urban development of the 1960s, destinations are, for much of the year, free from crowds of tourists. Plenty of churches and museums provide cultural enlightenment, and splendid late 19th-century spa resorts and casinos dole out satisfying entertainment.

Girls in traditional costume and clogs in Salers

Annual Variety
Sailing, windsurfing, canoeing, fishing and hiking are the main activities for summer visitors. Winter sees the gentle slopes called into service with ski resorts well known to the French but less vigorously marketed internationally than the Alpine stations. In the fall, a meeting of European hot air balloons takes place among the volcanoes.

Food
Local cuisine includes a great deal of freshwater fish: pike, perch, carp and trout. A noble tradition of sausage making, cured ham and all kinds of pork products dates from days when preserving meats was the only way to keep them through the long winter months. Light summer dishes are matched in winter by warming stews such as *potée auvergnate,* a hearty pot of cabbage and potatoes with bacon and sausages. Cabbage is matched in popularity only by the celebrated green lentils from le Puy.

Outstanding desserts include delicious puréed chestnuts from Ardèche and glazed shortcrust apple pie from Auvergne. Wines that once graced the tables of kings are gradually coming back into fashion. Order a St.-Pourçain from the Bourbonnais region, home of the royal house of Bourbon.

Massif Central

The ancient craft of cheese making at Roquefort-sur-Soulzon

OF TRUE LOVE AND BLUE CHEESE

Once upon a time on a hillside in the heart of France, a young shepherd boy was sitting at the entrance to his cave, lunching and munching on a tasty sandwich. In the distance he saw a beautiful shepherdess and ran to meet her, leaving his bread and cheese in the cave.

History doesn't tell whether the lovers found a happy ending, but the sandwich lived happily ever after. For the passionate swain recalled his long-lost snack, and returned to the caves some months later to find that the cool moist atmosphere had turned the moldy bread into blue veins, and so Roquefort cheese was born. By the time the Romans arrived in France, those caves were already full of cheeses for a discerning market. Today the queen of blue cheese is still made in the same way on the same site.

Although much commercially produced Roquefort is now made in factories as far south as Corsica, the real thing is still made at Roquefort-sur-Soulzon, south of Millau. The distinctive foil label stamped with a red sheep distinguishes that this cheese is the traditional blend of milk from Lacaune ewes and natural mold from two-month-old bread. The original cool damp caves under the village are open to lactose-tolerant visitors who marvel at the endless shelves of ripening cheeses.

Central France is duly proud of its cheese board; the beautiful Auvergne in particular has five distinguished cheeses. These are the widely appreciated Cantal; the lesser known Salers; creamy Saint-Nectaire, the long-matured favorite of King Louis XIV; and the veined specialties Fourme d'Ambert and Bleu d'Auvergne, a saltier alternative to Roquefort.

The cheeses feature in such regional specialty dishes as *tarte de St.-Nectaire*, and duck breast prepared with honey and Fourme d'Ambert. Every month from May to October sees at least one town or village hosting a cheese fair.

Hardy motorists for whom cholesterol holds no fears may scorn the healthy spa-town trail in favor of the cardiovascular white-knuckle thrill of a five-day drive along the cheese routes of the Puy-de-Dôme and Cantal areas. Road signs marked "Route des Fromages A.O.C. d'Auvergne" promise farmhouses, dairies, cellars and caves, as well as châteaux, parks and restaurants. Maps are available from most regional tourist offices.

CLERMONT-FERRAND

A town built on and of volcanic rock – even the Gothic Cathédrale Notre-Dame-de-l'Assomption is made of black lava – Clermont-Ferrand welcomes visitors but isn't overrun with camera-clicking foreigners.

Ideally, visitors should divide their time between the two historic quarters: Vieux (Old) Clermont and Montferrand. With plenty of pedestrian streets around the cathedral, Old Clermont is busy and attractive but for the occasional lapse to a modern color scheme. It's famous for its fountains great and small (see page 184). Nearby Montferrand, founded by the counts of Auvergne, has lovely rust-colored rooftops and neatly planned streets. It was originally a town in its own right before royal decree united it with Clermont in the 17th century.

Strolling by Colors

Walking is a pleasure and an education. Old quarters are color-coded, with themed signs and panels offering historic walks. Three trails begin from the main tourist office by Clermont's cathedral, the fourth by the art museum in Montferrand. Medallions featuring local heroes are embedded in the sidewalks to ensure you keep to the right path.

Massif Central

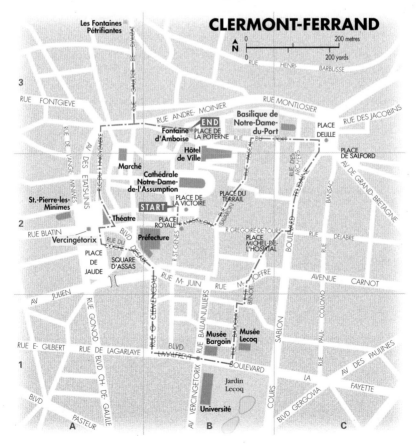

CLERMONT-FERRAND

Massif Central

A fountain in place du Terrail in Clermont

Local Heroes

The figure set in the streets of Montferrand is the much-loved society leper, the Countess G. Her husband bequeathed this amiable widow the city in 1196, and she in turn gave the citizens a charter and freedom to trade. Countess G, who suffered from leprosy, then devoted the rest of her life to charity work and running a leper colony with her son, Count Guillaume VIII of Auvergne. Other faces set in paving stones are those of Pope Urban II, Vercingétorix (see page 183), and the 17th-century mathematician and philosopher Blaise Pascal who invented the world's first adding machine.

The city has always bred pioneers such as the Michelin brothers, who created their tires here. The tradition of a city of thinkers continues at the Café des Augustes, 5 rue Sous-les-Augustins, where books, newspapers and magazines are swapped among tables as everyone, young and old, muses on the meaning of life and Pascal's view that "the heart has its reasons."

The book market is held every Saturday (except the second in the month) at place Delille, a Sunday flea market takes place at the bus depot, and merchants gather daily at the market at place St.-Pierre. Other passions are well served by the casino in nearby Royat, theater-opera house and circus school.

ESSENTIAL INFORMATION

TOURIST INFORMATION
place de la Victoire ☎ 04 73 98 65 00; www.ville-clermont-ferrand.fr Information and advice in English.

URBAN TRANSPORTATION
Although central Clermont-Ferrand is manageable on foot, bus service across town and to outlying districts is frequent and reliable. Tickets are available individually from the driver or in books (carnets) of 10 from tobacconists

(tabacs). Taxis may be hailed in the streets or call ☎ 04 73 31 53 15. SNCF rail services operate to Paris (☎ 08 36 35 35 35, toll call).

AIRPORT INFORMATION
Clermont-Auvergne Airport, just outside town at Aulnat, has scheduled domestic and European flights ☎ 04 73 62 71 00. A shuttle bus links the airport with the city center ☎ 04 73 84 72 57.

CLIMATE – Average highs and lows

JAN.	FEB.	MAR.	APR.	MAY	JUN.	JUL.	AUG.	SEP.	OCT.	NOV.	DEC.
5°C	7°C	13°C	16°C	20°C	24°C	27°C	26°C	23°C	16°C	10°C	6°C
41°F	45°F	55°F	61°F	68°F	75°F	81°F	79°F	73°F	61°F	50°F	43°F
-1°C	0°C	3°C	6°C	9°C	13°C	15°C	14°C	12°C	7°C	4°C	0°C
30°F	32°F	37°F	43°F	48°F	55°F	59°F	57°F	54°F	45°F	39°F	32°F

CLERMONT-FERRAND SIGHTS

Key to symbols

🔡 map coordinates refer to the Clermont-Ferrand map on page 181; sights below are highlighted in yellow on the map.

✉ address or location   ☎ telephone number

🕐 opening times   🚌 nearest bus or tram route

🍴 restaurant on site or nearby

Ⓜ nearest métro   ℹ information

💲 admission charge: $$$ more than €10, $$ €5–€10, $ less than €5

BASILIQUE DE NOTRE-DAME-DU-PORT

With splendid Romanesque architecture, Notre-Dame-du-Port justifiably is a World Heritage Site. A well from the earlier churches on the site may be seen in the crypt. This spacious building dates from 1150, and its 1843 octagonal tower perches proudly above the curves and right angles of this many-tiered classic of its type. A figure of Christ the King surrounded by cherubim sits above images of John the Baptist and Isaiah at the south entrance to the basilica. Within, there is true delight to be had in tracing the popular Bible stories carved into the capitals of the pillars. The most entertaining is the story of Adam and Eve, detailed in depictions of Eve eating the forbidden fruit of the vine (no apples in this Eden) and of a vivid moment of anger in which Adam grabs Eve by the hair and kicks her in an earthy manner.

🔡 C3   ✉ rue Notre-Dame-du-Port

VERCINGÉTORIX

In 52 BC a brave, 20-year-old Gallic chieftain saw off Julius Caesar's army as the Romans prepared to march through the Auvergne. Since then, the name Vercingétorix has been hailed with pride in the region despite him later being hauled off to Rome and imprisoned for six years before being executed by strangulation in 46 BC. In October 1903, he literally rode again when the town finally erected a statue of Vercingétorix on horseback, sculpted by Frédéric-Auguste

Romanesque style at Notre-Dame-du-Port

Bartholdi (1834-1905), who created the *Statue of Liberty*. Intriguingly, the town commissioned a full-size wooden version on wheels before the public would subscribe for the finished article. It was trundled around town until the residents agreed on the perfect site. And so Vercingétorix stands today, looking toward Puy-de-Dôme. Bartholdi's original bronze study is displayed beside art and artifacts from the medieval to the contemporary at Montferrand's Musée d'Art Roger-Quilliot.

🔡 A2

Vercingétorix Statue   ✉ place de Jaude

Musée d'Art Roger-Quilliot   ✉ place Louis-Deteix

☎ 04 73 16 11 30   🕐 Tue.–Sun. 10–6   Ⓜ Montesquieu

🚌 1, 9, 16 from place de Jaude; 17 from Gare SNCF

💲 $ (free first Sun. of the month)

WALK: AMONG THE FOUNTAINS

Refer to route marked on city map on page 181

Begin this 1.5-mile walk at place de la Victoire's fountain of Pope Urban II, pointing toward the Holy Land.

> *Take rue St.-Genès to place Royale with its 19th-century Renaissance-style Fontaine Royale. Rue Massillon twists into rue Savaron and place du Terrail, with galleried windows overlooking the cherubim of a 17th-century fountain.*

On rue Pascal, admire the elegant 18th-century house at No. 4, and the scalloped basin at the junction with rue du Port.

> *Take rue Notre-Dame-du-Port to the church (see page 183).*

Chubby cherubim at the Fontaine Delille

You can see Fontaine du Port's twin spouts from here. The road leads to place Delille, home to the chubby cheeks, thighs and pitchers of the Fontaine Delille.

> *Walk right on boulevard Trudaine. Fontaine de la Flèche is on the corner with rue des Archers. Farther along the boulevard, turn right on place Michel-de-l'Hospital.*

The 1661 Fontaine des Cercles is set into a wall.

> *Cross rue Maréchal-Joffre, taking rue St.-Benoît and rue Bardoux to pass the Musée Lecoq (natural history).*

Across boulevard Lafayette is the charming Jardin Lecoq, with a lake fed by a mythical animal's head fountain. By the gardener's hut is Jean Camus' white stone *Byblis Weeping*.

> *Leave the park toward boulevard Malfreyt and see the Egyptian obelisk known as la Fontaine de la Pyramide.*

This is dedicated to the Egyptian campaigns of local General Louis Desaix, and is opposite the archeological Musée Bargoin.

> *Continue to Fontaine de l'Hôtel-Dieu, erected in 1989, and take a right to rue Clemenceau.*

On the square d'Assas, the Fontaine du Roi-des-Eaux features a baroque-style Poseidon.

> *Rue du Coche leads to place Jaude and its modern water features. Pass a dinky Wallace drinking fountain by the theater. Follow rue du 11-Novembre and cross rue André-Moinier to rue Gaultier-de-Biauzat to visit the town's eccentric thermal spring grotto, La Fontaine Pétrifiante. Then return to rue André-Moinier and place de la Poterne.*

This the best photo opportunity of the day, the pretty Amboise Fountain set against the mountain-peaked skyline.

Musée Lecoq ✚ B1 ✉ 15 rue Bardoux ☎ 04 73 91 93 78 🕐 Tue.–Sat. 10–noon and 2–6, Sun. 2–6, May–Sep.; Tue.–Sat. 10–noon and 2–5, Sun. 2–5, rest of year 🎟 $ (free first Sun. of the month)
Musée Bargoin ✚ B1 ✉ 45 rue Ballainvilliers ☎ 04 73 91 37 31 🕐 Tue.–Sun. 10–6 🎟 $ (free first Sun. of the month)
Fontaine Pétrifiane ✚ A3 ✉ rue Gaultier de Biauzat ☎ 04 73 37 15 58 🕐 9–7:30, Jul.–Aug.; daily 9–noon and 2–6, rest of year 🎟 $

The village of Navacelles shelters in a massive glacial *cirque*

REGIONAL SIGHTS

AURILLAC

The man who gave the West the zero is honored with a statue in the main square of Aurillac. Pope Sylvester II is the most famous son of this fine town at the foot of the mountains. Monks educated the shepherd boy, who went on to study mathematics and medicine at the schools of Cordoba. Among his innovations was the concept of a clock worked by a system of weights and the introduction of Arabic numerals. In 999, he became the first French pope.

Aurillac has an art collection, museums of local culture and a museum of volcanoes to explore away from the heat of the sun or the rain. Outside, stroll through the old narrow streets and admire some fine houses in the historic quarter on the banks of the Jordanne river, with its Pont Rouge, named for the original red-painted wooden bridge that once stood here. Great Auvergnat produce is sold at the Wednesday and Sunday market.

⊞ A3

Tourist information ✉ place du Square ☎ 04 71 48 46 58; www.iaurillac.com

LES CAUSSES

The great river valley plateaus are known as les Causses, and the four great spaces between the Lot and the Languedoc's Mediterranean coast make for dramatic scenery, each plain ripped from its neighbors by great river gorges. The Causses of Sauveterre, Méjean, Causse Noir and Larzac offer wild, wind-swept countryside that serves as grazing ground for the sheep whose milk makes Roquefort cheese (see page 180). Rock formations protect towns and villages from the winds, and sweeping courses of long-gone glaciers and rivers have hewn vast natural amphitheaters out from the limestone, the best known being the Cirque de Navacelles. The other main attraction is underground, where potholes and caves open up into vast cathedral-like

Fine furnishings in the Château d'Anjony

spaces. These areas were relatively unknown outside the region until France's first great environmental protest in the 1970s, when the government's plan to develop a huge military base at Larzac eventually was defeated by the weight of public opinion. Once many of these strange landscapes were considered somewhat inaccessible, with access restricted to stone steps carved from the rock face and the old pilgrims' road across Larzac. Today, drivers can take the road along the Tarn Gorges (see page 188) and a toll-free section of the A75 highway across the Massif Central from St.-Flour to Montpellier.
✚ B1–B2

CHÂTEAU D'ANJONY

Lavish Renaissance frescoes, sumptuous tapestries and the rich tones of paintings commissioned by generations past bid you welcome not merely to a château, but to a genuine family home. Just as bookcases or CD racks inform you about new acquaintances, here solid wooden furnishings and extravagant decorative styles lend a personal insight into the fortunes and fashions of the Anjonys. Family portraits through the centuries go back to the days of the château's founder, the valiant and belligerent Louis II of Anjony. The 15th-century château has four round towers and overlooks the village of Tournemire, with its church built of local volcanic stone. Tournemire and Anjony have had a turbulent relationship over the years. After a quarrel over the land on which Louis II had built his château, the Tournemire and Anjony families fought a tournament to settle the dispute. By sundown, the Tournemires were the victors, with Louis and his sons slain. The families maintained hostilities until the 17th century, when Michel II of Anjony proposed to Tournemire heiress Gabrielle de Pesteils, and they all lived happily ever after.
✚ A3

GORGES DE L'ARDÈCHE

The very image of a rural French summer day is the sight of families by the waterside under the Pont d'Arc. This magnificent natural arch makes a fabulous 111-foot-high stone bridge spanning the Ardèche Gorge and is the undisputed star of the rugged Ardèche mountains between the Rhône and Cévennes valleys. Through the centuries, the river has carved a spectacular canyon, now classified as a natural park.

Excellent views are guaranteed along the gorge, and not only for drivers taking the D290 from Vallon-Pont-d'Arc to the Rhône, with its 12 designated viewing points en route. Lazy sunbathers tickle their toes in the water under the arch, and solo fishermen cast their lines from the rocks. Canoeists shoot the 25 rapids that cover 19 miles from Vallon to Pont-St.-Esprit. The adventure can take up to two days. Canoes can be rented at Vallon-Pont-d'Arc, where minibus shuttles link with Sauze, near St.-Martin-d'Ardèche, 20 miles downstream. Less energetic water travel is also available at a price. *Barques* carrying 4 to 6 passengers, and steered by two boatmen, may be reserved at the Vallon-Pont-d'Arc tourist office. The office can also advise on excursions to the various caves of the region (the Grottes d'Aven), where guides take visitors down to underground chambers of glistening stalactites and stalagmites. Recommendations vary according to the season.

The hillsides, with their steep paths above 1,000-year-old chestnut groves, are popular with hikers and mountain bikers in search of the perfect panorama. If the summer sun is too much, step into the cool shade of the 100 caves.

Many attractive towns and villages offer shady squares for a long, cool drink and a snack. At the delightful town of Aubenas, visit the elegant château with its 12th-century donjon , and see the dome of the Benedictine Chapelle St.-Benoît.

Don't leave the area without buying a can of the famous chestnut paste, *crème de marrons*. Delicious for cooking, it's available from shops or farmers' markets. Because of the afternoon heat, several

✉ Tournemire ☎ 04 71 47 61 67 🕐 Mon.–Sat. 11–6:30, Sun. 2–6:30, Jul.–Aug.; daily 2–6:30, Feb.–Jun. and Sep. 1 to mid-Nov. 💲 $$

CONQUES

The twin towers of Église St.-Foye once welcomed pilgrims to this picturesque hillside village in the Aveyron region, south of the Lot river. Today the charms are no less a lure to vacationers, wooed and won by dainty stone cottages, sloping rooftops and delightful country gardens. The name refers to the conch shell shape of the site. Pilgrims on their way to cross the Pyrénées made the fortunes of the village as they paid their respect at the shrine to the Christian martyr for whom the 11th-century church is named. A golden statue reliquary embossed with precious stones dates from the ninth century, and a superb interpretation of the Last Judgment is carved over the main doorway.

✚ A2

Tourist information ✉ place de l'Abbatiale
☎ 05 65 72 85 00; www.conques.com

Massif Central

towns hold midweek markets at night, an enchanting otherworldly experience marked by a wonderful atmosphere in local bars and sidewalk cafés. Check dates and addresses with tourist offices.

➕ C2

Tourist information (for Ardèche) ✉ 4 cours du Palais, 07000 Privas ☎ 04 75 64 04 66; www.ardeche-tourisme.com

Aubenas tourist information ✉ 4 boulevard Gambetta ☎ 04 75 89 02 03; www.inforoutes-ardeche.fr/tourisme/aubenas

Vallon-Pont-d'Arc tourist information ✉ 1 place de l'Ancienne Gare ☎ 04 75 88 04 01; www.vallon-pont-darc.com

Château d'Aubenas ☎ 04 75 87 81 11 🕐 Daily 11–5, in summer; 2–3, rest of year 📖 $

GORGES DU TARN

The most popular section of les Causses (see page 185) is this canyon dividing the *causses* of Méjean and Sauveterre. In summer, what is otherwise a peaceful and charming drive along the riverside D907b can resemble a crowded parking lot, as seemingly everyone from a 100-mile radius appears to have decided to take the same trip. Either grin and bear it in your quest for natural beauty, or do the trip before mid-July or after early September. The big attraction is the stretch of the riverbank between le Rozier-Peyreleau and Ste.-Énimie, wedged between 1,600-foot cliffs teeming with waterfalls. If you are fit, suitably shod and can find a place to park, follow marked trails up the rocks to gaze down on the shimmering waters below. Alternately, take a boat trip from la Malène through les Détroits (the straits).

➕ B2

Le Rozier-Peyreleau tourist information ✉ Siège au Rozier ☎ 05 65 60 60 89

Centre d'Information du Parc des Cévennes ✉ La Malène ☎ 04 66 48 50 77

LE LIORAN

From December to April, le Lioran is the capital of winter sports in the Cantal area. Nestled in pine forests just below the 4,245-foot Col de Cère, le Lioran attracts visitors year round. During the ski months, much of the attention is focused on nearby Super Lioran. The largest ski resort in the Massif Central, it's more a family destination than a chic jet-set spot. Cable cars and 24 ski lifts serve 40 miles of slopes and plenty of cross-country ski trails in winter and carry hang gliders and hikers to the crest of the 6,086-foot Plomb du Cantal and other peaks during summer and fall.

Tailor-made itineraries for touring the area – from torchlight ski rambles to mountain bike trails – are available year round. Since le Lioran isn't completely defined by mass-market winter sports, you can easily look beyond the obvious resort pizzerias to discover rustic taverns serving traditional mountain dishes.

➕ B3

Tourist information ✉ 15300 Lioran-et-Super-Lioran ☎ 04 71 49 50 08; www.lelioran.com

LE PUY-EN-VELAY

Crane your neck from the enchanting and awe-inspiring town, built in an old volcanic crater, to see the improbable chapel perched high on a rocky outcrop, way above the streets of le Puy-en-Velay. The 11th-century Chapelle St.-Michel-d'Aighuile sits like an eagle's nest on the horizon and upstages the town's cathedral, a similarly Moorish-style edifice with a rare vault of oblong domes and exquisite cloisters. Look above the cathedral for another rocky peak, capped by a 52-foot statue of the Madonna and Child. Climb up to the statue's viewing platform to look down at the many levels of this quaint town. For over 300 years, le Puy has been a center of lace-making – classes in the craft are held in the town center.

➕ C3

Tourist information ✉ place du Breuil ☎ 04 71 09 38 41; www.ot-lepuyenvelay.fr

RIOM

Until Clermont and Montferrand united to form Clermont-Ferrand (see pages 181–84), this city at the foot of the Puy-de-Dôme was the prime candidate for capital of the Auvergne. Its blend of volcanic rock and Renaissance architecture creates elegant streets and impressive private residences. The local

The Chapelle St.-Michel-d'Aighuile perches on a volcanic outcrop above le Puy-en-Velay

museum of the Auvergne is worth a visit, as is the Église Notre-Dame-du-Marthuret with its 14th-century statue La Vierge à l'Oiseau, with the infant Christ caressing a goldfinch. Appreciate excellent views over the rooftops from the city's old clock tower and visit the octagonal room housing the workings of the clock itself. A short excursion from the town takes in the ruined fortress of Tournoel, which looks down on the source of the region's famous Volvic mineral water spring. Visit the Maison de la Pierre in Volvic to learn about the region's lava stone.

➕ B4

Tourist information ✉ 16 rue du Commerce ☎ 04 73 38 59 45; www.riom-auvergne.com

Maison de la Pierre ✉ 63530 Volvic ☎ 04 73 33 56 92 🕐 Daily every hour 10–noon and 2–6, May–Sep.; 10–noon and 2–5, Mar.–Apr. and Oct. 1–Nov. 15 📖 $

LAND OF VOLCANOES

Far from the lunar landscape that its name evokes, Parc Naturel Régional des Volcans d'Auvergne is a verdant natural park, home to chamois, marmots and wild sheep. Kites and peregrine falcons patrol the skies around the highest peak, Puy de Sancy, and rare butterflies are attracted to colorful wild flowers. This largest ensemble of volcanoes in Europe boasts dome-shaped hills and craters shaped like egg cups. Although the volcanoes have been dormant for centuries, they still course with heat far below the surface – as the hot springs of the spa towns prove.

The biggest and best on the visitor trail, the 4,806-foot Puy de Dôme, has some remnants of a Roman temple, several postcard and souvenir hawkers and a spectacular view over the city of Clermont-Ferrand and south toward the Monts Dore.

Puy de Sancy, at 6,184 feet, has more than an hour's calf-straining hike from the top of the cable car route to reach the highest views over the Cantal massif. On the eastern slopes of the Monts Dore massif is the delightful little village of Besse-en-Chandesse, with its 15th-century houses and a museum of skiing. Real-life action takes place on the courses of Super-Besse, a few miles away.

Rangers organize short walks and weeklong treks through the park, but individuals seeking a brief taste of fresh air and scenery should drive on the D680 to the Pas de Peyrol. Here you can walk to the 5,863-foot Puy Mary and return to the car within an hour.

Because most of the undulating land remains too much of a challenge for town planners and road builders and because the army commandeered great swaths of land, the area is remarkably unspoiled. Most towns and villages retain their medieval charm. Hikers will notice lava stone huts and shelters, known as *burons*. This is where herdsmen live during summer when they bring their flocks from the valleys to the sunny slopes.

The story of the Auvergne volcanoes is told at Vulcania, the European vulcanology park near Clermont-Ferrand. The science park is hollowed into the landscape it represents and has underground exhibitions exploring the role of volcanoes in the creation of the earth and other planets in our solar system.

Centre d'Information du Parc Naturel Régional des Volcans d'Auvergne ✉ Monlosier, 63970 Aydat ☎ 04 73 65 64 00; www.volcan-auvergne.com
Vulcania, Parc Européen du Volcanisme ✉ route de Mazaye, 63230 St.-Ours-les-Roches ☎ 08 20 82 78 28 (toll call); www.vulcania.com 🕐 Daily 9–7, Jul.–Aug.; Mon.–Fri. 10–6, Sat.–Sun. 9–7, in Jun.; Wed.–Fri. 10–6, Sat.–Sun. 9–7, Apr.–May and Sep.–Oct.; Wed.–Sun. 10–6, in Mar. Also open late Feb. 🍴 3 Restaurants 💳 $$

Massif Central

Below: A dormant volcano in the Parc Naturel Régional des Volcans d'Auvergne

Opposite: Puy de Dôme seen across the surrounding fields

Massif Central

DRIVE: SPAS OF THE BELLE ÉPOQUE

Distance: 195 miles Time: 3 to 4 days

Discover the pleasures and leisures of a bygone era at a civilized pace. This summer drive through the Auvergne's countryside (some roads are closed in winter) takes in many of the bubbling springs where generations have come to enjoy the waters.

Ornate pergolas and regal architecture reflect the golden age of each favored resort. Even if you've no desire to sample the curative spring waters, you still will appreciate the ritual of afternoon tea, listening to music at the park bandstand and taking in evening entertainment. Nightfall means dressing in your best clothes for the casino, indulging in fine cuisine at an elegant restaurant or enjoying a night at the opera or even late-night flutters at the race track in Vichy. Known as queen of the spa towns, Vichy pampers the "haves" with all the pomp and splendor of the belle epoque and Second Empire.

Turn right from the N209 to the N9, then left on the D42. Turn left again to the D35, pausing in the exquisite village of Charroux. Continue on the D35, turning left on the D68 at St.-Bonnet-de-Rochefort. Head right on the D35 and left

Hot water can be enjoyed at Chaudes-Aigues

on the D37 to rejoin N9, passing Gannat to Riom (see page 188). Follow the D446 until turning right on the D985 to Châtelguyon.

At the spa resort of Châtelguyon, the style could best be described as art nouveau meets Hollywood. Guy de Maupassant was inspired to write *Mont-Oriol* after staying here.

Back to the D446, then take the D986 to Volvic (see page 189). From the D15 turn right on the D762 and left on the D941 via Clermont-Ferrand (see pages 181–84). Follow the D69B-D68 into Royat.

Just outside Clermont is the Roman-favored spa resort of Royat. Although its Source Eugénie spring is popular today with French women concerned about cellulite, visitors also visit the town's workshop, which specializes in cutting semi-precious stones. Attractive jewelry can be purchased at fair prices.

Back on the D68, turn left on the D941A, stopping at the Col de la Moreno. Then filter right on the D216–27 and join the D983-D996 to le Mont-Dore, stopping at the magnificent Col de Guéry, landscaped by volcanoes and glaciers.

In the heart of volcano country (see page 191), the mountain resort of le Mont-Dore was a place of worship long before the era of the body beautiful. Celts believed gods lived within the crater. Here the Romans built their largest temple to Mercury, some walls and steps of which remain. Nineteenth-century scientists chose the site for an observatory, and the 20th century saw the era of golf. Every generation comes for the views and thermal baths. The Byzantine spa and funicular railway are listed monuments.

Continue 3 miles along the D130 to la Bourboule.

With the "rock of the fairies," the wooded Park Fenêstre's little railway and lake, pastel-tinted bridges over the Dordogne and discreet grandeur, la Bourboule would be a joy at any altitude. Add pure air as refreshing as the waters of the spring, and you understand why it's so popular. Take the cable car to the Charlannes plateau at 4,100 feet. In winter, sports lovers come here to ski. In summer, parents bring asthmatic children here to breathe.

Head back to le Mont-Dore via the D130, then take the D996, turning left after Col de la Croix Morand on the D617. Take a right on the D5, pausing at Murol-Château, then join the D996. A left on the D150 leads into St.-Nectaire.

St.-Nectaire is a spa resort that boasts an interesting 12th-century church in the upper village of St.-Nectaire-le-Haut. Waters are said to help with weight loss and stress.

Follow the D996 to Issoire, then join the A75. Take the exit at junction 28, Rodez-St.-Flour center. Leave St.-Flour on the D921 to Chaudes-Aigues.

Europe's warmest natural springs produce 180-degree waters to heat Chaudes-Aigues itself. And this town is a delightful place to explore.

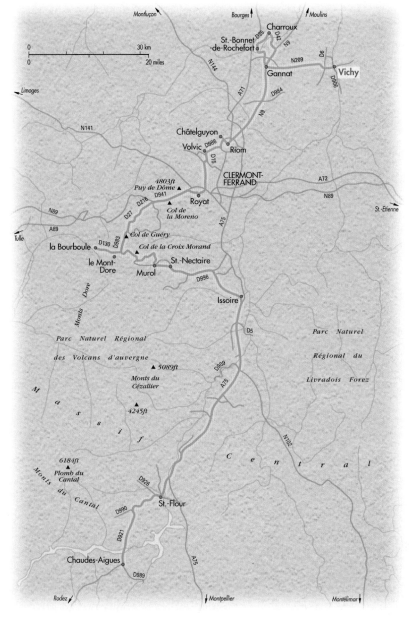

ALPS AND THE RHÔNE VALLEY

*"*DRAMATIC mountain ranges and a rich cultural heritage. This is the perfect country for walking, driving, skiing and developing an appetite.*"*

Opposite: The village of Combloux with stunning views of the Chaîne des Aravis mountains

Alps and the Rhône Valley

ALPS AND THE RHÔNE VALLEY

For the adventurer, this is the region of soaring glaciers and mountain ranges. For the trencherman, it's the pinnacle of haute cuisine. Whatever the lure, a vacation here is presented in wide screen. The grandeur of nature, lakes, mountains, gorges and vast areas of woodland may have been reined in by cable cars, modern roads and the architecture of electricity. Although electricity lines and power stations mar the occasional view, they do allow other vistas to be appreciated in comfort. Traffic fumes around the Mont-Blanc tunnel, which sometimes spoil summer panoramas, are the price paid for open borders with Italy, but the pristine waters of Lake Geneva (Lac Léman) show Swiss concern for cleanliness. The truth is that the region of the Rhône benefits from the environmental overspill of its neighbors, as well as from its own majestic Alpine pleasures of lakeside spas and ski resorts. Around the nougat town of Montelimar is the scenery of Provence. The Drôme and Ardèche landscapes are the continuation of the splendors of the Massif Central. Beaujolais and Macon have much in common with the slopes of Burgundy.

Whitewater rafting in the Sixt-Fer-à-Cheval nature reserve

Cosmopolitan Pleasures

The contrast between town and country, mountain resort and nature park is the main attraction of the area. Lyon is a city with a rich cultural and architectural heritage, yet it's just a short drive from many a rural idyll. Its key high-speed train link between Paris and the Mediterranean, and the famous Autoroute du Soleil guarantee Lyon's cosmopolitan mix of movers and shakers, as in its trading heyday on the Roman tin, and later silk, routes.

However, the regional capital has no monopoly on culture. In winter, the money moves to the mountains, and leisure resorts woo the arts. Great paintings from centuries past line gallery walls in towns such as Grenoble, and modern artists set up a colony in Pérouges.

Raise a Glass

A heritage of good food in cities and villages alike (see page 199) means that local wines may be found wherever you visit. Besides the wine of Beaujolais, the region has its red wines of Côtes du Rhône, the best known of which are Crozes-Hermitage and Condrieu. A small area of the Savoie produces splendid white wines. Try the clear and

Alps and the Rhône Valley

ALPS AND THE RHÔNE VALLEY

Skiers relax outside a mountain-top restaurant above Val d'Isère

fruity Cruet or Crépy, with its light intriguing bouquet from the Altesse vines. Locally popular everyday rosés and reds are produced here, too.

Capital of Winter Sports

Three Winter Olympic seasons – at Chamonix (1924), Grenoble (1968) and Albertville (1992) – and dozens of annual championship skiing events keep the French Alps in top form. With 180 resorts serving 3,600 miles of courses, this is the world's largest fully equipped skiing area. Three massive interconnected circuits offer unrivaled scope, each for the price of a single pass: les Portes de Soleil with 400 miles of linked runs along the Franco-Swiss border; les Trois Vallées, a similar circuit; and l'Espace Killy, named for Olympic gold medalist Jean-Claude Killy. The last contains 190 miles of connected slopes for serious downhill skiers.

The vast ski country has color-coded runs suitable for every ability: green for beginners, blue for intermediates, red for experienced skiers and black for James Bond-standard sportsmen. Lifts and cable cars are continually renewed and improved. Weekly passes are the

sensible option. Resorts range from the traditional mountain village, with its slate-roofed wooden chalets and cheery, old-fashioned knitwear boutiques, to the functional complexes built since the 1950s. Slopes and lifts reach the front doors of modern hotels. Megève, St.-Gervais and Val d'Isère are among traditional destinations safely wrapped in environmental protection orders. The tailor-made contemporary resorts include Avoriaz (a motorist-free zone), la Plagne and les Arcs.

Newer sports, such as snowboarding, are as well catered to as conventional skiing these days, and dog-sled rides, snowshoe hikes and adrenaline sports feature on many itineraries. Larger destinations now market themselves to non-skiers as well, packing the winter season with festivals on themes from film to stand-up comedy.

The region is big enough to cater to the lone adventurer as much as the sporting package tourist. Plenty of locations away from the ski hubs attract those who like to challenge the elements. Against the snows of winter and rock faces of summer, bright day-glo colors easily identify adventure-sports enthusiasts. The winter season is from early December to April, with good value weekend rates available outside French school holidays. There is no guarantee of good weather, but most destinations are equipped with snow-making machinery. Recent years have seen winters that are milder and later than the calendar assumes. Higher resorts are open earlier and continue into May. In summer, glacier skiing is an option at Val-Thorens, Val d'Isère, Tignes, la Plagne, les-Deux-Alpes and l'Alpe-d'Huez.

Tables of the Rhône

Food matters in the Rhône Valley. Where Paris sways between fashions, Lyon manages the complex balancing act of maintaining the finest traditions of gastronomy and steering each new wave. Maybe the common sense stems from the fact that the original innovators of Lyonaise cuisine were women (*les Mères,* the mothers).

There is life outside the important kitchens of the city. Lyon's bistros, known as *bouchons,* are lively, informal and welcoming establishments, serving up the famous *andouillette* (small sausage made of chitterlings) in mustard sauce; and *quenelles* (pike dumplings) in pink Nantua sauce.

After skiing, savor Savoyard favorites, including cheeses for all courses, the Tomme de Savoie, Beaufort, Emmental or Reblochon; a fondue with bread or raclette of melted cheese with ham as a warming fireside treat; or *tartiflette* (baked cheese and potatoes) as an informal snack. At the end of a meal, order walnut pie from Grenoble, a chocolate dessert from a Lyon confectioner, or in the fall, fresh wild berries from the woods.

Nyons produces the only *appellation d'origine contrôlée* olive oil in France. In the district of Drôme, the oil is outshone only by the value of the

Enjoying the heritage of good food in Lyon

legendary truffles. You will sometimes hear of a "truffle market" being held in town, but you will search in vain for neat tables of the sought-after delicacy. Chefs come with wads of bank notes to buy the best available, but the cash-only transactions take place in cafés and bars. Truffle farmers keep their wares discreetly in their deep coat pockets.

Secrets of the Greats

The great chefs of France still hail from Lyon and its outlying towns. Two legendary names are happy to pass on their skills at a price. Philippe Chavent holds court in the famous 16th-century Tour Rose (see page 205), where even absolute beginners can attend his cookery sessions. Individuals may enroll for the day at the National School of Culinary Arts at the Château de Viviers. Courses on the basics and classic French dishes are supervised by the maestro, seventh-generation chef Paul Bocuse.

École Nationale des Arts Culinaires
✉ Château du Viviers, 69131 Ecully (just outside Lyon) ☎ 04 78 43 36 10

Alps and the Rhône Valley

LYON

Lyon has scores of unmissable sights, but the greatest of them all is the city itself. Just like the Pyramids, St. Petersburg and Venice, the entire historic center of Lyon has been declared a World Heritage Site.

Almost 1,250 acres have been awarded monument status, so rich are the streets, hills and riverbanks in fabulously preserved memories of 2,000 dramatic years. Unlike ordinary

museums, this area is the vibrant, pulsating heart of France's second-busiest city. Rather than preserving the past under glass, the city center continues to develop with a keen eye on conservation. Parking lots are moved underground, and views remain unspoiled – except perhaps by the uninspiring pencil-shaped Credit Lyonnais tower.

The tower, along with the business and conference district, needn't concern you. With distinctive hills and a medieval quarter almost entirely

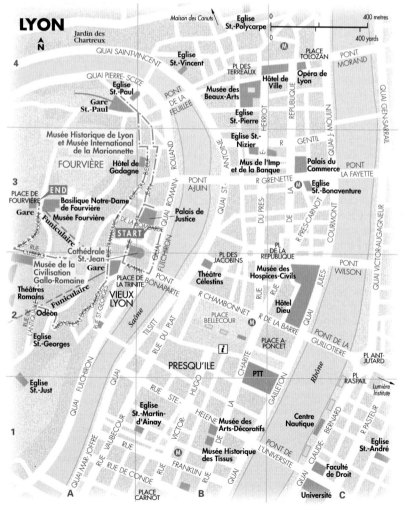

LYON

0   400 metres
0   400 yards

King Louis XIV parades on horseback at place Bellecour in the heart of old Lyon

surrounded by water, Lyon boasts enough historic landmarks to make the visitor feel comfortable about exploring on foot or by the well-organized public transportation system.

Since the city has never had time to stagnate, each era saw a new section of Lyon being developed. First to flourish were the hills of Fourvière and Croix-Rousse in 43 BC, when Romans and Gauls coexisted as the city proved a useful rallying point for Roman colonial armies marching north and west. As Rome declined and France grew, so did the medieval Vieux (Old) Lyon, below and between the hills.

The very center of this section is the Presqu'île, or peninsula (literally "nearly an island"). The dangling strip of land is almost completely surrounded by two rivers, the Saône and the Rhône. Most main sites may be found here and on the Fourvière bank of the Saône.

The church controlled medieval Lyon. Renaissance prosperity led to merchants and the monarchy taking over the city. Stunningly ostentatious houses sprung up during this period. The silk trade led to the development of the Croix-Rousse, and 19th-century civic confidence brought grand boulevards to the wider city.

Arts and Pleasures

Throughout its history, Lyon has garnered a deserved reputation as a center of good living. Gastronomically, the city is without equal (see page 198). Food is presented with a flourish, and shop windows and market stalls inspire unseemly drooling among passers-by. In fact, the local phrase for browsing for food is *lèche-vitrines*, literally meaning "window-licking."

Top-grade opera, ballet, concerts, theater and exhibitions run either in their formal fall-to-spring seasons or in world-class festivals, such as the biennial Contemporary Art Festival, held in odd years. Besides the great sites and monuments, at least two dozen fine museum collections are worth a visit.

Street culture is best seen in spectacular murals, painted walls on the outside of buildings. Trompe l'oeil fantasy worlds and famous faces from the city's past and present are favored themes. Bars and fashionable cafés buzz well into the night in the streets of Vieux Lyon. This is also the only French city aside from a seaside, mountain or lake resort to nurture a casino. Great shopping abounds around town, especially near place Bellecour and Part Dieu station.

As far from Hollywood as you could imagine, Lyon was the birthplace of cinema. Antoine Lumière encouraged his sons Louis and Auguste in their experiments, which in March 1895 resulted in the launch of the Lumière Cinématographe. The family's first film "Workers Leaving the Factory Gates" was an instant hit. The story of the brothers and the cinematic revolution that their work inspired is the theme of the Lumière Institute, a combined movie and museum complex that stands on the site of the family's groundbreaking first picture show.

Pick a Card

The essential companion for a city visit is the Lyon City Card. Valid for one, two or three days and sold at the tourist office, the pass offers unlimited use of public transportation, guided tours and river cruises, as well as admission to the main museums.

ESSENTIAL INFORMATION

TOURIST INFORMATION
• place Bellecour ☎ 04 72 77 69 69; www.lyon-france.com 🚇 Bellecour
• 3 avenue Aristide Briand ☎ 04 78 68 13 20 🚇 Gratte-Ciel

URBAN TRANSPORTATION
An excellent bus, tramway and subway system runs from 5 a.m. to midnight, and a funicular railway climbs Fourvière hill. Tourist offices and stations provide free route maps. Recognize stations by the sign M. Tickets, sold individually, in discounted books *(carnets)* of 10 or a one-day pass (Ticket Liberté) may be used on buses or subway. The Lyon City Card offers additional travel on riverboats as well as museum access are available from tourist offices. Taxis may be hailed in the streets or call ☎ 04 78 28 23 23 or 04 72 10 86 86. A high-speed train service from Perrache and Part-Dieu stations links Lyon with the rest of France – Paris in 2 hours 4 minutes, Marseille in 2 hours 45 minutes.

AIRPORT INFORMATION
Aéoport International de Lyon-Saint-Exupéry (☎ 04 72 22 72 21; www.lyon.aeroport.fr) is east of the city at Satolas. The Satobus shuttle operates between the airport and the railroad stations every 20 minutes ☎ 04 72 68 72 17; www.satobus.com

CLIMATE – Average highs and lows

JAN.	FEB.	MAR.	APR.	MAY	JUN.	JUL.	AUG.	SEP.	OCT.	NOV.	DEC.
5°C	8°C	12°C	14°C	20°C	23°C	27°C	26°C	22°C	17°C	10°C	7°C
41°F	46°F	54°F	57°F	68°F	73°F	81°F	79°F	72°F	63°F	50°F	45°F
0°C	1°C	3°C	5°C	10°C	14°C	17°C	16°C	12°C	8°C	4°C	2°C
32°F	34°F	37°F	41°F	50°F	57°F	63°F	61°F	54°F	46°F	39°F	36°F

Vieux Lyon from the Saône river with the Basilique Notre-Dame de Fourvière on the skyline

LYON SIGHTS

Key to symbols

🗺 map coordinates refer to the Lyon map on page 200; sights below are highlighted in yellow on the map.

✉ address or location ☎ telephone number
🕐 opening times Ⓜ nearest métro 🛈 information
🎟 admission charge: $$$ more than €10, $$ €5–€10, $ less than €5

CATHÉDRALE ST.-JEAN

Built between the 12th and 15th centuries, the cathedral has the expected Gothic facade and a grand rose window dating from 1393. St.-Jean still has its original 13th- and 14th-century stained glass. The main attraction for visitors is a 16th-century astronomic clock by Swiss craftsman Lippius. It chimes at noon, 2 p.m., 3 p.m. and 4 p.m.

🗺 A2, A3, B2, B3 ✉ place St.-Jean ☎ 04 78 42 28 25 🕐 Mon.–Fri. 8–noon and 2–7:30, Sat.–Sun. 8–noon and 2–5 Ⓜ Vieux Lyon 🎟 Free

FOURVIÈRE

A funicular train saves your breath for the breathtaking views from the top of the hill that dominates every other view of the city. A good place to start or finish any tour of Lyon, the hill shows off the rooftops of Vieux Lyon, the slopes of the Croix-Rousse and the Presqu'île to form the ultimate panorama. The views continue along a walkway to the Hauteurs Park and Jardin du Rosaire, which link the districts of St.-Jean and Loyasse. At the crest of

the hill is the chunky fortresslike Basilique Notre-Dame de Fourvière, opened in 1896. It's noteworthy for Byzantine mosaics, Gothic stained-glass windows, marble statues and its crypt. Nearby, the 12th-century oratory and 18th-century chapel, with its statue of the Virgin, are worth a visit. The Fourvière Museum has a splendid collection of sacred art. Television is beamed into local homes courtesy of a transmission tower reminiscent of Eiffel's in Paris.

🗺 A3

Musée de Fourvière ✉ 8 place Fourvière ☎ 04 78 25 13 01 🕐 Daily 10–noon and 2–6, Apr. 1 to early Dec. Ⓜ Vieux Lyon then funicular to Fourvière 🎟 $

MUSÉE DE LA CIVILISATION GALLO-ROMAINE

When Munatius Plancus founded the city of Lugdunum on the Fourvière hill in the ancient capital of Gaul, he simply wanted to provide shelter for the veterans of Julius Caesar's armies. He could not have imagined that so much of the original construction would still draw crowds 2,000 years later. Two Roman theaters from 15 BC still pull in huge audiences for summer classical and rock concerts. The 10,000-capacity open-air Théâtre and the Odéon, which once had a bronze roof, as well as traces of public baths, all can be explored free of charge. It's better, however, to pay to see the exhibitions at the adjacent Gallo-Roman Civilization Museum first to begin to understand life in Roman France. The museum is superbly designed with underground passages to keep the 21st century out of

The Roman Théâtre at Lyon could seat up to 10,000 people

sight. Intelligently displayed stone coffins, statues, bronze, mosaics, gold and silverware are explained using a wealth of English-language material.

➕ A2 ✉ Museum: 17 rue Cléberg. Theaters: 8 rue de l'Antiquaille ☎ 04 72 38 81 90 🕐 Museum: Tue.–Sun. 10–6, Mar.–Oct. Theaters: daily 7 a.m.–9 p.m., mid-Apr. to mid-Sep.; 7–7, rest of year 🚇 Vieux Lyon, then funicular to Minimes 💷 Museum $; theaters free

MUSÉE HISTORIQUE DE LYON ET MUSÉE INTERNATIONAL DE LA MARIONNETTE

Two enchantingly different museums share an elegant Renaissance home in the imposing mansion Hôtel de Gadagne: the Museum of Lyon History and the International Puppet Museum.

The Museum of Lyon History taste-fully presents the city from the Middle Ages to the 19th century. Just as the Gallo-Roman museum contains an impressive model of the first-century city, maps, drawings and engravings show the developing city through later centuries.

The International Puppet Museum has all manner of puppets that developed the nation's favorite creation, Guignol, which first was performed in the city. The fame of the satirical and politically incorrect

puppet show, with its farcical, conniving and nagging stereotypes, spread through France and the Continent.

➕ B3 ✉ 1 place du Petit-Collège ☎ 04 78 42 03 61 🕐 Wed.–Mon. 10:45–6 🚇 Vieux Lyon 💷 $ (free to all on Thu. ℹ The Zonzons company puts on Guignol performances for children Wed., Sat. and Sun. afternoons, and for adults on selected evenings at 2 rue Louis-Carrand (☎ 04 78 28 92 57)

PLACE BELLECOUR

The heart of Vieux Lyon, the Presqu'île and the city itself is the grand sweeping regal square midway between the two rivers. With glorious disregard for the limited land available on the peninsula, city fathers decided to create one of the biggest squares in Europe, with an elegant park at its center. The landscaping was designed by Robert de Cotle to disguise the fact that the Eastern section of the square is narrower than the west. Gravel paths and shady trees prove popular for the continual parade of visitors, watched over by a statue of a virile King Louis XIV on horseback, serving as a reminder that the square originally was known as place Royale. From the north, you've a good view of the Fourvière hill and basilica.

➕ B2 🚇 Bellecour

Lyon Town Hall – surrounded and adorned by statuary

WALK: WORLD HERITAGE SITE

Refer to route marked on city map on page 200

This 2-mile stretch of Renaissance houses, secret passageways and Roman theaters will give a flavor of the World Heritage Site in the center of Lyon.

From the 24 columns of the Palais de Justice, turn right along quai Fulchiron and right again into avenue Adolphe Max for Cathédrale St.-Jean.

Behind the cathedral, visit remains of St.-Etienne and Ste.-Croix churches. On rue de la Bombarde, pass the tax-collector's home Maison du Chamarier, the first Renaissance house in town. Cross rue St.-Jean, passing the Maison des Avocats and its magnificently arched gallery. In the 16th century, it was known as the Croix-d'Or Inn.

At 54 rue St.-Jean, enter the Grande Traboule through four buildings and courtyards before arriving at 27 rue du Bœuf. Double back to rue St.-Jean, and find the traboule opposite at No. 27, then walk through two small courtyards with 16th-century galleries to 6 rue des Trois-Maries. Then, return to rue St.-Jean and admire the architecture, especially at Nos. 24 and 28.

At place du Change, Maison Thomassin has a Gothic zodiac facade.

Follow rue Lainerie to the flamboyantly Gothic facade of No. 14. Continue on to the Romanesque and Gothic Église St.-Paul. Cross the square and take rue Juiverie. No. 4, the Maison Henri-IV, was built under the reign of François I.

At 8 rue Juiverie, the Maison Bullioud, with a gallery by Philibert Delorme, shows the skill of an architect who went to work for a king.

Continue to place du Petit Collège and its 16th-century Hôtel de Gadagne, home to the history museum (see page 204). Take rue du Bœuf to pause at No. 16 to appreciate the Tour Rose (pink tower) with its famous hanging gardens and break your journey at the splendid restaurant. Follow rue Tramassac until place de la Trinité. No. 2 rue St.-Georges leads you to some extraordinary oval galleries. Make your way up montée du Gourguillon, and then proceed right up rue de l'Antiquaille. Turn left at rue Cléberg to the Gallo-Roman museum, with access to the Roman theaters. Take a right on rue Roger Radisson to place Fourvière, the basilica, and panoramic views of the city from the esplanade.

Bacchus and friends celebrate with a glass or three of Beaujolais – a mural in the Juliénas winery

BEAUJOLAIS

Best known for its wines, Beaujolais country is a sunny distraction on the main highway to the south of France. Close enough to Lyon to benefit from the culture of gastronomy yet individual enough to retain its own flavors, this area of gentle hills and neat vineyards is pretty, welcoming and a pleasant detour from serious touring. Parts of the region have been dubbed Beaujolais Tuscany for the effect of the sunlight on rich golden stone. In Haut Beaujolais, villages are built of sturdy granite. Everywhere little churches prod the skyline, and wooden boards by the roadside invite drivers to stop and visit wine cellars.

The 54,000 acres between Mâcon and Lyon produce popular red wines. Unlike the vintages of neighboring Burgundy and the châteaux of Bordeaux, these don't change hands at hundreds of dollars per bottle. The vast majority of local wines are made to be shared informally around the dinner table.

There are three distinct types of Beaujolais: the highest-quality Beaujolais *crus,* the everyday Beaujolais *villages* and the famous Beaujolais *nouveau.* The Beaujolais *crus* comprise 10 fine wines – Brouilly, Chénas, Chiroubles, Côte-de-Brouilly, Fleurie, Juliénas, Morgon, Moulin-à-Vent, Régnié and Saint Amour. These are worth saving a few years.

Brouilly, in particular, is one of few red wines best served chilled. On the edges of the better slopes grow the Beaujolais *villages,* good-quality, everyday wines.

The vast majority of vineyards produce Beaujolais *nouveau,* bright red, fun and fruity country wine that is best drunk young – so young in fact that the third Thursday in November sees the famous Beaujolais Nouveau race. When the new wine is released at the stroke of midnight, vehicles hit the icy roads in a mad road race to be the first to bring the new wines to European capital cities, where commuters at railroad stations give their verdict to TV cameras.

Every other town seems to have its modest wine museum. One of the best is Le Hameau en Beaujolais (www.hameauenbeaujolais.com) in Romanèche-Thorins, which sits in the shadow of the windmill that gives its name to Moulin-à-Vent. Run by George Duboeuf, probably the finest name in Beaujolais viticulture, the tour features traditional wine making and modern bottling, audiovisual presentations and a wine tasting in the cellar. Rhône Tourist Board provides itineraries and details of cellar visits.

Comité Départemental du Tourisme du Rhône
✉ B.P. 5009, 69245 Lyon cedex 05 ☎ 04 72 61 78 90;
www.rhonetourisme.org

The Thiou river moats the Palais de L'Île in Annecy

REGIONAL SIGHTS

Key to symbols

🚼 map coordinates refer to the region map on page 197; sights below are highlighted in yellow on the map.

🖂 address or location ☎ telephone number

🕐 opening times 🍴 restaurant on site or nearby

🚌 nearest bus or tram route ℹ️ information

🎟 admission charge: $$$ more than €10, $$ €5–€10, $ less than €5

ANNECY

Postcard perfect, this charming town center – on the banks of the tourist-magnet lake of the same name – has a permanent air of having just been dusted. Fresh flowers perch on every surface; window sills, railings, bridges and even road sides are ablaze with color. Bracing fresh air and numerous waterways add to the air of constant cleanliness. Once upon a time, the air was less than fragrant and the water stagnant and polluted. Now the center of this wealthy town sparkles, and the waters are rich in trout and char. In season, the international crowds that fill the streets and line up for boat trips take the edge off the glow, but there is plenty to enjoy in the quaint, canal-veined quarter where the Thiou river flows into the lake. Enjoy Renaissance frescoes in the Église St.-Maurice, the water-bordered prison on the Palais de L'Île and an interesting local museum in the château that once was home to the counts of Geneva and dukes of Savoy.

🚼 B3

Tourist information 🖂 1 rue Jean-Jaures ☎ 04 50 45 00 33; www.lac-annecy.com

BOURGET, LAC DU

The spa town of Aix-les-Bains is the principal resort of this long, slender lake between high mountain ridges. With all the traditional diversions of a 19th-century spa resort, and enchanting promenade gardens, Aix is conducive to taking mountain air in a domestic environment. Modern water sports are available on the lake, and lunch cruises are ideal for admiring the scenery. Another interesting boat trip takes visitors to the final resting place of the dukes of Savoy, on the west bank of Lac du Bourget. Generations of the ruling family were interred at the mausoleum of Hautecombe Abbey at St.-Pierre-de-Curtille. The abbey was given a Gothic facelift in the 19th century and today is popular with lovers of Gregorian chant, who come to enjoy the services here. A pleasant walking tour from le Bourget-du-Lac, which has a notable 11th-century priory, leads up the slopes of Mont du

Alps and the Rhône Valley

The elephantine 1838 fountain commemorates the rebuilding of Chambéry

Chat and crosses the Col du Chat, culminating in excellent vistas.

🕂 B3
Tourist information ✉ place Maurice-Mollard, Aix-les-Bains ☎ 04 79 35 05 92; www.aixlesbains.com
Abbaye de Hautecombe ✉ 73310 St.-Pierre-de-Curtille ☎ 04 79 54 26 12 🕘 Wed.–Mon. 10–11:30, 2–5 💷 Donation

BRIANÇON

Since the days of the Roman Empire, Briançon has been the highest town in Europe. At 4,330 feet, the town is closer to the sun than any other, and accordingly the walls are liberally decorated with sundials. In the 18th century, these were painted on public buildings and churches, but by the 19th century they became the fashion for private houses. Frescoes with hour lines and mottos in Latin, French or local dialect range from naive clock faces to works of art in their own right. The sundial on the Cordeliers church has Louis XV ribbons and wreaths. Later domestic examples by the artist Zarbulla have trompe l'oeil birds and flowers, and young designers with a 21st century take on tradition are rediscovering the old art. Briançon stands at the crossroads of the Alps, with the Col de Montgenèvre kept open throughout the winter. The town is completely encased by citadel walls built by Louis XIV's legendary defensive architect Sébastien Le Prestre de Vauban, whose fortresses protected the entire nation's borders. This particular fortification has been embellished over the centuries, and extra forts have been added above the town. The town serves the ski resort of Serre-Chevalier.

🕂 C2
Tourist information ✉ 1 place du Temple ☎ 04 92 21 08 50; www.ot-briancon.fr

CHAMBÉRY

No one has heard of the Shroud of Chambéry. That is because when the dukes of Savoy moved their seat of government away from this Alpine town in the mid-16th century, the famous relic went with the power and the glory to the new capital in Turin. Today's administrators busy themselves with the affairs of the Savoie district, but memories of the way things once were may be discovered at the ducal château that dominates the town. Constantly reinvented and extended from the 13th to 19th centuries, the château's buildings include a beautiful Gothic chapel. Try to hear the grand carillon – a majestic peal of 70 bells from the chapel tower.

The old town around the château is a splendid labyrinth of winding streets and secret alleyways, similar to the *traboules* of Lyon. Private houses reflect the Italian influences of the Savoy dynasty, with ornate baroque stucco facades and wrought-iron decoration. Other streets have charming stone houses and shops with wooden shutters.

In the Curial quarter just outside the medieval district, the state seized Franciscan, Ursuline and other convents after the French Revolution. Napoléon himself decided to convert them into military barracks, along the lines of Les Invalides in Paris. Since 1975 the town has adapted the buildings as administrative and cultural centers. Other museums include the Musée Savoisien; the home of the writer Jean-Jacques Rousseau, which presents costumed tours in summer; and the Musée des Beaux-Arts, home to France's finest collection of Italian art outside the Louvre. Chambéry finally became French in 1860 after the treaty of Turin and a referendum among its citizens brought Savoy back within France's borders.

Savoy boasts that it's the home of true French gastronomy. All the elements of the national cuisine have origins in the regal demands of the former kingdom that stretched across the modern national borders of the Alps. Two-day cookery courses in town combine kitchen lore from the past 600 years with contemporary tips and recipes from top chefs.

➕ B3

Tourist information ✉ 24 boulevard de la Colonne ☎ 04 79 33 42 47; www.chambery-tourisme.com
Château des Ducs de Savoie ✉ Place du Château ☎ 04 79 33 42 47 🕐 Tours daily 10:30 (except Sun.), 2:30, 3:30 and 4:30, Jul.–Aug.; 2:30, May–Jun. and Sep. 📖 $
Musée des Beaux-Arts ✉ place du Palais Justice ☎ 04 79 33 75 03 🕐 Wed.–Mon. 10–noon and 2–6 📖 $

A sightseeing cruiser returns to Evian-les-Bains from Lake Geneva

EVIAN-LES-BAINS

Probably France's best-known mineral water, Evian made its name as a spa resort and still trades on the glories of its time as the elegant place to stay on the banks of Lac Léman (Lake Geneva). Guests at luxurious hotels with views across the Swiss border still spend their money on rejuvenating health treatments to reduce the stress lines grown at the roulette and blackjack tables of the flamboyant domed casino. Other visitors stay on their yachts in the marina. Those on modest budgets play miniature golf and enjoy the musical fountain.

Not all the thermal treatments are the exclusive province of the well-heeled. Simple rheumatic or post-natal cures are available at daily or single-session rates. Water sports, lake cruises and hikes are available for those wanting to explore. Regular festivals and exhibitions are among the on-site delights.

Evian is developing as something of a conference town, so out-of-season visitors might find themselves outnumbered by congress delegates sporting laminated name tags.

➕ C4

Tourist information ✉ place d'Allinges ☎ 04 50 75 04 26; www.eviantourism.com

A gondola lift provides the best view of Grenoble

GRENOBLE

Museums, parks, gardens and an air of civilization make Grenoble the perfect spot to recharge and reflect away from the ski society of the mountain resorts or rambler's solitude of the lake lands.

Cross the Isère river by the gondola lift *(téléphérique)* from the quai Stéphane Jay to the Fort de la Bastille, high above the university campus. Now home to a permanent exhibition of automobiles and motorbikes, the fort was originally a prison. City life begins behind the cable car station. Here from the neat Jardin de la Ville to the main square place Grenette and place St.-André is the hub of city life. The old city hall is now the Maison Stendhal, dedicated to the life of the author of *The Red and The Black*. Stendhal (real name Henry Beyle, 1783–1842) said of his hometown, "At the end of every street, there is a mountain." This fact is appreciated by drivers who can be at the ski resorts within half an hour.

Grenoble claims to have sown the seeds of the Revolution. When Louis XVI made moves to restrict local liberties, rioting citizens climbed onto the town roofs and attacked the army with tiles. The events of June 7, 1788, appropriately known as the Battle of Tiles, directly led the king to convene the Estates General in May 1789. The French Revolution was under way.

The defiant spirit continued, and the work of the French Resistance is celebrated in the modern Isère Resistance and Deportation Museum, featuring eyewitness accounts of life under the Nazi occupation.

The town is constantly modernized to meet new challenges. Since the 1968 Winter Olympics, the capital of the Alps has developed a lively arts scene to complement the sporting attractions.

In addition to theaters, a dance center and a respected chamber orchestra, the town has six museums. Visit the modern Musée de Grenoble, an example of 1990s architecture incorporating a medieval tower. Here is a spectacular art collection from the Old Masters to great moderns, including works by Marc Chagall, Pablo Picasso and René Magritte. Take the tram to Le Magasin, the national contemporary art center housed in Gustave Eiffel's splendid 1900 industrial building. For two weeks in December place Victor-Hugo is transformed into a Christmas market. One of the major seasonal fairs of the Alps, the event attracts up to 150,000 shoppers and revellers. Choirs singing carols, garlanded shopfronts and processions of children carrying lanterns set the scene for around 50 stalls selling traditional handmade gifts, cakes, candies and decorations.

✚ B2

Tourist information ✉ 14 rue de la République
☎ 04 76 42 41 41; www.grenoble-isere-tourisme.com
Le Magasin ✉ 155 cours Berriat ☎ 04 76 21 95 84
🕐 During exhibitions: Tue.–Sun. noon–7 🚋 Tram A
🍽 $ ⓘ Guided tours (free) Sat.–Sun. at 4
Musée de Grenoble ✉ 5 place Lavalette ☎ 04 76 63 44 44 🕐 Wed.–Mon. 11–7 (also Wed. 7–10 p.m.)
🍽 Restaurant and Café 🍽 $ ⓘ Guided tours Sat.–Sun. at 3
Maison Stendhal ✉ 20 Grande Rue ☎ 04 76 42 02 62 🕐 Tue.–Sun. 2–6, Easter–Oct. 31; Sat.–Sun. 2–6, rest of year 🍽 $

The Rhône-Alpes, extending as far as the Ardèche gorges, boasts nine nature parks and 28 nature reserves. Chamois and ibexes live among the firs, rhododendron and edelweiss, otters and beavers busy themselves at the water's edge, and deer and wild boars hide in the dense forest. Bird sanctuaries welcome snow finches and eagles.

Parc National des Ecrins

This European high mountain park is the largest national park in France. Small shepherds' villages make useful bases for hiking to the more accessible peaks. Tête de la Maye, at 8,265 feet, is a popular summer walk. Roads within the park link the eastern hamlets of Ailefroide, Pelvoux and Vallouise, where refreshments and supplies are available, for climbers heading to the Pré de Madame Carle. A mountain path with stunning views links the Pré to the Glacier Blanc. From the southern resort of la Chapelle-en-Valgaudemar, you can walk past waterfalls to the Lac du Lauzon. There is no entry to the park by road, but walkers can approach via the Oisans, Valgaudemar and Vallouise.

➕ B2–C2

Parc Naturel Régional du Queyras

The automobile-free village of St.-Véran, with its quaint sundials, fountains and crosses, is a charming time warp nestled in this protected area of mountain passes. A pilgrims' route from St.-Véran to the Chapelle Notre-Dame-de-Clausis is among the many paths through the peaks of the Italian border country. The contrast between the wooded slopes that mark much of the park and the Col d'Izoard route to Briançon is remarkable. The raw, rocky and barren landscape there is known as the Casse Déserte.

➕ C2

Parc National de la Vanoise

The great linked ski resorts of Courchevel, les Menuires, Méribel and Val Thorens bring a garland of ski lifts to the oldest national park in France. Protected since 1963, the 131,000-acre park, with its Italian neighbor the Grand Paradis, is one of the most-beautiful nature reserves in Europe. To the west, climbers head for Pralognan, while the hungry make their way to the cheese cellars of Champagny-en-Vanoise. Along the southern edge, visit Bonneval and other gorgeous simple villages of the Maurienne's Arc valley, where traditional stone chalets housed smallholders and their animals under the same roof. Hares, marmots and ermine live in la Grande Sassière.

➕ C3

NATURAL SPLENDOR

The warm colors of the fall in Queyras natural regional park

Alps and the Rhône Valley

Overhanging roofs are a feature of houses in the hilltop village of Pérouges

MONT-BLANC AND CHAMONIX

The highest peak in Europe at 15,771 feet, Mont-Blanc soars majestically above the granite needle peaks of the Aiguilles de Chamonix. Technically, it belongs to the neighboring town of St.-Gervais, but Chamonix, which incorporates the mountain in its name, has adopted the giant of the Alps. Chamonix is a hectic mixture of traditional Alpine chalets, serviceable hotel blocks and constant traffic clogging the road to the Mont-Blanc Tunnel to Italy. Despite all this and the tourist-ski-package industry that has all but swamped the town, Chamonix-Mont-Blanc remains a thrilling place to visit. This is due in part to the awe-inspiring peak that dared the first Alpine mountaineers in the 18th century. When Geneva scientist Dr. Michel-Gabriel Paccard returned from the summit in 1786, he started a tradition of climbing that remained a local diversion until the railroads reached the Alps in the 1860s. Suddenly Chamonix became popular not only for mountaineers but also for their fashionable friends who would enjoy hotel hospitality while watching the climbers through specially provided telescopes. A triumphant wave from the summit of Mont-Blanc would be the cue for champagne corks to pop in the resort. Natural wonders still upstage commercialism – with breathtaking glaciers such as the Glacier des Bossons dropping nearly 12,000 feet. Don't forget your passport if you want to take the spectacular six-stage cable car ride over Mont-Blanc via the Aiguille du Midi to la Palud in Italy. You will need it for the bus ride back through the tunnel.

➕ C3

Tourist information ✉ 85 place du Triangle de l'Amitié, Chamonix-Mont-Blanc ☎ 04 50 53 00 24; www.chamonix.com

PÉROUGES

Named for the Italian weavers from Perugia who founded the village, this imposing fortified settlement perches on a hilltop northeast of Lyon. Houses lining the picturesque narrow, cobbled streets have mullioned windows and overhanging roofs. A busy artists' community still thrives here, even if most of its output is designed for the tourist market. The central place du Tilleul is named after the old linden tree that still grows in the center. Visit the fortified church.

➕ A3

Tourist information ✉ Entrée de la Cité ☎ 04 74 61 01 14; www.perouges.org

Opposite: Mont-Blanc viewed from the Col des Saisies

DRIVE: LAKES AND PEAKS

Distance: 294 miles Time: 4 days

Starting and finishing at the cultural oasis of Grenoble (see page 210), this drive takes in nature's grandeur and sophisticated resorts in equal measure. In general, thanks to various Olympic seasons, Alpine roads are first class. But even in summer it's important to check road and weather reports before embarking on a long drive. Local tourist offices can advise about snow and road forecasts and offer alternate routes for any leg of the itinerary.

Leave Grenoble on the north bank of the Isère, following the D512 to St.-Pierre-de-Chartreuse.

From their secluded monastery in the forest, the Carthusian monks gave the world the green liqueur known as Chartreuse. Made from a secret blend of 130 wild herbs and plants added to brandy and honey, the heady

drink is now manufactured in Voiron (an easy drive west along the D520), where cellar tours and tastings of Chartreuse, both the green and milder yellow variety, are offered. At la Correrie, just northwest of St.-Pierre-de-Chartreuse, a museum tells the story of the 11th-century monastic order.

Continue on the D512, then take the D912 over the Col du Granier to Chambéry (see page 208). The N201 follows the east bank of Lac du Bourget to Aix-les-Bains.

The popular resort (see page 207) has plenty of distractions for the active and passive visitor. A trip to the Roman remains provides insight into the lives of those who first exploited the potential of the town.

Leave town on the N201, then turn right onto the D911. After la Tropaz, turn left to cross the Chéran river on the D31, then right on the D5 to rejoin the D911. Turn left on the D912 to Annecy (see page 207), climbing the Montagne du Semnoz and crossing the Col de Leschaux. Follow the D909 via Thônes to la Clusaz.

Mushrooms, cheese and summer skis keep the winter sport resort of la Clusaz alive all

The popular spa resort of Aix-les-Bains sits by the Lac du Bourget

through the summer. Skiing on grass is an option for the hardened athlete, and demonstrations of Reblochon cheese-making in large copper cauldrons, sampling matured cheeses and admiring traditional chalet-roofing skills are essential parts of summer festivals. Mid-September sees a mushroom fair when locals gather chanterelles and other wild fungi from the woods.

The D909 continues over the Col des Aravis to Flumet, where the D218B leads over the Col des Saisies. At the D925, turn left toward Bourg-St.-Maurice, making the most of a thrilling drive featuring a veritable catalog of spectacular Alpine scenery.

Bourg-St.-Maurice, with its 15th-century wooden houses and Renaissance porches, is best known for les Arcs ski resort. The Academy Music Festival takes place during the last two weeks of July. Gifted young musicians from France and abroad attend exclusive master classes, and 20,000 visitors enjoy a fabulous season of free concerts and recitals in churches and public squares in outlying villages. Golf, hiking and tennis are among summer sports, and the terrace cafés around Grand Rue bustle year round.

Take the D902 to Val d'Isère.

Ride the winter cable cars in summer for great views, or use this most popular of ski resorts in a narrow valley as a base for hiking or horseback riding through the spectacular countryside. Experts can take advantage of summer glacier skiing. In summer, Val d'Isère is a venue for the Savoy Music Festival.

The same road continues to Col de l'Iseran. One of the highest roads in Europe at 9,085 feet, the road up the Col de l'Iseran took 20 years to build and is often closed well past spring. However, it's well worth the effort for the impressive views it affords over the mountains of the Parc National de la Vanoise.

Still on the D902, pass through Bessans, Lanslevillard and Lanslebourg. Take a right on the N6, turning right at Sollières on the D83–D215 to Modane.

Modane is mostly used as a junction for hikers and travelers changing courses in mid-Alp. Walkers passing through the town may be treated to an unexpected musical soundtrack as students from Modane's Music School rehearse through open windows. The old center is the quartier du Pâquier, clustered around the parish church with its simple bell tower. Across town, Lutraz's Rizerie des Alpes is a Greek-style temple.

Follow the N6 to St.-Jean-de-Maurienne. Three fingers of the hand that baptized Christ are represented on the coat of arms of St.-Jean-de-Maurienne, which acquired these relics of John the Baptist back in the sixth

Alps and the Rhône Valley

century. See the 11th-century portal of Église Notre-Dame and the 15th-century cathedral and cloister. Secular attractions include a museum of knives and the Saturday market.

The D926 leads to Col de la Croix-de-Fer. The austere iron cross gives its name to a popular leg of the Tour de France. This section of the drive, from Col de la Croix-de-Fer to Défilé de Maupas, is a fabulous combination of all that is exciting about driving in the region – emerging from rock tunnels over the dramatic Arvan Gorge, leaning into sharp twists and turns of a mountain climb and awesome views of the Combe d'Olle and Défilé de Maupas.

Take the D926-D526-N91 toward Grenoble. At Vizille, take the D101 to the D524 via Uriage-les-Bains into Grenoble.

La Clusaz tourist information ☒ place Eglise ☎ 04 50 32 65 00; www.laclusaz.com

Les Arcs-Bourg St.-Maurice ☒ place Gare, 73706 Les Arcs/Bourg St.-Maurice ☎ 04 79 07 12 57; www.lesarcs.com

Val d'Isère tourist information ☒ Maison de Val-d'Isère ☎ 04 79 06 06 60; www.valdisere.com

Valfréjus-Modane tourist information ☒ Les Mélèzets, 73500 Valfréjus ☎ 04 79 05 33 83; www.valfrejus.com

St.-Jean-de-Maurienne tourist information ☒ Ancien Évêché, place de la Cathédrale ☎ 04 79

83 51 51; www.ville-saint-jean-de-maurienne.fr

Musée de la Grande Chartreuse ☒ 38380 St.-Pierre-de-Chartreuse ☎ 04 76 88 60 45 ⏱ Daily 9:30–6:30, Jul.–Aug.; 9:30–noon, and 2–6:30, May–Jun. and in Sep.; 10–noon and 2–6 in Apr. and Oct. 📷 $

Caves de la Chartreuse ☒ 10 boulevard Kofler, 38500 Voiron ☎ 04 76 05 81 77 ⏱ Daily 9–11:30 and 2–6:30, Apr.–Oct.; Mon.–Fri. 9–11:30 and 2–5, rest of year 📷 Free

The garden in the cathedral cloister at St.-Jean-de-Maurienne

The modern village of Vassieux-en-Vercors nestles in the foothills of the Vercors massif

VERCORS

Pine-forested slopes and limestone river gorges mark this majestic mountain range. The largest national park in France lies at the heart of the massif and proves a magnet to serious hikers who plan week-long treks around the inland cliff faces and dramatic waterfalls. Local drivers seem to have no fear negotiating the narrow roads of the Grands Goulets, which have been cut out of the rock face. During World War II, the name Vercors became synonymous with the heroism of the French Resistance. The movement eventually incurred the wrath of the German forces, who bombed the region in 1944 and razed the villages of St.-Nizier, la Chapelle and Vassieux-en-Vercors. Rebuilt after the war, Vassieux now is home to the Mémorial de la Résistance du Vercors. At the very end of the gorges of the Bourne and Grands Goulets, the fast-flowing waters meet at Pont-en-Royans before spilling into the Isère river. Come here to walk the narrow streets and marvel at the perilously suspended houses.
✚ A2–B2
Pont en Royans tourist information ✉ grande Rue
☎ 04 76 36 09 10
Mémorial de la Résistance du Vercors ✉ 26420 Vassieux-en-Vercors ☎ 04 75 48 26 00 🕓 Daily 10–6, Apr.–Sep.; daily 10–5, Oct. 1 to mid-Nov. and mid-Dec. through Dec. 31; Wed.–Sun. 10–5, rest of year 🎟 $

VIENNE

South of Lyon on the Rhône, Vienne is the second capital of Roman Gaul. Less well known to visitors than the remains in Lyon (see pages 200–205), it outlines its heritage through the legendary July jazz festival in the Théâtre Antique, the biggest and best of the town's treasures. Don't miss the section of fourth-century road in the Jardin Public and an 85-foot-high obelisk from the old circus. In place du Palais is the Temple of Augustus and Livia, dating from 25 BC. It became a Christian church in medieval times and was reincarnated as a post-revolutionary Temple of Reason, courthouse and museum. Mosaics and sculpture are displayed in the Musée de L'Ancienne (sixth century) Église St.-Pierre. The Cathédrale St.-Maurice, has Romanesque sculpture, a Gothic facade and 16th-century Flemish tapestries.
✚ A3
Tourist information ✉ cours Brillier ☎ 04 74 53 80 30; www.vienne-rhone-alpes.org
Théâtre Antique ✉ rue du Cirque ☎ 04 74 85 39 23 🕓 Daily 9:30–1 and 2–6, Apr.–Aug.; Tue.–Sun. 9:30–1 and 2–6, Sep–Oct.; Tue.–Sat. 9:30–12:30 and 2–5, Sun. 1:30–5:30, rest of year 🎟 $
Musée de l'Ancienne Église St.-Pierre ✉ place St.-Pierre ☎ 04 74 85 20 35 🕓 Tue.–Sun. 9:30–1 and 2–6, Apr.–Oct.; Tue.–Fri. 9:30–12:30 and 2–5, Sat.–Sun. 2–6, rest of year 🎟 $

BURGUNDY AND THE EAST

"B ETWEEN two worlds, the land of the mountains and vines celebrates the arts of good living, endurance and neighborliness. "

Opposite: An elegant house peers above the trees in the town of la Petite Pierre

BURGUNDY AND THE EAST

There is a gentle quality to this part of eastern France. Here great vineyards spread over a softly undulating landscape, with none of the rugged scrubland of the south. The mountains of the Jura are strangers to the razzmatazz of the Alps. Even disputed border towns paint quaint images from the pages of a children's book.

Disputed Lands

The regions of Alsace and Lorraine are an intriguing blend of French and German culture, for centuries pawed this way and that by warring neighbors. At the end of each 20th-century war, both were returned to France. The legacy is a wealth of contrasting influences on food, dialects and building style. Mixed parentage is a boon for the Alsace capital Strasbourg. An international city like New York, Brussels and Geneva, Strasbourg is home to the European Parliament. Besides Teutonic timbered houses, Alsatian towns and villages, such as Riquewhir and Hunspach, are famed for abundant floral displays in windows and storks nesting on chimney stacks.

The least-known region of France is Franche-Comté, a land of deep forests, running waters and the snowcapped mountain peaks of the Jura mountains. Its sobriquets include: Little Scotland for its lakes; Little Ireland for its moors, bogs and streams; and Little Canada for its gorges and expanses of tall trees.

Endurance

The occupations of cheese making, freshwater fishing and wine producing are key to the region, as are its less trumpeted winter-sports resorts. But don't overlook another aspect that lends character – the fierce independence of the people of the Jura. The fortified hill town of Belfort is known for holding

Vines skirt a rocky outcrop near the Burgundian village of Époisses

out against invasion months longer than many bigger cities. Present-day endurance is typified by the February Transjurassienne – a 47.5-mile World Cup class cross-country skiing rally along the Swiss border. The event attracts 90,000 participants who ring cowbells, light torches at nightfall and bake heart-shaped gingerbread to comfort the last brave competitors.

Despite the fact that the French Formula One Grand Prix is run at Magny-Cours, Burgundy should be enjoyed at a more leisurely pace. Besides vines (see pages 232–233), the countryside is dotted with hilltop Romanesque churches and simple

Cistercian abbeys. Even the cattle – cream-colored and elegant Charolais – are picturesque.

Canals

The ideal way to discover Burgundy is from the water. The Loire, Seine and Rhône rivers freshen a 750-mile network of canals. Small motor boats can be rented from a half-day to the full season, and many floating hotels ply the water and serve good local food. A good starting point is the town of Auxerre. The best sightseeing waterways are the canals de Bourgogne and du Nivernais. The French canal network extends as far as the Atlantic.

Burgundy and the East

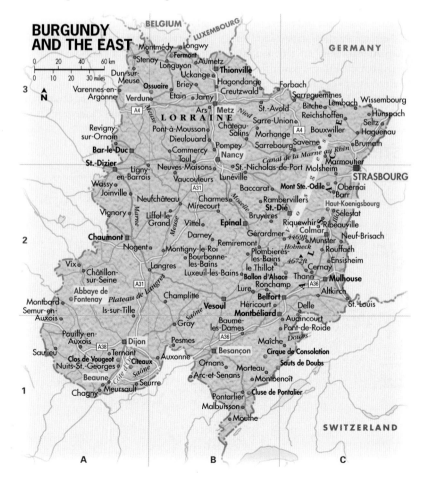

STRASBOURG

Strasbourg redefines cosmopolitan. With the German border just across the Rhine, the city is a shuttlecock in the nationality tussles of Alsace, creating a unique Franco-German style from its architecture to its dinner plates. Strasbourg is also the site of the European Parliament. So as you admire trellised timbering on quaint old houses, your ears may ring to an international hum of voices and accents more usually heard in an airport lounge.

In countless atmospheric restaurants, waiters slip effortlessly from French to Spanish to Greek to English as they flourish trays of authentic Alsatian sauerkraut and beer.

Fortunately, the institutions of an international capital are far enough away from the historic center for the heart of Strasbourg to retain its centuries-old charm. Dominated by a magnificent cathedral and embraced by the meandering Ill river, the old quarter combines a striking German postcard image of charming cobbled streets and tall gabled buildings with unmistakably French warmth.

Getting Around

Strasbourg is a city for *flâneurs* (strollers). Wander among the three main squares: the places de la Cathédrale, Gutenberg and Kléber. Bicycles may be rented at the Tour des Ponts-Couverts in Petite France. Trams are useful for crisscrossing the city, and taxis are plentiful. The boat trip along the Ill and Rhine rivers is a relaxing option – and it's free to holders of the Strasbourg Pass, which offers a combination of free and discounted admissions to museums, sites, tours and concerts over three days; available from the tourist office and hotels.

Music

Music is an essential part of Strasbourg life. Annual traditions range from a

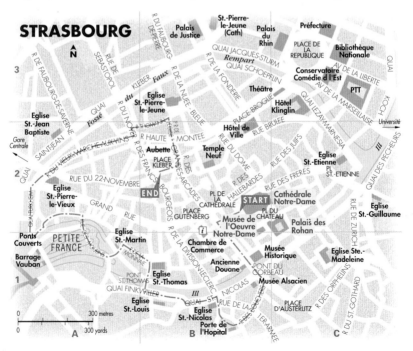

Burgundy and the East

celebration of street musicians in August to the September, classical Musica Festival. Opera and concerts catering to the diplomatic and political community are of a high standard. In summer months, folk concerts are held outside the Palais Rohan, in the flood-lit Orangerie park and in main squares.

Christmas

Alsace believes not only in Father Christmas, but also in Santa Claus' inspiration, St. Nicholas. St. Nicholas' Day is celebrated December 5 with partying in the streets, and the Christmas season continues until Christmas eve. The town prides itself on the size of its Christmas tree, adorned with humongous mock fruits. Gift ideas abound at the huge Christkindelsmärik, a market of wooden chalets that sprawls from place de la Cathédrale to the other two squares. A monthlong December tradition since 1570, the market is bathed in twinkling lights and lays out an array of hand-carved toys and fragrant candles. Hot mulled wine and spiced cakes provide seasonal fuel to sustain shopping.

The Marseillaise

On April 24, 1792, Frédéric de Dietrich, the first elected mayor of Strasbourg, commissioned composer Rouget de Lisle to write a stirring marching song for the volunteer soldiers of the Army of the Rhine. The next morning, Rouget de Lisle had completed the song, which was adopted by the Federates of Marseille. And so the French national anthem, the *Marseillaise*, was born.

Shopping

Even outside the Christmas season, most days promise at least one market: flea markets at rue du Viel-Hôpital; a book market at place Gutenberg; and various produce markets around town for picking up foods and souvenirs. Saturday is the farmers' market on place du Marché-aux-Poissons. Plenty of shops in the old quarter sell antiques, as well as clothes and crafts, but prices are geared to the international market. Locals tend to stick to Les Halles shopping mall, across the river.

ESSENTIAL INFORMATION

TOURIST INFORMATION
17 place de la Cathédrale ☎ 03 88 52 28 28; www.strasbourg.com

URBAN TRANSPORTATION
Trams and buses cross the city. Buy tickets from machines at bus and tram stops and validate before boarding. Route maps are available from the tourist office; for information ☎ 03 88 77 70 70. Taxi stands operate from the railroad station, place Kléber and place Gutenberg ☎ 03 88 36 13 13

AIRPORT INFORMATION
Strasbourg International Airport ☎ 03 88 64 67 67. Connections link to most European capitals. A taxi ride to the city center takes about 20 minutes. A shuttle bus runs every 15 minutes (every 30 minutes Sat. p.m. and Sun. a.m.).

CLIMATE – Average highs and lows

JAN.	FEB.	MAR.	APR.	MAY	JUN.	JUL.	AUG.	SEP.	OCT.	NOV.	DEC.
4°C	5°C	10°C	15°C	19°C	22°C	24°C	24°C	20°C	14°C	8°C	4°C
39°F	41°F	50°F	59°F	66°F	72°F	75°F	75°F	68°F	57°F	46°F	39°F
-2°C	-2°C	1°C	5°C	9°C	12°C	14°C	13°C	10°C	6°C	2°C	0°C
28°F	28°F	34°F	41°F	48°F	54°F	57°F	55°F	50°F	43°F	36°F	32°F

Glorious stained glass in Cathédrale Notre-Dame

STRASBOURG SIGHTS

Key to symbols

✚ map coordinates refer to the Strasbourg map on page 222; sights below are highlighted in yellow on the map.

✉ address or location ☎ telephone number
🕐 opening times 🚌 nearest bus or tram route
🍴 restaurant on site or nearby ℹ information
🎫 admission charge: $$$ more than €10, $$ €5–€10, $ less than €5

CATHÉDRALE NOTRE-DAME

Work started in 1176 and continued for more than 250 years on the undisputed masterpiece of the city. Floodlit by night, the Gothic facade becomes the world's most beautiful gilded casket. Whatever the time of day, this magnificent frontage is breathtaking, from the ornate porch up past numerous saintly statues to its single open-work octagonal spire which ascends 466 feet above the town and the Alsace plain. Step inside for wonders that never cease. Evocative shadows painted by stained-glass windows pour on splendid statuary. Pride of place goes to the Pilier des Anges, a pillar dressed with ranks of angels telling the story of the Last Judgment.

Behind the column is the famous 16th-century astronomical clock. Arrive at 12:30 p.m. for its automated pageant of the Apostles and the Ages of Man. The clock's main performance is a ticket-only event. It may be booked at the postcard stand from 9 a.m. to 11:30 a.m. or with the cashier at the south doorway from 11:50 a.m. to 12:20 p.m. During other times, there is no charge for witnessing the figure of Death announce that each of us is another hour nearer the grave.

✚ B2 ✉ place de la Cathédrale ☎ 03 88 43 60 32 🕐 Daily 7–11:30 and 12:40–7, except during Mass 🎫 Free (tower $; clock $) 🚌 A, D

MUSÉE DE L'OEUVRE NOTRE-DAME

Many of the greatest original architectural treasures of the cathedral are displayed here, free from the ravages of pollution. The stone masons of Chartres worked on the statuary, and the elegant features of saints and biblical characters can be fully appreciated in close proximity. Modern copies have taken their place within the cathedral. Examples to seek out include The Wise and Foolish Virgins, with the famous image of the seduced maiden about to undo her dress, and the architect's original drawings of the spire. This 14th-century building – originally used by workers who built and cleaned the cathedral – is worth a visit in its own right. Discover graceful tiny spiral staircases, pretty courtyards and a medicinal herb garden.

✚ B2 ✉ 2 place du Château ☎ 03 88 52 50 00 🕐 Wed.–Mon. 10–6 🚌 A, D 🎫 $

PALAIS DES ROHAN

The one-time residence of the prince bishops of Strasbourg, no strangers to court intrigue, Palais des Rohan is a typical example of mid-18th-century Classical flamboyance. Balustrades and galleries line the courtyard and bull's-eye windows stud the roofs. It's now home to a fine-arts museum on the first floor, decorative-arts museum on the ground floor and archeological museum in the basement.

✚ C2, B2, C1 ✉ 2 place du Château ☎ 03 88 52 50 00 🕐 Wed.–Mon. 10–6 🚌 A, D 🎫 $

WALK: MEDIEVAL CHURCHES AND LA PETITE FRANCE

Refer to route on city map on page 222

Opposite the cathedral, the Pharmacie du Cerf (the oldest pharmacy in France) has fabulous 15th-century arches carved with branches and reptiles.

Take rue Mercière, then the second left into rue du Vieux-Marché-aux-Poissons.
The Ancienne Douane, at the end of the street by the river, is largely a 1950s reconstruction of the original 14th-century bonded customs warehouse. It houses a good restaurant.
Cross the river on Pont du Corbeau and follow rue des Bouchers to the hospital gateway.
The hospital's 17th-century observatory is a remodeling of the 13th-century original. The 15th-century Chapelle St.-Erhard became the hospital's Anatomy Hall.
Rue St.-Nicolas leads to the river bank; bear left past Église St.-Nicolas then cross the river on Pont St.-Thomas. Ahead to your right is Église St.-Thomas. Turn left on rue de la Monnaie, then take the first bridge on your left to rue des Moulins and the old tanners' district.
The twists and turns of the river proved ideal for water mills, which were essential for leather workers. This former industrial district is now one of the prettiest corners of town.
The second promontory on the left is square des Moulins. Turn back, then left and left again onto square Louise Weiss and the yellow, blue, white and terra-cotta house fronts of la Petite France.
The chocolate-box charm has a much earthier history. Here, veterans of 16th-century battles with Italy were quarantined for venereal disease. Since locals blamed the French for the disease, "la Petite France" became the nickname for syphilis.

At the tip of quai de la Petite-France are the Ponts Couverts: once timber-covered bridges, now stone, with three defensive towers offering fabulous views of the river and the Barrage Vauban, a 17th-century defensive dam. The viewing platform is the perfect spot for photographs of Petite France's low-sweeping *Sleeping Beauty* roofs, shady dappled banks reflected in still waters and panoramic vistas leading to the cathedral.
Follow quai Turkheim to place St.-Pierre-le-Vieux.
At Église St.-Pierre-le-Vieux, admire the 15th-century panels of Christ's Passion.
Turn right on rue du Vieux-Marché-aux-Vins, left on rue du Noyer and right on rue Thomann to place St.-Pierre-le-Jeune.
Église St.-Pierre-le-Jeune has medieval frescoes and a 12th-century bell tower.
Petite rue de l'Église and rue des Grandes-Arcades lead into the Renaissance place Kléber.

Burgundy and the East

The Ponts Couverts – once timber-covered, now stone – are guarded by defensive towers

Burgundy and the East

REGIONAL SIGHTS

Key to symbols

🟥 map coordinates refer to the region map on page 221; sights below are highlighted in yellow on the map.
⊠ address or location ☎ telephone number
◎ opening times 🚌 nearest bus or tram route
🍴 restaurant on site or nearby 🛈 information
💰 admission charge: $$$ more than €10, $$ €5–€10, $ less than €5

BEAUNE

Although Dijon may be the capital of the Burgundy region, Beaune is capital of the wine. This incredibly beautiful town in the midst of the area's grandest vineyards is simply exquisite.

See for yourself the elegant patchwork of many-colored glazed tiles above the carved gables and palatial pillars of the Hôtel Dieu of the Hospices de Beaune. No photograph will ever do it full justice. This building, with its courtyard and centuries-old pharmacy, was established as a hospital in 1443, a function it continued to fulfill until 1971. Visit the marvelous vaulted sick room, laid out like a church with 230-foot rows of wooden beds, each big enough for two patients and separated by heavy red drapes. These would be pulled back so the sick could participate in religious services. Nuns still care for elderly residents who reside in less public rooms.

The hospice hosts the annual charity wine auctions in October, setting the annual price for classic Burgundy wines and continuing until the last candle on the auctioneer's platform flickers out. An exhibition gallery contains the hospice's art treasures, including Roger van de Weyden's polyptych *The Last Judgment*. More spiritual sustenance is contained at the 12th- to 13th-century Collégiale Notre-Dame, which has remarkable tapestries displayed only in warm seasons.

Opposite the Hôtel Dieu, the Marché aux Vins tempts the palate for wine tasting and shopping. The town has plenty of first-class restaurants for sampling wines, with cooking of the highest standard.

Walk around the town walls, which now hide wine cellars. Visit the Museum of Burgundy Wine. The tourist office can arrange excursions to visit vineyards. July sees weekend baroque concerts at the principal sites. However, since air-conditioning isn't available, seasonal temperatures can make 90 minutes inside the Hôtel Dieu's sick room very uncomfortable. Open-air performances in the courtyard are more advisable.

🟥 A1

Tourist information ⊠ 1 rue de l'Hôtel-Dieu ☎ 03 80 26 21 30; www.ot-beaune.fr

Musée de Hôtel Dieu ⊠ 2 rue de l'Hôtel-Dieu ☎ 03 80 24 75 75 ◎ Daily 9–6:30, late Mar. to mid-Nov.; 9–11:30 and 2–5:30, rest of year 💰 $$

Collegiale Notre-Dame (Tapisseries) ⊠ place Notre-Dame ◎ Mon.–Sat. 9:30–12:30 and 2–5, Sun. 2–5 💰 Free

Musée de Vin de Bourgogne ⊠ rue d'Enfer ☎ 03 80 22 08 19 ◎ Daily 9–12:30 and 1:30–6, Apr. 1–late Nov.; daily 10–noon and 2–5:30, in Mar. and late Nov.; Wed.–Mon. 10–noon and 2–5:30, rest of year 💰 $

Grape lesson: Statuette in the Museum of Wine

Opposite: The magnificent gables and glazed tiles of the Hôtel Dieu of the Hospices de Beaune

EASTERN PROMISE DELIVERS AT THE TABLE

Burgundy's wealth is displayed at its tables. Great chefs – such as Bernard Saulieu, a gourmet legend – are attracted here by excellent produce, and others arrive, retire and turn restaurateur, serving simple classics after careers in other fast lanes. MGM star Leslie Caron turned her back on Hollywood to run an inn, La Lucarne aux Chouettes in Villeneuve-sur-Yonne. The star of *Gigi* and *An American in Paris* fell in love with an old ruined building and converted it into a hotel. She now serves quail and lamb to guests on the terrace overlooking the 13th-century bridge over the Yonne river.

The ultimate poultry comes from Bresse, where free-range birds are fed on creamy milk and wheat and prepared with reverence. Even in the simplest restaurant, menu favorites include escargots and the famous boeuf Bourguignon.

Alsace cuisine is hearty. Best known is *choucroute*, the mountain of cabbage, pork and sausages. Try Baeckeoffe, pork and mutton marinated for 24 hours in white wine. *Flammekueche*, or *tarte flambée*, is an essential part of tavern culture. Between a pizza and a pancake, the flat dough is covered with sweet or savory toppings and baked on a wooden board for 90 seconds.

Traditionally, one tears a strip of the flam', rolls it like a cigar and munches it with the fingers as an accompaniment to beer and good cheer.

Lorraine is famous for its egg, cheese and bacon quiche. Patés and stews are prepared with fruits, including local Mirabelle golden plums, which are also found in jams and desserts.

Franche-Comté's smoked meats and fish are staples. The true star of a meal is the cheese course. Mont d'Or is matured in a box of spruce wood, but the ultimate flavor is that of the Comté cheese, often compared to a fine wine. The herds and pastures that create the milk, as well as the 18-month ripening process, are strictly controlled.

Franche-Comté produces many excellent wines. *Vins jaunes* (yellow wines), in essence white wines that may be matured for up to 100 years, are something of a rarity. Beer-making Alsace is also famous for whites: Pinot Noir, Pinot Gris, Riesling and Gerwürzstraminer. Toul and Moselle wines are served in Lorraine, where fruits flavor beers, ciders and liqueurs.

Wines of the Alsace region on a traditional barrow cart in Riquewhir

Merchant houses with sharply pointed roofs in the center of Colmar

COLMAR

With narrow streets, tall gabled merchant houses and 16th-century timbered fronts tapering up to sharply pointed roofs, Colmar is the ultimate Alsatian town. Each turn in the old quarter seems to lead to another storybook address. Most picturesque, with turrets, wooden galleries and cascades of seasonal flowers, is the Maison Pfister at the pretty corner of the rues Mercière and des Marchands. Another photo opportunity is the early 17th-century Renaissance Maison des Têtes at 19 rue des Têtes, liberally decorated with images of faces and heads. The town is one of those that gives you a reason to gasp every few yards, but the effect is slightly marred by crowds in vacation season. Don't let it keep you from visiting the engaging Krutenau district in Little Venice, where little bridges span the Lauch and church towers and willow trees frame every snapshot. The Musée d'Unterlinden, in a former Dominican convent, has many fine German paintings and works by 20th-century artists. Its treasure is Matthias Grünewald's 1515 Issenheim Altar, with its vivid depiction of the Redemption of Christ.

🕂 C2

Tourist information ✉ 4 rue d'Unterlinden ☎ 03 89 20 68 92; www.ot-colmar.fr
Musée d'Unterlinden ✉ 1 rue d'Unterlinden ☎ 03 89 20 15 50 🕐 Daily 9–6, Apr.–Oct.; Wed.–Mon. 10:30–4:30, rest of year 🎟 $$

CÔTE D'OR

A ribbon of less than 10,000 acres of land produces some of the world's most sought-after wines. This area, south of Dijon, is known as the Côte d'Or (golden slopes). The northern section, the Côtes de Nuit, produces celebrated reds, while the southern half, the Côtes de Beaune, makes red and white. It's like traveling through an expensive wine list, each village a legend among fine wines. Meursault, Montrachet, Chambertin – these familiar names are modest settlements since land is too valuable for vines to be built on. Roadside signs offer tastings *(dégustation)* in cellars *(caves)*, and the winemakers often will escort visitors to view the vines. Because of inheritance laws, farmers often own two rows of vines in one field and half a row in another a mile away. Each strip gets a unique degree of sunshine, thus the subtle variation in taste and huge difference in prices.

🕂 A1

Angels keep watch over the effigy of Philip the Bold in Dijon's Fine Arts Museum

DIJON

The dukes of Burgundy ran an empire that extended as far north as Flanders, and their seat at Dijon is a rich and prosperous city. The former ducal palace at the 17th-century place de la Libération houses the Musée des Beaux-Arts (Fine Arts Museum) with fascinating Gothic kitchens and superb sculpture galleries. See Claus Sluter's *Well of Moses*, in which Moses may be identified by his horns. Stroll through the oldest quarter with 16th-century houses, and note the little owl carved into the back of Église Notre-Dame, on rue de la Chouette. The front of the church has a mechanical clock made in 1383. Dijon streets were among the first in France to have sidewalks. Gastronomy and wine have long been associated with the city. When besieged by the Swiss, the city ended the 16th-century conflict with a gift of wine. Attacking soldiers simply fell asleep after overindulging. Visit the Amora Museum of Mustard and buy a jar of the famous condiment. The other treat is *crème de cassis* (blackcurrant liqueur), which when mixed with white wine, ideally bourgogne alligoté, makes the aperitif known as Kir, named for a mayor of the city.
➕ A1

Tourist information ✉ 34 rue des Forges & place Darcy ☎ 03 80 44 11 44; www.ot-dijon.fr
Musée des Beaux-Arts ✉ Palais des États-de-Bourgogne (entrance: cour de Bar) ☎ 03 80 74 52 09 🕐 Wed.–Mon. 10–6 💲 $ (free to all on Sun.)
Musée des la Moutarde Amora ✉ 48 quai Nicolas-Rolin ☎ 03 80 44 11 44 🕐 Tours are given Mon.–Sat. at 3, mid-Jun.–mid-Sep.; Wed. and Sat. at 3, rest of year ✋ Free

FONTENAY

Burgundy was the cradle of the Cistercian movement, founded by St. Bernard of Clairvaux at Citeaux Abbey, near Dijon. St. Bernard rebelled against the ostentation of other abbeys and established a new order of simplicity and tranquility for pure meditation. No site reflects his ideals better than the Abbey of Fontenay, set in wooded Burgundy countryside. Restored at the beginning of the 20th century, its cloisters and halls remain masterpieces of calm, even during the peak summer season. The uncomplicated architecture contrasts dramatically with medieval chapels and cathedrals found elsewhere in France.
➕ A2
Abbaye de Fontenay ✉ 21500 Montbard ☎ 03 80 92 15 00, book in advance 🕐 Guided tours depart daily at 10, 11, noon, 2, 3, 4 and 5, Apr. 1 to mid-Nov.; unguided visits 10–noon and 2–5, rest of year ✋ $

HAUT-KOENIGSBOURG

The largest château in Alsace is every inch the European castle: vast rose-red sandstone walls with tendrils of green creeper spreading across them, round and square towers, suits of armor, even spindly trees growing in tiny courtyards among the turrets. The Château of Haut-Koenigsbourg in the Vosges mountains has been rebuilt several times since its first incarnation as a stronghold of Emperor Frederick of Hohenstaufen in 1114. The castle was destroyed in 1462 and 1633, and the ruins eventually were presented in 1899 to the German Kaiser Wilhelm II, who commissioned a re-creation of the medieval version. Work on the reconstruction lasted from 1901 to 1908. On a clear day, the view from the top is magnificent, with vistas across the Rhine valley. To the east, you can see the edge of Germany's Black Forest.

➕ C2

Château du Haut-Koenigsbourg

✉ 67600 Orschwiller ☎ 03 88 82 50 60 🕐 Daily 9–6, Jun.–Sep.; 9–noon and 1–6, Apr.–May; 9–noon and 1–5, in Oct.; 9–noon and 1–4, Nov. 1–early Jan. and early Feb.–Mar. 31 💰 $$

METZ

Metz is a town with a long history but a young heart. The townsfolk became French only in 1918, after a long period of German rule. Perhaps because its national identity is less than a century old, the town has a definite buzz in its cafés and bars. Chart the political fortunes of Metz through its buildings. Late-19th-century edifices, including the railroad station, have a Germanic appearance, while the attractive confection of Cathédrale St.-Etienne belongs to the great French Gothic period. Each era has added stained-glass windows to the church,

which now displays 1.5 acres of kaleidoscopic colored glass from the 13th, 15th and 16th centuries, as well as modern panes by Marc Chagall. Sébastien Le Prestre de Vauban fortified Metz (locals pronounce it "Mess") with a ring of châteaux; the last vestige is the imposing Porte des Allemands, a miniature castle gateway facing the German border. In 1603, Henri IV offered Jews protection in the Saint-Ferroy quarter, where they had lived since the 11th century. The present neo-Roman synagogue was built in 1850. Admire the lawns and flower beds of the elegant place de la Comédie during the day, but the best time to enjoy Metz is after dark. Collaboration with the electricity company creates stunning illuminations, as the bridges and buildings glow with warm light that shows off the local sandstone to remarkable effect.

➕ B3

Tourist information ✉ place d'Armes ☎ 03 87 55 53 76; www.tourisme.mairie-metz.fr

The rose-colored Château of Haut-Koenigsbourg

St. Vincent Requests the Pleasure

It happens every year in a different village of the Côte d'Or (see page 229), surrounding the old walled city of Beaune. On the last weekend of January, more than 200,000 visitors descend on the chosen village to drink the place dry as about 800 inhabitants cheerily pour out 24,000 liters of hugely expensive burgundy into 160,000 commemorative wine glasses.

While most of the year is spent producing wine, mid-winter is party time. This is when the feast of St. Vincent, the patron saint of winegrowers, is celebrated with a formal procession, a formal Mass and an informal carnival. It's known as the St.-Vincent Tournante (turn), because the venue changes every year, as Montrachet and Mussigny, Fixin and Rully takes its turn to host the event.

In preparation for the festival, the village lays down wines for a decade and the children create thousands of paper flowers to bring summer to the winter gardens and streets. When the bands strike up Saturday morning, the red-robed

brotherhood Chevaliers de Tastevin and members of the 19th-century Société d'Entre Aide des Vignerons begin to march down the main road. Dozens of statues of the saint are hoisted through the crowds, and the doors of wine cellars fling open to serve the very best of their recent vintages. Then for the next two days, revelers swill wine without a whiff of aggression or loutishness. Consider it a civilized joy.

As you push your way through the tidal surge of humanity, keep tight hold of the wine glass, slung on a strap around your neck. This engraved glass, sold around town for 30 or 40 francs, is your passport to unlimited free tastings of wines that ordinarily are way beyond the average budget. Weave from cellar to cellar, as every hour another vintage is uncorked.

"The wine is to the table as the flower is to the garden," the signs proclaim. "Drink and you die. Don't drink and you die. So drink," reason banners draped across house fronts.

Children can sup milkshakes at the village pump, and trays of cakes and sandwiches are sold to those without tickets to the grand banquet being served at the edge of town. Tickets costing about 1,000 francs pay for a seven- or eight-course meal cooked by the finest chefs in France. An equal number of extremely rare wines accompanies every dish. Less expensive is the public ball, with dancing in the streets late into Saturday night, before the tasting starts again Sunday morning.

Whatever time you decide to leave, it's best to make arrangements in advance for local accommodations or a taxi back to Dijon or Beaune. Visitors can never quite keep up with the locals. The sound of celebrations will ring in your ears as you pass the church or the eye of a stone statue of Bacchus dressed for the procession. Blame the unseasonable sunshine or perhaps the afterglow of a particularly fruity vintage, but you will swear that he winks *au revoir.*

The St.-Vincent Tournante is but one of many wine festivals throughout the year. Most take place in autumn, from the folk festival around the centuries-old wine presses of the dukes of Burgundy in Chénove to the celebrations of the new wines at Nuits St.-Georges. Les Trois Gloirieuses is a series of November events at Clos de Vougeot, Mersault and Beaune. Featuring the legendary auction at the hospice (see page 227), the event is considered the highlight of the serious wine lover's calendar.

Summer events include the May Day Wine Fair at Chablis and August festivals in Pouilly-sur-Loire, Dijon and Beaune.

Robes are donned for celebrations toasting the patron saint of winegrowers, St. Vincent

Elegant stairway in the fine arts museum at Nancy

NANCY

The historic capital of Lorraine is a masterpiece of 17th- and 18th-century town planning. Take in the baroque, ornate gilding on gateways and railings around the city, best appreciated in the main square, place Stanislas. The square is named after Stanislas Leczinski, Duke of Lorraine and former King of Poland, who brought numerous artists to his court and gave the city its rococo flourishes. The gracefully proportioned square was laid out from 1752 to 1760, and its fountains, several palaces and the Hôtel de Ville are best appreciated from a table at a fashionable restaurant.

Despite this, baroque isn't the style for which Nancy acquired its reputation. To the world, Nancy is the city of art nouveau.

Gallé, Prouvé and Daum glass may be enjoyed around town, and many art-nouveau architectural gems line the streets. Even banks are worth a visit for more than changing traveler's checks.

Jacques Gruber's 1901 glass roof of Credit Lyonais brings a delicate and harmonious touch of green and purple coloring through the clematis that winds around the bank's initials "C.L." The BNP (Banque National de Palis) is a nouveau take on a Germanic style that is more Alsace than Lorraine.

Houses worth photographing include the looming Villa Majorelle and the extravagantly shuttered Villa Marguerite. Visit the Brasserie Excelsior for its original furnishings and stained glass.

The School of Nancy Museum, a gift to the town by the owner of a department store who amassed an enviable collection of furniture and glassware, also has fascinating grounds with a remarkable folly of underground fish pools and an aquarium.

Other treats include a fine arts museum and some enchanting gardens along the waterways. Nancy celebrates Christmas early, with delightful St. Nicholas Day partying in the streets for the children on December 6. Adults appreciate the beat of the Pulsations Jazz Festival in October.
✚ B3

Tourist information ✉ place Stanislas ☎ 03 83 35 22 41; www.ot-nancy.fr

Musée de l'École de Nancy ✉ 36 rue du Sergent-Blandan ☎ 03 83 40 14 86 🕐 Wed.–Sun. 10:30–6 📖 $

VERDUN

Verdun is a small town in eastern France that cast a long shadow over the 20th century. From February 1916 until October 1917, the German high command attempted to bleed France dry at a cost of 800,000 lives. More than 80 years after the Great War, visitors still come here to shake their heads and ponder the terrible cost of humanity. A center for world peace is a worthy institution, but the most powerful and eloquent arguments come from the unending sea of graves at Douaumont, watched over by its stark white memorial tower. Here, too, the Tranchée des Baïonnetles recalls the men of the 137th Infantry Regiment, who were buried alive in a trench. The stars and stripes fly

Windowboxes drip with flowers in the village of Riquewhir

alongside the *tricolor* outside the Citadelle Souterraine, an exhibition about the living conditions of soldiers during the battle, and at the American Cemetery at nearby Romagne-sous-Montfaucon, the largest U.S. graveyard in Europe.

✚ B3

Tourist information ✉ place de la Nation ☎ 03 29 86 14 18; www.verduntourisme.com

VOSGES

The Vosges mountains, the sister range to Germany's Black Forest, neatly divide the regions of Alsace and Lorraine. An area rich in woodlands, ruined castles and health spas, it's a favored retreat in summer months and an alternative to the Alps during the ski season. Year round, wine lovers follow the route du Vin, which takes in many enchanting medieval villages tucked among vineyards that produce the region's Riesling, Gewürztraminer and Tokay wines. Just north of Colmar (see page 229), the jewel of the wine trail is the cobbled village of Riquewhir. With pots of geraniums in the windows and a 13th-century gate tower at the main entrance, it's the perfect spot to take a break from any journey. The northern Vosges are now a protected natural park, but some of the more spectacular views may be found in the southern Vosges. Here summits known as *ballons* reach heights of up to 4,672 feet.

✚ C2–C3

Riquewhir tourist information ✉ 2 rue de la lère Armée, 683C ☎ 08 20 36 09 22 (toll call); www.ribeauville-riquewhir.com

DRIVE: DISCOVERING THE FRANCHE-COMTÉ

Distance: 209 miles Time: 4–5 days

This drive takes you along two of this undiscovered region's rivers, the Doubs and the Ognon and features some splendid towns and lush green scenery. Multicolored roof tiles and neat wood piles outside farmhouses contrast with high, defensive city walls and imaginative architecture. Start and finish the tour in the watchmakers' city of Besançon, wrapped in a loop of the Doubs. Art festivals, an art gallery and museums cover themes from the French Resistance to time itself.

Take the N83 along and across the Doubs, filtering right on the D463 after l'Isle-sur-le-Doubs. Follow signs into Montbéliard.
This city of princes is famed for its annual book fair and its 12th-century château with Renaissance adornments. Visit the 16th-century market buildings, a Peugeot automobile museum, more than a motorshow, a celebration of 20th-century popular culture, introduced by a virtual reality version of T.V's Columbo.
From the D438, take the N83 via Argiesans, then the D47A into Belfort.

The huge 36-foot-high sandstone lion that guards the château from its perch on a rock 230 feet high is the symbol of plucky little Belfort. The territory has a history of heroism, and Frédéric Auguste Bartholdi, builder of the *Statue of Liberty*, sculpted its lion to guard the main route from the Vosges to the Jura. The streets bustle and views are great.
Follow the N19 to Ronchamp.
On a hill to the west of Ronchamp is the remarkable 1950-54 Notre-Dame-du-Haut. The most famous creation of architect Le Corbusier, the church has a distinctive sweeping roof reminiscent of a melting Noah's ark. Within the church, find works by Marc Chagall and Henri Matisse. The site has welcomed pilgrims for centuries.
Today's long drive follows the Ognon river. Take the N19 towards Lure, turn left on the D64 then follow the D486 to Villersexel. Turn right to the D9 and left to the D49, which becomes the D15 at Montbozon. Go left on the D67 at Marnay and right on the D459 turning left after Ougney on the D10. Turn right on the N73/D973 to Dole.
Gateway to the Jura and capital of Franche-Comté until the 17th century, Dole gained new fame as birthplace of Louis Pasteur. His childhood home is now a museum. Picturesque narrow streets and carved doorways characterize the old quarter around the 16th-century church, with its 246-foot tower. Many

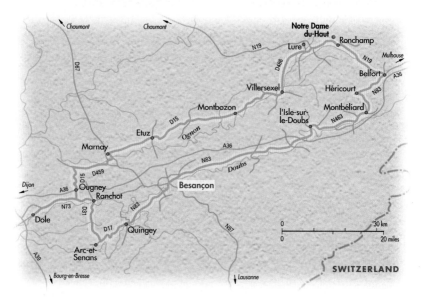

The late 17th-century ramparts of the citadel at Besançon

churches, chapels, convents and cloisters beckon you to explore. The town is a popular starting point for river trips on the Doubs.

Back up the N73 to Ranchot, turn right on the D31 following signs on the D17 for Arc-et-Senans.

It's incredible that Claude-Nicolas Ledoux's beautiful Classical architecture served as an industrial plant, but this World Heritage Site was the Royal Saltworks (Saline Royale). Built between 1775 and 1779, the saltworks for 120 years burned wood from the nearby forest to extract salt from the water of Salins les Bains.

Continue on the D17, filtering onto the N83, which leads back to Besançon.

Belfort tourist information ✉ 2 bis rue Clemenceau ☎ 03 84 55 90 90

Besançon tourist information ✉ 2 place de la 1ère-Armée-Française ☎ 03 81 80 92 55; www.besancon.com

Dole tourist information ✉ 6 place Jules-Grévy ☎ 03 84 72 11 22; www.dole.org

Montbéliard tourist information 1 rue Henri-Mouhot ☎ 03 81 94 45 60; www.agglo-montbeliard.fr/tourisme

Ronchamp tourist information ✉ place du 14-Juillet ☎ 03 84 63 50 82; www.tourisme-ronchamp.fr.st

Musée de l'Aventure Peugeot ✉ Carretour de l'Europe, 25600 Sochaux ☎ 03 81 99 42 03 ⊙ Daily 9–7, Apr.–Sep.; 10–6, rest of year 🍴 $

La Chapelle Notre-Dame-du-Haut ✉ 70250 Ronchamp ☎ 03 84 20 65 13 ⊙ Daily 9:30–6:30, Apr.–Sep.; 10–4, rest of year 🍴 $$

Maison Natale de Louis Pasteur ✉ 43 rue Pasteur Dole ☎ 03 84 72 20 61 ⊙ Mon.–Sat. 10–6, Sun. noon–6, Jul.–Aug.; Mon.–Sat. 10–noon, and 2–6, Sun. 2–6, Apr.–Jun. and Sep.–Oct.; Sat. 10–noon and 2–5, Sun. 2–5, rest of year 🍴 $

Saline Royale ✉ 25610 Arc-et-Senans ☎ 03 81 54 45 45 ⊙ Daily 9–7, Jul.–Aug.; 9–6 in Jun. and Sep.; 9–noon and 2–6, Apr.–May and in Oct.; 10–noon and 2–5, rest of year 🍴 $$

CHAMPAGNE AND THE NORTH

*"*F*ROM white cliffs and Gothic cathedrals to a land of forests and sparkling wine, the north lets you rediscover wide-open spaces. "*

Opposite: Ornate clock tower and facade of the Town Hall at Calais

Champagne and the North

CHAMPAGNE AND THE NORTH

Visitors often dismiss France north of Paris as little more than a shortcut to Britain and Belgium. But shrug away these regions and you're missing out on some of the most charming corners of the country, with unspoiled walled towns, dramatic Gothic cathedrals and celebrated champagne bubbles.

From the Battlefields

The green, pleasant land hides the scars of battles. The Somme and Flanders fields are still dotted with poppies and broken by countless war cemeteries and memorials. Historic wars and treaties between France and England litter local history books – Agincourt, Crécy and the Cloth of Gold Field are indicated from the roadside. At Compiègne in Picardy, visit the old railroad carriage where Germany signed the armistice of World War I and later forced France to surrender on the same site.

The fields that saw so much blood are mainly farmland today, and fresh vegetables contribute to much of the rural economy. Industrialized developments outside principal towns center on pharmaceuticals in Reims and mail-order clothing in Lille Métropole.

The area suffered considerably with the running down of the traditional mining industry. The former pit at Lewarde, near the bell-ringing town of Douai, is now an excellent museum showing the daily life of miners and their families over the past 100 years.

Other mines and slag heaps have been redeveloped as dry ski slopes.

Food

Food is generally less extravagant and ostentatious than in Paris, Lyon and Burgundy to the south, but it's full of delicious local flavors. You can still find some of France's best restaurants in rural locations, but simple local fare in family-run restaurants in the Nord-Pas de Calais is a cheering experience. Savory filled pastries *(tartes)* made with maroilles cheese or leeks *(poireaux)* are a particular favorite. The filling main course is *carbonade flamande,* a hearty stew. Along the coast, fresh fish is a specialty. Etaples, outside Le Touquet, has a restaurant run by fishermen themselves, and the region has many local variants on *soupe de poisson* (fish soup). Ardennes pâté is legendary (see page 248).

Beers

Champagne of course grows its wines, and bars in the region will serve bubbly not only by the bottle but also by the glass (ask for a *coupe* or a *flute*). Elsewhere is beer country. The hops of Artois and Flanders create many fabulous ales, including monastic brews. The area around Cassel has some great beers, and in Lille, Les Trois Brasseurs restaurant brews its own. There are four main types of beer: *blonde, brune, rousse* and the local specialty *blanche de Lille,* usually served with a slice of lemon.

Estaminets

Breweries and gin distilleries (see page 247) often organize guided tours and tasting sessions, but the place to stop for a drink in the north, especially near Cassel, is an *estaminet*. These are small local bars in towns and villages, often the front room of a private house, sometimes open for just a few hours.

The Hautvillers vineyards cover the gently sloping hillside near Épernay

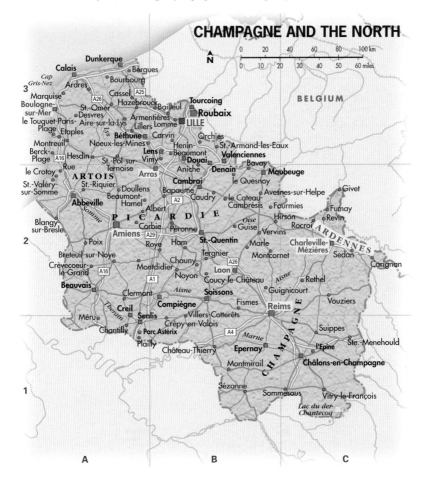

CHAMPAGNE AND THE NORTH

0 20 40 60 80 100 km
0 10 20 30 40 50 60 miles

N

Cap Gris-Nez
Calais
Dunkerque
Bergues
Bourbourg
Ardres
Marquise
Boulogne-sur-Mer
le Touquet-Paris-Plage
Étaples
Montreuil
Berck-Plage
le Crotoy
St.-Valéry-sur-Somme
Abbeville
Blangy-sur-Bresle
Poix
Breteuil-sur-Noye
Crèvecoeur-le-Grand
Beauvais
Méru
Chantilly
Creil
Senlis
Clermont
Compiègne
Parc Astérix
Plailly

Cassel
Hazebrouck
St.-Omer
Desvres
Aire-sur-la-Lys
Lillers
Béthune
Noeux-les-Mines
Hesdin
St.-Pol-sur-Ternoise
Rue
St.-Riquier
Doullens
Beaumont-Hamel
Albert
Corbie
Amiens
Roye
Ham
Montdidier
Noyon

Bailleul
Armentières
Lomme
Carvin
Lens
Vimy
Aniche
Bapaume
Caudry
Péronne
St.-Quentin
Chauny
Tergnier
Laon
Coucy-le-Château
Soissons
Fismes
Villers-Cotterêts
Crépy-en-Valois
Château-Thierry
Montmirail
Sézanne

Tourcoing
Roubaix
LILLE
Orchies
Hénin-Beaumont
Douai
Denain
Cambrai
le Quesnoy
le Cateau-Cambrésis
Guise
Vervins
Marle
Montcornet
Rethel
Guignicourt
Reims
Épernay
Sommesous

BELGIUM

St.-Armand-les-Eaux
Valenciennes
Bavay
Maubeuge
Avesnes-sur-Helpe
Fourmies
Hirson
Rocroi
Charleville-Mézières
Sedan
Carignan
Vouziers
Suippes
l'Épine
Châlons-en-Champagne
Ste.-Menehould
Vitry-le-François

Givet
Fumay
Revin
ARDENNES

ARTOIS
PICARDIE
CHAMPAGNE

Somme
Oise
Aisne
Aisne
Marne
Lac du der-Chantecoq

Lys
Thérain

A26
A25
A16
A2
A29
A1
A16
A26
A4

3

2

1

A   B   C

Champagne and the North

LILLE

For years Lille was the best-kept secret in France. Despite having charming cobbled streets of elegant 17th- and 18th-century houses, broad Flemish squares and the richest art gallery outside Paris, the city was tucked away in a coal-mining region and therefore scorned by Parisians and ignored by tourists. Then came TGV high-speed trains, which brought Europe's key capitals within an easy commute. The city was reborn.

Shopping is a main attraction. The Euralille mall, by the station, and the pedestrian streets around rue de Béthune have big stores, and the chic boutiques in Vieux Lille (the old quarter) have the top names in fashion.

The first weekend in September sees the *Braderie de Lille* a citywide garage sale, with 125 miles of sidewalks taken over as every family in town trades around the clock. Subways run all night, and every restaurant serves mussels and fries.

Eating out is a social occasion. Intimate and charming restaurants line rue de Gand in the old town, and lively bars and bistros cluster around the former market Halles on rue Solférino for the younger crowd. Forty percent of the population is under 25, many attending the city's respected universities. Louis Pasteur was the first dean of the science faculty at the University of Lille.

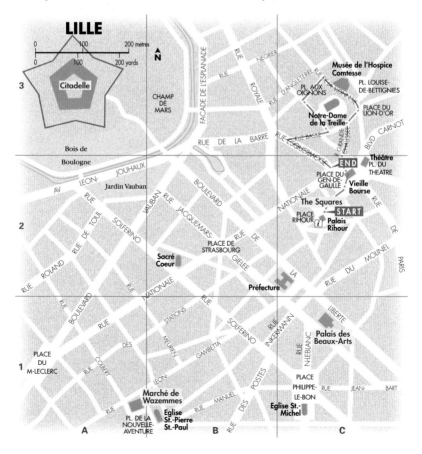

The cloistered courtyard in the Vieille Bourse serves as a book market

ESSENTIAL INFORMATION

TOURIST INFORMATION
• Palais Rihour, place Rihour ☎ 03 20 21 94 21; www.lilletourism.com 🚇 Rihour
• Lille-Europe Station 🚇 Gare Lille-Europe
• Lille-Airport

Stewards in yellow jackets provide tourist and shopping information on central streets.

URBAN TRANSPORTATION
Two subway lines and more than 70 bus routes serve central Lille and the metropolitan area as far as the Belgian border. Two tramways link the city with Tourcoing and Roubaix. Integrated ticketing means that any single journey may be taken using one or all of the bus, tram or subway lines. Tickets are sold individually or in books (carnets) of 10, and a one-day Pass Journée is available. The Lille Métropole City Pass gives free access to museums, monuments and attractions and use of public transportation for 1, 2 or 3 days; available from the tourist office (www.cdt-nord.fr). Services run from 6 a.m. to midnight. No public transportation operates on May 1. Information, tickets and assistance are available from Lille-Flandres Station ☎ 03 20 40 40 40. Taxis can be hailed from stands outside main stations. Or book: ☎ 03 20 06 06 06. Lille-Europe Station has fast train links to northern Europe (Brussels 35 minutes, Paris 1 hour and 12 minutes, London via Channel Tunnel 2 hours). Local services depart from the platforms of Lille-Flandres Station (500 yards away); For information ☎ 08 36 67 68 69 (daily, 24 hours; toll call).

AIRPORT INFORMATION
Lille Airport, 5 miles out of town at Lesquin has international and domestic services ☎ 03 20 49 68 68; www.lille.aeroport.fr. A regular shuttle bus runs to Lille-Europe Station.

CLIMATE – Average highs and lows											
JAN.	FEB.	MAR.	APR.	MAY	JUN.	JUL.	AUG.	SEP.	OCT.	NOV.	DEC.
5°C	6°C	9°C	12°C	17°C	20°C	22°C	23°C	19°C	15°C	9°C	7°C
41°F	43°F	48°F	54°F	63°F	68°F	72°F	73°F	66°F	59°F	48°F	45°F
1°C	1°C	3°C	5°C	8°C	11°C	13°C	13°C	11°C	7°C	4°C	2°C
34°F	34°F	37°F	41°F	46°F	52°F	55°F	55°F	52°F	45°F	39°F	36°F

Lille Sights

Key to symbols

⊞ map coordinates refer to the Lille map on page 242; sights below are highlighted in yellow on the map.

⊠ address or location ☎ telephone number

◎ opening times ▣ nearest bus or tram route

⋔ restaurant on site or nearby

◉ nearest métro/subway station(s)

ℹ information 🎫 admission charge: $$$ more than €10, $$ €5–€10, $ less than €5

Citadelle

The magnificent fortress surrounded by trees has been the hub of the French army for 300 years. Louis XIV's "Queen of Citadels" was a town in its own right – its five-sided star-shaped design inspired the U.S. Pentagon. The main entrance, Porte Royale, has a Latin-inscribed regal façade and 13-foot-thick walls. Designed for 1,200 men, the garrison remains home to 1,000 soldiers, including members of the French Foreign Legion. The elegant parade ground, arsenal and chapel may be visited by appointment with the tourist office on Sunday afternoons from May through August. The first governor of the garrison was its architect Sébastien Le Prestre de Vauban, and the second was d'Artagnan, hero of *The Three Musketeers*. The fortress stands in the Bois de Boulogne, 124 acres of wooded parkland that are home to Sunday joggers and a zoo.

⊞ A3 ⊠ avenue du 43ème-Régiment-d'Infantrie
☎ 03 20 21 94 21 (tourist office) ◎ Tours depart Sun. 3–5 ▣ 14 🎫 $$

Marché de Wazemmes

No mere market, this is an occasion – a multicultural Sunday morning in the streets around Église St.-Pierre St.-Paul and place de la Nouvelle-Aventure. Antiques and kittens are sold on the sidewalks, and produce stalls are piled to creaking with plump, fresh chicory and ripe tomatoes. For pâté and cheeses, try the brick market hall. Sounds of an accordion from a pavement café mingle with the spiel of traders selling fresh mint from old bicycles. All is handshakes, backslapping and *bonhommie*.

The smell of Sunday lunch is overwhelming. Huge pans of paëlla are stirred outside many ethnic restaurants, and giant rôtisseries turn dozens of roast chickens.

⊞ A1 ⊠ Place de la Nouvelle-Aventure ◎ Sun. mornings and holidays ⋔ Bars, cafés and food stalls ◉ Gambetta

Palais des Beaux-Arts

France's second national art collection after the Louvre was originally built from 1885 to 1892 and reopened in 1997 after six years of renovation. No one should miss the museum's celebrated works by Francisco José de Goya: a pair of wicked portrayals of youth and old age, *Les Jeunes* and *Les Vieilles*. Deep red walls and high ceilings provide the perfect backdrop to a

Place du Général-de-Gaulle sits at the heart of Lille

veritable banquet of French, Flemish and European masterpieces from the 17th century to the Impressionists. A Renaissance gallery and Sébastien Le Prestre de Vauban's original citadel models take up the basement.

✚ C1 ✉ place de la République ☎ 03 20 06 78 00 🕐 Wed.–Sun. 10–6 (also Fri. 6–7 p.m.), Mon. 2–6; closed holidays. Closed first weekend in Sep.
🍴 Café and restaurant with terrace 🚇 République
♿ $

THE SQUARES

The heart of Lille is place du Général-de-Gaulle. Often transformed into park or fairground when the city is in party mood, it's the venue for the Christmas Ferris wheel, which affords unrivaled views across the city. Everyone meets at the central fountain with its statue of *Déesse* (Goddess), a spiritual symbol of civic courage during a siege in 1792. The main theater is the former guardhouse. The tiered roof topped with golden figures next door is the 1936 home of the local paper *La Voix du Nord*, dominating the square along with Europe's largest bookstore the Furet du Nord. Restaurants, cafés and bars buzz until the wee hours. Behind the elegant Vieille Bourse (see page 246) is place du Théâtre, the neoclassical Opera House and the magnificent belfry of the imposing chamber of commerce.

✚ C2 🚇 Rihour

Vieille Bourse – Lille's most beautiful site

WALK: OLD TOWN

Refer to route marked on city map on page 242

**This 1.5-mile stroll is around the 17th-
and 18th-century quarter.**

*Leave the tourist office at Palais Rihour, a
former chapel of the dukes of Burgundy,
and cross place du Général de Gaulle.
Walk through the Vieille Bourse.*
Vieille Bourse is Lille's most beautiful site. It
is a cluster of private houses, where
merchant stalls in the cloistered courtyard
serve as a flower and book market and refuge
for chess players.

*Rue de la Bourse leads to rue de la
Grande-Chaussée.*
An iron arm above the corner shop points
you in the right direction. D'Artagnan lived at
Nos. 20 and 26.

*Turn right along rue des Chats-Bossus; on
your left you may admire the fabulous
Breton art deco mosaic frontage of
l'Huitrière restaurant. Continue to place
du Lion-d'Or, then rue de la Monnaie.*
Visit Musée de l'Hospice Comtesse, a 13th-
century hospital that now houses a museum

focusing on Flemish life and art from the 15th
through 17th centuries. Noteworthy features
include a fabulous blue-tiled kitchen and a
medicinal herb garden.

*Continue along the road and turn left on
rue au Péterinck, past 18th-century
weavers' houses to place aux Oignons.*
The name has nothing to do with the onions
sold in the nearby market; rather it's a
corruption of donjon (dungeon). Little
alleyways lead to place Gilleson, where long
ago stood the château of the counts of
Flanders. The foundation stone of Cathédrale
Notre-Dame de la Treille was laid in 1854.
However, although the chapel and apse were
built by the end of the 19th century and the
city welcomed its first bishop in 1913,
construction was abandoned in 1947, leaving
Lille with three-quarters of a cathedral until
1999. Notre-Dame now has an oddly
industrial modern frontage and piazza, with
magnificent doors by Holocaust survivor
sculptor Georges Jeanclos.

*Take rue du Cirque, and turn right on rue
Basse to see the antique shops. Then go
left to the bustling rue Esquermoise, with
its legendary tea shop Meert at No. 27, a
few steps from place du Général de Gaulle.*

Champagne and the North

The town of Roubaix has become a mecca for clothes shopping

LILLE MÉTROPOLE

The larger metropolitan area around Lille boosts its population from around 150,000 to almost a million and laps over the Belgian border. An integrated public transportation system of trams, buses and subways enables a local ticket to take you from a museum in one town to an opera in the next. Pretty gardens line the roads to the two major satellite towns, Tourcoing and Roubaix, each 30 minutes away. Tourcoing is a major cultural center with music festivals and an enchanting free Fine Arts Museum, where priceless canvases are hung on a whim. One month you may find Impressionists next to Pablo Picasso, the next might see Old Masters sharing a wall with a local experimental artist. Once home to the textile mills and factories of the north, Roubaix is now a mecca for clothes shopping. McArthur Glenn is where top brands sell at 30 to 40 percent below usual prices. The presigious 19th century Museum of Arts and Industry has reopened in a converted art deco swimming pool with a stunning multicolored sunset window. Villeneuve d'Ascq, just 15 minutes from central Lille, is home to the Modern Art Museum, which has excellent displays of all major art movements of the 20th century. The building is set in a park where locals walk their dogs beside sculptures by Pablo Picasso and his contemporaries. A river trip along the Deûle from Lille includes a visit to the 200-year-old distillery at Wambrechies. Original equipment from the early 1800s makes *genièvre* (a juniper gin) and an associated 40-proof *Vieux Malt* that would be at home in the highlands of Scotland.

Tourcoing tourist information ✉ 9 rue de Tournai ☎ 03 20 26 89 03

Roubaix tourist information ✉ rue de la Tuilerie ☎ 03 20 65 31 90

Musée des Beaux-Arts ✉ 2 rue Paul Doumer, 59200 Tourcoing ☎ 03 20 28 91 60 🕐 Wed.–Mon. 1:30–6; closed holidays 🚇 Tourcoing Centre 💵 Free

McArthur Glenn ✉ 44 Mail de Lannoy, 59100 Roubaix ☎ 03 28 33 36 00 🕐 Mon.–Fri. 10–7, Sat. 9:30–7 🚇 Euroteleport

Musée de l'Art Moderne ✉ 1 allée du Musée, 59650 Villeneuve d'Ascq ☎ 03 20 19 68 68 🕐 Wed.–Mon. 10–6 🚇 Pont de Bois, then bus 41 to Parc-Urban-Musée 💵 $$

Distillerie Claeyssens ✉ 1 avenue des Châteaux, 59118 Wambrechies ☎ 03 20 14 91 91; www.wambrechies.com 🕐 Tours depart Tue.–Thu. at 11 and 3, Sat. at 4:30 and Sun. at 3 and 4:30 🚌 9 Wambrechies Château 💵 $

REGIONAL SIGHTS

Key to symbols

🟩 map coordinates refer to the region map on page 241; sights below are highlighted in yellow on the map.

✉ address or location   ☎ telephone number

🕐 opening times   🚌 nearest bus or tram route

🍴 restaurant on site or nearby   ℹ information

💳 admission charge: $$$ more than €10, $$ €5–€10, $ less than €5

AMIENS

The miracle of Amiens is its vast Gothic cathedral. During the bombings of the 20th-century wars, when much of the surrounding medieval town was destroyed, France's largest cathedral remained untouched. Similarly, during the Revolution, when images of saints outside most churches and cathedrals were decapitated, the faces on rows of apostles and prophets around the three main porches remained intact. Built in less than 50 years, this 13th-century marvel of engineering has a 139-foot-high nave. Later treasures include 3,650 carved figures in the 16th-century choir and an impressive baroque pulpit. Explore the surviving medieval

Lovely Louvergny in the Ardennes

quarter behind the cathedral and Jules Verne's house. The town was a Celtic settlement on the Somme river until taken by the Romans under Julius Caesar as a strategic point on routes to the north. The Somme feeds Amiens' unusual private market gardens Les Hortillonnages, floating plots of land served by narrow canals *(rieux)*. Boat trips around the gardens provide a delightful diversion.
🟩 A2

Tourist information ✉ 6 bis rue Dusevel ☎ 03 22 71 60 50; www.amiens.com

ARDENNES

The town of Charleville-Mézières (see page 250) is a perfect base for exploring the wooded countryside of the Ardennes. Deep forests straddle the border with present-day Belgium, and it's impossible today to imagine the huge tracts of woodland flattened during the last war in Germany's final assault on the Allies. By the 1970s, the forests were as rich as ever. Following the river Meuse provides spectacular scenery. The Massif Ardennais is a perfect backdrop high above, and the river gorge below is equally dramatic. Explore on horseback, by boat or on foot; details are available from Charleville tourist office. Each month, forest rangers lead escorted treks to discover wildlife, wild fruits and mushrooms in the woods. Strong mushrooms and wild boar dominate the flavors in bistro and restaurant fare, which includes famous pâtés and smoked meats. Boar is best served with a potato and onion dish known as *la bayenne.* The health-conscious will treasure one of the local cheeses: rocroi, which is strong in flavor but low in fat.
🟩 C2

Departmental tourist information: Comité Départemental du Tourisme des Ardennes ✉ 22 place Ducale, 08107 Charleville Mézières ☎ 03 24 56 06 08; www.ardennes.com

Opposite: Inside the vast cathedral at Amiens

The arcaded place des Héros in Arras

ARRAS

Amid the countless World War I cemeteries, Arras, with its arcaded squares and high gabled houses, was once the capital of Artois and gave its name to fine tapestries. The stunning 17th- and 18th-century architecture in the wide squares, place des Héros and Grand Place, is a miraculous reconstruction since the original buildings were destroyed in the war. Fortunately, a network of passages linked the town's cellars, and the original plans for every building were discovered therein. The 16th-century town hall, which was also rebuilt and boasts a fabulous belfry, stands over the entrance to these tunnels, known as Les Boves. During the war, the tunnels extended to the trenches and an underground railway and telephone system communicated with the front. Visit the tunnels, then climb the belfry for good views. The war memorial lists the names of 36,000 soldiers whose bodies were never found. The awe-inspiring Canadian Monument at Vimy Ridge is 7 miles away (see page 255).
🕂 B2

Tourist information ✉ Hôtel de Ville, rue Jacques le Caron ☎ 03 21 51 26 95; www.ot-arras.fr
Les Boves ✉ place des Héros ☎ 03 21 51 26 95 🕐 Daily 9–6:30, May–Sep.; 9–noon and 2–6, rest of year 🚻 $

BOULOGNE

France's largest fishing port, Boulogne has a bustling commercial center with a lively market and one of the world's greatest cheese shops, Philippe Olivier, on rue Thiers. Leave the shoppers behind and climb Grande Rue to the upper town. Untouched by wartime bombings, the old town is completely walled, with just four entrances. Tree-lined paths top the ramparts and make for a pleasant walk. Fortifications enclose the 19th-century domed basilica, attractive cobbled streets and the moated medieval château, now a museum. Summer sees a music festival on the ramparts. Down by the port is Nausicaä, a fascinating sea-life center, and a wide beach. As a ferry port for Britain, English is spoken widely here.
🕂 A3

Tourist information ✉ 24 quai Gambetta ☎ 03 21 10 88 10; www.boulogne.com
Nausicaä ✉ boulevard Ste.-Beuve ☎ 03 21 30 99 99; www.nausicaa.fr 🕐 Daily 9:30–8, Jul.–Aug.; 9:30–6:30, rest of year. Closed early to late Jan. 🍴 Restaurant and bistro 🚻 $$ ($$$ Jul.– Aug., some weekends and during school holidays)

CHARLEVILLE-MÉZIÈRES

The ninth-century town of Mézières was a fortified buffer zone between France and its enemies in the low countries. Bruised by the centuries, it declined when Charles de Gonzague, Duke of Nevers and Mantua, built splendidly Ruritanian Charleville, and rivalry between the two towns ensued until they merged in 1966. Charleville's main square, place Ducale, with its honeyed buildings framed by forest treetops, looks like a fairy tale illustration, never more so than during the triennial International Marionette Festival, scheduled for September 2003 and 2006. Known as the City of Puppets, Charleville hosts the Institut National de la Marionnette, the world's leading school

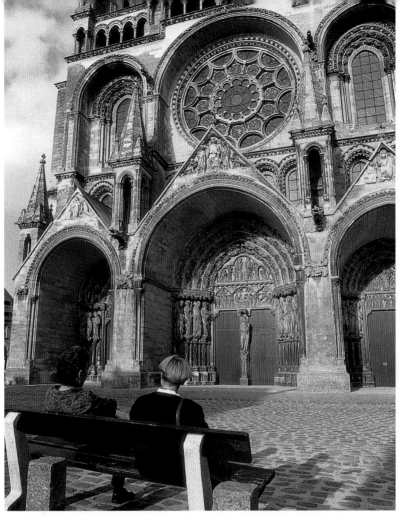

Inset porchways are a feature of the west front of the Gothic cathedral of Notre-Dame in Laon

for puppeteers with its incredible clock called the Grand Marionnettiste (Puppet Master). A two-story delight, the clock transforms itself into a puppet show every hour from 10 a.m. to 9 p.m. For more reflective moments, the Arthur Rimbaud Museum evokes the life and work of the young poet, born in Charleville in 1854.

✚ C2
Tourist information ✉ 4 place Ducale
☎ 03 24 55 69 90

LAON

The seven towers of the cathedral in the hilltop city of Laon can be seen for miles around. On closer inspection, it should come as no surprise that the glorious Notre-Dame, built in 1235, inspired the Gothic design of its more famous namesake in Paris. The highlight of the walled town, the cathedral has brooding inset porchways that frown across the parvis under the twin towers of the west front. Inside, discover two rose windows, lovely old stained glass, a splendid 387-foot-long nave and a beautiful cloister. During the 9th and 10th centuries, Laon was the capital of France. There is plenty of medieval architecture to appreciate, including the leaning tower of the 13th-century Porte de Soissons. Upper town treasures are best explored on foot, so leave your car in the lower town and take the automated monorail to the top of the hill.

✚ B2
Tourist information ✉ place du Parvis-Gautier de Mortagne ☎ 03 23 20 28 62; www.ville-loan.fr

Champagne and the North

Champagne stored in the cellars of Veuve Cliquot in Reims

DISCOVERING CHAMPAGNE

There is no such thing as French champagne; there is just champagne. If made anywhere else, it's simply sparkling wine. Only champagne from Champagne is champagne.

The unknown alchemy in the cellars and soil, which creates this special wine (locals swear one may drink until dawn and never know a hangover) was discovered by Dom Pérignon, a monk who added yeast to speed the winemaking at the Hautvillers Abbey. Visit the abbey and the neighboring village as part of a trail through Champagne country. The tourist office in Reims provides routes that feature Châlons-en-Champagne and Château-Thierry, plus some small private cellars. Base yourself in Epernay or Reims, where the great champagne houses are. Neither city has a subway since they are riddled with tunnels where bottles are stored.

Many larger houses offer escorted tours of their cellars. Some are simple, educational walks through chalk tunnels where staff explain winemaking from pressing to blending red and white grapes with cane sugar. Stored neck down in wooden racks, bottles must be twisted an eighth of a turn every day in a process called *remuage*. Each *remueur* turns 40,000 bottles daily.

Tours of this special underworld vary from Champagne Piper-Heidsieck's automated ride through Hollywood glamour, which whisks visitors to the set of *Casablanca* and sells souvenir Marilyn Monroe's monogrammed ice bucket in Reims, to Champagne Mercier's miniature train ride past thousands of bottles and a gallery of 19th-century posters in Epernay.

Pay around $40 in September for a day working the harvest: Volunteers are given breakfast, a champagne banquet in a cellar, a museum tour and a bottle to take home in return for a morning spent picking the Pinot Noir, Pinot Meunier and Chardonnay grapes – all the while sipping bubbly in the fields from a glass around your neck.

Reims tourist information (see page 253)
Epernay tourist information ✉ 7 avenue de Champagne ☎ 03 26 55 33 00; www.ot-epernay.fr
Regional tourist information: Comité Régional du Tourisme de Champagne-Ardenne ✉ B.P. 319, 51013 Châlons-en-Champagne Cedex ☎ 03 26 21 85 80; www.tourisme-champagne-ard.com

REIMS

Reims is rich. The wealth of the city was built on the popping of champagne corks (see page 252), but its history is richer than the fizz in its cellars. Clovis, France's first Christian king, was crowned here, and Joan of Arc led the Dauphin to his coronation in Reims. The city has overseen 25 Sunday morning coronation processions to the cathedral, from Louis VIII in 1223 to Charles X in 1825. That magnificent cathedral is the essential visit, however brief your stay. A gentle giant that wears sunlight like a coronation robe, the front combines the best of all of France's Gothic cathedrals: stone lacework on the twin towers and 56 statues of kings, each one 14.5 feet high, arranged above the rose window. The most famous figure on the facade is the Angel, the city symbol whose enigmatic smile rivals that of the *Mona Lisa*. The edifice was restored after artillery damage in World War I, and its 20th-century prize is the window by Marc Chagall, among some stunning 13th-century glass. Check out a fascinating 15th-century astronomical clock with moving figures depicting the Adoration of the Magi and the Flight into Egypt. A sound-and-light show tells the cathedral's story in July and August.

Don't miss the Archbishops' Palace (Palais du Tau) nearby – a World Heritage Site like the cathedral – where remains of many of the cathedral's original damaged statues, replaced during renovation, can be seen close up. The Fine Arts Museum has paintings from the Renaissance to the 20th century. The Roman era is recalled by the Porte de Mars, a splendid ocher-colored stone archway that now stands forlornly at the heart of a traffic interchange on the edge of town. Horse-

Joan of Arc is celebrated in the center of Reims

drawn carriage tours depart from the cathedral parvis in July and August, except Tuesdays and rainy days.

The city's wealth is the only barrier to true relaxation. Shops and restaurants may appear smug, but there is little real street life – many of Reims' citizens indulge themselves in private. The exception is summertime (late June to late August), when Les Flâneries Musicales, a season of free concerts established by Yehudi Menuhin, brings the world's greatest musicians playing Mozart, Bach and Gershwin in churches and parks.

🚩 B2

Tourist information ✉ 2 rue Guillaume-de-Machault ☎ 03 26 77 45 25; www.tourisme.fr/reims

Palais du Tau ✉ place du Cardinal-Luçon ☎ 03 26 47 81 79 🕐 Daily 9:30–12:30 and 2–6, mid-Mar. to mid-Nov.; Mon.–Fri. 10–noon and 2 and 5, Sat.–Sun. 10–noon and 2–5, rest of year 💵 $

Musée des Beaux-Arts ✉ 8 rue Chanvy ☎ 03 26 47 28 44 🕐 Wed.–Mon. 10–noon and 2–6 💵 $ (free first Sun. of the month)

DRIVE: THE OPAL COAST AND OLD WALLED TOWNS

Distance: 160 miles Time: 3 days

With a coast that has attracted pioneers from aviation to the Channel Tunnel and a hinterland rich in history, the Pas de Calais has plenty of tales to tell along its pretty valleys and byways.

From Calais, with its famed Auguste Rodin statue outside the ornate town hall belfry, take the D940 south toward Boulogne-sur-Mer.

Follow the Côte d'Opale (Opal Coast) of the English Channel with ferries and tunnel trains from Calais. Blériot-Plage is named for the aviator who first flew the Channel from here in 1909. The cliffs Cap Gris-Nez and Cap-Blanc Nez are signposted from the road. Explore Boulogne (see page 250).

Continue on the D940 to Etaples, then take the N39 to Le Touquet.

The seaside and casino resort is known as Paris-Plage due to its popularity with wealthy weekenders. Built by the British, who take 20-

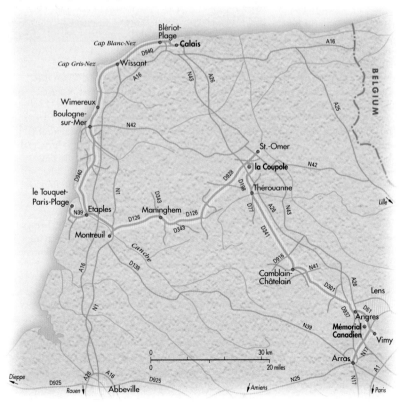

On the beach at the pleasure resort of Le Touquet

minute flights from Britain to an airstrip by one of three golf courses, this early-20th-century pleasure ground remains fashionable. Enjoy thalassotherapy, great food and shopping. Pine groves hide houses of a style the Brits call "Snow White Perpendicular."

From the N39 turn right to the N1 and right to the D138 and the D901 to Montreuil.

High on a hill above the Canche river, the old walled town of Montreuil-sur-Mer with quaint, cobbled streets is, despite the name, 10 miles from the sea. *Les Misérables* was set here, and townsfolk re-enact scenes from the novel on summer evenings. An 11th-century church and good restaurants are among quieter town alternatives.

Return to the N1, then take the D907 to the D126. Turn right on D343 at Maninghem and continue for 3 miles. Rejoin the D126, then turn left on D928 into St.-Omer.

Fast highways to Paris mean most travelers miss the delights of another walled town, St.-Omer, with a Gothic cathedral and unusual farms on waterlogged marshes, where farmers tend fields of lettuce from flat-bottomed boats.

Leave on the D928 to Abbeville then the D210 signed for Helfault and La Coupole.

A Nazi rocket bunker, La Coupole, serves as a moving museum, with two remarkable audiovisual presentations: one showing rocket science from wartime weaponry to the Apollo missions and the other revealing life in

occupied France through thousands of home movies and family photographs.

Take the D198 to Thérouanne, picking up the D341. Just after Camblain-Châtelain, go left on the D301 and filter left to turn right on the D937. Turn left at Angres on the D51 to Vimy. After 4 miles, look for signs to the Mémorial Canadien.

On the battlefield of April 1917 – land France later gave to Canada – Walter Allward's white stone cenotaph, Mémorial de Vimy (Parc Commémoratif), dominates the Douai plain. The inscription reads: "To the valor of their countrymen in the Great War and in memory of their 60,000 dead, this monument is raised by the people of Canada." At its foot, the figure of Mother Canada weeps for her sons. Visitors may walk front-line trenches and in summer explore tunnels behind the lines.

Take the N17 to Arras (see page 250).

Le Touquet tourist information ✉ Palais de l'Europe, place de l'Hermitage ☎ 03 21 06 72 00; www.letouquet.com

Montreuil-sur-Mer tourist information ✉ 21 rue Carnot, La Guinguette ☎ 03 21 06 04 27

St.-Omer tourist information ✉ 4 rue du Lion d'Or ☎ 03 21 98 08 51; www.tourisme.fr/saint-omer

La Coupole ✉ 62504 St.-Omer ☎ 03 21 93 07 07 🕙 Mon.–Fri. 9:30–6:30, Sat.–Sun. 10–7, Apr.–Sep.; daily 9:30–6:30, rest of year. Closed first half of Jan. 🍴 Café 🎫 $$

Mémorial de Vimy ✉ 62580 Vimy ☎ 03 21 48 72 29 🕙 Daily dawn–dusk. Tours 10–6, Apr.–Nov. 🎫 Free

HOTELS AND RESTAURANTS

The hotels and restaurants in this book were selected by local specialists and include establishments in several price ranges. Since price is often the best indication of the level of facilities and quality of service, a three-tiered price guide appears at the beginning of the listings. Because variable rates will affect the amount of foreign currency that can be exchanged for dollars (and thus affect the cost of a room or a meal), price ranges are given in the local currency.

Although price ranges and operating times were accurate at press time, this information is always subject to change without notice. If you're interested in a particular establishment, it is always advisable to call ahead to book. The larger and more expensive hotels, and the better-known restaurants, are more likely to have someone who speaks English on staff; smaller establishments may not.

Facilities for travelers with disabilities vary greatly, it is advisable to contact an establishment directly to determine whether your needs can be met. Some older buildings may not be suitable for visitors with limited or impaired mobility.

Accommodations
Accommodations have been selected with two considerations in mind: a particularly attractive character or sense of local flavor, or a convenient or central location. Remember that centrally located hotels fill up quickly, especially during summer vacation periods; make reservations well in advance. In-room bathrooms (sometimes referred to as "en-suite facilities") may not be available in smaller budget hotels.

Room rates for French hotels normally includes a light breakfast of rolls or croissants and coffee. Some hotels offer a rate that includes an evening meal (known as *demi-pension*).

Eating Out
Listed restaurants range from upscale places suitable for an elegant evening out to small cafés where you can stop and take a leisurely break from a busy day of sightseeing. Some are close to attractions; where this is the case, there is a cross-reference under the attraction listing. Other eating possibilities are the cafeterias and restaurants on the premises of museums and galleries.

French food has a justifiable reputation as among the best in the world. From the simplest offering of an oven-fresh baguette with a melt-in-the-mouth omelet, to the most elaborate and imaginatively prepared menu *gastronomique* of a famous chef, you will be delighted by your meals in France. So relax and take your time as the French do; a meal here is not just a remedy for hunger, but an experience to enjoy at leisure and a feast for eye and palate, enhanced by the hospitality and good service of your host.

Opposite: Eating out in style

Paris – Île de France

KEY TO SYMBOLS

- 🏨 hotel
- 🍴 restaurant
- ✉ address
- ☎ telephone number
- 🕐 days/times closed
- Ⓜ nearest metro/tube/subway station(s)
- 🚌 nearby bus/trolley-bus/tram route(s).
- ⛴ ferry
- AX American Express
- DC Diners Club
- MC MasterCard
- VI VISA

Hotel
Price guide: double room with breakfast for two people
- **$$$** over €150
- **$$** €75–€150
- **$** under €75

Restaurant
Price guide: dinner per person, excluding drinks
- **$$$** over €40
- **$$** €20–€40
- **$** under €20

A TASTE OF VAN GOGH

Van Gogh's last supper was most likely taken at the Auberge Ravoux at Auvers-sur-Oise. The café is therefore an ideal place to dine and toast this remarkable artist. Close by is a museum devoted to the now-illegal liqueur favored by the Impressionists, absinthe, which made the art go stronger back in the 19th century (see page 50). The old style of the café remains as in those times, but today safer aperitifs are served.

Paris– Île de France

AUVERS-SUR-OISE

🍴 Auberge Ravoux $$
The restaurant serves lunch to those who come to discover the last home of Vincent van Gogh upstairs. Reservations are essential.
✉ Maison de Van Gogh, 52 rue du Général de Gaulle ☎ 01 30 36 60 63 🕐 Closed Sun. dinner and Mon. dinner   AX DC MC VI

CHARTRES

🍴 Le Buisson Ardent $$
A stone's throw from the cathedral, this restaurant blends contemporary cuisine with traditional local recipes.
✉ 10 rue au Lait ☎ 02 37 34 04 66 MC VI

🏨 Grand Monarque $$
The former coaching inn is now a smoothly operated hotel, with individually styled rooms.
✉ 22 place des Épars ☎ 02 37 18 15 15; fax 02 37 36 34 18   AX DC MC VI

FONTAINEBLEAU

🏨 L'Aigle Noir $$$
The elegant hotel faces the château. Its renowned restaurant ($$$) caters to upmarket diners.
✉ 27 place Napoléon-Bonaparte, 77300 ☎ 01 60 74 60 00; fax 01 60 74 60 01   AX DC MC VI

PARIS

🏨 Agora $$
This good value, mildly eccentric hotel is centrally located just yards from the Chatelet-Les-Halles RER train station. The cheerful reception staff speak English.
✉ 7 rue de la Cossonnerie, 75001 ☎ 01 42 33 46 02; fax 01 42 33 80 99 Ⓜ Les Halles; RER Chatelet-Les-Halles   AX MC VI

🍴 Beauvilliers $$$
Decorated like a 19th-century show-girl's dressing room, the restaurant has an indulgent menu and a decadent atmosphere that could make a silver wedding seem illicit.
✉ 52 rue Lamark, 75018 ☎ 01 42 54 54 42 🕐 Closed Mon. lunch and Sun. Ⓜ Lamarck-Caulaincourt   AX DC MC VI

🍴 Bofinger $
Ask for a table under the dome at this chic restaurant, known for traditional oyster and foie-gras dishes and reliable menus.
✉ 5 rue de la Bastille, 75004 ☎ 01 42 72 87 82 Ⓜ Bastille   AX DC MC VI

🍴 Les Bookinistes $$
Protégés of the great chef Guy Savoy prepare imaginative, reasonably priced food in this corner restaurant. Enjoy smart service and the rare vegetarian menu.
✉ 53 quai des Grands-Augustins, 75006 ☎ 01 43 25 45 94 🕐 Closed Sat. lunch and Sun. Ⓜ Saint Michel   AX DC MC VI

🍴 Brasserie Flo $$
In this backstreet restaurant hear the clatter of platters and yells of barmen as waiters slice through the crowds carrying trays of seafood and ice, cheese and bamboo.
✉ 7 cour des Petites-Écuries, 75010 ☎ 01 47 70 13 59 Ⓜ Château d'Eau   AX DC MC VI

🏨 La Bretonnerie $$
Antique furnishings fill the old-style rooms of the family-run hotel. Parking may be arranged in advance.
✉ 22 rue Ste.-Croix de la Bretonnerie, 75004 ☎ 01 48 87 77 63; fax 01 42 77 26 78 🕐 Closed in Aug. Ⓜ Hôtel de Ville   MC VI

🍴 Café Beaubourg $
Watch street entertainers outside the Pompidou Center while savoring salads and fashionable food.
✉ Rue St.-Martin 75004 ☎ 01 48 87 63 96 Ⓜ Châtelet Les Halles   AX DC MC VI

🍴 Chez Georges $$$
Journalists and bankers dine elbow to elbow and lunch secrets are confided over turbot in a *sauce béarnaise* and good steaks.
✉ 1 rue du Mail, 75002 ☎ 01 42 60 07 11 🕐 Closed Sun. Ⓜ Sentier   AX MC VI

🏨 Chopin $–$$
At the end of a glass-roofed gallery of toy shops, the homey spot has rooms overlooking courtyards.
✉ 10 boulevard Montmartre ,46 passage Joufroy, 75009 ☎ 01 47 70 58 10; fax 01 42 47 00 70 Ⓜ Grands Boulevards   MC VI

⌂ Crillon $$$

Arguably the most prestigious hotel in town, the Bernstein and Presidential apartment are ideal for those with elastic wallets.

✉ 10 place de la Concorde, 75008 ☎ 01 44 71 15 00; fax 01 44 71 15 02 🚇 Concorde   AX DC MC VI

🍴 La Fontaine de Mars $$

Red-checked tablecloths and polished copper decorate this café. Lunches are a good value.

✉ 129 rue St.-Dominique, 75007 ☎ 01 47 05 46 44 🚇 École Militaire   AX DC MC VI

🍴 Le Fouquet's Barriere $$$

This restaurant is a Champs-Élysées institution, where people-watching has been refined into an art form.

✉ 99 avenue des Champs-Élysées, 75008 ☎ 01 47 23 50 00 🚇 George V   AX DC MC VI

🍴 Le Grand Vefour $$$

The decor is opulent, the wine cellar is great, and Guy Martin's cuisine is faultless. Make a reservation well in advance and you might enjoy lunch for €50.

✉ 17 rue de Beaujolais, 75001 ☎ 01 42 96 56 27 🚇 Closed Sat.–Sun. 🚇 Palais Royal Musée du Louvre   AX DC MC VI

⌂ L'Hôtel $$$

Oscar Wilde died here, and cabaret-singer Mistinguette's boudoir is among the rooms in what is one of the most expensive hotels on the left bank.

✉ 13 rue des Beaux-Arts, 75006 ☎ 01 44 41 99 00; fax 01 43 25 64 81 🚇 St.-Germain-des-Près   AX DC MC VI

⌂ Jeu de Paume $$$

A 17th-century courtyard leads to this former tennis court on the quieter and more elegant of the Seine islands.

✉ 54 rue St.-Louis-en-l'Île, 75004 ☎ 01 43 26 14 18; fax 01 40 46 02 76 🚇 Pont Marie   AX DC MC VI

⌂ Méridien Montparnasse $$$

Glass, chrome and jazz give an international buzz to the modern hotel by the TGV station.

✉ 19 rue du Commandant-René-Mouchotte, 75014 ☎ 01 44 36 44 36; fax 01 44 36 47 00 🚇 Montparnasse-Bienvenue   AX DC MC VI

⌂ Meurice $$$

Fling open a tall bedroom window and look over the gardens of the Tuileries. The palatial hotel is furnished to glorious effect.

✉ 228 rue de Rivoli, 75001 ☎ 01 44 58 10 10; fax 01 48 58 10 15 🚇 Tuileries   AX DC MC VI

⌂ Millennium Opera Paris $$$

The newly refurbished delight features a glass dome and country-house good taste in the rooms.

✉ 12 boulevard Haussmann, 75009 ☎ 01 49 49 16 00; fax 01 49 49 17 00 🚇 Opéra   AX DC MC VI

⌂ Le Pavillon Bastille $$

Opposite the opera building, the discreet town house blends traditional and contemporary styles.

✉ 65 rue de Lyon, 75012 ☎ 01 43 43 65 65; fax 01 43 43 96 52 🚇 Bastille   AX DC MC VI

⌂ Pavillon de la Reine $$$

These converted royal apartments are a rarity among the garret-like accommodations of the Marais.

✉ 28 place de Vosges, 75003 ☎ 01 40 29 19 19; fax 01 40 29 19 20 🚇 St.-Paul   AX DC MC VI

🍴 Pavillon Puebla $$–$$$

Christian Vergès' fabulous hideaway hunting lodge is the place to enjoy classic Catalan and Gascony cuisine with a contemporary twist.

✉ Parc des Buttes Chaumont, 75019 ☎ 01 42 08 92 62 🚇 Closed Sun.–Mon. 🚇 Buttes-Chaumont   AX MC VI

🍴 Le 59 Poincaré $$$

It's here, rather than at his satellite restaurants, that Alain Ducasse proves himself a master of traditional French cuisine.

✉ 59 avenue Raymond-Poincaré, 75016 ☎ 01 47 27 59 59   AX DC MC VI

🍴 Au Pied de Cochon $$

At the last great market restaurant in town, join revelers for onion soup and pig's trotters at dawn.

✉ 6 rue Coquillère, 75001 ☎ 01 40 13 77 00. 🚇 Châtelet Les Halles   AX DC MC VI

🍴 Polidor $

At this last of the left bank eateries, students and visitors share long wooden tables and waitresses are honest about the dish of the day.

✉ 41 rue Monsieur-le-Prince, 75006 ☎ 01 43 26 95 34 🚇 Odéon   No credit cards

⌂ Prima Lepic $

The popular, but still individual, small hotel thrives in the heart of the Montmartre village.

✉ 29 rue Lépic, 75018 ☎ 01 46 06 44 64; fax 01 46 06 66 11 🚇 Blanche MC VI

🍴 La Régalade $$

When Yves Camborde left the Crillon, he brought his distinctive style of cuisine to this sleepy residential quarter. It's worth the trek from the city center.

✉ 49 avenue Jean-Moulin, 75014 ☎ 01 45 45 68 58 🚇 Closed Sun.–Mon. 🚇 Porte d'Orléans   VI

🍴 Rendezvous de la Marine $

Despite being gentrified, this bank of the canal still has a good blue-collar bistro, which serves generous portions of homey cooking.

✉ 14 quai de la Loire, 75019 ☎ 01 42 49 33 40 🚇 Closed Sun.–Mon. 🚇 Jaurès   MC VI

⌂ Le Rives de Notre-Dame $$$

The delightful 16th-century house, located on the banks of the Seine, boasts bright decor and attentive service.

✉ 15 quai St.-Michel, 75005 ☎ 01 43 54 81 16; fax 01 43 26 27 09 🚇 St.-Michel   AX DC MC VI

🍴 Rotisserie du Beaujolais $$

Perhaps the best-kept secret in Paris, this country-style bistro is run by the same team that operates the legendary Tour d'Argent opposite. Fabulous regional dishes are prepared in the traditional manner.

✉ 19 quai de Tournelle, 75005 ☎ 01 43 54 17 47 🚇 Closed Mon. 🚇 Maubert Mutalité   MC VI

⌂ St.-James Paris $$$

This is the only private château-hotel in Paris, with a garden terrace restaurant, faultless service and comfortable rooms and suites. It's a jet-setters' home away from home.

✉ 43 avenue Bugeaud, 75016 ☎ 01 44 05 81 81; fax 01 44 05 81 82 🚇 Porte Dauphine   AX DC MC VI

⌂ St.-Merry $$–$$$

The Gothic interior is actually the exterior of the 16th-century church

KEY TO SYMBOLS

- ⊞ hotel
- �𝄙 restaurant
- ⊠ address
- ☎ telephone number
- ⏱ days/times closed
- Ⓜ nearest metro/tube/subway station(s)
- 🚌 nearby bus/trolley-bus/tram route(s).
- ⛴ ferry
- AX American Express
- DC Diners Club
- MC MasterCard
- VI VISA

Hotel

Price guide: double room with breakfast for two people

$$$	over €150
$$	€75–€150
$	under €75

Restaurant

Price guide: dinner per person, excluding drinks

$$$	over €40
$$	€20–€40
$	under €20

HOTEL DU JEU-DE-PAUME

The Hotel du Jeu-de-Paume, located on Île St.-Louis, is one of Paris' more imaginative conversions. From the archway leading to the hotel's former 17th-century royal jeu de paume – or indoor tennis court – the interior decor offers a change of pace for the visitor bored with efficient but dull whitewash and chrome. A glass elevator affords a superb view of the courtyard and its galleries, cleverly redone as comfortable breakfast and lounge areas, and centuries-old beams grandly support this airy central well. All rooms are individually furnished, and those under the eaves have little private spiral staircases to the sleeping area. The hotel also boasts its own sauna.

⊠ 54 rue St.-Louis-en-l'Île, Île St.-Louis (Pont Marie) ☎ 01 43 26 14 18; fax 01 40 46 02 76 Ⓜ Pont-Marie AX DC MC VI

---

of St.-Merry. Original flying buttresses plunge through room No. 9.

⊠ 78 rue de la Verrerie, 75004 ☎ 01 42 78 14 15; fax 01 40 29 06 82 Ⓜ Châtelet AX MC VI

⊞ St.-Michel $

Excellent value, the Mecelle family's clean, basic hotel is on an unexpectedly peaceful street in bustling St.-Michel.

⊠ 17 rue Gît-Le-Coeur, 75006 ☎ 01 43 26 98 70; fax 01 40 46 95 69 Ⓜ St.-Michel No credit cards

𝄙 Le Train Bleu $$$

This station restaurant is a concoction of luxuriant red drapes and extravagant gilts and mirrors. Solemn mustached waiters don ankle-length starched aprons.

⊠ Place Louis-Armand, Gare de Lyon, 75012 ☎ 01 44 75 76 76 Ⓜ Gare de Lyon AX DC MC VI

⊞ Vendôme $$$

A few yards from the Ritz and the best-kept secret on the square, the small hotel blends luxury with an informal touch.English-speaking staff and easily accessible from the highway.

⊠ 1 place Vendôme, 75001 ☎ 01 55 04 55 00 (800 525 4800 from U.S.); fax 01 49 27 97 89 Ⓜ Concorde AX DC MC VI

VERSAILLES

𝄙 Le Potager du Roy $$

This neat restaurant is by Église St.-Louis, between the palace kitchen garden and the railroad station. Veal and pâté standards are offered.

⊠ 1 rue du Maréchal-Joffre, 78000 ☎ 01 39 50 35 34 ⏱ Closed Sat. lunch, Sun. dinner and Mon. Ⓜ RER C Versailles Rive Gauche AX MC VI

⊞ Trianon Palace $$$

Opened in 1910, the hotel offers timeless tranquility with views over its extensive grounds and the forest of Versailles. A health center provides regal pampering.

⊠ 1 boulevard de la Reine, 78000 ☎ 01 30 84 38 00; fax 01 39 49 00 77 Ⓜ Versailles Rive Droit AX DC MC VI

BAYEUX

⊞ Churchill $–$$

Conveniently located for the cathedral and tapestry, this hotel has a pretty courtyard and offers home-cooked meals.

⊠ 14–16 rue St.-Jean, 14404 ☎ 02 31 21 31 80; fax 02 31 21 41 66 ⏱ Closed Nov. 11–Feb. 28 AX MC VI

𝄙 Le Lion d'Or $

Step inside the airy, salmon-pink dining room of this old post inn for classic Normandy dishes with flair.

⊠ 71 rue St.-Jean ☎ 02 31 92 06 90 ⏱ Closed Dec. 20–Jan. 20 AX DC MC VI

CAEN

𝄙 La Bourride $$$

A gastronomic peak among many good local restaurants, la Bourride serves lobster and tripe classics in a cozy stone dining room.

⊠ 15–17 rue du Vaugueux, 14000 ☎ 02 31 93 50 76 ⏱ Closed early to late Jan., mid-Aug. to early Sep., Sun. dinner and Mon. AX DC MC VI

CARNAC

⊞ Le Bateau Ivre $–$$

Guests tend to stay in for the wholesome cooking served in the restaurant. Rooms have views over the beach or the garden.

⊠ 71 boulevard de la Plage, 56340 ☎ 02 97 52 19 55; fax 02 97 52 84 94 ⏱ Closed in Jan. AX DC MC VI

𝄙 Le Ratelier $$

This vine-covered house in a quiet corner of town has a loyal clientele who treasure dishes such as pan-fried foie gras with a rhubarb compote.

⊠ 4 chemin du Douët, 56340 ☎ 02 97 52 05 04 ⏱ Closed Jan. 15–Feb. 7, Sun. dinner and Mon. Oct.–Mar. MC VI

CLECY

𝄙 Au Site Normand $

Airy rooms make up the traditional timbered house. The restaurant ($–$$) has choices to suit most budgets and offers vegetarian dishes.

⊠ 1 rue des Châtelets, 14570

☎ 02 31 69 71 05; fax 02 31 69 48 51   AX DC MC VI

DEAUVILLE

🏨 Normandy Barriere $$$
Traditional Norman timbering accentuates the luxury seaside hotel. An indoor pool, casino and golf are among attractions.
✉ 38 rue Jean-Mermoz, 14800
☎ 02 31 98 66 22; fax 02 31 98 66 23 AX DC MC VI

🍴 Le Spinnaker $$
Wash down Normandy seafood in this promenade favorite with good wines or local farmhouse cider.
✉ 52 rue Mirabeau ☎ 02 31 88 24 40 🕐 Closed Jan., Nov. 12–21 and Mon. Sep.–Jun., Tue. Oct.–Apr. AX DC MC VI

DINAN

🏨 Avaugour $$
The two old stone buildings offer lovely views of the ramparts and the hotel garden. An enthusiastic staff and pleasant restaurant ($$) add to the appeal.
✉ 1 place du Champ ☎ 02 96 39 07 49; fax 02 96 85 43 04 🕐 Closed Nov. 17–Dec. 15 and Jan. 10–Mar. 10 AX DC MC VI

DINARD

🏨 Inter Hôtel Balmoral Minotel $
The pleasant, old-style hotel is near the seashore and most town-center attractions.
✉ 26 rue du Maréchal-Leclerc, 35800 ☎ 02 99 46 16 97; fax 02 99 88 20 48 🕐 Closed Nov. 15–Dec. 15 AX DC MC VI

🍴 La Salle à Manger $
The cheery dining room specializes in local fish dishes, prepared traditionally. Book in advance.
✉ 25 boulevard Féart ☎ 02 99 16 07 95   MC VI

ÉTRETAT

🏨 Le Donjon $$
The romantic, ivy-covered 19th-century château boasts a charming patio garden high above the town; restaurant is elegantly furnished.
✉ Chemin de St.-Clair, 76790
☎ 02 35 27 08 23; fax 02 35 29 92 24   AX DC MC VI

GIVERNY

🍴 Les Jardins de Giverny $$
English is spoken here – and loudly. This is the usual feeding post for those doing the garden visit.
✉ On the D5 at Giverny ☎ 02 32 21 60 80 🕐 Closed Feb., Nov. 1–15, Mon. and dinner except Sat. AX MC VI

HONFLEUR

🍴 L'Assiette Gourmande $$$
Escargots, oysters and tarte St.-Jacques are among specialties of Gérard Bonnefoy's highly regarded quayside establishment.
✉ 2 quai Passagers, 14600
☎ 02 31 89 24 88 🕐 Closed mid-Nov. to late Feb., Mon. in Sep.–Jun. and Sun. dinner AX DC MC VI

🏨 L'Écrin $$
The elegant manor house has regal rooms and a sumptuous salon.
✉ 19 rue Eugène-Boudin ☎ 02 31 14 43 45; fax 02 31 89 24 41 AX DC MC VI

LE MONT-ST.-MICHEL

🏨 Les Terasses Poulard $–$$
The welcoming inn may be crowded during school holidays. La Mère Poulard restaurant ($) is famous for its secret omelet recipe.
✉ Grande Rue, 50116 ☎ 02 33 60 14 09; fax 02 33 60 37 31   AX MC VI

NANTES

🍴 Auberge du Château $–$$
Opposite the château, this spot offers value-priced meals and fine Loire wines.
✉ 5 place de la Duchesse-Anne, 44000 ☎ 02 40 74 31 85   MC VI

🏨 Jules Verne $–$$
Double glazing makes up for the small rooms in this popular hotel near place Royale.
✉ 3 rue du Couëdic, 44000 ☎ 02 40 35 74 50; fax 02 40 20 09 35 AX DC MC VI

QUIMPER

🏨 Château de Guilguiffin $$
The enchanting 18th-century château is in the heart of a family-owned estate with three rooms and two suites available for guests. English is spoken.

✉ 29710 Landudec; D765 from Quimper, 11 miles, then D784
☎ 02 98 91 52 11, fax 02 98 91 52 52   AX DC MC VI

🍴 L'Ambroisie $–$$$
Classic Breton dishes with fresh produce are prepared with flair by Monsieur Guyon. Travelers on a budget should try the excellent lunch menu.
✉ 49 rue Elie-Fréron ☎ 02 98 95 00 02   MC VI

RENNES

🍴 Le Corsaire $–$$
Locals return time and again for classic dishes and good wines.
✉ 52 rue Antrain, 35700 ☎ 02 99 36 33 69   AX DC MC VI

🏨 Lecoq-Gadby $$
In its own elegant gardens, the hotel has well-furnished rooms with parquet floors and Oriental rugs.
✉ 156 rue Antrain, 35000 ☎ 02 99 38 05 55; fax 02 99 38 53 40 AX DC MC VI

ROUEN

🏨 Le Cardinal $
Top-floor rooms afford good cathedral views.
✉ 1 place de la Cathédrale, 76000
☎ 02 35 70 24 42; fax 02 35 89 75 14
🚇 Théâtre des Arts   MC VI

🏨 Dieppe $$
Comfortable hotel located opposite the railroad station.
✉ place Bernard-Tissot, 76000
☎ 02 35 71 96 00; fax 02 35 89 65 21
🚇 Gare-Rue Verte   AX DC MC VI

🍴 Gill $$$
The specialty of this imposing riverside restaurant is pigeon stuffed with liver.
✉ 9 quai de la Bourse, 76000
☎ 02 35 71 16 14 🕐 Closed in mid-Apr., late Aug., Sun. dinner Oct.–Apr. and Mon. 🚇 Théâtre des Arts AX DC MC VI

🏨 Lisieux $
Overlooking the cathedral from modest rooms, the medium-size hotel has a welcoming staff.
✉ 4 rue de la Savonnerie ☎ 02 35 71 87 73; fax 02 35 89 31 52
🕐 Closed late Dec.–early Jan.
🚇 Théâtre des AX DC MC VI

KEY TO SYMBOLS

🏨 hotel
🍴 restaurant
✉ address
☎ telephone number
🕐 days/times closed
Ⓜ nearest metro/tube/subway station(s)
🚌 nearby bus/trolley-bus/tram route(s)
⛴ ferry
AX American Express
DC Diners Club
MC MasterCard
VI VISA

Hotel

Price guide: double room with breakfast for two people

$$$ over €150
$$ €75–€150
$ under €75

Restaurant

Price guide: dinner per person, excluding drinks

$$$ over €40
$$ €20–€40
$ under €20

DISCOVER THE LOGIS

For a true taste of regional France, venture away from the international chain hotels and grand restaurants and watch for the yellow and green fireplace logo of Logis-de-France. Established by government initiative after World War II, these small, usually family-run establishments will prepare an unforgettable *menu de terroir* for well under €20. These meals are inspired by and created from local produce, often by a son or daughter who has been sent to study at one of the great culinary schools and returned with skills to make the most of regional bounty. Dining rooms are furnished with a homey touch, and hotel facilities are graded from one to three fireplaces. The Logis-de-France website has English descriptions of member hotels and restaurants:
www.logis-de-france.fr/us/index.htm.
☎ 01 45 84 83 84.

🍴 Les Nymphéas $$

Good fish and game dishes are the mark of this small house with a beamed carriage entry and garden.
✉ 9 rue Pie, 76000 ☎ 02 35 89 26 69 🕐 Closed Aug. 26–mid-Sep., Sun. dinner and Mon. Ⓜ Théâtre des Arts AX DC MC VI

ST.-MALO

🍴 À la Duchesse Anne $$$

The 1920s-style dining room, within the historic walled town, specializes in seafood dishes, plus the celebrated house foie gras.
✉ 5 place Guy-la-Chambre, 35400 ☎ 02 99 40 85 33 🕐 Closed Dec.–Jan.; Wed.., Sun. dinner and Mon. lunch in Summer MC VI

🏨 France et Châteaubriand $–$$

Napoleon III-style salons and comfy rooms overlook the port in the house where the author Châteaubriand was born. English is spoken.
✉ place Châteaubriand BP 77, 35412 ☎ 02 99 56 66 52; fax 02 99 40 10 04 AX DC MC VI

ST.-VAAST-LA-HOUGUE

🏨 Hotel de France et des Fuchsias $–$$

A remarkable climbing fuchsia envelops this family-run hotel. Its excellent restaurant ($$), serving the local catch, is popular with discerning locals and visitors alike.
✉ 20 rue du Maréchal-Foch ☎ 02 33 54 42 26; fax 02 33 43 46 79 🕐 Closed Jan. 4–Feb. 28 AX DC MC VI

Loire Valley – Atlantic Coast

AMBOISE

🏨 Choiseul $$–$$$

Just outside the royal estate, this luxury hotel has a pool and a renowned restaurant ($$$) where Pascal Bouvier's cuisine may best be enjoyed at lunch ($$).
✉ 36 quai Guinot ☎ 02 47 30 45 45; fax 02 47 30 46 10 AX DC MC VI

ANGERS

🏨 Anjou $–$$

Art-deco mosaics, stained-glass windows and elegant lounges adorn Corine and Alain Rio's imposing hotel. The Renaissance-style Salamandre gourmet restaurant ($$) specializes in regal hunting dishes.
✉ 1 boulevard Maréchal-Foch ☎ 02 41 88 24 82; fax 02 41 87 22 21 AX MC VI

AZAY-LE-RIDEAU

🏨 🍴 Grand Monarque $–$$

Enjoy wine from the château's cellar at the restaurant of this friendly hotel. The menu ($$–$$$) includes fresh catch from the Loire.
✉ 3 place de la République, 37190 ☎ 02 47 45 40 08; fax: 02 47 45 46 25 🕐 Closed mid-Dec. to Jan 31., Mon., Fri. lunch and Sun. dinner Oct.–Mar. AX DC VI

🏨 Manoir de la Rémonière $$

Opposite the more-famous château, this 15th-century manor house stands within an 82-acre park and bird sanctuary. The Indre river forms part of the estate boundary. Reservations are essential between Halloween and Easter.
✉ Cheillé, 37190; D17 signed for la Rémonière ☎ 02 47 45 24 88; fax 02 47 45 45 69 No credit cards

BIARRITZ

🍴 Campagne et Gourmandise $$

This Basque villa offers views of the Pyrénées. The creative menu includes oxtail en croute, roast sea bass with wild mushrooms, a fish *pot-au-feu*, and traditional desserts.
✉ 52 avenue Alan-Seeger ☎ 05 59 41 10 11 🕐 Closed in Feb., school holidays, Sun. dinner in winter and Wed. MC VI

🏨 Palais $$$

The essential hotel of Biarritz was built for an empress. It has a hair salon and a heated seawater pool. The restaurant, Villa Eugénie ($$$), has splendid Landais cuisine.
✉ 1 avenue de l'Impératrice, 64200 ☎ 05 59 41 64 00; fax 05 59 41 67 99 AX DC MC VI

BLOIS

🏨 Holiday Inn Garden Court $

International comforts are standard in the contemporary chain hotel.
✉ 26 avenue Maundoury, 41000 ☎ 02 54 55 44 88; fax 02 54 74 57 97 AX DC MC VI

BORDEAUX

🏨 Burdigala $$$
A comfortable hotel with a generous buffet breakfast and health center.
✉ 115 rue Georges-Bonnac, 33000
☎ 05 56 90 16 16; fax 05 56 93 15 06
Ⓜ Mériadeck AX DC MC VI

🏨 Grand Hôtel Français $–$$
Spacious air-conditioned rooms fill this imposing city-center institution.
✉ 12 rue du Temple ☎ 05 56 48 10 35; fax 05 56 51 76 18
Ⓜ Gambetta AX DC MC VI

🏨 Normandie $–$$
The hotel's modern rooms are near most attractions.
✉ 7 cours du 30-Juillet ☎ 05 56 52 16 80; fax 05 56 51 68 91
Ⓜ Quinconces AX DC MC VI

🍽 Pavillon des Boulevards $$$
Chef Denis Franc is widely regarded as a master of Bordelais cuisine. Innovative meals may be enjoyed in the dining rooms or the garden.
✉ 120 rue Croix-de-Seguey
☎ 05 56 81 51 02 Ⓒ Closed early Jan., mid-Aug., Sat. lunch and Sun.
Ⓜ Barrière du Médoc AX DC MC VI

🍽 La Tupina $$
Wholesome Gascon food is the house specialty. Winter log fires add to the cozy mood.
✉ 6 rue Porte-de-la-Monnaie
☎ 05 56 91 56 37 Ⓒ Closed national holidays and Sun.
Ⓜ Salinières AX DC MC VI

CHAUMONT

🍽 La Chancelière $$
Gaze at the river and enjoy local Loire poultry and game.
✉ 1 rue Bellevue ☎ 02 54 20 96 95
AX MC VI

CHENONCEAUX

🏨 Le Bon Laboureur $–$$
Enjoy old-fashioned hospitality, shared by superb restaurant ($–$$$).
✉ rue Bretonneau, 37150 ☎ 02 47 23 90 02; fax 02 47 23 82 01
DC MC VI

COGNAC

🏨 Hôtellerie les Pigeons Blancs $–$$
Guests stay for lunch in the restaurant ($$), where fish is cooked in – what else – cognac.
✉ 110 rue Jules-Brisson, 16100
☎ 05 45 82 16 36; fax 05 45 82 29 29
AX DC MC VI

FONTEVRAUD

🍽 La Licorne $$–$$$
This smart house is an ideal spot to discover Loire specialties, including Sandre and the langoustine ravioli.
✉ Allée Ste.-Catherine ☎ 02 41 51 72 49 Ⓒ Closed Dec.–Jan., Mon. and Wed. in winter and Sun. dinner
AX DC MC VI

🏨 Hôtellerie du Pieuré St.-Lazare $
Surprisingly inexpensive, these comfortable accommodations are in a former priory. A private restaurant in the cloister ($$) serves Loire specialties.
✉ Abbaye de Fontevraud, rue St. Jean de L'Habit BP 14, 49590 Fontevraud l'Abbaye ☎ 02 41 51 73 16; fax 02 41 51 75 50 AX MC VI

ORLEANS

🍽 Eugène $
The lively bistro offers standard ingredients and a good wine list.
✉ 24 rue Ste.-Anne ☎ 02 38 53 82 64 AX MC VI

POITIERS

🏨 Le Grand Hôtel $
Art-deco stylings and courtyard tranquility mark the hotel.
✉ 28 rue Carnot, 86000 ☎ 05 49 60 90 60; fax 05 49 62 81 89
AX DC MC VI

🍽 Maxime $–$$
Enjoy the flavors of roast pigeon or green apple sorbet chez Christian Rougier.
✉ 4 rue St.-Nicholas ☎ 05 49 41 09 55 Ⓒ Closed mid-Jul., mid-Aug. and Sat.–Sun. AX DC MC VI

SAUMUR

🏨 Anne d'Anjou $
By the banks of the Loire, this charming 18th-century house has Louis XVI decor and a fabulous main staircase. A pleasant restaurant ($$) can be found at the bottom of the garden.
✉ 32–33 quai Mayaud, 49400
☎ 02 41 67 30 30; fax 02 41 67 51 00
AX DC MC VI

🍽 Le Calyce $$–$$$
Spices tickle good basic ingredients in the dining room of the peaceful Close des Bénédictines hotel.
✉ St.-Hilaire-St.-Florent; N147, D751 from Saumur, 2 miles west
☎ 02 41 67 28 48 Ⓒ Closed Dec.–Jan. AX MC VI

TOURS

🏨 🍽 Jean Bardet $$–$$$
This old-style hotel-restaurant ($$$) has a kitchen garden that provides the herbs and vegetables selected and prepared by the renowned chef.
✉ 57 rue Groison, 37100 ☎ 02 47 41 41 11; fax 02 47 51 68 72
Ⓒ Restaurant closed Mon. in Nov.–Mar.; Mon. lunch in Apr.–Oct.; and Sun. dinner AX DC MC VI

VILLANDRY

🏨 Le Cheval Rouge $
The modest village hotel and restaurant ($) is near the château.
✉ 37510 Villandry ☎ 02 47 50 02 07; fax 02 47 50 08 77 MC VI

Dordogne

ALBI

🍽 Moulin de la Mothe $$–$$$
The charming location on the banks of the Tarn boasts a good wine list.
✉ Rue de la Mothe ☎ 05 63 60 38 15 Ⓒ Closed Nov. and Feb. school vacation, Sun. dinner except Jul.–Aug. and Wed. AX DC MC VI

🏨 La Réserve $$
Set on the banks of the Tarn, the hotel has a pool and tennis courts.
✉ Route de Cordes, 81000
☎ 05 63 60 80 80; fax 05 63 47 63 60
Ⓒ Closed early Nov.–late Apr
AX DC MC VI

AUBUSSON

🏨 Le Lion d'Or $
Frédéric Chaussoy's modest hotel also has a dining room with inexpensive country food ($).
✉ Place d'Espagne, 23200
☎ 05 55 66 13 88; fax 05 55 66 84 73
AX DC MC VI

Dordogne

Dordogne

KEY TO SYMBOLS

⊞ hotel
🍴 restaurant
✉ address
☎ telephone number
🕐 days/times closed
Ⓜ nearest metro/tube/subway
station(s)
🚌 nearby bus/trolley-bus/tram
route(s).
⛴ ferry
AX American Express
DC Diners Club
MC MasterCard
VI VISA

Hotel
Price guide: double room with
breakfast for two people
$$$ over €150
$$ €75–€150
$ under €75

Restaurant
Price guide: dinner per person,
excluding drinks
$$$ over €40
$$ €20–€40
$ under €20

REGIONAL DELICACIES

Provence's natural abundance of
fresh fruits, vegetables and fish
means that local food is both rich
and healthy. Some foods are
particular to the region, such as
the delicious tapenade, a paste
of black olives, capers and
anchovies, and aioli, a rich garlic
and olive oil mayonnaise. Both
may be served with crudités, a
selection of raw crunchy
vegetables. Two classic soups
come from Provence: *soupe au
pistou*, a basil-rich minestrone,
and the Marseille classic fish
stew bouillabaisse. The latter is
served with *rouille*, a spicy red
paste that is spread on croutons,
which are sprinkled with grated
cheese and floated in the soup.
The soup often is served as a
main course. Most vegetables are
seasonal, except for
ratatouille with zucchini and
tomato, which is available year
round. The most famous summer
dish is *salade niçoise*, which
varies from street to street but
should include anchovies,
tomato, potato, hard-boiled egg
and beans.

BERGERAC

🍴 Le Cyrano $–$$
The pleasant restaurant serves
value-priced meals with local wines.
✉ 2 boulevard Montaigne ☎ 05
53 57 02 76 🕐 Closed one week in
Dec., Sat. lunch; Sun. except
national holidays MC VI

BEYNAC ET CAZENAC

⊞ Pontet $
In this family-run hotel is a
restaurant that serves good, local
dishes ($).
✉ Village center, 24220 ☎ 05 53
29 50 06; fax 05 53 28 28 52
🕐 Closed in Jan. AX DC MC VI

CAHORS

🍴 Le Balandre $$
Regulars savor pan-fried foie gras
and truffles with poached eggs at
tables dappled by sunlight through
century-old windows.
✉ 5 avenue Château-de-Freycinet
☎ 05 65 53 32 00 🕐 Closed Sun.
dinner and Mon. in winter AX DC
MC VI

⊞ Château de Mercuès $$$
The former residence of the
count-bishops of Cahors is now a
château hotel-restaurant ($$$$)
serving fine duck, pâté and truffle-
based cuisine.
✉ Mercuès, 46090; D911 from
Cahors, 3 miles northwest ☎ 05 65
20 00 01; fax 05 65 20 05 72
🕐 Closed Nov. 1–Easter AX DC
MC VI

CASTELNAU-DE-LÉVIS

🍴 La Taverne $$$
In the former village bakery, Bruno
Besson has created an intimate
bistro for his hearty regional dishes.
✉ Castelnau-de-Lévis, 81150
☎ 05 63 60 90 16; fax 05 63 60 96 73
🕐 Closed three weeks in Oct., Sun.
dinner and Mon. AX DC MC VI

LIMOGES

⊞ Jeanne-d'Arc $
Despite the railroad opposite, this is
a charming, well-run hotel.
✉ 17 avenue de Gaulle, 87000
☎ 05 55 77 67 77; fax 05 55 79 86 75
🕐 Closed Dec. 23–Jan. 1 AX DC
MC VI

🍴 Philippe Redon $–$$
Contemporary style decorates the
dining room. The chef shows a
talent for updating the classics.
✉ 3 rue d'Aguesseau ☎ 05 55 34
66 22 🕐 Closed early Jan. and
early Aug., Mon. lunch and Sun.
AX DC MC VI

MOISSAC

⊞ Le Pont Napoléon $
This place is a treat for its air-
conditioned rooms and pastel decor.
Developed by Michel Dussau,
dashing protégé of the great Alain
Ducasse, the restaurant is worth a
visit in its own right ($$–$$$).
✉ 2 allées Montebello, 82200
☎ 05 63 04 01 55; fax 05 63 04 34 44
🕐 Closed in mid-Jan. and Wed.
AX DC MC VI

MONTAUBAN

🍴 Cuisine d'Alain $$–$$$
This restaurant's modestly priced
dishes are prepared with local
market produce.
✉ Opposite SNCF Villebourbon
railroad station ☎ 05 63 66 06 66,
fax 05 63 66 19 39 AX DC MC VI

⊞ Ingres $$
Comfortable rooms make up the
hotel near the Tarn river.
✉ 10 avenue Mayenne, 82000
☎ 05 63 63 36 01; fax 05 63 66 02 90
AX DC MC VI

PÉRIGUEUX

⊞ Périgord $
Yvonne Vallejo's hotel has parking
and a restaurant ($) serving simple
food. Book in advance.
✉ 74 rue Victor-Hugo, 24000
☎ 05 53 53 33 63; fax 05 53 08 19 74
🕐 Closed late Oct.–early Nov,. Feb.
school vacations, Sun. dinner and
Sat. Oct.–Feb. MC VI

LA ROQUE-GAGEAC

⊞ Belle Étoile $
This small hotel offers a garden and
an air-conditioned restaurant ($).
Eccentric rules allow dogs in the
dining room but not in the rooms.
✉ 24250 la Roque-Gageac ☎ 05
53 29 51 44; fax 05 53 29 45 63
🕐 Closed Nov.–Mar. Restaurant
closed Mon. and Wed.lunch
Apr.–Oct. AX DC MC VI

Pyrénées, Provence – Côte d'Azur

SARLAT-LA-CANEDA

🏨 La Madeleine $–$$
Flower-decked balconies welcome you to this stylish hotel, which includes a restaurant ($).
✉ 1 place de la Petite-Rigaudie, 24200 ☎ 05 53 59 10 41; fax 05 53 31 03 62 ⏰ Closed early Jan.–early Feb. Restaurant closed mid-Nov. to mid-Mar. AX DC MC VI

Pyrénées

BAYONNE

🍴 Auberge du Cheval Blanc $$–$$$
Jean-Claude Tellechea handles Basque dishes with modern flair in this old coaching inn.
✉ 68 rue Bourgneuf ☎ 05 59 59 01 33 ⏰ Closed Feb., first week of Aug., Sun. dinner and Mon. except Jul.–Aug. AX DC MC VI

🏨 Le Grand Hôtel $–$$
Relish the warm welcome at this old-fashioned hotel and restaurant ($) near the beach.
✉ 21 rue Thiers, 64100 ☎ 05 59 59 62 00; fax 05 59 59 62 01 ⏰ Restaurant closed Sat.–Sun, except Jul.–Aug. AX DC MC VI

CARCASSONNE

🏨 Hôtel de la Cité $$$
The luxury choice boasts Gothic furnishings. Its restaurant ($$$) is ideal for special celebrations.
✉ Place de l'Église, La Cité 11000 ☎ 04 68 71 98 71; fax 04 68 71 50 15 ⏰ Closed early Dec. to mid-Jan. AX DC MC VI

🍴 Le Donjon $
Enjoy a traditional southwestern cassoulet at this stylish restaurant.
✉ 2 rue du Comte-Roger, La Cité, 11000 ☎ 04 68 71 08 80 ⏰ Closed Sun. dinner Nov.–Mar. AX DC MC VI

CASTRES

🏨 Renaissance $
This building is 17th century in style and the red-brick bathrooms are the last word in modern good taste.
✉ 17 rue Victor-Hugo, 81100 ☎ 05 63 59 30 42; fax 05 63 72 11 57 ⏰ Restaurant closed in Aug., Dec. 22–30, Mon. lunch and Sun. AX DC MC VI

LOURDES

🏨 Grand Hôtel de la Grotte $
Fabulous mountain views and spacious rooms distinguish this place from dozens catering to the unending stream of visitors. A restaurant ($) is on the premises.
✉ 66 rue de la Grotte, 65100 ☎ 05 62 94 58 87; fax 05 62 94 20 50 ⏰ Restaurant closed Nov.–Mar. AX DC MC VI

🍴 Le Magret $$–$$$
As the name implies, this is the place to choose for duck breast cooked traditionally.
✉ 10 rue des 4-Frères-Soulas ☎ 05 62 94 20 55 ⏰ Closed in mid-Jan. and Mon. AX DC MC VI

LUCHON

🏨 Étigny $
Opposite the spa and park is the comfortable hotel and restaurant ($–$$) specializing in regional dishes.
✉ 31110 Luchon ☎ 05 61 79 01 42; fax 05 61 79 80 64 MC VI

ST.-JEAN-DE-LUZ

🏨 Parc Victoria $$$
In its own park, the hotel has rooms decorated in the 1930s style and a good restaurant ($$$).
✉ 5 rue Cépé, 64500 ☎ 05 59 26 78 78; fax 05 59 26 78 08 ⏰ Closed Nov. 15–Mar. 15 AX DC MC VI

ST-JEAN-PIED-DE-PORT

🏨 Les Pyrénées $$
The Basque hotel has accommodations to gracious standards and its restaurant ($$$) offers the best in local cuisine.
✉ 19 place Charles-de-Gaulle, 64220 ☎ 05 59 37 01 01; fax 05 59 37 18 97 ⏰ Closed Jan. 5–28 AX DC MC VI

TOULOUSE

🏨 Beaux Arts $$
Opposite the Pont Neuf and near the art museum, the hotel has windows that overlook the Garonne.
✉ 1 place du Pont-Neuf, 31000 ☎ 05 34 45 42 42; fax 05 34 45 42 43 Ⓜ Esquirol AX DC MC VI

🏨 Grand Hôtel Capoul $$
Modern plate glass and light wood design fit the hotel, in the heart of the Toulouse nightlife district.
✉ 13 place Wilson, 31000 ☎ 05 61 10 70 70; fax 05 61 21 96 70 Ⓜ Jean-Jaurès AX DC MC VI

🏨 Grand Hôtel de l'Opéra $$
The Florentine splendor of the brick facade continues in the tastefully decorated rooms.
✉ 1 place du Capitole, 31000 ☎ 05 61 21 82 66; fax 05 61 23 41 04 Ⓜ Capitole AX DC MC VI

🍴 Les Jardins de l'Opéra $$$
This is the fine dining address of Toulouse, where deals are toasted and anniversaries celebrated.
✉ 1 place du Capitole ☎ 05 61 23 07 76 Ⓜ Capitole AX DC MC VI

🍴 7 Place St.-Sernin $
The fashionable dining room offers a lighter, stylish take on local cuisine.
✉ 7 place St.-Sernin ☎ 05 62 30 05 30 Ⓜ Capitole AX MC VI

Provence – Côte d'Azur

AIX-EN-PROVENCE

🍴 L'Amphityron $$
Dine among magnolias and choose the market-fresh dish of the day.
✉ 2-4 rue Paul-Doumer ☎ 04 42 26 54 10 ⏰ Closed late Aug., Mon. lunch and Sun. MC VI

🏨 Augustins $$
The popular, small hotel sits on a side street off cours Mirabeau.
✉ 3 rue Masse, 13100 ☎ 04 42 27 28 59; fax 04 42 26 74 87 AX DC MC VI

🏨 Château de la Pioline $$$
Don't be put off by signs for les Milles business area. This splendid château outside town offers breakfast on the terrace overlooking peaceful gardens and woodland. A restaurant ($$$) is on site.
✉ 13546 les Milles; D9 from Aix, 3 miles southwest ☎ 04 42 20 07 81; fax 04 42 52 27 28 AX DC MC VI

🍴 Clos de la Violette $$$
The great table of Aix specializes in truffle dishes in winter and *petits farcis* of Provençal vegetables in summer. Book well in advance.

Provence – Côte d'Azur

KEY TO SYMBOLS
- 🏨 hotel
- 🍴 restaurant
- ✉ address
- ☎ telephone number
- 🕐 days/times closed
- Ⓜ nearest metro/tube/subway station(s)
- 🚌 nearby bus/trolley-bus/tram route(s).
- ⛴ ferry
- AX American Express
- DC Diners Club
- MC MasterCard
- VI VISA

Hotel
Price guide: double room with breakfast for two people
- $$$ over €150
- $$ €75–€150
- $ under €75

Restaurant
Price guide: dinner per person, excluding drinks
- $$$ over €40
- $$ €20–€40
- $ under €20

TWO FOR ONE

Double your pleasure and your fun at more than 40 French regional cities and towns from Aix-en-Provence to Versailles. The promotional "Bon Week-end en Villes" offers two nights of hotel accommodation for the price of one for any stay beginning on a Friday or Saturday night. The offer is good from Nov. 1 through Mar. 31, although some cities/towns run it year-round. Reservations must be made through the town tourist office at least one day in advance. In return you will receive a welcoming gift plus details of discounted leisure and cultural activities. A directory listing all participating cities and hotels is available from the French Tourist Office or by writing to the Club Bon Week-end en Villes.
✉ Club Bon Week-end en Villes, TDC. B.P. 251, 59665 Villeneuve d'Ascq cedex, France; www.bon-week-end-en-villes.com

✉ 10 avenue Violette ☎ 04 42 23 30 71   AX MC VI

🏨 Grand Hôtel Mercure Roi René $$
This hotel's air-conditioned rooms sit away from the town center.
✉ 24 boulevard du Roi-René, 13100 ☎ 04 42 37 61 00; fax 04 42 37 61 11 AX DC MC VI

ANTIBES

🍴 Le Bacon $$$
Sophisticated establishment offering high-class seafood and spectacular views over the bay.
✉ Boulevard Bacon, 06600 ☎ 04 93 61 50 02 🕐 Closed Nov.–Jan. and Mon. in Sep.–Jun. AX DC MC VI

ARLES

🏨 Calendal $
Pastel rooms of the pretty city-center base overlook the garden. Book a garage space well in advance.
✉ 22 place du Dr.-Pomme, 13200 ☎ 04 90 96 11 89; fax 04 90 96 05 84 AX DC MC VI

🍴 La Paillotte $
A simple dining room that offers genuine Provençale flavors and good local wines.
✉ 28 rue du Dr.-Fanton ☎ 04 90 96 33 15   AX DC MC VI

AVIGNON

🍴 La Fourchette $
This great bistro, always busy, serves delicious, simply prepared plats du jour, local Rhône wines and good humor.
✉ 17 rue Racine ☎ 04 90 85 20 93 MC VI

🏨 Mirande $$$
This one-time cardinal's palace is now one of France's most elegant hotels, with a superb restaurant ($$–$$$) supervised by a disciple of Alain Ducasse.
✉ 4 place de l'Amirande, 84000 ☎ 04 90 85 93 93; fax 04 90 86 26 85 AX DC MC VI

🍴 Le Vernet $–$$$
Dine by lamplight in this charming walled garden. An innovative flair distinguishes traditional dishes.
✉ 58 rue Joseph-Vernet ☎ 04 90 86 64 53   AX MC VI

BIOT

🏨 Domaine du Jas $$–$$$
Comfortable rooms, efficient service, a pool and garage parking are all hotel features.
✉ 625 route de la Mer, 06410 ☎ 04 93 65 50 50; fax 04 93 65 02 01 🕐 Closed mid-Nov. to Feb. 28 MC VI

🍴 Les Terraillers $$$
A 16th-century pottery is the setting for plates of Claude Jacques' sophisticated cuisine, which has wooed nearly every food critic in France.
✉ 11 route Chemin-Neuf ☎ 04 93 65 01 59 🕐 Closed Mon. lunch and Wed.   AX MC VI

CAGNES-SUR-MER

🏨 Cagnard $$–$$$
Manorial comforts characterize this delightful hotel and its fabulous dining room ($$$). In summer, the restaurant's paneled ceiling slides away for dining under the stars.
✉ 45 rue Sous-Barri, Haut-de-Cagnes, 06800 ☎ 04 93 20 73 21; fax 04 93 22 06 39 🕐 Restaurant closed Nov. 1 – mid. Dec. and Thu. lunch   AX DC MC VI

CANNES

🍴 Les Mesclun $$
Although it's just a couple of streets from the seashore razzmatazz, this place offers just well-prepared food.
✉ 16 rue St.-Antoine ☎ 04 93 99 45 19 🕐 Closed mid-Nov. to mid-Dec., Wed. and lunch   AX MC VI

🍴 Villa des Lys $$$
A talented team prepares classic French dishes. This restaurant may soon outclass some bigger names on the Croisette.
✉ Hôtel Majestic, 14 boulevard de la Croisette ☎ 04 92 98 77 41 🕐 Closed mid-Nov. to late Dec. AX DC MC VI

🏨 Villa de l'Olivier $–$$
The informal hotel overlooks the old town and is near the beach.
✉ 5 rue des Tambourinaires, 06400 ☎ 04 93 39 53 28; fax 04 93 39 55 85 AX DC MC VI

Provence – Côte d'Azur

CORSICA – ERBALUNGA

Castel Brando $–$$
The Pieri family's 19th-century mansion with shady gardens is near the charming fishing port of Erbalunga.
✉ Erbalunga village; D80 from Bastia, 7 miles north ☎ 04 95 30 10 30; fax 04 95 33 98 18 ⊙ Closed mid-Oct. to mid-Mar. AX MC VI

GRASSE

🏨 🍽 Bastide St.-Antoine $$$
Jacques Chibois' renowned hotel-restaurant is a champion of the flavors of Provence, from the sea to the olive grove.
✉ 48 avenue Dunant ☎ 04 93 09 16 48; fax 04 92 42 03 42 AX DC MC VI

🏨 La Rivolte $$
Enjoy marvelous palm-fringed views of the town and sea from this comfortable 19th-century mansion with well-tended gardens.
✉ Chemin des Lierres, 06130 ☎ 04 93 36 81 58; fax 04 93 36 87 29 DC MC VI

MARSEILLE

🍽 Les Arcenaulx $$
A bibliophile's delight: Restaurant tables are set up in a quayside bookshop. Family favorites include Daube de Sanglier and the morning's fresh catch.
✉ 25 cours d'Estienne-d'Orves ☎ 04 91 59 80 37 AX DC MC VI

🏨 St.-Ferréol's Hôtel $
On a pedestrian-friendly street near the old port, this hotel provides a whirlpool bath for aching muscles.
✉ 19 rue Pisançon, 13001 ☎ 04 91 33 12 21; fax 04 91 54 29 97 AX DC MC VI

MENTON

🍽 Au Pistou $
Taste good mariners' fare at harborside tables.
✉ 9 quai Gordon-Bennett ☎ 04 93 57 45 89 ⊙ Closed mid-Nov. to mid-Dec. and Mon. MC VI

🏨 Prince de Galles $–$$
The pleasant hotel includes a modest restaurant ($).
✉ 4 avenue Général-de-Gaulle,

06500 ☎ 04 93 28 21 21; fax 04 93 35 92 91 ⊙ Restaurant closed mid-Nov. to mid-Dec. AX DC MC VI

MONACO – MONTE CARLO

🏨 Paris $$$
If you plan to stay in Monaco, do it in style at this extravagant hotel, where no stone is left ungilded.
✉ Place du Casino, 98000 ☎ (00 377) 92 16 30 00; fax (00 377) 92 16 38 50 AX DC MC VI

MONTPELLIER

🍽 Brasserie le Théatre $–$$
The restaurant has a walled garden and a pleasant dining room.
✉ 22 boulevard Victor-Hugo ☎ 04 67 58 88 80 AX DC MC VI

🏨 Guilhem $–$$
Look out at the cathedral garden from a stylishly restored room in this cluster of renovated old houses.
✉ 18 rue Jean-Jacques Rousseau, 34000 ☎ 04 67 52 90 90; fax 04 67 60 67 67 AX DC MC VI

🍽 Le Jardin des Sens $$$
Probably the finest meals between Marseille and the Spanish border are encountered in the Pourcel twins' smart dining room.
✉ 11 avenue St.-Lazare ☎ 04 99 58 38 38 ⊙ Closed Mon. and Wed. lunch and Sun. AX DC MC VI

NARBONNE

🍽 Agora $
The restaurant's generous platter of tapas or the value plat du jour are perfect for a simple lunch.
✉ 2 place de l'Hôtel-de-Ville ☎ 04 68 90 10 70 VI

🏨 Auberge des Vignes $–$$
Relax in a room with a view in the heart of a wine-making estate. The restaurant ($) offers excellent value.
✉ Domaine de L'Hospitalet, 11100; Route de Narbonne Plage, 6 miles east ☎ 04 68 42 28 50; fax 04 68 45 28 78 MC VI

🍽 David Moreno $–$$$
Great value-priced lunches and quality dinners are served on the abbey's olive-tree-bordered terrace.
✉ Abbaye de Fontfroide ☎ 04 68 41 86 00 ⊙ Closed Nov.–Mar. and Mon., except Jul.–Aug. AX DC MC VI

NICE

🍽 Flo $–$$
The kitchen is center stage in this flamboyant restaurant dramatically housed in an old theater.
✉ 4 rue Sacha-Guitry ☎ 04 93 13 38 38 AX DC MC VI

🍽 La Mérenda $$
This place is a favorite with locals, who love the great salads and tarts. In season book in person: The restaurant has no telephone.
✉ 4 rue de la Terrasse ⊙ Closed 1 week Easter, 3 weeks in Aug. and Sat.–Sun. No credit cards

🏨 Négresco $$$
The flamboyant doorman sets the tone for a hotel styled from Hollywood's heyday. Memorable meals are prepared at the fabulous Négresco restaurant ($$–$$$).
✉ 37 promenade des Anglais, 06000 ☎ 04 93 16 64 00; fax 04 93 88 35 68 AX DC MC VI

🏨 La Pérouse $$–$$$
An unexpected quiet spot, just a stroll from the old town, offering unmatchable views.
✉ 11 quai Rauba-Capéu, 06000 ☎ 04 93 62 34 63; fax 04 93 62 59 41 AX DC MC VI

🏨 Petit Palais $$
Prettily furnished rooms make up this charming house.
✉ 10 avenue E.–Bieckert, 06000 ☎ 04 93 62 19 11; fax 04 93 62 53 60 AX DC MC VI

NÎMES

🍽 L'Enclos de la Fontaine $$–$$$
At festival and féria time, it's almost impossible to get a table at this charming restaurant. Brandade de Morue – salt cod with crème fraîche – is a specialty.
✉ Quai de la Fontaine ☎ 04 66 21 90 30 AX MC VI

ORANGE

🏨 Arène $
Centrally located hotel with a friendly staff and snug, tastefully furnished rooms.
✉ Place de Langes, 84100 ☎ 04 90 11 40 40; fax 04 90 11 40 45 ⊙ Closed Nov. 9–31 AX DC MC VI

Provence – Côte d'Azur

KEY TO SYMBOLS

- 🏨 hotel
- 🍴 restaurant
- ✉ address
- ☎ telephone number
- 🕐 days/times closed
- Ⓜ nearest metro/tube/subway station(s)
- 🚌 nearby bus/trolley-bus/tram route(s).
- ⛴ ferry
- AX   American Express
- DC   Diners Club
- MC   MasterCard
- VI   VISA

Hotel
Price guide: double room with breakfast for two people
$$$ over €150
$$ €75–€150
$ under €75

Restaurant
Price guide: dinner per person, excluding drinks
$$$ over €40
$$ €20–€40
$ under €20

MASTERING THE MENU

Since the French take their food seriously, menus, even in modest bistros, are rarely dumbed down. Freely exploring the main a la carte selections can seriously bruise your wallet, but every restaurant must offer at least one fixed-price, set menu. With a restricted choice of two or three courses, this will provide not only the best value in the restaurant but usually the best reflection of the regional cuisine. Most places have two or three set menus, ranging from the budget-minded *"menu express"* to a *"menu degustation"* offering haute cuisine at a set price. This gastronomic indulgence might feature an appetizer, starter course, fish course, meat course, salad or vegetable dish, cheese, dessert and homemade candies. Lunchtime menus are often 20 to 50 percent cheaper than evening meals, and by going with bargain daily specials (plat du jour) you can enjoy a true taste of France for around €15.

🍴 Le Parvis $$
Fennel and local herbs flavor traditional meals in this stylish venue close to the Roman theater.
✉ 3 cours Pourtoules ☎ 04 90 34 82 00 🕐 Closed Nov., Sun. dinner, except summer, and Mon.   AX DC MC VI

PERPIGNAN

🍴 La Passerelle $–$$
Close to the palace, this unassuming bistro serves fresh fish with no frills.
✉ 1 cours Palmarole ☎ 04 68 51 30 65   AX DC MC VI

🏨 Villa Duflot $$
Big bedrooms and bathrooms are hallmarks, as are lovely breakfasts.
✉ rond-point Albert Donnezan (Serrat d'en Vaguer), 66000 ☎ 04 68 56 67 67; fax 04 68 56 54 05 AX DC MC VI

PONT-DU-GARD

🏨 Bégude St.-Pierre $$
The 17th-century building sits amid extensive grounds. The restaurant ($$) serves well-prepared local fare.
✉ 30210 Pont-du-Gard ☎ 04 66 63 63 63; fax 04 66 22 73 73   AX DC MC VI

ST.-JEAN-CAP-FERRAT

🏨 Grand-Hôtel du Cap-Ferrat $$$
The private estate sits on the tip of the peninsula with its own park. The restaurant ($$$) is renowned.
✉ 1 boulevard Général-de-Gaulle, 06230 ☎ 04 93 76 50 50; fax 04 93 76 04 52 🕐 Closed Jan. 3–Mar. 3 AX DC MC VI

ST.-RAPHAËL

🍴 L'Abousier $$–$$$
Taste fabulous Mediterranean flavors in this popular restaurant.
✉ 6 avenue de Valescure ☎ 04 94 95 25 00 🕐 Closed Dec. 21–Jan. 5, Sun. dinner in winter and Mon. AX MC VI

🏨 La Potinière $–$$
Set in pine and eucalyptus trees, this hotel is a haven of tranquility.
✉ 169 avenue de Boulouris, 83700; N98 from St.-Raphaël, 3 miles east ☎ 04 94 19 81 71; fax 04 94 19 81 72 AX DC MC VI

ST.-REMY-DE-PROVENCE

🍴 Café des Arts $
Part bistro and part art gallery, this is where locals find hearty fare.
✉ 30 boulevard Victor ☎ 04 90 92 13 41 🕐 Closed Nov.–Mar. and Wed. AX MC VI

🏨 Domaine de Valmouriane $$
A traditional Provençal 18th-century house, with an individual style.
✉ Petit route des Baux, 13210; D99 from St.-Rémy, 1.5 miles west, D27 towards les Baux, 1.5 miles south ☎ 04 90 92 44 62; fax 04 90 92 37 32 AX DC MC VI

ST.-TROPEZ

🍴 L'Olivier $$–$$$
Good, sensibly priced meals are served in a pretty garden.
✉ route des Carles ☎ 04 94 55 82 55   AX MC VI

🏨 Sube $$
Luxurious hotels now abound in St.-Tropez, but this simpler delight gives a taste of how things were.
✉ Quai Suffren, 83990 ☎ 04 94 97 30 04, 04 94 54 89 08   AX DC MC VI

SALON DE PROVENCE

🏨 Abbaye de Ste.-Croix $$–$$$
The fabulous 12th-century monastery offers glorious views and a top-class restaurant ($$$).
✉ Route du Val de Cuech, 13300 ☎ 04 90 56 24 55; fax 04 90 56 31 12 🕐 Closed mid-Nov. to mid-Mar. Restaurant closed Mon. lunch and Thu. lunch   AX DC MC VI

VENCE

🍴 Le Vieux Couvent $$–$$$
In a former chapel, the restaurant offers fresh lamb from nearby Alpine slopes and Mediterranean seafood.
✉ 37 avenue Toreille ☎ 04 93 58 78 58 🕐 Closed mid-Jan. to mid-Mar. and Wed.   MC VI

🏨 Villa Roseraie $$
This unique and welcoming hotel has a personality all its own.
✉ Avenue Henri-Giraud, 06140 ☎ 04 93 58 02 20; fax 04 93 58 99 31 AX MC VI

Massif Central

AUBENAS

🍴 Le Fournil $–$$
The comfort of the old stone dining room is reflected in Michel Leynaud's cuisine. Leave space for the *tarte au praline*.
✉ 34 rue de 4-Septembre ☎ 04 75 93 58 68 ⊙ Closed in Feb., two weeks in Jun., Nov. school vacations, Dec. 22–Jan. 3., Sun. dinner and Mon. AX MC VI

🏨 La Pinède $
A warm welcome is waiting in the family-run hotel, which has its own pool, parkland and restaurant ($–$$).
✉ 07200 Aubenas; on the D235 ☎ 04 75 35 25 88; fax 04 75 93 06 42 ⊙ Closed Dec. 25–Jan. 1 VI

AURILLAC

🍴 À la Reine Margot $–$$
Honest regional food is prepared with rare skill and flair and served with the utmost professionalism.
✉ 19 rue Guy-de-Veyre ☎ 04 71 48 26 46 ⊙ Closed two weeks Feb., Sun. dinner and Mon. AX MC VI

🏨 Grand Hôtel de Bordeaux $–$$
Rooms in this old-fashioned establishment vary from smart to dowdy, but service is always polite.
✉ 2 avenue de la République, 15000 ☎ 04 71 48 01 84; fax 04 71 48 49 93 AX DC MC VI

CHAUDES-AIGUES

🏨 Thermal du Ban $
The modern spa hotel offers well-equipped accommodations.
✉ Chaudes-Aigues, 15110; south end of village ☎ 04 71 23 51 06; fax 04 71 23 58 46 ⊙ Closed Oct.–Apr. MC VI

CLERMONT-FERRAND

🍴 Bistroquet le Bouchon $
Specialties of Auvergne and old Lyon line the inexpensive menu.
✉ 4 rue Ste.-Eutope ☎ 04 73 36 22 19 ⊙ Closed Sun. MC VI

🍴 Emmanuel Hodencq $$
Try pan-fried foie gras at Clermont-Ferrand's cutting-edge spot, both on the plate and in the decor.
✉ Place Marché-St.-Pierre

☎ 04 73 31 23 23 ⊙ Closed national holidays, Feb. holidays, early Sep., Sun. and Mon. AX DC MC VI

🏨 Frantour Arverne $–$$
Close to Notre-Dame du Port, the restaurant affords good city views.
✉ 16 place Delille, 63000 ☎ 04 73 91 92 06; fax 04 73 91 60 25 AX DC MC VI

🏨 Novotel $$
A poolside restaurant and air-conditioned rooms are features of this hotel on the outskirts of town.
✉ 32–34 rue G.–Besse-ZI, le Brezet Est, 63100 ☎ 04 73 41 14 14; fax 04 73 41 14 00 AX DC MC VI

CONQUES

🏨 Grand Hôtel Ste.-Foy $$
The rustic hotel-restaurant ($$) sits opposite the historic abbey church.
✉ Conques 12320 ☎ 05 65 69 84 03; fax 05 65 72 81 04 ⊙ Closed Nov. 1–Easter AX DC MC VI

SUPER-LIORAN

🏨 Remberter Saporta $
The hotel has a pool in the garden for exercise outside the ski season. Simple meals are served in the restaurant ($).
✉ 6 route Rocher du Cerf ☎ 04 71 49 50 28; fax 04 71 49 52 88 ⊙ Closed several weeks in spring and mid-Sep. to mid-Dec. MC VI

LA MALÈNE

🏨 Manoir de Montesquiou $$
A dozen comfortable rooms make up the attractive 15th-century manor house. The restaurant ($) offers views of the grounds.
✉ La Malène, 48210 ☎ 04 66 48 51 12; fax 04 66 48 50 47 ⊙ Closed Oct. 31–Mar. 31 DC MC VI

LE PUY-EN-VELAY

🏨 Bristol $
Monsieur Vallet welcomes guests to the main hotel and its modern annex, with family rooms, garage parking and a restaurant ($).
✉ 7 avenue Foch, 43000 ☎ 04 71 09 13 38; fax 04 71 09 51 70 ⊙ Closed three weeks in Mar. and three weeks in Nov. AX DC MC VI

🍴 Tournayre $–$$
Try the inexpensive set menu for flavorsome country dishes, or venture onto the main carte for delights such as lobster and red mullet cannelloni.
✉ 12 rue Chênebouterie ☎ 04 71 09 58 94 ⊙ Closed in Jan., Sun. dinner and Mon. AX MC VI

RIOM

🏨 Anémotel $
The modern hotel-restaurant ($) has air-conditioned rooms.
✉ Les Portes de Riom, 63200 ☎ 04 73 33 71 00; fax 04 73 64 00 60 AX MC VI

🍴 Le Flamboyant $$
Good food is tastefully presented at reasonable prices.
✉ 21 bis rue de l'Horloge ☎ 04 73 63 07 97 ⊙ Closed two weeks Sep., Sun. dinner and Mon. AX DC MC VI

VICHY

🏨 Les Célestins $$–$$$
Rooms overlook the spa or the park, and the two restaurants include a simple bistro ($) or fine dining at Les Jardins de l'Empereur ($$$). All is smart, yet comfortably informal.
✉ 111 boulevard des États-Unis ☎ 04 70 30 82 00; fax 04 70 30 82 01 AX DC MC VI

🍴 Table d'Atoine $$–$$$
The menu may suggest traditional cuisine, but food here, from steak to stuffed pasta, has a modern presentation.
✉ 8 rue Burnol ☎ 04 70 98 99 71 ⊙ Closed early Mar., mid-Nov., Sun. dinner and Mon. MC VI

VOLVIC

🏨 La Rose des Vents $
Lovely views await at this hotel with a garden and pool. A restaurant ($–$$) is on site.
✉ Route de Pontgibaud, 63530 Luzet; D986 from Volvic, 2½ miles west ☎ 04 73 33 50 77; fax 04 73 33 57 11 ⊙ Closed Jan.-Mar.; Mon. lunch, except for dinner in summer; and Sun. dinner AX MC VI

Rhône Valley

KEY TO SYMBOLS

🏨 hotel
🍴 restaurant
✉ address
☎ telephone number
🕐 days/times closed
Ⓜ nearest metro/tube/subway station(s)
🚌 nearby bus/trolley-bus/tram route(s).
⛴ ferry
AX   American Express
DC   Diners Club
MC   MasterCard
VI   VISA

Hotel

Price guide: double room with breakfast for two people
$$$ over €150
$$ €75–€150
$ under €75

Restaurant

Price guide: dinner per person, excluding drinks
$$$ over €40
$$ €20–€40
$ under €20

SIMPLE DELIGHT

Although often overshadowed by the gastronomic fireworks of the Burgundy region next door, Franche-Comte region's tables are appetizing as well. Smoked meats and fish are staples, but the true star of a meal is the cheese course. Mont d'Or is matured in a spruce box, and the flavor of Comte cheese has often been compared to fine wine, so strictly controlled are the herds that create the milk and the long ripening process (up to 18 months). The region also produces excellent wines. Vins jaune (yellow wines) are something of a rarity: heady evaporated white wines matured a little over six years that may be kept for up to a century.

Alps - Rhône Valley

AIX-LES-BAINS

🏨 Agora $
Surprises hide in the basement of this budget address: a pool, sauna, steam room and power shower.
✉ Rue de Chambéry, 73100 ☎ 04 79 34 20 20; fax 04 79 34 20 30 AX DC MC VI

🍴 Le Grand Café Adélaïde $$
Images of the resort's heyday provide a backdrop to the innovative meals enjoyed in this restaurant.
✉ Avenue Marlioz ☎ 04 79 61 79 79 AX DC MC VI

ANNECY

🏨 Best Western Carlton $–$$
The 1930s-style hotel is close to the lake and the sights of the old town.
✉ 5 rue des Glières, 74000 ☎ 04 50 10 09 09; fax 04 50 10 09 60 AX DC MC VI

🍴 Le Clos des Sens $$–$$$
Enjoy fine dining in an idyllic old-town setting, where freshwater fish and farm fare are specialties.
✉ 13 rue J.-Mermoz ☎ 04 50 23 07 90 🕐 Closed in Jan., Sat. lunch, Sun. dinner and Mon. AX DC MC VI

BRIANÇON

🏨 Vauban $
A genuine family welcome awaits at the hotel. Reliable home cooking is served in the restaurant ($–$$).
✉ 13 avenue Gén de Gaulle ☎ 04 92 21 12 11; fax 04 92 20 58 20 🕐 Closed Nov. 1 to mid-Dec. MC VI

CHAMBÉRY

🏨 Château de Candie $$–$$$
A 14th-century Savoyard castle furnished with frescoes and a pleasant restaurant ($–$$).
✉ rue du Bois de Candie, 73000 Chambéry-le-Vieux; N201 from Chambéry, 3 miles north ☎ 04 79 96 63 00; fax 04 79 96 63 10 AX MC VI

🍴 L'Essentiel $$–$$$
Scrumptious desserts follow imaginative fish dishes, all washed down with Savoy wines.
✉ 183 place de la Gare ☎ 04 79 96 97 27 🕐 Closed Sun. except lunch in Jul.–Aug. and Sat. lunch AX MC VI

CHAMONIX

🍴 Atmosphère $–$$
Traditional dishes offer good value, but the view of Mont Blanc is priceless.
✉ 123 place Balmat ☎ 04 50 55 97 97 AX MC VI

🏨 Jeu de Paume $$–$$$
The classic wooden chalet has a restaurant ($$$), pool and sauna.
✉ 705 route du Chapeau, le Lavancher, 74400 N 506 from Chamonix, 4 miles northeast ☎ 04 50 54 03 76; fax 04 50 54 10 75 🕐 Closed in May, Jun. and mid-Sep. to Nov. 30 AX DC MC VI

LA CLUSAZ

🏨 Chalets de la Serraz $–$$
The traditional chalet's comfortable rooms pamper the sporty types who use the gym and pool when not on the slopes. Savoyard favorites are served in the restaurant ($–$$).
✉ Route du Col des Aravis; D909 from la Clusaz, 3 miles south ☎ 04 50 02 48 29 🕐 Closed May and Oct. AX DC MC VI

EVIAN-LES-BAINS

🍴 La Toque Royale $$$
Sumptuous ingredients and spices are treated with high respect. This spot is ideal for celebration or consolation after a session at the gaming tables.
✉ Casino Royal, avenue de Narvik ☎ 04 50 26 87 10 🕐 Closed in mid-Jan. and Sun. AX DC MC VI

🏨 La Verniaz $$
Guests who stay in chalets with lake views get a generous taste of the high life. The restaurant menu ($$–$$$) features French favorites.
✉ route d'Abondance, 74500 ☎ 0450 75 04 90; fax 04 50 70 78 92 🕐 Closed mid-Nov. to mid-Feb. AX MC VI

GRENOBLE

🍴 À Ma Table $$–$$$
The memorable house specialties of this unpretentious and intimate restaurant include caramelized sea bream. Book in advance.
✉ 92 cours Jean-Jaurès ☎ 04 76 96 77 04 🕐 Closed Aug., Sat. lunch, Sun. and Mon. MC VI

Burgundy and the East

Le Grand Hôtel $–$$
This great location near the museum offers air-conditioned rooms and a better-than-average breakfast.
✉ 5 rue de la République, 38000 ☎ 04 76 44 49 36; fax 04 76 63 14 06 AX DC MC VI

LYON

Château Perrache $$–$$$
Rooms are big and lounges reflect an art-nouveau flair. A standard restaurant ($$) is on site.
✉ 12 cours de Verdun-Rambaud, 69002 ☎ 04 72 77 15 00; fax 04 78 37 06 56 🚇 Perrache AX DC MC VI

Les Eaux Vives $$–$$$
The Hôtel Métropole's popular riverside restaurant lets you appreciate the classics without breaking the bank.
✉ 85 quai Joseph-Gillet ☎ 04 72 10 44 45 🚇 Henon AX DC MC VI

Paul Bocuse $$$
This place is simply the best.
✉ 40 rue de la Plage, Collonges-au-Mont-d'Or; D433, D51 from Lyon, 8 miles north ☎ 04 72 42 90 90 AX DC MC VI

Sofitel Royal $$–$$$
The Sofitel Royal is renowned for its lavish bedrooms and bathrooms and the professionalism of the staff.
✉ 20 place Bellecour, 60002 ☎ 04 78 37 57 31; fax 04 78 37 01 36 🚇 Bellecour AX DC MC VI

La Tour Rose $$$
The charming and beautifully converted 16th-century convent is also home to Philippe Chavent's legendary restaurant ($$$).
✉ 22 rue du Boeuf, 69005 ☎ 04 78 92 69 10; fax 04 78 42 26 02 🚇 Vieux Lyon AX DC MC VI

PEROUGES

Hostellerie du Vieux Pérouges $$–$$$
One of the oldest hotels in France, this comfortable establishment has great views and an excellent restaurant ($$$).
✉ Place Tilleul, 01800 ☎ 04 74 61 00 88; fax 04 74 34 77 90 MC VI

ROMANÈCHE-THORINS – BEAUJOLAIS
Les Maritonnes $
This is a useful overnight stop for those who may have overindulged in vineyard and cellar tours. The restaurant ($$–$$$) serves escargot and *quenelle-de-brochet* (pike patty) to show off the local wine.
✉ Route de Fleurie, 71570 ☎ 03 85 35 51 70; fax 03 85 35 58 14 🕐 Closed Dec. 16–Jan. 25. Restaurant closed Sun. dinner and Mon. AX DC MC VI

ST. VÉRAN

Grand Tétras $
Friendly service and home cooking can be expected in the dining room of this small hotel ($) in Queyras' best-known village.
✉ Village center 05350 ☎ 04 92 45 82 42 🕐 Closed Apr. 1 to mid-May and mid-Sep. to mid-Dec. MC VI

VASSIEUX-EN-VERCORS

Allard $
Henri Allard's friendly hotel offers a fitness center, sauna and restaurant ($–$$).
✉ Vassieux-en-Vercors, 26420 ☎ 04 75 48 28 04; fax 04 75 48 26 90 🕐 Closed mid-Oct. to mid-Dec. MC VI

VIENNE

Hôtel des 7 Fontaines $
Spacious rooms fill the large house, which is set in parkland just five minutes out of town.
✉ Les 7 Fontaines, 38200 ☎ 04 74 85 25 70; fax 04 74 31 74 47 🕐 Closed Nov.–Mar. AX MC VI

Pyramide $$
Although the hotel with gardens is lovely, the main attraction is the restaurant ($$$), which holds its own against the best Lyon can offer.
✉ 14 boulevard Fernand-Point, 38200 ☎ 04 74 53 01 96 🕐 Closed Feb. and Tue.–Wed. AX DC MC VI

Burgundy and the East

ARBOIS

Le Caveau d'Arbois $–$$
This place is known for hearty family cooking, popular fish dishes and terrines.
✉ 3 route de Besançon ☎ 03 84 66 10 70 AX MC VI

Moulin de la Mère Michelle $$
Accommodations are in a restored water mill and outbuildings around a waterfall. A restaurant ($$) is on site.
✉ Les Planches-en-Arbois, 39600 ☎ 03 84 66 08 17; fax 03 84 37 49 69 🕐 Restaurant closed Mon.–Fri. lunch AX MC VI

BEAUNE

Le Jardin des Remparts $$–$$$
A local favorite, the restaurant boasts a great wine cellar and fabulous food – from mouth-watering beef and seafood to the delicate pear sorbet.
✉ 10 rue Hôtel-Dieu ☎ 03 80 24 79 41 🕐 Closed Feb., early Aug.; Mon., except national holidays; and Sun. MC VI

Poste $$
The rooms of this lovely old white house either face the ramparts of the old town or overlook the local vineyards.
✉ 5 boulevard Clémenceau, 21200 ☎ 03 80 22 08 11; fax 03 80 24 19 71 AX DC MC VI

BELFORT

Grand Hôtel du Tonneau d'Or $$
This place is popular during festivals; it's advisable to book in advance to avoid disapointment. A restaurant ($$) is on site.
✉ 1 rue Reiset, 90000 ☎ 03 84 58 57 56; fax 03 84 58 57 50 AX DC MC VI

Le Molière $–$$
The flair of a woman's touch is evident in the popular restaurant's traditional dishes.
✉ 6 place Étuve, 90000 ☎ 03 84 21 86 38 AX DC MC VI

BESANÇON

Castan $$
The hotel is set in a converted 17th-century town house. The rooms are attractively decorated and give a characterful and warm touch.
✉ 6 square Castan, 25000 ☎ 03 81 65 02 00; fax 03 81 83 01 02 🕐 Closed three weeks in Aug. and Dec. 26–Jan. 2 AX MC VI

Burgundy and the East

KEY TO SYMBOLS

- ⊞ hotel
- ❙❙ restaurant
- ✉ address
- ☎ telephone number
- ⏰ days/times closed
- Ⓜ nearest metro/tube/subway station(s)
- 🚌 nearby bus/trolley-bus/tram route(s)
- ⛴ ferry
- AX American Express
- DC Diners Club
- MC MasterCard
- VI VISA

Hotel
Price guide: double room with breakfast for two people

$$$	over €150
$$	€75–€150
$	under €75

Restaurant
Price guide: dinner per person, excluding drinks

$$$	over €40
$$	€20–€40
$	under €20

BREAKFAST AT PAUL'S

Paul doesn't have the biggest or most varied breakfast in Lille, but it does have the best. This bakery opposite the Vieille Bourse is the place to go for fresh bread and croissants, homemade jam, and creamy, piping-hot chocolate first thing in the morning. Breakfast, served on solid wooden tables against the blue-and-white tiled walls and heavy tapestries of the bread and cake shop, is the perfect way to start the day. But meals also are served until the wee hours, and it would be a pity to dismiss this elegant bakery as a mere breakfast place or tearoom. Up a curving wooden staircase is the bright and airy second-floor dining room, which provides echoes of a more elegant era.

✉ Paul, 8 rue de Paris (Rihour) ☎ 03 20 78 20 78.

❙❙ Vauban $
The popular dining room sits at the Citadel gate.

✉ Citadelle ☎ 03 81 83 02 77 ⏰ Closed Dec. 20–Feb. 20; Mon., except summer lunch; and Sun. dinner　AX MC VI

COLMAR

⊞ Le Maréchal $$–$$$
The 16th-century hotel is home to l'Echevin restaurant ($$$), a favorite for excellent Alsatian cuisine.

✉ 4-b place des Six-Montagnes-Noires, 68000 ☎ 03 89 41 60 32; fax 03 89 24 59 40　AX MC VI

❙❙ Rendez Vous de Chasse $$$
Regional and classic French standards are served in the finer of the Hôtel Bristol's two restaurants. The Auberge restaurant ($) is ideal for simple occasions.

✉ 7 place de la Gare ☎ 03 89 41 10 10　AX MC VI

DIJON

❙❙ Le Bistrot des Halles $
Flavorful food and wine are standbys at the reliable market restaurant.

✉ 10 rue Bannelier ☎ 03 80 49 94 15 ⏰ Closed Sun. dinner　MC VI

⊞ Jacquemart $
Quaint streets behind the palace aren't ideal for vehicles, so park elsewhere and walk to this charming hotel in a 17th-century house.

✉ 32 rue Verrerie, 21000 ☎ 03 80 60 09 60; fax 03 80 60 09 69　MC VI

METZ

❙❙ Brasserie Flo $–$$
Step inside the grand Napoleon III dining rooms for huge seafood platters and local specialties.

✉ 2 bis rue Gambetta ☎ 03 87 55 94 95　AX DC MC VI

⊞ Cathédrale $
This is a great base for sightseeing – with the cathedral, marketplace and river at your doorstep.

✉ 25 place Chambre, 57000 ☎ 03 87 75 00 02; fax 03 87 75 40 75　AX MC VI

MONTBÉLIARD

❙❙ La Tour Henriette $$–$$$
Lamb and fish are served with a smile in the best Comtoise fashion.

✉ 59 faubourg de Besançon ☎ 03 81 91 03 24 ⏰ Closed mid-Jul. to mid-Aug., Sun. dinner and Sat.　AX MC VI DC

MONTBARD – FONTENAY

⊞ L'Écu Coupat Pere et Fils $
The restaurant ($–$$$) in the hotel has both budget and gastronomic menus featuring local dishes.

✉ 7 rue Auguste Carré, 21500; D905, D32 to Fontenay Abbey, 4 miles northeast ☎ 03 80 92 11 66; fax 03 80 92 14 13 ⏰ Closed Tue. lunch mid-Nov. to mid-Apr.　AX DC MC VI

NANCY

⊞ Albert 1er Astoria $
The convenient hotel offers parking and an English-speaking staff.

✉ 3 rue de l'Armée Patton, 54000 ☎ 03 83 40 31 24; fax 03 83 28 47 78　AX DC MC VI

❙❙ Excelsior Flo $–$$
This lively restaurant specializes in oysters and a visit will also please those interested in art-nouveau decor.

✉ 50 rue Poincaré ☎ 03 83 35 24 57　AX DC MC VI

RIQUEWIHR

⊞ Couronne $–$$
Roomy accommodations fill the pretty 15th-century building.

✉ 5 rue de la Couronne, 68340 ☎ 03 89 49 03 03; fax 03 89 49 01 01　AX MC VI

❙❙ Table du Gourmet $$$
Savor textbook Alsace cooking by award-winning chef Jean-Luc Brendel. Let your waiter guide your discovery of the region's finer flavors.

✉ 5 rue de la 1ère-Armée ☎ 03 89 49 09 09 ⏰ Closed mid-Jan. to Feb. 28, Wed. lunch and Tue.　AX MC VI

STRASBOURG

❙❙ Bierstub l'Ami Schutz $–$$
The traditional Alsace restaurant resides in the pretty waterside district.

✉ 1 rue Ponts Couverts ☎ 03 88 32 76 98 ⏰ Closed national holidays　AX DC MC VI

🍴 Buerehiesel $$$

Chef Antoine Westermann prepares inventive gastronomy in this old farmhouse.

✉ 4 parc de l'Orangerie ☎ 03 88 45 56 65 🕐 Closed First half of Jan., 3 weeks in Aug. and Tue.–Wed AX DC MC VI

🏨 Cathédrale $–$$

Opposite the cathedral, this is an unrivaled central spot, especially during the Christmas market season.

✉ 12–13 place de la Cathédrale, 67061 ☎ 03 88 22 12 12; fax 03 88 23 28 00 AX DC MC VI

🏨 Dragon $$

From the 17th-century house, on a quiet street, take an easy stroll to Petite France and the markets.

✉ 2 rue de l'Écarlate, 67000 ☎ 03 88 35 79 80; fax 03 88 25 78 95 AX DC MC VI

🏨 Rohan $–$$

Rooms range from rustic to baroque in this peaceful hotel.

✉ 17–19 rue du Maroquin, 67000 ☎ 03 88 32 85 11; fax 03 88 75 65 37 AX DC MC VI

<h3>VERDUN</h3>

🏨 Château des Monthairons $$

This 19th-century château sits in extensive grounds. Dine well at the restaurant ($$–$$$).

✉ 55320 les Monthairons; D34 from Verdun, 10 miles south ☎ 03 29 87 78 55; fax 03 29 87 73 49 🕐 Closed Jan. 1 to mid-Feb. AX DC MC VI

🍴 Hostellerie du Coq Hardi $$$

Relish old-fashioned dining in the hotel ($–$$) of the same name. Wonderful plates of hare and beef are followed by flambéed plums.

✉ 8 avenue de la Victoire ☎ 03 29 86 36 36 🕐 Closed Fri. AX DC MC VI

Champagne and the North

<h3>AMIENS</h3>

🏨 Grand Hôtel de l'Univers $

The large house contains well-equipped rooms and a leafy garden.

✉ 2 rue de Noyon, 80000 ☎ 03 22 91 52 51; fax 03 22 92 81 66 AX DC MC VI

🍴 Marissons $$

Within a choir's chant of the cathedral, diners indulge in dishes such as duck with foie gras.

✉ Pont Dodane ☎ 03 22 92 96 66 AX DC MC VI

<h3>ARRAS</h3>

🍴 La Faisanderie $$–$$$

The best food in town, including a fabulous cheeseboard, is served in the evocative 17th-century cellars.

✉ 45 Grand-Place ☎ 03 21 48 20 76 🕐 Closed early Jan., Aug. 3–24; school holidays; Sun. dinner and Mon. AX DC MC VI

🏨 Trois Luppars $

This oldest house on the main square was lovingly restored by the present owners.

✉ 49 Grand-Place, 62000 ☎ 03 21 07 41 41; fax 03 21 24 24 80 AX MC DC VI

<h3>BOULOGNE-SUR-MER</h3>

🍴 La Matelote $$–$$$

Tony Lestienne's fish-based menu always proves excellent value.

✉ 80 boulevard Ste.-Beuve ☎ 03 21 30 17 97 🕐 Closed Dec. 24–Jan. 10, Sun. dinner, except Jul.–Aug. and holidays AX MC VI

🏨 Metropole $

This hotel has a friendly, family welcome and a small garden.

✉ 51 rue Thiers, 62200 ☎ 03 21 31 54 30; fax 03 21 30 45 72 🕐 Closed Dec. 21–Jan. 5 AX MC VI DC

<h3>CALAIS</h3>

🍴 Le Channel $–$$$

Taste the best Dover sole this side of the Channel in this unpretentious seashore dining room.

✉ 3 boulevard de la Résistance ☎ 03 21 34 42 30 🕐 Closed late Jul. to mid-Aug., late Dec. to mid-Jan. and Tue. and Sun. dinner AX DC MC VI

🏨 Metropol $

This is probably the smartest hotel in town. Rooms have sea views.

✉ 43 quai du Rhin, 62100 ☎ 03 21 97 54 00; fax 03 21 96 69 70 🕐 Closed Dec. 19–Jan. 3 AX DC MC VI

<h3>CHARLEVILLE-MÉZIÈRES</h3>

🍴 Clef des Champs $$

The small restaurant serves inventive cuisine prepared by an enthusiastic, informal young team.

✉ 33 rue du Moulin ☎ 03 24 56 17 50 🕐 Closed Sun. dinner and Mon. MC VI

🏨 Paris $

This unassuming central hotel offers clean, basic rooms.

✉ 24 avenue G.-Corneau, 08000 ☎ 03 24 33 34 38; fax 03 24 59 11 21 🕐 Closed Dec. 24–Jan. 3 AX MC VI

<h3>EPERNAY</h3>

🍴 Le Théâtre $$

Well-judged menus are served at the popular local restaurant. In the evening, revelers take over from the more sober business lunchers.

✉ 8 place Mendès-France ☎ 03 26 58 88 19 🕐 Closed 3 weeks in Feb., 2 weeks in Jul., 1 week at Christmas, Tue.dinner and Wed. all year, Sun. dinner mid-Nov. to mid-Mar. MC VI

<h3>LAON</h3>

🏨 Hostellerie St.-Vincent $

Comfortable rooms fill a modern building. Follow signs toward the industrial zone.

✉ Avenue Charles-de-Gaulle, 02000 ☎ 03 23 23 42 43; fax 03 23 79 22 55 🕐 Closed 3 weeks at Christmas AX MC VI

🍴 La Petite Auberge $$–$$$

Taste a hint of the Mediterranean in the sauces and flavors of this bistro's dishes.

✉ 45 boulevard Brossolette ☎ 03 23 23 02 38 🕐 Closed Easter, in Aug., Sat. lunch and Sun. AX MC VI

<h3>LILLE</h3>

🏨 Alliance $$–$$$

This former convent has air-conditioned rooms.

✉ 17 quai du Wault, Lille Couvent des Minimes, 59027 ☎ 03 20 30 62 62; fax 03 20 42 94 25 AX DC MC VI

🏨 Carlton $$$

The comfortable hotel has a fabulous cupola bedroom on the roof that affords the best panoramic view over the city center.

✉ 3 rue de Paris, 59026 ☎ 03 20 13 33 13; fax 03 20 51 48 17 🚇 Rihour AX DC MC VI

Champagne and the North

Champagne and the North

KEY TO SYMBOLS

- 🏨 hotel
- 🍴 restaurant
- ✉ address
- ☎ telephone number
- 🕐 days/times closed
- Ⓜ nearest metro/tube/subway station(s)
- 🚌 nearby bus/trolley-bus/tram route(s).
- 🚢 ferry
- AX American Express
- DC Diners Club
- MC MasterCard
- VI VISA

Hotel

Price guide: double room with breakfast for two people

$$$	over €150
$$	€75–€150
$	under €75

Restaurant

Price guide: dinner per person, excluding drinks

$$$	over €40
$$	€20–€40
$	under €20

CHOOSING A WINE

Whether choosing a wine or a stunning fall outfit, it pays to read the label in France. Unlike in the United States, the name of the grape variety tends not to be shown on the label; the main reference is more likely to be the region or the estate where the wine was produced. There are four main catagories: *A.O.C. (appellation d'origine controlée),* stating that the wine is made from grapes grown in a specified area and to an agreed-on standard; *V.D.Q.S. (vin delimité de qualité superieure),* or top-grade country wine; *vin de pays,* an honest open wine from a particular region; and *vin de table,* an everyday drinking wine that may be made fom a blend of grapes from various sources. Look for Chardonnays in Burgundy and eastern France, and the spicy grenache in the southwest.

🍴 La Compostelle $–$$

Charming little dining rooms and a glazed Renaissance courtyard enliven this one-time rest house for pilgrims heading for Santiago de Compostela.

✉ 4 rue St.-Étienne ☎ 03 28 38 08 30 Ⓜ Rihour   MC VI

🏨 Grand Hôtel Bellevue $$–$$$

The young Wolfgang Amadeus Mozart stayed here. Today's visitor can choose rooms overlooking the main square.

✉ 5 rue Jean-Roisin, 59800 ☎ 03 20 57 45 64; fax 03 20 40 07 93 Ⓜ Rihour   AX DC MC VI

🍴 A L'Huîtrière $$$

Behind an art-deco fish shop, the eatery offers renowned dining and a lunch menu of excellent value.

✉ 3 rue des Chats-Bossus ☎ 03 20 55 43 41 🕐 Closed Sun. dinner   AX DC MC VI

MONTREUIL-SUR-MER

🍴 Auberge de la Grenouillère $$–$$$

Known affectionately to its English-speaking fans as the Froggery, this snug farmhouse offers unforgettable food. Order from the most expensive menu midweek, and you may stay overnight to sleep off the meal at no extra charge.

✉ La Madelaine-sous-Montreuil; D917, D139 from Montreuil, 1.5 miles west ☎ 03 21 06 07 22 🕐 Closed in Jan. and Tue.–Wed., except Jul.–Aug.   AX DC MC VI

REIMS

🏨 Boyer-Les Crayères $$$

The opulent Champagne lifestyle exudes from this romantic mini-estate. The house is all marble and columns, with rooms designed for indulgence.

✉ 64 boulevard Henri-Vasnier, 51100 ☎ 03 26 82 80 80; fax 03 26 82 65 52 🕐 Closed Dec. 23–Jan. 13   AX DC MC VI

🍴 Le Vigneron $$–$$$

The chef uses the local fizz to flavor everything from turbot to desserts.

✉ Place Paul-Jamot ☎ 03 26 79 86 86 🕐 Closed Dec. 24–Jan. 1, 2 weeks in Aug., Sat. lunch and Sun.   MC VI

ROUBAIX

🍴 Chez Charly $–$$

Thoughtful menus offer good food with no fuss. Prices are reasonable, but the classy apple tart is a must at any price.

✉ 127 avenue Lebas ☎ 03 20 70 78 58 🕐 Closed Easter, Aug. and Sun.   MC VI

ST.-OMER

🍴 Le Cygne $–$$

Ask for a table in the smart first-floor dining room, where locals lunch on traditional dishes.

✉ 8 rue Caventou ☎ 03 21 98 20 52 🕐 Closed Aug. 16–23, Sun. dinner and Mon.   AX DC MC VI

SIGNY-L'ABBAYE

🏨 Auberge de l'Abbaye $

Monsieur Lefebre's welcome is always genuine, either in the agreeable restaurant ($) or showing guests around the eccentrically proportioned rooms.

✉ Place Briand, 08460 ☎ 03 24 52 81 27; fax 03 24 53 71 72   MC VI

LE TOUQUET-PARIS-PLAGE

🍴 Flavio $$–$$$

This restaurant is renowned for its fish soups, Flavio skillfully treads the line between familiarity and fine dining. It's the secret favorite of many off-duty food critics.

✉ 1 avenue du Verger ☎ 03 21 05 10 22 🕐 Closed Jan.–Feb. and Mon. except Jul.–Aug.   DC MC VI

🏨 Westminster $$–$$$

Something of an institution with a fine restaurant ($$$), the Westminster is at the heart of le Touquet's social scene.

✉ 5 avenue du Verger, 62520 ☎ 03 21 05 48 48; fax 03 21 05 45 45   AX DC MC VI

TOURCOING

🍴 La Baratte $–$$$

A local caterer was persuaded by friends and family to open his own restaurant. The result is this club-like atmosphere.

✉ 395 rue Clinquet ☎ 03 20 94 45 63 🕐 Closed Feb. school holidays, Aug., Sun. and Mon. dinner and Sat.   AX MC VI

ESSENTIAL
INFORMATION

"PLANNING advice and practical travel tips "

The information in this guide has been compiled for U.S. citizens traveling as tourists.

Travelers who are not U.S. citizens, or who are traveling on business, should check with their embassies and tourist offices for information on the countries they wish to visit.

Entry requirements are subject to change at short notice, and travelers are advised to check the current situation before they travel.

France – Essential Information

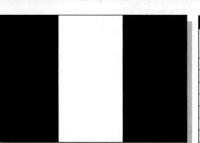

● Required   ● Recommended   ○ Not required

Passport	●
Visa	○
Travel, medical insurance	●
Round-trip or onward airline ticket	○
Local currency	●
Traveler's checks	●
Credit cards	●
First-aid kit and medicines	●
Health inoculations	○

BEFORE YOU GO

PASSPORTS

Each person traveling must have a passport. A visa isn't required for a tourist or business stay up to 90 days.

Passport application forms can be obtained from any federal or state court or post office authorized to accept passport applications; apply early, since processing can take several months. U.S. passport agencies have offices in major cities; check the Yellow Pages (U.S. Government, State Department) for the nearest one. You also can request an application form from the National Passport Information Center: ☎ (900) 225-5674 (35¢ per minute) or ☎ (888) 498-3648. ($4.95 per call) Passport information and application forms are available on the U.S. State Government internet site at www.travel.state.gov.

Photocopy the identification page of your passport; leave one copy with a relative or friend in case of emergency, and carry one with you in case the passport is lost or stolen while traveling. If this occurs, inform the local police immediately and contact the nearest U.S. embassy or consulate. The U.S. State Department has a 24-hour traveler's hotline: ☎ (202) 647-5225.

Passports must be shown whenever you board an international flight or cross an international border. In practice, however, border controls have been relaxed between many European Union (EU) member countries.

TRAVEL INSURANCE

Before departing, make sure you are covered by insurance that will reimburse travel expenses if you need to cancel or cut short your trip due to unforeseen circumstances. You also will need coverage for property loss or theft, emergency medical and dental treatment, and emergency evacuation if necessary. Before taking out additional insurance, check whether your current homeowners or medical coverage already includes travel abroad.

If you make a claim your insurance company will need proof of the incident or expenditure. Keep copies of any police report and related documents, or medical bills or statements.

● Required   ● Recommended   ○ Not required

Driver's license	●
International Driving Permit	●
Car insurance (for non-rental cars)	●
Car registration (for non-rental cars)	●

See also DRIVING section

WHEN TO GO

The moderate northerly climate of France is affected by various factors. The Gulf Stream has a warming, if sometimes wet, influence on its Atlantic coastline, while Mediterranean destinations have mostly sunny skies and warm temperatures. Inland, the altitude of the Pyrénées and the Alps bring cooler temperatures; the Alps are especially popular with winter skiers. The southwest area of Aquitaine, including the Dordogne, has hot summers.

French school vacations are in July and August, so June and September are good months to visit, with fine weather and fewer crowds.

IMPORTANT ADDRESSES

French Government Tourist Office
444 Madison Avenue
New York, NY 10022
☎ (212) 838-7800
Fax (212) 838-7855
www.franceguide.com

French Government Tourist Office
Maison de la France
20 avenue de l'Opéra
75001 Paris, France
☎ 01 42 96 70 00
Fax 01 42 96 70 11

American Embassy
2 avenue Gabriel
75008 Paris, France
☎ 01 43 12 22 22
Fax 01 42 66 97 83
American Citizens Services: Mon.–Fri. 9–3

TIME ZONES

PARIS	NEW YORK	CHICAGO	DENVER	SAN FRANCISCO
12:00 noon	6 hours behind France	7 hours behind France	8 hours behind France	9 hours behind France

277

France – Essential Information

CUSTOMS

YES
Duty-free limits on goods brought in from non-European Union countries:
200 cigarettes or 100 cigarillos or 50 cigars or 250 g. tobacco; 2 L wine; 1 L alcohol over 22% volume; 2 L alcohol under 22%; 50 g perfume; 250 ml. toilet water; plus any other duty-free goods (including gifts) to the value of €45. There is no limit on the importation of tax-paid goods purchased within the European Union, provided they are for your own personal use. There are no currency regulations. On returning to the United States, you will be required to complete a customs declaration form. You are allowed $400 worth of goods or gifts (including items purchased in duty-free shops); keep sales slips and have them ready for inspection. The duty-free exemption can include 100 cigars and 200 cigarettes, as well as 1L of wine, beer or liquor if you are 21 or older.

NO
No unlicensed drugs, weapons, ammunition, obscene material, pets or other animals, counterfeit money or copied goods, meat or poultry.

MONEY

France's currency is the euro (€), a currency shared by 11 other European Union countries. The euro is divided into 100 cents (¢). The denominations of euro bills are 5, 10, 20, 50, 100, 200 and 500 euros. There are coins of 1, 2, 5, 10, 20 and 50¢ and €1 and €2. You can exchange dollars or traveler's checks (chèques de voyage) at a bank (banque) or an exchange office (bureau de change).

Exchange rate at press time: $1 = €1.02

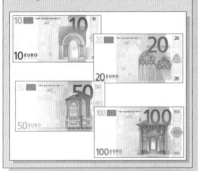

COMMUNICATIONS

POST OFFICES

Buy stamps (timbres) at a post office (une poste), newsstand (une marchande de journaux) or tobacconist (distinguished by its red Tabac sign). Hours of out-of-town post offices may vary.

Mailboxes are yellow and are wall mounted or freestanding. For posting abroad, use the slot marked département étrangers.

TELEPHONES
Phone booths with instructions in English are easy to find. Most phones are operated with a phone card (télécarte), which can be bought from post offices, newsstands and many tobacconists (€7.41or €14.74 values). You

can use credit cards in some booths.

Phoning within France
All telephone numbers are 10 digits, and include the regional code. Numbers beginning 08.00 are toll free; those beginning 08.36 are charged at premium rate. For national directory inquiries dial 12.

Phoning France from abroad
The country code for France is 33. To phone France from the United States or Canada, omit the first zero from the French number, and add the prefix 011 33.
Example: 01 22 33 44 55 becomes 011 33 1 22 33 44 55.

Phoning from France
To phone the United States or Canada from France, prefix the area code and number with 00 1.
Example: (111) 222-3333 becomes 00 1 111 222-3333.

To call international information dial 003312 plus the country prefix as above.

To call the operator dial 3123 for any country.

TIPS AND GRATUITIES

Tips (pourboires) are welcomed, but not expected

Restaurants (service is almost always included)	change
Cafés/bars	change
Porters	€1–2
Chambermaids	€2
Taxis	€1–2
Cloakroom attendants	50¢–€1

EMERGENCY NUMBERS

Police (police)	17
Fire service (pompiers)	18
Ambulance (ambulance)	15

Emergency calls are free from phone booths.

France – Essential Information

HOURS OF OPERATION

- Stores Tue.–Sat.
- Museums/monuments
- Offices Mon.–Fri.
- Pharmacies
- Banks Mon.–Fri.
- Post offices Mon.–Fri.

7 8 9 10 11 12 1 2 3 4 5 6 7

Many stores close on Sunday and all or half day on Monday, although opening hours are longer in resort areas and major towns and cities. Small stores close for lunch and in the south of France in the heat of the summer, lunch may extend to 4 p.m., but then the store will stay open later in the evening.

Out-of-town banks may stay closed on Monday, while city banks may open on Saturday morning.

Post offices close at noon on Saturday, small offices close for lunch weekdays.

National museums are closed on Tuesday (except Versailles, the Trianon Palace and the Musée d'Orsay which are closed Monday). Municipal museums are closed on Monday. Museum times vary considerably, and it's best to check before a visit.

NATIONAL HOLIDAYS

Banks, businesses and most stores close on these days:

Jan. 1	New Year's Day
Mar./Apr.	Easter Monday
May 1	May Day
May 8	VE Day
May	Ascension Day
May/Jun.	Pentecost Monday
Jul. 14	Bastille Day
Aug. 15	Assumption of the Virgin
Nov. 1	All Saints' Day
Nov. 11	Armistice Day
Dec. 25	Christmas Day

RESTROOMS

Restrooms (les toilettes or WC, pronounced vay-say in French) are more common in larger towns, often located near a public space or amenity. You may still find the old-fashioned "squat" variety and hygiene is usually of a reasonable standard. There is a small fee to use facilities in train stations. If you need to use the restroom in a café or bar, buy a drink first.

HEALTH ADVICE

MEDICAL SERVICES

Private medical insurance is recommended. Visitors from non-EU countries have to pay for all medical treatment; keep all receipts and medicine labels to claim on your travel insurance. If you wish to see an English-speaking doctor (un médecin) ask at your consulate or hotel.

DENTAL SERVICES

A dentist (un/une dentiste) charges for treatment. Emergency help is available from dentists listed in the yellow pages (les pages jaunes). Check that your private medical insurance covers dental treatment.

SUN ADVICE

The yearly average for sunshine is high: 2,500 hours (3,000 hours along the coast). Summers, particularly July and August, can be dry and hot, especially in the south. When outside wear a hat and drink plenty of fluids. On the beach a high factor sunscreen is essential.

DRUGS

Prescription medicines and medical advice can be obtained from a pharmacy (une pharmacie), designated by a green cross sign. If you need medicines outside regular hours, information about the nearest 24-hour facility is posted on the door of all pharmacies.

SAFE WATER

It's safe to drink tap water, but never drink from a fountain marked "eau non potable" ("not drinking water"). Many French people prefer the taste of bottled mineral water (eau minérale en bouteille), which is widely available. A less expensive alternative is eau de source, or spring water.

PERSONAL SAFETY

To lessen the risk of theft or injury through crime, try not to be conspicuous by wearing expensive jewelry or carrying valuables. Criminals frequent tourist attractions, stores, markets and all transportation, while theft from rental vehicles

with non-local license plates is common.

Your passport, money and credit cards should be kept hidden inside clothing, and only necessary money or cards carried.

If you should get into trouble contact the police (see Emergency Numbers), and if required the nearest U.S. embassy.

FIRE SERVICE 18
(Pompiers)

AMBULANCE 15
(Ambulance)

279

France – Essential Information

NATIONAL TRANSPORTATION

AIR *(avion)*

Airports for the major cities in France are served by Air Inter Europe and Air France, while many U.S. operators provide regular flights to Paris. For details on local and international Air France flights, call (800) 237-2747 in the United States or contact your travel agent. For Air France information in France, call 08 02 80 28 02.

Paris has two airports – Roissy-Charles de Gaulle (Roissy-CDG) to the north, and Orly to the south. Both are connected to the center of Paris by the RER B (Orly also connected by RER C) railroad, and other public transportation is easily available. For daily flight information, call 01 48 62 22 80 (Roissy) or 01 49 75 15 15 (Orly). General information about the airports is provided by Aérports de Paris (ADP), who have customer service desks in the main terminals; website www.adp.fr.

Many of the main cities described in this guide can be reached from Paris by plane, including Bordeaux, Clermont Ferrand, Lille, Lyons, Marseille, Nice, Rennes, Strasbourg and Toulouse. Other regional airports can provide connections to smaller towns; contact Air France.

TRAIN *(train)*

The state rail company is the Société Nationale des Chemins de Fer Français (SNCF). Trains are fast, reliable and comfortable, with numerous discounts available. A "turn-up-and-go" car-carrying service from Calais (Le Shuttle) and a Paris–London passenger train (Eurostar) both run through the tunnel under the English Channel. For SNCF details, call 08 36 35 35 35 (toll call) and for Eurostar details, call 08 36 35 35 39 (English speaking; toll call).

BUS *(autobus)*

Bus services in cities are excellent, but rural areas may be less well served. Long-distance bus stations are usually close to railroad stations, and major train and bus services usually co-ordinate (a long-distance bus is called a *car*). Bus services shown on train timetables are run by the SNCF, and rail tickets are often valid for them. The Eurolines international bus network operates in France; ☎ 08 36 69 52 52 (toll call).

FERRY *(ferry)*

There are frequent sailings to southern England from ports along the English Channel. P&O Stena Line (☎ 08 02 01 00 20) and Seafrance (☎ 08 25 04 40 45 Mon.–Fri.; 03 31 46 80 00 Sat.–Sun.) operate from Calais in the north. P&O Portsmouth (☎ 08 03 01 30 13) operate from Le Havre and Cherbourg in Normandy. Brittany Ferries (☎ 08 03 82 88 28) sail from Caen, Cherbourg, St. Malo and Roscoff along the Normandy and Brittany coasts.

Some Mediterranean ferries operate in summer only and require reservations. SNCM offers sailings to Corsica from Marseille, Toulon and Nice. For details, call 08 36 67 95 00; website www.sncm.fr.

PHOTOGRAPHY

You will never be short of subjects to shoot in France. There is the huge variety of architecture – cathedrals, churches and châteaux – and diverse landscapes from mountain to seashore. If it's a gloomy day get closer for interesting details. The common 100 ASA film should be fine for most scenes. In general, if you're taking a picture inside a building seek permission if possible. The same applies when taking someone's portrait. And always buy a postcard: most are of good quality and will suffice if any accidents happen to your film.

Photographic films and batteries are widely available in France and developing services can be found in most towns and even in large villages in tourist areas such as Brittany and the southwest. Specialized developing stores provide a one- or 24-hour express service but French pharmacies do not provide developing services. Large stores such as Leclerc and Carrefour, which are present in or around most towns, provide developing services up to 30 percent cheaper than the specialized stores.

MEDIA

France's national newspapers *(journaux)* include the conservative *Le Figaro*, the authoritative liberal *Le Monde*, the socialist *Libération*, the communist *L'Humanité*, the catholic *La Croix* and the ever-popular sports paper *L'Equipe*. Regional newspapers are also widely read.

In larger cities, American newspapers (usually previous-day editions) and magazines are available; the most common are *USA Today*, the international edition of the *New York Herald Tribune* and *Time* magazine. They can be purchased at central rail stations and airports, as well as newsstands and tobacconists.

The national radio and television network enters into healthy competition with independent stations. *Le journal télévisé*, broadcast at meal times (1 p.m. and 8 p.m.) on France 2 and TF1, is watched by the majority of French people.

On the radio you can pick up "Voice of America", Radio Canada, or BBC broadcasts, and larger hotels often have satellite or cable connections that broadcast BBC channels, the British Sky network or CNN.

ELECTRICITY

France has a 220-volt power supply. Electrical sockets take plugs with two round pins; American appliances will need a plug adapter and will require a transformer if they don't have a dual-voltage facility.

France – Essential Information

DRIVING REGULATIONS

DRIVE ON THE RIGHT
Drive on the right-hand side of the road; passing is on the left. At intersections in urban areas yield to traffic coming from the right, often shown by signs saying *Priorité à droite*. Major roads have priority over side roads or upcoming intersections, shown by the sign *Passage protégé*. Vehicles in a traffic circle have priority over traffic entering it, shown by the sign on the approach saying *Vous n'avez pas la priorité* or *Cédez le passage*.

SEAT BELTS
Must be worn in front seats at all times and in rear seats where fitted.

MINIMUM AGE
The minimum age for driving a car is 18. However, car rental agencies stipulate a minimum age of 21 years – some companies 25 years – and the driver to have held a driver's license for at least a year.

BLOOD ALCOHOL
The legal blood alcohol limit is 0.05 percent. Random breath tests are carried out frequently, especially late at night.

TOLLS
There are tolls on many limited-access highways (*autoroutes à péage*), which are identified on route signs with an A. Collect a ticket on entry and keep it in a safe place: you must show the ticket and pay when exiting. Cash and credit cards are accepted. Tolls are more expensive than in the United States.

ADDITIONAL INFORMATION

Although a valid American driver's license is acceptable, an International Driving Permit (IDP) is recommended; some rental firms require it, and it can speed up formalities if you are involved in an accident. An IDP contains your photograph and confirms you hold a valid driver's license in your own country; it has a standard translation in several languages. The permit is available from AAA travel agencies.

A Green Card (international motor insurance certificate) is recommended if you are driving a private car; see page 276 for more information.

A free road map of France produced by the French Ministry of Transport can be obtained free from all garages displaying the sign *Bison Futé* (wily buffalo). Less conjested routes are marked on the map as well as lists of hotels, restaurants, garages and information centers.

You may find another driver flashing their headlights at you, this usually means they are claiming right of way and you should allow them to pass.

SPEED LIMITS

REGULATIONS
Traffic police can impose severe on-the-spot fines.

Toll highways (*autoroutes à péage*) **130 kph (80 mph)**
Outer lane minimum **80 kph (49 mph)**
Non-toll highways and divided highways **110 kph (68 mph)**

Main roads **90 kph (55 mph)**

Urban areas (indicated by place-name signs) **50 kph (31 mph)**

Speed limits are reduced by 20 kph on toll highways and 10 kph on main roads in wet weather, and by 80 kph on toll highways in foggy conditions (visibility less than 50 meters).

CAR RENTAL

The leading rental firms have offices at airports and train stations. Insurance is obligatory and a major credit card is usually required. Hertz offers discounted rates for AAA members. For reservations:

	UNITED STATES	FRANCE (toll calls)
Alamo	(800) 327-9633	08 03 35 23 52 (Europcar)
Avis	(800) 331-2112	08 02 05 05 05
Budget	(800) 527-0700	08 00 10 00 01
Hertz	(800) 654-3001	08 01 34 73 47

FUEL

Gas stations are generally easy to find, and highway service areas are open 24 hours. Although the leaded variety is still available, gas (*essence*) is mostly unleaded (*sans plomb*) and sold in liters; diesel fuel also is easily available. Credit cards are widely accepted; many pumps read cards directly, so the customer doesn't have to pay at the counter. Gas stations are less common in rural areas, and some close on Sunday.

PARKING

Parking is usually regulated along the roads of urban areas, although it is forbidden on many streets in central Paris. Only park in white spaces: unmarked spaces are free, those marked *Payant* require payment. Yellow or other markings are reserved for certain vehicles. A dotted yellow line on the edge of a sidewalk indicates you can drop off or collect passengers. Coin-operated meters on the sidewalk allow parking for up to two hours. Most towns have parking lots close to the center.

AAA

 AAA AFFILIATED MOTORING CLUB
Fédération Française des Automobiles-Clubes et des Usagers de la Route (FFAC)

8 place de la Concorde, F-75008 Paris, France
☎ 01 53 30 89 30; fax 01 53 30 89 29

If you break down while driving, ☎ 08 00 08 92 22 (FFAC breakdown service; toll free).
Not all automobile clubs offer full services to AAA members.

BREAKDOWNS/ACCIDENTS

If you are involved in an accident call 17 for police assistance. There are orange emergency telephones every 2 kms on highways.

Most car rental firms provide their own free rescue service; if your car is rented, follow the instructions given in the documentation. Use of a car-repair service other than those authorized by your rental company may violate your agreement.

ROAD SIGNS

French traffic signs consist of six main types. Symbols in red triangles are warnings and those in a red circle state a ban. Red triangles also indicate the right of way at intersections. Blue circular signs give obligatory commands but symbols in blue rectangles only indicate or provide information. Red-and-blue circlular signs declare parking restrictions: A red cross indicates no stopping, a slanted red bar no parking.

Route bends to left

Route has priority at intersection

CEDEZ LE PASSAGE

Give way

VOUS N'AVEZ PAS LA PRIORITÉ

Vehicles on traffic circle have priority

ROAD SIGNS (continued)

No passing

No entry

Oncoming vehicles have priority

No U turns

Ahead only

Keep right

One-way traffic

No through road

No stopping

End of restriction

France – Essential Information

PRONUNCIATION

You'll be well received if you try to pronounce words correctly. However, don't worry too much about rolling your r's – the French realize how difficult it can be.

Final consonants are seldom pronounced: the masculine adjective *ouvert* (open) is "oo-vair"; the feminine *ouverte*, "oo-vert." The final consonant in words like *vin* or *bon* makes the last vowel nasal.

h is silent	*hôtel* [o-tel]
th is t	*thé* [tay]
ch is sh	*chambre* [shombr]
ou is full	*vous* [vu]
u is tight	*menu* [meuh-nu]
c and *g* before *a, o, u*	*car* [car], *gare* [gar]
c and *g* before *i* or *e*	*merci, bagages* [si, gazh]
ç is soft before an *a*	*ça* [sa]
gn as in union	*agneau* [an-yo]

AIRPORT

airport	*l'aéroport*
arrivals	*arrivées*
departures	*départs*
check-in	*l'enregistrement*
information	*information;*
	renseignements
ticket	*un billet*
flight	*un vol*
baggage	*les bagages*
baggage check	*contrôle des*
	bagages
passport	*le passeport*
passport control	*contrôle des passe-*
	ports
window seat	*place côté fenêtre*

MEETING PEOPLE

hello, good morning	*bonjour*
good evening	*bonsoir*
Mr., Mrs., Miss	*monsieur, madame,*
	mademoiselle
excuse me	*excusez-moi*
Do you speak English?	*Parlez-vous anglais?*
yes, no	*oui, non*
I'm sorry	*pardon*
please	*s'il vous plaît*
thank you	*merci*
I am American	*Je suis américain(e)*
We are American	*Nous sommes américain*
My name is...	*je m'appelle...*
I don't understand	*je ne comprends pas*
How are you?	*Comment allez-vous?*
That's fine, OK	*ça va, d'accord*
goodbye	*au revoir*
see you later	*à bientôt*

HOTEL

hotel, inn	*hôtel, auberge*
I have a reservation	*J'ai une réservation*
Do you have...	*Avez-vous...*
a room available?	*une chambre disponible?*
a single room?	*une chambre pour une personne?*
twin beds?	*une chambre à deux lits?*
a double room?	*une chambre pour deux personnes?*
What floor?	*À quel étage?*
Is there an elevator?	*Y a-t-il un ascenseur?*
room service	*service d'étage*
manager	*le directeur*
The check, please	*La note, s'il vous plaît*

EATING OUT

A table for two, please	*Une table pour deux, s'il vous plaît*
Do you have a set menu?	*Avez-vous un menu à prix fixe?*
first course	*entrée*
main course	*plat principal*
cheese	*fromage*
dessert	*dessert*
wine list...	*carte des vins...*
red, white, rosé	*rouge, blanc, rosé*
a glass	*un verre*
bottle, half	*une bouteille, une demi-*
carafe, half	*un pichet, un demi-*
mineral water	*eau minérale*
What is that? (in menu)	*Qu'est-ce que c'est?*
bread	*du pain*
beef	*boeuf*
chicken	*poulet*
duck	*canard, caneton*
ham	*jambon*
lamb	*agneau*
pork	*porc*
pâté	*terrine/pâté*
mixed seafood	*fruits de mer*
mussels	*moules*
salmon	*saumon*
eggs	*oeufs*
coffee...	*café...*
small, black	*un expresso noir*
white	*au lait*
large white	*grand crème*
tea, with milk	*thé, au lait*
The restroom, please?	*Les toilettes, s'il vous plaît?*
The check, please	*L'addition, s'il vous plaît*
Thank you, that was very good	*Merci, c'était très bon*

DIRECTIONS

Where is/are…	Où se trouve/trouvent…
Turn left/right	Tournez à gauche/à droite
Go straight	Continuez tout droit ahead
Take the first left/right	Prenez la première à gauche/droite

POST OFFICE

post office	la poste
A stamp for…	Un timbre pour…
America, please	l'Amérique, s'il vous plaît
this letter	cette lettre
these letters	ces lettres
this postcard	cette carte postale
this parcel	ce paquet
mailbox	boîte aux lettres
for abroad	autres destinations

TELEPHONE CALLS

phone booth	une cabine téléphonique
phone card	une télécarte/carte de téléphone
operator	le/la standardiste
long-distance	interurbain (France), international
collect call	un appel en PCV

SHOPPING

bakery	une boulangerie
delicatessen	une charcuterie
newsstand	un tabac
bookshop	une librairie
grocery store	un supermarché
Have you got…?	Avez-vous…?
How much?	Combien?
I'm just looking, thank you	Je regarde seulement, merci
change	la monnaie
a shopping bag, please	un sac, s'il vous plaît

PHARMACY

painkiller	un calmant
antiseptic	de l'antiseptique
bandage	un pansement
sanitary napkin	des serviettes hygiéniques
tampons	des tampons
razor blades	des lames de rasoir
suntan lotion	de la lotion solaire
absorbent cotton	des coton hydrophile

EMERGENCIES

police (17)	la police
ambulance (15)	une ambulance
fire service (18)	les sapeurs-pompiers
emergency services	police secours
policeman	un gendarme
police station	une gendarmerie
first aid	les premiers soins
auto accident	un accident de voiture

Emergency calls are free from phone booths.

TRANSPORTATION

railroad station	la gare
subway	le métro
train	le train
platform	le quai
ticket office	le guichet
bus station	la gare routière
bus	l'autobus, un bus
long-distance	un autocar, car
bus stop	un arrêt de bus
ticket	un billet
one-way to…	un billet simple pour…
round-trip to…	un aller-retour pour…
timetable	un horaire
Is this the bus/train to…	Est-ce bien le train/bus pour…

MONEY

Do you accept…	Acceptez-vous…
this credit card?	cette carte de crédit?
traveler's checks?	les chèques de voyage?
ATM	un guichet automatique

NUMBERS

1, 2, 3	un, deux, trois
4, 5, 6	quatre, cinq, six
7, 8, 9, 10	sept, huit, neuf, dix
11. 12, 13	onze, douze, treize
14, 15	quatorze, quinze
16, 17	seize, dix-sept
18, 19	dix-huit, dix-neuf
20, 21	vingt, vingt-et-un
30, 40	trente, quarante
50, 60	cinquante, soixante
70	soixante-dix
80	quatre-vingt
90	quatre-vingt-dix
100, 101	cent, cent-et-un

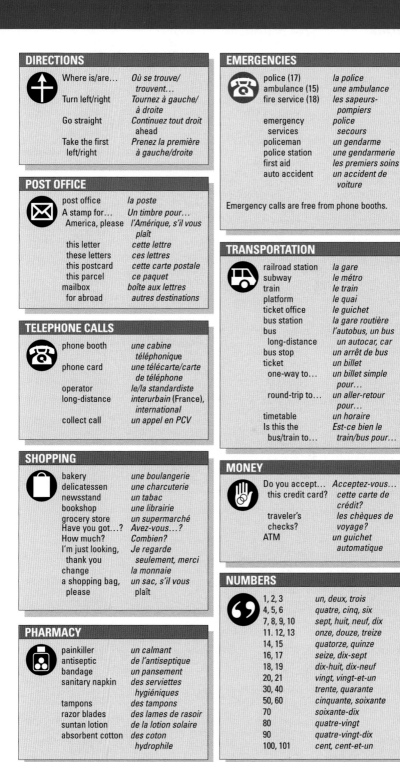

Index

Index

Acknowledgements

The Automobile Association wishes to thank the following photographers and libraries for their assistance in the preparation of this book:
MICHAEL BUSSELLE 116/7, 232/3; DIAF 50, (J P Garcin), 117 (J P Garcin), 154 (J P Garcin), 182 (J D Sudres), 209 (D Thiery), 247 (P Cheuva), 248 (R Maxin), 252 (J D Sudres); FRENCH PICTURE LIBRARY/BARRIE SMITH 97(t), 97(b), 180, 191, 192, 212, 216, 231; ROBERT HARDING PICTURE LIBRARY 19, 89, 204; HULTON GETTY COLLECTION 21; JOHN MILLER 164, 250; PICTURES COLOUR LIBRARY 87, 90, 128, 168, 203; SPECTRUM COLOUR LIBRARY 12/3, 65, 88, 110, 111, 113, 129, 130, 131, 199, 201, 205, 225, 229, 243, 246, 254/5; WORLD PICTURES 16/7, 132, 151, 183, 244/5; www.euro.ecb.int/(euro notes) 277.

The remaining pictures are held in the Association's own library (AA PHOTO LIBRARY) with contributions from the following photographers:
A Baker 74, 142, 146, 150, 153, 156/7, 160, 162, 169, 172; P Bennett 94, 94/5, 122, 126, 133, 134, 134/5, 138; S L Day 69, 75, 76/7; J Edmanson 6, 91, 92/3, 102, 103; P Kenward 11, 34, 48, 86, 114/5, 120, 121, 141, 278; R Moore 23, 62, 68, 70, 72/3, 77, 80, 92, 96, 99, 159, 176, 179; R Moss 26, 196, 277(t); D Noble 24, 51, 53, 54, 55; T Oliver 185, 186/7, 189, 190, 218, 238, 241, 249; K Paterson 30/1, 35, 47, 277(b); K Reynolds 124, 125; B Rieger 27, 37, 39; D Robertson 224, 234, 235, 251, 253; C Sawyer 46, 58, 64, 70/1, 72, 78, 79; M Short 3, 220, 226, 227, 237(t), 237(b); B Smith 60, 100/1, 104, 109, 112, 118, 119, 136, 173, 207, 208, 210, 213, 215; T Souter 32, 36, 40, 42, 44, 45, 256; R Strange 14/5, 56, 67, 84, 148, 152, 157, 161, 163, 174, 175, 194, 198, 206, 211, 216/7; J A Tims 41, 43, 49.